European Sources of

European Sources of Human Dignity

A COMMENTED ANTHOLOGY

Mette Lebech

PETER LANG

Oxford • Bern • Berlin • Bruxelles • New York • Wien

Bibliographic information published by Die Deutsche Bibliothek
Die Deutsche Bibliothek lists this publication in the Deutsche Nationalbibliografie;
detailed bibliographic data is available on the Internet at
?http://dnb.ddb.de.

A catalogue record for this book is available at the British Library.

Library of Congress Cataloging-in-Publication Data:

Names: Lebech, Mette, author.
Title: European sources of human dignity : a commented anthology / Mette Lebech.
Description: 1 [edition]. | New York : Peter Lang, 2019. | Includes bibliographical
references and index.
Identifiers: LCCN 2019008338 | ISBN 9781788745246 (alk. paper)
Subjects: LCSH: Dignity--History--Sources.
Classification: LCC BJ1533.D45 L43 2019 | DDC 323.09--dc23 LC record available at
https://lccn.loc.gov/2019008338

Cover image: 'Untitled 15, November 1999' by Eva Weis Bentzon.

ISBN 978-1-78874-524-6 (print) • ISBN 978-1-78874-521-5 (ePDF)
ISBN 978-1-78874-522-2 (ePub) • ISBN 978-1-78874-523-9 (mobi)

© Peter Lang AG 2019

Published by Peter Lang Ltd, International Academic Publishers,
52 St Giles, Oxford, OX1 3LU, United Kingdom
oxford@peterlang.com, www.peterlang.com

Printed in Germany

To the memory of
Rie Lebech († 22 November 2015) and
Peter Kemp († 3 August 2018)

As a first formulation let us say: *Human dignity consists in our recognising that each human being, including ourselves, has intrinsic value and is a valuer in his own right.*

The term 'recognising' means in this context 'attributing intrinsic value to.' The first formulation can, then, be developed into this somewhat more elaborate formulation: Human dignity consists in our attributing intrinsic value to both

(i) each person's having intrinsic value for himself and to his being himself a valuer; and
(ii) the kind of relationship that thereby becomes possible between people, viz. personal interrelationship.

— AXEL STERN: 'On Value and Human Dignity',
in *Listening*, 1975, Spring, p. 83.

Contents

Acknowledgements   xi

Introduction   1

PART I   Ancient Sources   9

CHAPTER 1
The Greek Vocabulary of Importance
as Reflected in Aristotle   11

CHAPTER 2
The Roman Integration of Status
and State Observed in Cicero   27

CHAPTER 3
The Dead Sea Scrolls and the Biblical Heritage   57

PART II   Medieval Sources   63

CHAPTER 4
Patristic and Carolingian Sources   65

CHAPTER 5
Scholastic Sources   83

CHAPTER 6
Late Medieval Sources   119

PART III   Early Modern Sources   129

CHAPTER 7
Renaissance, Reformation and the New World   131

CHAPTER 8
Absolutism and Counterreformation   153

CHAPTER 9
The Enlightenment and its Discontents   165

PART IV   Modern Sources   193

CHAPTER 10
The French Revolution   195

CHAPTER 11
Industrialisation and Democracy   265

CHAPTER 12
The Impact of the Second World War   283

Conclusion   309

Bibliography   311

Index   335

Acknowledgements

This work was begun more than twenty-five years ago. Many people have helped towards its realisation on its long journey, not least the two people to whom it is dedicated, sharing the desire to see it finished and in print. I hope it still is of consolation to them, now they are on the 'other side'.

Many thanks are due to Jeremy Corley, John Glucker, Amos Edelheit, Stella Sørensen, John Flood, Harry McCauley, William Desmond, Andrea Robiglio, Jacob Rendtorff, Stephan Steiner, Maria José Vega, Klaus Schulte and Hilda Schulte Middelboe for many helpful suggestions and feedback. Thanks are also due to James McEvoy† for help with translations, some dating back to when the anthology was first begun, and for countless wonderful discussions, not least of the prayer framing the present work. My language specific proof readers, Elena Garcia, Helle Gjellerup, Anna Marie Lebech Sørensen, James Smith and Amos Edelheit all deserve thanks for their kind and sustained attention to detail. The mistakes and faults remaining are of course my own.

I would also like to thank my head of department Philipp Rosemann, for kindly leaving me alone over the summer of 2018 so I could finish the manuscript. The many helpers in the computer centre and the library at Maynooth University deserve thanks as well. Christabel Scaife, commissioning editor at Peter Lang, is due thanks for bravely commissioning the cumbersome project with all its many bits and for clearing the complex questions of copyright over the span of an entire year, together with Philip Dunshea, Tony Mason and the careful setters, who took the project to completion.

Finally, thanks are due to the Maynooth University Publication Fund and to the National University of Ireland for financial support as well as to Eva Weis Bentzon for the use her work for the cover.

Rights to reprint have been obtained from the publishers of *The Complete Works of Aristotle*, the Revised Oxford Translation, vols I–II, ed. Jonathan Barnes (Princeton, NJ: Princeton University Press, 1984); Cicero, *On Invention*, Vol II, trans. H. M. Hubbell, Loeb Classical Library

Volume 386 (Cambridge, MA: Harvard University Press, first published 1949) (Loeb Classical Library ® is a registered trademark of the President and Fellows of Harvard College); Kant: *Practical Philosophy*, ed. Mary Gregor (Cambridge: Cambridge University Press, 1996) and Pico della Mirandola, 'Oration on the Dignity of Man', trans. E. L. Forbes, in *The Renaissance Philosophy of Man*, eds Cassirer, Kristeller and Randall (Chicago and London: University of Chicago Press, 1948). Permission has been granted by Brepols to print an earlier version of the translation of *De dignitate conditionis humanae* by myself and James McEvoy† and by the Otto-Karrer-Vorlesung to reprint and translate Otto Karrer's 'The dignity of the human person'. Permission has likewise been obtained from Königshausen und Neuman to create a cover that recalls the cover of my *On the Problem of Human Dignity*, published with them in 2009, to which this is a companion volume. Every effort has been made to trace any other copyright holder and to obtain their permission for the use of copyright material. The publisher apologises for any errors or omissions in the above list and would be grateful for notification of any corrections that should be incorporated in future reprints or editions of this book.

Celbridge, 10 November 2018,
Feast of St Leo the Great

Introduction

This anthology started out as an appendix to my doctoral thesis, which was published under the title *On the Problem of Human Dignity* (2009). For the purpose of constructing a theory about what human dignity is, the texts in the collection were chosen according to the criterion that 'human dignity', 'dignity' or any derivatives thereof were used in them. This criterion still governs the collection, as many readers may still be in need of constructing such a theory. The now much expanded collection allows for doing that in different ways and can be consulted for many different reasons relating to ethics, theology, history or law. Introductions and comments frame the texts nevertheless, so that they form a kind of patchwork, the pattern of which reflects my own understanding of human dignity, as presented in *On the Problem of Human Dignity* and sharpened during the work with the present anthology.

In that first work, I proposed, in terms not unlike those of Alex Stern quoted above, an argument for human dignity being implicitly and quasi-necessarily intuited as the fundamental value of the subject of human experience. I moreover argued that this intuition allows it to function as a constitutional principle, and indeed as the constitutional principle founding human rights. The history of the conceptualisation of human dignity as a constitutional principle is the account of how that intuition came to play the role of being foundational for law on the national and international level. This history reflects political history in that it tracks the history of constitutional law, the constitution of states and the development of the understanding of citizenship. It also reflects the history of religions, culture and philosophy as far as various types of anthropology account for the value attributed to the human being at any given time. The decisive question this history addresses is how the fundamental value of the human being come to determine political status. Politics alone cannot account for the ontological status of the human being. Religion on its own cannot accord political status. Thus, a standoff between politics and

religion creates an equilibrium without which both are incapable of protecting human dignity. More than portraying competing traditions, this history testifies to a balance to be celebrated, a means between extremes surmounting potential conflict at any time.

The present anthology presents textual evidence of this history. Different, even rival, interpretations already exist of this history as well as of the various texts that document it. This is why there is a need for a comprehensive compendium like this one, to facilitate the probing of the various interpretations against the texts themselves.

Rival interpretations form competing traditions, which all converge, however, on understanding human dignity as the constitutional principle of human rights. Jacques Maritain famously maintained (UNESCO, 1949, 16) that the use of the principle of human dignity as the basic principle of human rights could be agreed to by everyone, as long as no one asked what exactly it meant. The acute desire for peace and the experience of the principle's practical necessity adequately explained the principle's function as a *topos* in the political landscape in the aftermath of the Second World War. Despite the general wisdom of not asking for the meaning of the principle in order to preserve a delicate peace, I will continue to claim that human dignity does in fact mean something, maybe despite ourselves, namely, as defended in *On the Problem of Human Dignity*, the fundamental value of the human being. I am confident in doing that because I think it unlikely that it will compromise peace. Stern puts the same intuition differently: 'Human dignity consists in our recognising that each human being, including ourselves, has intrinsic value and is a valuer in his own right'. I am not suggesting Maritain would not agree to this. He probably would. Yet, according to his intuition, it may well be that this is not saying enough about human dignity, or that it may indeed be saying too much. In the light of the Christian tradition, it may be saying too little. In particular, it may make too little of the need for grace and actions in keeping with this dignity, and underestimate the deformation of human dignity that happened when man fell, and consequently the value of the salvation brought by Christ. For a secularist sensibility, it may be saying too much, as far as it recognises ultimate value to every human being, those conceived outside a parental project along with those whose life is a burden to themselves

and to others. At any rate: how can one say anything about human dignity after Auschwitz? Nevertheless, the flippancy of reducing human dignity to an abstract principle (such as autonomy, freedom, rationality, normality or the ability to choose one's own nature) testifies to the gap between the need for discussion about it and the difficulty of speaking of it. Yet, the experience that gave rise to the human rights tradition of the United Nations is as uncompromising in its focalisation of all traditions as is the need to move beyond either flippancy or silence.

Besides the Christian and secular traditions, other traditions, the role and importance of which should not be underestimated, are focalised in the human rights tradition. They meander through the history of human dignity complicating, upsetting and facilitating the equilibrium between the two first. Jewish, masonic, left-wing, right-wing, conservative and liberal traditions can be traced; the Islamic tradition has until recently had only indirect importance in Europe. In the stream of traditions, the human being finds himself now attracted to this and now convinced by something else. Esoteric and science fiction traditions swirl at the edges, together with other traditions not interested in the human being for its own sake, where they therefore contribute to the conceptualisation history of human dignity only by eschewing the question.

Do we presently experience the falling apart of the human rights tradition in its basic principle under the pressures of vice, competition and the fear of death? All spiritual traditions interpret these natural factors as well as their need for harmonisation by reason, but none of them can interpret the tensions away. This may allow us to understand each tradition conceptualising human dignity as finalised by its commitment to it and to respect it for that. Then the falling apart can be experienced as a falling towards a new balance as humanity takes its next step.

The present anthology attempts to explain what happened from the time human dignity was identified in those exact terms ('human dignity') until the formulation in which it had initially been broadcast was quietly left aside. This initial broadcast took the form of a prayer said during every mass throughout the Latin Patriarchate (i.e. western Europe) from the time of the liturgical reforms of Charlemagne until the liturgical reforms of the Catholic Church after the Second Vatican Council. The prayer not only

discretely occupies the background of this study, but also determines its cut-off point. The removal of the prayer from the offertory after 1965 was followed by the beginning of the abortion debates. Hereafter the literature debating the content of the concept virtually exploded, and one would have to devote a separate volume to it if one were to do it justice.

In contrast with the definite cut-off point, the first part collecting ancient sources leading up to the prayer's inception, presents sources in Greek, Latin and Hebrew that illuminate the early history and linguistic ancestry of the expression 'human dignity'. The insistence on the centrality of the expression 'human dignity', with its linguistically related expressions, stems from the desire not to pre-empt what human dignity *means* or indeed to mistake it for the reasons given for it. Thus texts concerning the iconicity of God or microcosmic status have only been included to the extent they make use of the expression. Both of these images express the idea that human beings as such have fundamental value by explaining why they have that. They express it in different ways, however, as God's image and as the sum of creation respectively, and therefore are more like *reasons* for human dignity than conceptualisations of human dignity itself. As the conceptualisation history of human dignity as a constitutional principle begins with the occurrence of the expression 'human dignity' and its linguistically related expressions, the first part is schematic in its representation of the cultural sources that influenced the conceptualisation of human dignity in Europe, since the expression as such rarely occurs.

The collection and analysis of the non-European sources lies outside the scope of the present work. Iberian, Finno-Ugric and Slavonic sources have been left out due to a regrettable lack of linguistic competences. The reason for including accounts often referred to as authoritative on the topic of human dignity more extensively than their use of the expression 'human dignity' would warrant, is that they have played an important role in the debates about human dignity. Lesser-known treatments of the subject are included, as are also fragments from well-known or representative authors. The resulting collection aims to be as enlightening as possible, leaving it possible to interpret the texts according to different traditions while also providing an interpretative key by the framework proposed. The collection is of course not, and could not be, exhaustive.

The conception of the state and of its role in European history, which guides the conceptualisation of a constitutional principle relied upon here, owes much to Edith Stein's phenomenological *An Investigation Concerning the State* (1922). Stein regards the state as expressing itself essentially in the making of positive law, for which it may give itself a 'constitution' (whether formally adopted or not), a set of principles, to which its laws are meant to conform. As it is in relation to the constitutional state that a constitutional principle makes sense and can matter, a constitutional principle cannot exist or have any meaning apart from it. Human dignity can and does have such meaning, albeit not *as* a constitutional principle. Human dignity can serve as a constitutional principle precisely because it has a meaning that anchors it ontologically in the lives of those who socially construct the state, a meaning they take an interest in seeing formalised in a formal constitution so that they can hold the state responsible for respecting it. As the status of the citizen, in contrast with human dignity, depends on the state, the citizens of a state do not necessarily coincide with those who are subject to it (slaves, for example, are not citizens). Citizens are representatives of the state in that they freely participate in the law-making process also by upholding the laws and have an interest in constituting or recognising the state as theirs.

The four parts of the present anthology reflect four states of the state thus understood in Europe, each characterised by typical ways of identifying who counts as citizen in the state, and therefore standing in a specific and recognisable tension with the state taking human dignity as its constitutional principle.

Part I assembles texts written in the landscape of ancient city-states and empires, in which women, slaves and foreigners, and indeed most peasants, were not (regarded as, constituted as, socially constructed as) citizens. The idea that human beings have dignity because they are human is present, but it is of little consequence for political institutions, although it may have played a role in the arguments against aristocracy and for democracy in the form that all *free men* have dignity.

Part II includes texts authored under the demise, the resurgence and the relapse of empire and the emergence of kingdoms centred on tribal loyalties. The idea that human beings have dignity because they are human

was present and taught by the Church, which performed many roles of public utility because of it. Citizenship mattered little outside the city-states, whose constitutions, like those of their ancient predecessors, did not expect an active political role from women, slaves and peasants. Baptism, in contrast, gives rights in Christendom in a manner that look like citizen rights, since it gives right to participate in the life of the Church and access to receive other sacraments.

Part III gathers texts from the period during which the modern European state emerged from kingdoms in a relentless competition between royal families and empires resulting in a gradual alignment of the different tensions along fault lines of national sentiment. During this period, the status of the cities' merchants and the rights of the professions were negotiated with the landed classes whose privileges made them the dominant element at court. Correspondingly, the money economy gradually overtook the land-based one while law courts and parliaments created a political space for negotiation 'at home' in the sovereign colonial nation-states. Here, government granted citizenship and took an interest in discussions of constitutional law as it related to the aboriginal inhabitants of the colonies and to imported slaves.

Part IV assembles texts written at the time of and after the French revolution, which specifically proclaimed the right of citizens to men outside the ranks of the aristocracy. The institution of aristocracy gradually lost its relevance as the economy definitively turned from land-based to money-based, to wage-earner-based production forms. The abolition of slavery occurred gradually until machines and wage earners completely replaced its economic 'necessity'. Constitutions were now used as means for politically excluded classes to claim inclusion in the political decision making process, and amid liberal, socialist and anarchist claims, women organised to obtain access to education, suffrage, the professions and the labour market. After the Second World War, human dignity became, as a constitutional principle, synonymous with democracy and was used as a political tool to abolish privilege and claim equality before the law of all human beings.

The processes of (trans)formation of states underlying the distinctions between epochs transpire in the conceptions of human dignity that

occur in the period during which they obtain, but the two only sometimes coincide to address the question of citizenship. Conceptions of human dignity, apart from the colouration they take from their period, are as varied as flowers of the field, reflecting personal genius, religious affiliation, locality, culture, language and community. The fact that customs provide a kind of framework in relation to which understandings of human dignity occur may make the investigation appear like a catalogue of appalling cultural double standards to some. However, what we are really seeing is the tension between the possibility of a personal commitment to a fundamental value and the state's being constructed through political effort to measure up to this value. If we find it shocking that the state has only the commitment to human dignity we make it have, we are merely beginning to realise the enormous task that is political responsibility. The different periods demonstrate ways in which human beings have attempted to do better in different ways, but they also show that we do not seem to be able to do better in every way simultaneously. An attitude is therefore called for that does not dismiss the advances made by one period just because it did not get everything right.

Women's voices often produce what seems to be a shift of topic, a breach of style or a disturbance. An effort has been made to integrate them for at least two reasons: Women have often played the role of making up for cultural insufficiencies, and consequently been conceived as both having and not having human dignity. Because the disturbance of the inclusion itself, better than any attempt at explanation, illustrates the effects of the customary framework, I have left and cherished the voices as wonderful and as awkward as they are. Also: women's role as mothers and educators have given them a position throughout history in counterpoise to politics, relativising it, by occupying the private realm. From this position, which also is a privileged position in relation to the state, they have in their caring for family members, the young, the sick, the old, the poor and their husbands, valued human dignity. It must not be forgotten for it being gentle that caring constitutes the perhaps most essential form of leadership in the struggle for the recognition of human dignity.

Lastly, although a particular understanding of human dignity may be in the interest of the state, whether as emerging or consolidating, the

recognition of human dignity does not have any direct relationship with the state: states can obtain irrespective of the level of respect for human dignity expressed in their laws. It requires the intervention of human beings to hold the state to account for its respect for human dignity, and when citizens do not agree on the implications of the principle, this holding to account is complicated accordingly.

In what follows, the original texts are provided along with their translations into English to avoid ambiguities arising from translation alone and to fill in the etymological context of the expression. Throughout, authors and texts appear in approximate chronological order, although I have refrained from dating the texts presented in Parts I and II, since these are a matter of scholarly debate. The presence of the expression **human dignity** (or of words or phrases linguistically related to it) stands out in bold in the texts and translations for the sake of facilitating the use of the anthology. When occasionally translations are my own, this has been indicated. Existing translations have been adapted only if it was necessary in order to understand the use of the expression human dignity in them. Quotation marks have been somewhat standardised.

PART I

Ancient Sources

Three ancient civilisations lie at the origin of what we today call Europe: the Greek, the Roman and the Jewish. They all shared an understanding of the human being as an exceptional being with a naturally privileged position in the cosmos in relation to the animals. The Greeks and the Romans explained this position by intellect (νοῦς/*ratio*), the Jews furthermore by the creation of the human being in the image of God.

If social organisation, science or religion needed justification or regulation, reference was made to this place at the summit of the natural order. Rational nature accounted for the dignity of the human being but slavery was also 'natural'. Nature's resources and regenerative powers seems here to break against its intelligibility assigning a social order of its own devising; at the outset, human nature was understood not only as privileged and admirable, but also as exposed to irrationality and to some extent corrupt.

Aristotle was a keen explorer of nature's intelligibility. Human nature was to him both biological and political, due to the faculty of reason, which he understood to mark human affairs essentially. When Aristotle's texts were translated into Latin during the Middle Ages, *dignitas* translated both *axia* and *axioma*, value and principle, features of reason and politics alike. Both of these meanings therefore came to contribute to the meaning of dignity, identifying what is important for the functioning of the city as well as for reason as such.

Cicero's background in law and politics enabled him to launch and sustain the originally Greek idea of Natural Law as distinct from the law of the particular state. His perspective was *cosmo-politan*, because he was aware of possible universal political implications of Roman Imperialism: his society was in fact already an empire state, not a city-state. Nature was all the more strongly appealed to as what lay beyond controversy, and the argument was advanced that human dignity is something human beings

have 'by nature', and which obligates them to stay in control of themselves by means of reason.

The Jews were a people on the coast of the Mediterranean, who came first under Greek and then under Roman imperial power. In the centuries up to the birth of Christ, what we today call the Jewish Bible or the Old Testament had not been finalised, although the 'Law' and the 'Prophets' had been. In Second Temple Judaism, Pharisees, Sadducees and Essenes provided different interpretations of the common legacy of 'the Scriptures' for religious Jews. The texts presented here are selected because they make use of the expression, which in modern legal Hebrew translates into human dignity, *kvod ha-adam*. The expression is not found in the Bible of today, whether Jewish or Christian, but it is found three times in the Dead Sea Scrolls, probably consisting of the library of the Essenes, found in Qumran 1947–56. In translations of those texts for the English speaking public of today, the expression features as 'the glory of Adam'.

The Greek Vocabulary of Importance as Reflected in Aristotle

The Latin translators of Aristotle translated both ἀξίωμα and ἀξία by *dignitas*. Dignity, accordingly, has drawn upon the meanings expressed in both of these terms: it is a non-demonstrable startingpoint or principle, and it is desert or merit, that is, what gives rights, the proper attitude towards which is respect. The source of both duty and rights, dignity is associated with moral weight or importance, and in Rome *dignitas* also meant office, that is, both duty and status, which gave both tasks and entitlements. This spectrum of meaning is the reason why we talk about dignity, and in particular human dignity, as a basic value and a principle.

For Aristotle, as for any Greek, the value possessed by human individuals was variable according to standards socially constructed by any society, even if an ideal of ἰσονομία seemed to most a necessary requirement for the proper functioning of society. The Greeks were aware that in an oligarchy riches would count, in democracy status as a free man, high birth or virtue in an aristocracy, and sheer power under a tyrannical rule. Aristotle, for one, being a foreigner in Athens, was sensitive to the relativity of respect for human status as well as to the fundamental importance rationality bestows on the human being as such. He regarded rationality, and in particular intuition (νοῦς), in which first principles are grasped, as what sets human beings apart. Reason's value is grasped intuitively as an implicit corrective to state-organisation, an intuition of natural justice. Because rationality relies on identification, memory and the possession of the universal, the process of induction at the basis of experience cannot be further accounted for than through these. The importance of rationality cannot be either; it relies on itself for importance. In this sense, rationality is itself a beginning, a principle or an axiom, and this beginning is what accounts for dignity.

Therefore, the intuition of dignity also cannot be further accounted for. It is basic. That humans have dignity is therefore part and parcel of their rationality, which, according to Aristotle's definition of man as a 'rational animal', is part of what they are.

The Greek text is taken from the Loeb edition, with the omission of some footnotes pertaining to variants in manuscripts and earlier editions, deemed to be of no consequence for the present inquiry. Latin translations are those used by the editors of Thomas Aquinas' *Opera Omnia* (Commissio Leonina), as this exemplifies a translation that does not differ in its use of *dignitas* from the versions of the *Aristoteles Latinus*. The English translation is that of the revised Oxford translation, edited by Jonathan Barnes.

Posterior Analytics

In the *Posterior Analytics* Aristotle accounts for scientific knowledge. He makes it clear that all knowledge cannot be scientific, but that scientific knowledge on the contrary must rely on non-demonstrable first principles. These must be taken for granted for scientific demonstration to begin. Such principles are called ἀξιώματα, or in Latin *dignitates*. Hence a dignity is a kind of origin (also ἀρχή, αἴτιον), which cannot be demonstrated because it lies at the basis of all knowledge, and must be taken for granted in order for learning to take place. It is something of basic importance, which influences whatever comes after it.

For the Greeks, as well as later for the Romans, people in authority were thought to be important in this way: their authority consisted in a similar prerogative of initiative, and they were therefore called οἱ ἄξιοι. The Romans referred to the holding of office by the same term: *dignitas*. What axioms and authority have in common is that they both have 'things following from them' – whether because they order it, or because they entail it. Our use of 'principle' has the same twofold use: it can refer to a basic rule, the consequences of which are implied in it or, with the spelling 'principal', it can refer to the head of a school. *Princeps*, from which we have *prince*, derives its meaning from the same root. What we designate

by the terms *axiom*, *dignity* and *basic principle* is accordingly a source of spontaneous and self-reliant regulation, which initiates, and in this sense is unfounded and first.

I, 2 (72a7–72a24)

Ἐκ πρώτων δ' ἐστὶ τὸ ἐξ ἀρχῶν οἰκείων· ταὐτὸ γὰρ λέγω πρῶτον καὶ ἀρχήν. ἀρχὴ δ' ἐστὶν ἀποδείξεως πρότασις ἄμεσος, ἄμεσος δὲ ἧς μὴ ἔστιν ἄλλη προτέρα. πρότασις δ' ἐστὶν ἀποφάνσεως τὸ ἕτερον μόριον, ἓν καθ'ἑνός, διαλεκτικὴ μὲν ἡ ὁμοίως λαμβάνουσα ὁποτερονοῦν, ἀποδεικτικὴ δὲ ἡ ὡρισμένως θάτερον, ὅτι ἀλεθές. ἀπόφανσις δὲ ἀντιφάσεως ὁποτερονοῦν μόριον. ἀντίφασις δὲ ἀντίθεσις ἧς οὐκ ἔστι μεταξὺ καθ'αὑτήν. μόριον δ' ἀντιφάσεως τὸ μὲν τὶ κατὰ τινος κατάφασις, τὸ δὲ τὶ ἀπό τινος ἀπόφασις. ἀμέσου δ'ἀρχῆς συλλογιστικῆς θέσιν μὲν λέγω ἣν μὴ ἔστι δεῖξαι μηδ' ἀνάγκη ἔχειν τὸν μαθησόμενόν τι· ἣν δ' ἀνάγκη ἔχειν τὸν ὁτιοῦν μαθησόμενον, ἀξίωμα· ἔστι γὰρ ἔνια ποιαῦτα· τοῦτο γὰρ μάλιστ' ἐπὶ τοῖς τοιούτοις εἰώθαμεν ὄνομα λέγειν. θέσεως δ'ἡ μὲν ὁποτερονοῦν τῶν μορίων τῆς ἀποφάνσεως λαμβάνουσα, οἷον λέγω τὸ εἶναί τι ἢ μὴ εἶναί τι,

Ex primis autem est, quod ex propriis principiis est. Idem enim dico primum et principium. Est autem principium demonstrationis propositio inmediata. Inmediata autem est qua non est altera prior. Propositio autem est enunciationis altera pars, unum de uno. Dialectica similiter est accipiens quamlibet. Demonstrativa autem determinate alteram, quoniam uerum est. Enunciatio autem contradictionis quamlibet partem. Contradictio autem est oppositio cui non est medium secundum se. Pars autem contradictionis que quidem aliquid de aliquo est, affirmatio est, que uero est aliquid ab aliquo, negatio est. Inmediati autem principii sillogistici positionem dico quam non est monstrare, neque necesse est habere docendum aliquem. **Quam uero necesse est habere quemlibet docendum, dignitatem vel maximam**

Depending on things that are primitive is depending on appropriate principles; for I call the same thing primitive and a principle. A principle of a demonstration is an immediate proposition, and an immediate proposition is one to which there is no other prior. A proposition is the one part of a contradiction, one thing said of one; it is dialectical if it assumes the other one that is true. A statement is either part of a contradiction. A contradiction is an opposition which of itself excludes any intermediate; and the part of a contradiction saying something *of* something is an affirmation, the one saying something *from* something is a denial. An immediate deductive principle I call a posit if one cannot prove it but it is not necessary for anyone who is to learn anything to grasp it; **and one which it is necessary for**

ὑπόθεσις, ἡ δ'ἄνευ τούτου ὁρισμός. ὁ γὰρ ὁρισμὸς θέσις μέν ἐστι· τίθεται γὰρ ὁ ἀριθμητικὸς μονάδα τὸ ἀδιαίρετον εἶναι κατὰ τὸ ποσόν· ὑπόθεσις δ' οὐκ ἔστι· τὸ γὰρ τί ἐστι μονὰς καὶ τὸ εἶναι μονάδα οὐ ταὐτόν.

propositionem; sunt enim quedam huiusmodi; hoc enim 'maxime' in huiusmodi consueuimus nomen dicere. Positionis autem que quidem est quamlibet partium enunciationis accipiens, ut dico esse aliquid aut non esse, suppositio est. Que vero sine hoc diffinitio est: diffinitio enim positio quidem est; ponit enim arithmeticus unitatem hoc indiuisibile esse secundum quantitatem; suppositio autem non est. Id enim quod quid est unitas et esse unitatem non idem est.

anyone who is to learn anything whatever to grasp, I call an axiom (for there are some such things); for we are accustomed to use this name especially of such things. A posit which assumes either of the parts of a contradiction – i.e., I mean, that something is or that something is not – I call a supposition; one without this, a definition. For a definition is a posit (for the arithmetician posits that a unit is what is quantitatively indivisible) but not a supposition (for what a unit is and that a unit is are not the same).

Aristotle distinguishes suppositions, propositions, definitions and axioms, and affirms a need for depending on 'primitives' or appropriate principles in all kinds of knowledge. All demonstration relies on insight into 'primitives' of which we have intuition gained through induction. Definitions formulate these insights and make them accessible to demonstration, but without induction or intuition there would be no definition in the first place, as demonstration is mainly useful to criticise or disprove definitions, not to establish them. This is also the case for axioms: they are indemonstrable, and only show themselves in their 'consequences' – that is, in what can be deduced from them, or learnt, when they are grasped. Axioms, in other words, are intelligible in what they ground or what follows from them. They are distinct from propositions or definitions in that they are indispensable for the learning process. Their necessity is teleological. They are relative only to what follows from them. This is what is meant by the fact that they are prior, first or basic. They formulate the necessary conditions for thought and impress this requirement on the learning process, of which demonstration is the most important part. Without them, the

learning process would disintegrate, as they, properly speaking, constitute its form. From this, we may conclude that in the same way as axioms are basic to demonstration but cannot be proven, so dignity is basic to what follows from it (rights and duties). However, like axioms, dignity cannot be proven. Axioms and dignity are alike in that they must be relied upon, so that what follows from them may not disintegrate. This is what it means to claim that dignity is fundamental.

This impression is reinforced by the following passage, in which it is stated that axioms are what demonstration is *from*, and hence what conditions and validates it. Demonstration *depends* on its basic principles.

I, VII (75a38–75b3)

Τρία γάρ ἐστι τὰ ἐν ταῖς ἀπο-δείξεσιν, ἓν μὲν τὸ ἀποδεικνύ-μενον τὸ συμπέρασμα (τοῦτο δ' ἐστὶ τὸ ὑπάρχον γένει τινὶ καθ'αὑτό), ἓν δὲ τὰ **ἀξιώ-ματα** (ἀξιώματα δ' ἐστὶν ἐξ ὧν), τρίτον τὸ γένος τὸ ὑπο-κείμενον, οὗ τὰ πάθη καὶ τὰ καθ'αὑτὰ συμβεβηκότα δηλοῖ ἡ ἀπόδειξις.

Tria enim sunt in demonstrationibus, unum quidem quod demonstratur, conclusio; hoc autem est quod inest alicui generi per se. Aliud autem **dignitates; dignitates autem sunt ex quibus est.** Tercium autem genus subiectum, cuius passiones et per se accidencia ostendit demonstratio.

For there are three things in demonstrations: one, what is being demonstrated, the conclusion (this is what belongs to some genus in itself); one, the **axioms (axioms are the things on which the demonstration depends);** third, the underlying genus of which the demonstration makes clear the attributes and what is accidental to it in itself.

Axioms, together with the demonstrations based on them, form part of the science that they found. They constitute its basic principles, from which the science derives, and cannot be separated from it. They therefore inform this science and in a sense define it. Basic principles must be assumed or accepted for the inquiry to begin, not only because of what follows from them, but also because they cannot in themselves be proven apart from the coherence that they lend to the science they found.

I, X (76b13–15)

Πᾶσα γὰρ ἀποδεικτικὴ ἐπι-
στήμη περὶ τρία ἐστίν, ὅσα τε
εἶναι τίθεται (ταῦτα δ'ἐστὶ τὸ
γένος, οὗ τῶν καθ'αὑτὰ παθη-
μάτων ἐστὶ θεωρητική), καὶ
τὰ κοινὰ λεγόμενα **ἀξιώματα,**
ἐξ ὧν πρώτων ἀποδείκνυσι,
καὶ τρίτον τὰ πάθη, ὧν τί
σημαίνει ἕκαστον λαμβάνει.

Omnis enim demonstra-
tiua sciencia circa tria est:
quecunque esse ponuntur
(hec autem sunt genus,
cuius per se passionum
speculatiua est), et que
communes dicuntur **dig-
nitates,** ex quibus primis
demonstrant, et tercium
passiones, quarum quid sig-
nificet unaqueque accipit.

For every demonstrative science has to do with three
things; what it posits to
be (these form the genus
of what it considers the
attributes that belong to
it in itself); and what are
called the common **axioms,**
the primitives from which
it demonstrates, and thirdly
the attributes, of which it
assumes what each signifies.

The ability to take something intelligently for granted that is implied in demonstration seems to be what is characteristic of rationality (II, 19 (99b20–100b17)). Intelligence itself is fundamental in that by definition it takes something for granted (namely the 'primitives' or appropriate principles through which understanding is held as explanation for something). It also is prior or first, in the sense that it cannot be further explained or derived from anything else. The fact that human beings are the kind of animals that are rational means that they are of the kind that is capable of this sort of intuitive activity, basic to demonstration. The activity also accounts for the fact that they learn to take those things for granted which they ought to take for granted, that is, the things that are truly first. To some degree, all animals have this capacity to learn, but humans have it eminently, in that they possess the universal through abstraction sustained by memory.

In Aristotle's dictionary, principle (ἀρχή) is defined as 'that from which a thing can first be known' (*Metaphysics* V, 1013a14–15). Therefore, if an axiom is a first principle, it is not only that from which some thing can first be known, but that from which things *as such* can first be known. In this sense, rationality can be said to be the principle of principles, the principle, namely, which is an absolute beginning. The fact that human beings are rational animals means for Aristotle that they in this manner reflect the absolute beginning, and therefore are absolute beginnings in themselves:

that their knowledge as such cannot be any further founded but must in the last resort rely on itself as rational.

If we further ask what category of being such a principle as rationality belongs to, we note that his definitions of ἀρχή all *relate* various things. A principle in Aristotle's view is in fact closer to being a relation (namely of foundation, of beginning or of originating), than it is to being a substance. This, surprisingly, echoes throughout the *Ethics*, where worth (ἀξία) is explicitly characterised as a term of relation. These things taken together make it more likely that Aristotle would regard ἀξίωμα (*dignitas*) as being of the category of relation, than that he would consider it to be a substance or a thing of any other kind. This is part of what justifies an understanding of dignity as a value, a value being, like ἀξία, a term of relation denoting a claim to have something follow from it.

The Nicomachean Ethics

In the *Nicomachean Ethics* Aristotle treats of value (ἀξία) in three contexts. They all have to do with the value of a person: and this has occasioned ἀξία to be translated by 'desert', 'merit' or 'claim' in English, whereas the Latin translated it by *dignitas*, just as ἀξίωμα was translated with *dignitas*. Ἀξία, in fact, is distinctive of the good or perfect man. The 'great-souled' (Ross translates μεγαλόψυχος with 'proud') has dignity. This dignity is defined as his claim to goods external to himself, in particular to honour, and it relies not only on his natural greatness but also on his moral goodness. The great man, in fact, would not be great without at the same time being also good. His *valour* – to use a decidedly out of date expression rendering exactly what ἄξιος means – is a whole, integrating all his natural and moral attributes. His virtues express it in their individuality, but none of them – whether natural or moral – can be missing without seriously diminishing the overall impression.

IV, 3 (1123a34–1125a31)

Ἡ δὲ μεγαλοψυχία περὶ μεγάλα μὲν καὶ ἐκ τοῦ ὀνόματος ἔοικεν εἶναι, περὶ ποῖα δ᾽ ἐστὶ πρῶτον λάβωμεν· διαφέρει δ᾽ οὐθὲν τὴν ἕξιν ἢ τὸν κατὰ τὴν ἕξιν σκοπεῖν. δοκεῖ δὴ μεγαλόψυχος εἶναι ὁ μεγάλων αὑτὸν **ἀξιῶν ἄξιος** ὤν· ὁ γὰρ μὴ κατ᾽**ἀξίαν** αὐτὸ ποιῶν ἠλίθιος, τῶν δὲ κατ᾽ἀρετὴν οὐδεὶς ἠλίθιος οὐδ᾽ ἀνόητος. μεγαλόψυχος μὲν οὖν ὁ εἰρημένος. ὁ γὰρ μικρῶν **ἄξιος** καὶ τούτων **ἀξιῶν** ἑαυτὸν σώφρων, μεγαλόψυχος δ᾽ οὔ· ἐν μεγέθει γὰρ ἡ μεγαλοψυχία, ὥσπερ καὶ τὸ κάλλος ἐν μεγάλῳ σώματι, οἱ μικροὶ δ᾽ ἀστεῖοι καὶ σύμμετροι, καλοὶ δ᾽ οὔ. ὁ δὲ μεγάλων ἑαυτὸν **ἀξιῶν ἀνάξιος** ὢν χαῦνος· ὁ δ᾽ μειζόνων ἢ **ἄξιος** οὐ πᾶς χαῦνος. ὁ δ᾽ἐλαττόνων ἢ **ἄξιος** μικρόψυχος, ἐάν τε μεγάλων ἐὰν τε μετρίων, ἐάν τε καὶ μικρῶν **ἄξιος** ὢν ἔτι ἐλαττόνων αὑτὸν **ἀξιοῖ** καὶ μάλιστα ἂν δόξειεν ὁ μεγάλων **ἄξιος**· τί γὰρ ἂν ἐποίει, εἰ μὴ τοσούτων ἦν **ἄξιος**; ἔστι δὴ ὁ μεγαλόψυχος τῷ μὲν μεγέθει ἄκρος, τῷ δὲ ὡς δεῖ μέσος (τοῦ γὰρ κατ᾽**ἀξίαν** αὑτὸν **ἀξιοῖ**)· οἱ δ᾽ ὑπερβάλλουσι καὶ ἐλλείπουσιν. Εἰ δὴ μεγάλων ἑαυτὸν **ἀξιοῖ ἄξιος** ὤν, καὶ μάλιστα τῶν μεγίστων, περὶ ἓν μάλιστα ἂν εἴη.

Magnanimitas autem circa magna quidem et ex nomine videtur esse. Circa qualia autem est primum accipiamus. Differt autem nihil habitum vel eum qui secundum habitum intendere. Videtur autem magnanimus esse qui magnis se ipsum **dignificat dignus** existens. Qui enim non secundum **dignitatem** id facit insipiens. Eorum autem qui secundum virtutem nullus insipiens neque stultus. Magnanimus quidem igitur qui dictus est. Qui enim parvis **dignus** et his **dignificat** se ipsum temperatus, magnanimus autem non; in magnitudine enim magnanimitas quemadmodum et pulcritudo in corpore magno; parvi autem formosi et commensurati, pulcri autem non. Qui autem magnis se ipsum **dignum** facit **indignus** existens, chaunus. Qui autem maioribus quam **dignus** non omnis chaunus. Qui autem minoribus quam **dignus** pusillanimis sive magnis sive moderatis sive parvis **dignus** existens adhuc minoribus se ipsum dignificet. Et maxime utique videbitur qui magnis **dignus**; quid enim utique

Pride seems even from its name to be concerned with great things; what sort of great things, is the first question we must try to answer. It makes no difference whether we consider the state or the man characterized by it. Now the man is thought to be proud who thinks himself **worthy** of great things, being **worthy** of them; for he who does so beyond his **deserts** is a fool, but no excellent man is foolish or silly. The proud man, then, is the man we have described. For he who is **worthy** of little and thinks himself **worthy** of little is temperate, but not proud; for pride implies greatness, as beauty implies a good-sized body, and little people may be neat and well proportioned but cannot be beautiful. On the other hand, he who thinks himself **worthy** of great things, being **unworthy** of them, is vain; though not every one who thinks himself **worthy** of more than he really is **worthy** of is vain. The man who thinks himself **worthy** of less than he really is **worthy** of is unduly humble, whether his **deserts** be great or moderate, or his **deserts** be small but his

faceret nisi talibus esset **dignus**? Est autem magnanimus magnitudine quidem extremus, eo autem quod ut opportet medius, eo enim quod secundum **dignitatem** se ipsum **dignificat**; hi autem superabundant et deficiunt. Si autem utique magnis se ipsum **dignificat dignus** existens, et maxime maximis, circa unum maxime utique erit.

claims yet smaller. And the man whose **deserts** are great would seem *most* unduly humble; for what would he have done if they had been less? The proud man, then, is an extreme in respect of the greatness of his claims, but a mean in respect of the rightness of them; for he **claims what is in accordance** with his **merits**, while the others go to excess or fall short. If, then, he **deserves and claims** great things, and above all the greatest things, he will be concerned with one thing in particular.

ἡ δ' ἀξία λέγεται πρὸς τὰ ἐκτὸς ἀγαθά· μέγιστον δὲ τοῦτ' ἂν θείημεν ὃ τοῖς θεοῖς ἀπονέμομεν, καὶ οὗ μάλιστ' ἐφίενται οἱ ἐν ἀξιώματι, καὶ τὸ ἐπὶ τοῖς καλλίστοις ἆθλον· τοιοῦτον δ' ἡ τιμή· μέγιστον γὰρ δὴ τοῦτο τῶν ἐκτὸς ἀγαθῶν. περὶ τιμὰς δὴ καὶ ἀτιμίας ὁ μεγαλόψυχός ἐστιν ὡς δεῖ. καὶ ἄνευ δὲ λόγου φαίνονται οἱ μεγαλόψυχοι περὶ τιμὴν εἶναι· τιμῆς γὰρ μάλισθ' οἱ μεγάλοι ἀξιοῦσιν ἑαυτούς, κατ' ἀξίαν δέ. ὁ δὲ μικρόψυχος ἐλλείπει καὶ πρὸς ἑαυτὸν καὶ πρὸς τὸ τοῦ μεγαλοψύχου ἀξίωμα· ὁ δὲ χαῦνος πρὸς ἑαυτὸν μὲν ὑπερβάλλει, οὐ μὴν τόν γε μεγαλόψυχον. ὁ δὲ μεγαλόψυχος, εἴπερ τῶν μεγίστων ἄξιος, ἄριστος ἂν

Dignitas autem dicitur ad ea quae exterius **bona**. Maximum autem hoc utique ponemus quod diis attribuimus et quod maxime desiderant qui in **dignitate** et quod in optimis praemium. Tale autem **honor**. Maximum enim utique hoc eorum quae exterius bonorum. Circa honores utique et inhonorationes magnanimus est ut oportet. Et sine ratione autem videntur magnanimi circa honorem esse. Honore enim maxime magni **dignificant** se ipsos secundum **dignitatem**. Pusillanimis autem deficit et ad se ipsum et ad magnanimi **dignitatem**. Chaunus vero et ad se

Desert is relative to external goods; and the greatest of these, we should say, is that which we render to the gods, and which people of **position** most aim at, and which is the prize appointed for the noblest deeds; and this is **honour**; that is surely the greatest of external goods. Honours and dishonours, therefore, are the objects with respect to which the proud man is as he should be. And even apart from argument it is with honour that proud men appear to be concerned; for it is honour that they chiefly **claim**, but in accordance with their **deserts**. The unduly humble man falls short both in

εἴη· μείζονος γὰρ ἀεὶ ὁ βελτίων **ἄξιος,** καὶ μεγίστων ὁ ἄριστος· τὸν ὡς ἀληθῶς ἄρα μεγαλόψυχον δεῖ ἀγαθὸν εἶναι. καὶ δόξειεν [ἂν] εἶναι μεγαλοψύχου τὸ ἐν ἑκάστῃ ἀρετῇ μέγα· οὐδαμῶς γ' ἂν ἁρμόζοι μεγαλοψύχῳ φεύγειν παρασείσαντι, οὐδ' ἀδικεῖν· τίνος γὰρ ἕνεκα πράξει αἰσχρὰ ᾧ γ' οὐθὲν μέγα; καθ' ἕκαστα δ' ἐπισκοποῦντι πάμπαν γελοῖος φαίνοιτ' ἂν ὁ μεγαλόψυχος μὴ ἀγαθὸς ὤν. οὐκ εἴη δ' ἂν οὐδὲ τιμῆς **ἄξιος** φαῦλος ὤν. τῆς ἀρετῆς γὰρ ἆθλον ἡ τιμή, καὶ ἀπονέμεται τοῖς ἀγαθοῖς. ἔοικε μὲν οὖν ἡ μεγαλοψυχία οἷον κόσμος τις εἶναι τῶν ἀρετῶν· μείζους γὰρ αὐτὰς ποιεῖ, καὶ οὐ γίνεται ἄνευ ἐκείνων. διὰ τοῦτο χαλεπὸν τῇ ἀληθείᾳ μεγαλόψυχον εἶναι· οὐ γὰρ οἷόν τε ἄνευ καλοκἀγαθίας.

ipsum quidem superabundat, non tamen ad magnanimum. Magnanimus autem, si quidem maximis **dignus,** optimus utique erit. Maiori enim semper melior **dignus** et maximis optimus. Ut vere ergo magnanimum oportet bonum esse. Videtur autem esse magnanimi quod in unaquaque virtute magnum. Et nequaquam utique congruit magnanimo fugere commoventem neque iniusta facere; cuius enim gratia operabitur turpia cui nihil magnum? Secundum singula autem intendenti omnino derisibilis videbitur utique magnanimus non bonus existens; non erit autem utique neque honore **dignus** pravus existens, virtutis enim praemium honor et attribuitur bonis. Videtur quidem igitur magnanimitas ut ornatus quidam esse virtutum; maiores enim ipsas facit et non fit sine illis. Propter hoc difficile secundum veritatem magnanimum esse; non enim possibili sine bonitate.

comparison with his own merits and in comparison with the proud man's **claims.** The vain man goes to excess in comparison with his own merits, but does not exceed the proud man's claims. Now the proud man, since he **deserves** most, must be good in the highest degree; for the better man always **deserves** more, and the best man most. Therefore, the truly proud man must be good. And greatness in every excellence would seem to be characteristic of a proud man. And it would be most unbecoming for a proud man to fly from danger, swinging his arms by his sides, or to wrong another; for to what end should he do disgraceful acts, he to whom nothing is great? If we consider him point by point, we shall see utter absurdity of a proud man who is not good. Nor, again, would he be **worthy** of honour if he were bad; for honour is the prize of excellence and it is to the good that it is rendered. Pride then seems to be a sort of crown of the excellences; for it makes them greater, and it is not found without them. Therefore, it is hard to be truly proud; for it is impossible without nobility and goodness of character.

What we learn from this passage is that the term ἀξία largely corresponds to worth or value, whereas the good (ἀγαθόν) is entirely distinct. It is not a coincidence that the theory of values is called 'axiology' – it relies in fact on this early Greek distinction. The subjective dimension inherent in the understanding of a value, in contradistinction to the understanding of a good, is quite obviously present to Aristotle's mind here and even more so in the following passage.

V, 3 (1131a10–28)

Dignity, being not merely a sense of one's own worth, but also a claim to external goods (in particular to honour), defines justice. Justice is, in fact, according to an old saying criticised by Plato in the first book of the *Republic*, 'to give to everyone according to their dignity'. Hence, when dignity is dependent both on the social system and on virtue, justice must be a balancing act between claimants of various substance and quality in a given society. It is, to use language, which will only become current when the Latin *ius* is translated into the more subjective-sounding 'right' in the modern English natural rights tradition, *a balancing act between rights*.

Ἐπεὶ δ' ὅ τ' ἄδικος ἄνισος καὶ τὸ ἄδικον ἄνισον, δῆλον ὅτι καὶ μέσον τί ἐστι τοῦ ἀνίσου, τοῦτο δ' ἐστὶ τὸ ἴσον· ἐν ὁποίᾳ γὰρ πράξει ἐστὶ τὸ πλέον καὶ τὸ ἔλαττον, ἐστὶ καὶ τὸ ἴσον. εἰ οὖν τὸ ἄδικον ἄνισον, τὸ δίκαιον ἴσον· ὅπερ καὶ ἄνευ λόγου δοκεῖ πᾶσιν. ἐπεὶ δὲ τὸ ἴσον μέσον, τὸ δίκαιον μέσον τι ἂν εἴη. ἔστι δὲ τὸ ἴσον ἐν ἐλαχίστοις δυσίν. ἀνάγκη τοίνυν τὸ δίκαιον μέσον τε καὶ ἴσον εἶναι [καὶ πρός τι καὶ τισίν], καὶ ᾗ μὲν μέσον, τινῶν (ταῦτα δ' ἐστὶ πλεῖον

Quia autem et iniustus inaequalis et iniustum inaequale, manifestum quoniam et medium aliquod est iniusti [inaequalis?]; hoc autem est aequale, in quali enim operatione est plus et minus, est et aequale. Si igitur inuistum inaequale, iustum aequale, quod et sine ratione videtur omnibus; quia autem aequale medium, iustum medium quoddam utique erit. Est autem aequale ut in minimis duobus. Necessarium

Since the unjust man is unequal and the unjust act unequal, it is clear that there is also an intermediate for the unequal. And this is the equal; for in any kind of action in which there is a more and a less there is also what is equal. If, then, the unjust be unequal, the just is equal, as all men suppose it to be, even apart from argument. And since the equal is intermediate, the just will be an intermediate. Now equality implies at least

καὶ ἔλαττον), ᾗ δ' ἴσον ἐστίν,
ἐν δυοῖν, ᾗ δὲ δίκαιον, τισίν.
ἀνάγκη ἄρα τὸ δίκαιον, ἐν
ἐλαχίστοις εἶναι τέτταρσιν·
οἷς τε γὰρ δίκαιον τυγχάνει ὂν
δύο ἐστί, καὶ ἐν οἷς [τὰ πράγ-
ματα] δύο. καὶ ἡ αὐτὴ ἔσται
ἰσότης οἷς καὶ ἐν οἷς. ὡς γὰρ
ἐκεῖνα ἔχει [τὰ ἐν οἷς], οὕτω
κἀκεῖνα ἕξει· εἰ γὰρ μὴ ἴσοι,
οὐκ ἴσα ἕξουσιν, ἀλλ' ἐντεῦθεν
αἱ μάχαι καὶ τὰ ἐγκλήματα,
ὅταν ἢ ἴσοι μὴ ἴσα ἢ μὴ ἴσοι
ἴσα ἔχωσι καὶ νέμωνται. ἔτι ἐκ
τοῦ **κατ' ἀξίαν** τοῦτο δῆλον·
τὸ γὰρ δίκαιον ἐν ταῖς δια-
νομαῖς ὁμολογοῦσι πάντες
κατ' ἀξίαν τινὰ δεῖν εἶναι, τὴν
μέντοι ἀξίαν οὐ τὴν αὐτὴν
λέγουσι πάντες [ὑπάρχειν],
ἀλλ' οἱ μὲν δημοκρατικοὶ
ἐλευθερίαν, οἱ δ' ὀλιγαρχικοὶ
πλοῦτον, οἱ δ' εὐγένειαν, οἱ δ'
ἀριστοκρατικοὶ ἀρετήν. ἔστιν
ἄρα τὸ δίκαιον ἀνάλογόν τι.
τὸ γὰρ ἀνάλογον οὐ μόνον
ἐστὶ μοναδικοῦ ἀριθμοῦ ἴδιον,
ἀλλ' ὅλως ἀριθμοῦ· ἡ γὰρ ἀνα-
λογία ἰσότης ἐστὶ λόγων, καὶ
ἐν τέτταρσιν ἐλαχίστοις.

igitur iustum et medium et
aequale esse et ad aliquid et
quibusdam. Et secundum
quod quidem medium,
aliquorum, haec autem sunt
plus et minus; secundum
quod autem aequale est,
duobus; secundum quod
autem iustum, aliquibus et
ad aliquos, ad alios enim est.
Necessarium ergo iustum
in minimis esse quatuor;
quibus enim iustum con-
tingit ens, duo sunt, et in
quibus, res, duae. Et eadem
erit aequalitas quibus et
in quibus; ut enim illa
habent, quae in quibus, sic
et illa habent, quae quibus,
si enim non aequales, non
aequalia habebunt. Sed
hinc pugnae et accusationes,
quando vel aequales non
aequalia vel non aequales
aequalia habent et in distri-
butione suscipiunt. Adhuc
ex eo quod **secundum
dignitatem** hoc manifes-
tum. Iustum enim in dis-
tributionibus confitentur
omnes **secundum digni-
tatem** quandam oportere
esse. **Dignitatem** quidem
non eandem dicunt omnes
existere, sed democratici
quidem libertatem, oligar-
chiki autem divitias, quidam
autem generis nobilitatem,
aristocratici autem vir-
tutem. Est ergo iustum
proportionale quidem,

two things. The just, then,
must be both intermediate
and equal and relative (i.e.
for certain persons). And
qua intermediate it must
be between certain things
(which are respectively
greater or less); qua equal,
it involves *two* things; qua
just, it is for certain people.
The just, therefore, involves
at least four terms: for the
persons for whom it is in
fact just are two, and the
things in which it is manifested, the objects, are two.
And the same equality will
exist between the persons
and between the things concerned; for as the latter –
the things concerned – are
related, so are the former;
if they are not equal, they
will not have what is equal,
but this is the origin of quarrels and complaints – when
either equals have and are
awarded unequal shares,
or unequal equal shares.
Further, this is plain from
the fact that awards should
be **according to merit**; for
all men agree that what is
just in distribution must be
according to merit in some
sense, though they do not
all specify the same sort of
merit, but democrats identify it with the status of freeman, supporters of oligarchy
with wealth (or with noble

proportionale enim non solum est monadici numeri proprium, sed totaliter numeri. Proportionalitas enim aequalitas est proportionis. Et in quatuor minimis.

birth), and supporters of aristocracy with excellence. The just, then, is a species of the proportionate (proportion being not a property only of the kind of number which consists of abstract units, but of number in general). For proportion is equality of ratios, and involves four terms at least.

Aristotle here gives expression to the experience that various social groups and even entire societies value things differently and also value human beings differently. To him, therefore, worth (ἀξία) is not objective in the sense that the good (ἀγαθόν) is, rather it is dependent on the valuer who sets a price on the good. In relation to men, it is the status (the right to claim) which is recognised to them. Value, as distinct from the good, is what the good is recognised to be. Value was thus for Aristotle, as it is for the moderns, determining of the valuers, so it can define a group, who in virtue of their allegiance to the value constitute themselves as such (e.g. democrats, aristocrats). Hence democracy does not only recognise freeman's status to be the qualifying criterion for political status or dignity, democrats are in fact *defined* by their acceptance of the value of the freeman as being that which merits recognition of political rights. In this sense, modern democracy might be defined by its recognition of the value of intrinsic human dignity as explicitated by the human rights tradition.

Because acceptance makes up the character of the one who accepts (and of the society that adopts) the values, these are tried out in human relationships, where they become obvious for the valuer as well as for his or her fellows, in particular in intimate relationships such as friendship. This is why Aristotle regarded friendship as being in practical terms the equalising factor in human society.

VIII, 8 (1159a32–1159b1)

Because dignity defines justice, it also plays a role in friendship, which in
turn both defines and relies on justice. Friendship is, so to speak, the regulative ideal of justice in that it relies on the activity of friendliness (φιλεῖν),
as it is those who exercise the activity of friendliness *according to dignity*
(it is unclear whether this dignity pertains to the lover or to the beloved
or to both individually), who build a lasting friendship. Friendliness is in
its formal aspect what Kant later will call 'respect'. It has as its content the
entire substance of the moral life. Aristotle does not think that only the
love of lasting friendship measures up to the worth of the other. On the
contrary, for Aristotle, there cannot be many friends but only a few, due
to limited lifespan of the individual. Moreover, not everyone is worthy of
friendship. However, the lasting quality of the friendship – of whatever
kind it is – shows that a balance has been reached in it, where the other is
recognised for the worth he has, neither more nor less, whether this be of
the useful, the pleasant or the intrinsic kind.

Μᾶλλον δὲ τῆς φιλίας οὔσης ἐν τῷ φιλεῖν, καὶ τῶν φιλο-φίλων ἐπαινουμένων, φίλων ἀρετῇ τὸ φιλεῖν ἔοικεν· ὥστ' ἐν οἷς τοῦτο γίνεται **κατ' ἀξίαν**, οὗτοι μόνιμοι φίλοι καὶ ἡ τούτων φιλία.	Magis autem amicitia existente in amare et ama-toribus amicorum laudatis, amicorum virtus amare videtur. Quare in quibus hoc fit **secundum digni-tatem**, isti mansivi amici et talium amicitia.	Now since friendship depends more on loving, and it is those who love their friends that are praised, loving seems to be the characteristic excellence of friends, so that it is only those in whom this is found **in due measure** that are last-ing friends, and only their friendship that endures.

The Oxford translation here misses a point of the Greek, which the Latin
picks out very well: it is not only that those who love in due measure can be
lasting friends, it is also that the friendship lasts because they love according to the dignity of the beloved. This can of course be said to be to love
in due measure, and the translation expresses this meaning well. Even so,
the objective standard, set by the dignity of the other, is not underlined
in the English to the same extent as it is in the Latin (and in the Greek),

and it is likely that the objective note was intended by Aristotle. Friends are lasting friends because they are loved and esteemed as they deserve to be loved and esteemed, and because they love and esteem as their friends deserve to be loved and esteemed. They are in other words not deceived, either about the true value of the other or about their own worth.

If Aristotle had an understanding of human dignity, it is to be assembled from the preceding fragments. He did understand humans to be rational animals and reason to be fundamental in the sense that it laid its own foundations in intuition. Reason, hence, as far as it specifies a kind among animals, could be said, for Aristotle, to qualify these same animals with a 'fundamentality' that we could call dignity, and which is inherent in their very specificity. Human dignity would thus consist in the rationality determining the human kind as such.

Can we conclude from this that Aristotle had a concept of human dignity? This seems to be precluded by the fact that there is, according to Aristotle, no continuity between the principle of human dignity, derived from the rationality defining the human species, and the ethico-legal consequences to be drawn from it within a given social system. Aristotle admitted slavery and the subordination of women and was by no means an egalitarian. He rather argued for a pragmatic traditionalism based on a meritocracy. His recognition of various degrees of rationality to human beings may reflect that rationality cannot thrive in the presence of tyranny, but he did not contemplate the possibility of a status above the law of any particular society, which could correspond to the status of human dignity. He might have regarded such an idea as utopian, and looked upon it perhaps with suspicion. Yet, he did regard rationality to originate by itself, so he would have had the ressources to understand the idea.

That status in any given society is accorded for reasons other than that of humanity does not entail that human dignity is not at all respected in that society. It does mean however, that family connections, gender, money, merit and means play a role in how society responds to needs and establishes status in that society, and that human dignity is not the constitutional principle determining the laws of that society.

Dignity being the claim to goods external to oneself, and human beings being rational animals, human dignity would mean for Aristotle the claim

to exterior goods that the rational animal lays upon its surrounding world. This claim, or entitlement, would be what is experienced as desert, even if it is not linked to doing but to being. The idea of human dignity, however, though it is present in Aristotle, is so only in the margin as an idea that seems to have to be thought if we want to regard human beings as rational animals.

CHAPTER 2

The Roman Integration of Status and State Observed in Cicero

In Cicero, the concept of dignity is quite clearly thought out as a moral, legal and political fact, due to temperance, physical appearance and social organisation, and entitling the bearer to respect and honour. This is in many ways identical to Aristotle, also for the political context, in which *dignitas* was commonly used to designate an office. However *human* dignity is slightly more clearly conceptualised in Cicero than it is in Aristotle: it is the quality in humans commanding respect and honour. However, Cicero only once uses the phrase *human dignity* (6, *De Off.* 106) and in that context, the legal consequences of the term *dignitas* are not evoked, but only mastery over the passions. Even so, the idea that human nature (in virtue of which all humans are equal and in search of each other's company) should found the laws of the state is somehow, perhaps remotely, regulative for Cicero's ideal of a Republic. What is certain is that it constitutes a good argument, universally understood and therefore carrying a lot of political weight. Cicero the orator knows instinctively to distinguish between advantageous aspects of human dignity and disadvantageous ones, because he instinctively knows where it is good (and where it is possible) to steer the state.

Cicero's cosmopolitan experience, gained from contemplating the possibility of extending Roman Law to the ends of the known world, forced him to think in general terms and on a much larger scale than Aristotle. The challenge of universalism implicit in Roman imperialism also forced Cicero to think in more egalitarian terms even if he may well have been as enclined towards aristocracy as was Aristotle. Cicero did in fact understand himself to be a bridge between Greek and Roman culture, making accessible Greek refinement to his pragmatic co-citizens. He understood himself to transliterate the Aristotelian heritage into his Roman idiom and make

it serve the purpose of educating young Romans for public life, an activity through which he could have an influence on the Roman ruling cast.

Both texts and translations are taken from the Loeb editions.

De Inventione

Book II, Cap. LII–LV (157–169)

In the early work *De Inventione* dignity plays an important role. The definition: *dignitas est alicuius honesta et cultu et honore et verecundia digna auctoritas* – dignity is the possession of distinguished authority which merits respect, honour and reverence – allows Cicero to speak about the dignity of various things. There is a dignity of virtue, of knowledge and of truth, of people, and of their appearance, in so far, precisely, as each of these commands respect. (Only an untranslatable Latin expression, which Cicero in fact does not use, could shorten this definition further: *dignitas observanda est*). He in turn defines both justice and respect in terms of dignity thus creating a circular argument establishing justice, respect and dignity as complementary or co-original concepts, relying on each other for their definition.

Justice he defines as *habitus animi communi utilitate conservata suam cuique tribuens dignitatem* – the mental habit of giving every one according to merit while preserving the common advantage. Respect or reverence (*observantia*) he characterises as that *per quam homines aliqua dignitate antecedentes cultu quodam et honore dignantur* – by which people of some dignity are deigned to be worthy of cult and honour (*dignantur* could also be translated as 'deemed', 'recognised', 'accorded' or 'given'). Neither of these characterisations, however, serves the purpose of being the startingpoint of a more thorough inquiry. They rather form part of a catalogue of the moral virtues, that is, of the honourable attitudes.

Dignity, however, is not only honourable, it is also useful, like glory, importance and friendship. It is closely related to office or rank of either a charismatic or an institutionalised kind, because it is the root of right and duty simultaneously. The translation used in fact mistakenly renders it with an 'office'. From the context, however, dignity is more broadly defined by the honour and cult that is due to the authority it gives than is an office, and this serves to illustrate that dignity is not strictly speaking identical with an office. In fact, Cicero comes close to arguing – as Boethius will do later – that dignity should be the reason why someone would be conferred with an office in the first place, so that people be given only the offices they merit. Merit (*dignitas*), Boethius would claim, is not given by the office, but ought to precede it and be the ground for the authority it gives power to exercise. What is illustrated in Cicero's agreement with Boethius is that office, merit, desert, right and duty all have their common root and explanation in the concept of dignity. Translations therefore from time to time use these concepts interchangeably. Cicero, given his understanding of moral virtue and its relationship with state requirements, would quite likely have agreed with Boethius. What he insists on, however, is not that the office as such merits respect, but that dignity merits authority. The advantage or usefulness of dignity to which Cicero points, stands in contrast to its honourability but is not a negation of it. Dignity is mostly useful to provide for the needs of the body, though it may be advantageous in other ways too. Cicero understands the honourable and useful goods mentioned to contribute not only to the material security of the citizen in possession of them, but also to that of the state and of its power and reputation. For the sake of glory and security, the state thus has an interest in the protection of the dignity and other honourable and useful goods of its citizens. This understanding of dignity as both useful and honourable assures its place not only in the moral sphere but also in the political. An instinctive insight into how to balance these spheres against one another is in Cicero's case reinforced by rhetorical training and practice. It is also, however, a lawyer's or a politician's skill and Cicero possessed a good deal of both.

(157) LII. Rerum expetendarum tria genera sunt; par autem numerus vitandarum ex contraria parte. Nam est quiddam quod sua vi nos alliciat ad sese, non emolumento captans aliquo, sed trahens sua **dignitate**, quod genus virtus, scientia, veritas. Est aliud autem non propter suam vim et naturam, sed propter fructum atque utilitatem petendum; quod genus pecunia est. Est porro quiddam ex horum partibus iunctum, quod et sua vi et **dignitate** nos illectos ducit et prae se quandam gerit utilitatem, quo magis expetatur, ut amicitia, bona existimatio. Atque ex his horum contraria facile, tacentibus nobis, intellegentur. (158) Sed ut expeditius ratio tradatur, ea quae possimus brevi nominabuntur. Nam in primo genere quae sunt honesta appellabuntur; quae autem in secundo, utilia. Haec autem tertia, quia partem honestatis continent et quia maior est vis honestatis, iuncta esse omnino et duplici genere intelleguntur, sed in meliorem partem vocabuli conferantur et honesta nominentur. Ex his illud conficitur ut petendarum rerum partes sint honestas et utilitas, vitandarum turpitudo et inutilitas. His igitur duabus rebus res duae grandes sunt attributae, necessitudo et affectio; quarum altera ex vi, altera ex re et personis consideratur. De utraque post apertius perscribemus; nunc honestatis rationes primum explicemus.

LII. There are three kinds of things to be sought, and on the opposite side an equal number to be avoided. There is, namely, something which draws us to it by its intrinsic merit, not winning us by any prospect of gain, but attracting us by its own **worth**; to this class belong virtue, knowledge and truth. But there is something else that is to be sought not because of its own merit and natural goodness, but because of some profit or advantage to be derived from it. Money is in this class. There is, furthermore, something which unites qualities from both these classes; by its own merit and **worth** it entices us and leads us on, and also holds out to us a prospect of some advantage to induce us to seek it more eagerly. Examples are friendship and a good reputation. And these will easily suggest their opposites without our saying more. But that the principle may be stated more concisely, we shall give them names in a few words. The things in the first class will be called honourable, those in the second advantageous. Because the third group possesses some of the characteristics of honour, and because honour is a higher quality, we may apply the better term to them and call them honourable, although it is understood that they are undoubtedly complex and belong to both groups. From this it follows that honour and advantage are the qualities of things to be sought, and baseness and disadvantage, of things to be avoided. These two classes – things to be sought and things to be avoided – are related to two important circumstances – necessity and affection. Necessity is considered with reference to force, and affection with reference to events and persons. We shall write at

length with somewhat more detail about both later in the book. Now let us explain the nature of what is honourable.

(159) LIII. Quod aut totum aut aliqua ex parte propter se petitur, honestum nominabimus. Quare, cum eius duae partes sint, quarum altera simplex, altera iuncta sit, simplicem prius consideremus. Est igitur in eo genere omnes res una vi atque uno nomine amplexa virtus. Nam virtus est animi habitus naturae modo atque rationi consentaneus. Quamobrem omnibus eius partibus cognitis tota vis erit simplicis honestatis considerata. Habet igitur partes quattuor: prudentiam, iustitiam, fortitudinem, temperantiam.

(160) Prudentia est rerum bonarum et malarum neutrarumque scientia. Partes eius: memoria, intellegentia, providentia. Memoria est per quam animus repetit illa quae fuerunt; intellegentia, per quam ea perspicit quae sunt; providentia, per quam futurum aliquid videtur ante quam factum est.

Iustitia est habitus animi communi utilitate conservata suam cuique tribuens dignitatem. Eius initium est ab natura profectum; deinde quaedam in consuetudinem ex utilitatis ratione venerunt; postea res et ab natura profectas et ab consuetudine probatas legum metus et religio sanxit. (161) Naturae ius est quod non opinio genuit, sed quaedam in natura vis insevit, ut religionem, pietatem, gratiam, vindicationem, observantiam, veritatem. Religio est, quae superioris cuiusdam naturae, quam divinam vocant, curam caerimoniamque affert: pietas, per quam sanguine coniunctis patriaeque benivolum officium et diligens

LIII. We shall call honourable anything that is sought wholly or partly for its own sake. Now, since it has two divisions, one simple and the other complex, let us consider the simple one first. Everything in this class is embraced in one meaning and under one name, virtue. Virtue may be defined as a habit of mind in harmony with reason and the order of nature. Therefore, when we have become acquainted with all its parts we shall have considered the full scope of honour, pure and simple. It has four parts: wisdom, justice, courage, temperance.

Wisdom is the knowledge of what is good, what is bad and what is neither good nor bad. Its parts are memory, intelligence, and foresight. Memory is the faculty by which the mind recalls what has happened. Intelligence is the faculty by which it ascertains what is. Foresight is the faculty by which it is seen that something is going to occur before it occurs.

Justice is a habit of mind which gives every man his desert while preserving the common advantage. Its first principles proceed from nature, then certain rules of conduct became customary by reason of their advantage; later still both the principles that proceed from nature and those that had been approved by custom received the support of religion and the fear of the law. The law of nature is that which is not born of opinion, but implanted in us by a kind of innate instinct: it includes religion, duty, gratitude, revenge, reverence and truth. Religion is that which brings men to serve and worship a higher order

tribuitur cultus; gratia, in qua amicitiarum et officiorum alterius memoria et remunerandi voluntas continetur; vindicatio, per quam vis aut iniuria et omnino omne, quod obfuturum est, defendendo aut ulciscendo propulsatur; **observantia, per quam homines aliqua dignitate antecedentes cultu quodam et honore dignantur;** veritas, per quam immutata ea quae sunt aut ante fuerunt aut futura sunt dicuntur.

of nature, which they call divine. Duty is the feeling, which renders kind offices and loving service to one's kin and country. Gratitude embraces the memory of friendships and of services rendered by another and the desire to requite these benefits. Revenge is the act of defending or avenging ourselves and so warding off violence, injury or anything, which is likely to be prejudicial. **Reverence is the feeling by which men of distinguished position are held worthy of respect and honour.** Truth is the quality by which events in the past, present and future are referred to without alteration of material fact.

(162) LIV. Consuetudine ius est, quod aut leviter a natura tractum aluit et maius fecit usus, ut religionem; aut si quid eorum quae ante diximus ab natura profectum maius factum propter consuetudinem videmus, aut quod in morem vetustas vulgi approbatione perduxit; quod genus pactum est, par, iudicatum. Pactum est quod inter aliquos convenit; par, quod in omnes aequabile est; iudicatum, de quo alicuius aut aliquorum iam sententiis constitutum est. Lege ius est, quod in eo scripto, quod populo expositum est, ut observet, continetur.

LIV. Customary law is either a principle that is derived only in a slight degree from nature and has been fed and strengthened by usage – religion, for example – or any of the laws that we have mentioned before which we see proceed from nature but which have been strengthened by custom, or any principle which lapse of time and public approval have made the habit or usage of the community. Among these are covenants, equity and decisions. A covenant is an agreement between some persons. Equity is what is just and fair to all. A decision is something determined previously by the opinion of some person or persons. Statute law is what is contained in a written document which is published for people to observe.

(163) Fortitudo est considerata periculorum susceptio et laborum perpessio. Eius partes magnificentia, fidentia, patientia, perseverantia. Magnificentia est rerum magnarum et excelsarum cum animi ampla quadam et splendida propositione cogitatio atque administratio; fidentia est per quam magnis

Courage is the quality by which one undertakes dangerous tasks and endures hardships. Its parts are highmindedness, confidence, patience, perseverance. Highmindedness consists in the contemplation and execution of great and sublime projects with a certain grandeur and mag-

et honestis in rebus multum ipse animus in se fiduciae certa cum spe collocavit; patientia est honestatis aut utilitatis causa rerum arduarum ac difficilium voluntaria ac diuturna perpessio; (164) perseverantia est in ratione bene considerata stabilis et perpetua permansio.

Temperantia est rationis in libidinem atque in alios non rectos impetus animi firma et moderata dominatio. Eius partes continentia, clementia, modestia. Continentia est per quam cupiditas consili gubernatione regitur; clementia, per quam animi temere in odium alicuius inferioris concitati comitate retinentur; modestia, per quam pudor honesti curam et stabilem comparat auctoritatem. Atque haec omnia propter se solum, ut nihil adiungatur emolumenti, petenda sunt. Quod ut demonstretur neque ad hoc nostrum institutum pertinet et a brevitate praecipiendi remotum est. (165) Propter se autem vitanda sunt non ea modo quae his contraria sunt, ut fortitudini ignavia et iustitiae iniustitia, verum etiam illa quae propinqua videntur et finitima esse, absunt autem longissime, quod genus, fidentiae contrarium est diffidentia et ea re vitium est; audacia non contrarium, sed appositum est ac propinquum et tamen vitium est. Sic uni cuique virtuti finitimum vitium reperietur, aut certo iam nomine appellatum, ut audacia, quae fidentiae, pertinacia, quae perseverantiae finitima est, superstitio, quae religioni propinqua est, aut sine ullo certo nomine. Quae omnia item uti contraria rerum bonarum in rebus vitandis reponentur.

nificence of imagination. Confidence is the quality by which in important and honourable undertakings the spirit has placed great trust in itself with a resolute hope of success. Patience is a willing and sustained endurance of difficult and arduous tasks for a noble and useful end. Perseverance is a firm and abiding persistence in a well-considered plan of action.

Temperance is a firm and well-considered control exercised by the reason over lust and other improper impulses of the mind. Its parts are continence, clemency and modesty. Continence is the control of desire by the guidance of wisdom. Clemency is a kindly and gentle restraint of spirits that have been provoked to dislike of a person of inferior rank. Modesty is a sense of shame or decency which secures observance and firm authority for what is honourable. All these qualities are desirable for their own sake, though no profit be connected with them. To prove this is not pertinent to our present purpose nor is it consistent with the brevity required in a textbook. On the other side the qualities to be avoided for their own sake are not only the opposites of these – as, for example, cowardice is the opposite of courage, and injustice of justice – but also those qualities which seem akin and close to these but are really far removed from them. To illustrate, diffidence is the opposite of confidence, and therefore is a vice; temerity is not opposite to courage, but borders on it and is akin to it, and yet is a vice. In a similar way each virtue will be found to have a vice bordering upon it, either one to which a definite name has become attached, as temerity which borders on courage, or stubbornness, which

borders on perseverance, or superstition which is akin to religion; or one without any definite name. All of these as well as the opposites of good qualities will be classed among things to be avoided.

Ac de eo quidem genere honestatis quod omni ex parte propter se petitur, satis dictum est.

Enough has been said about the kind of honourable thing that is sought entirely for its own sake.

(166) LV. Nunc de eo in quo utilitas quoque adiungitur, quod tamen honestum vocamus, dicendum videtur. Sunt igitur multa quae nos cum **dignitate** tum quoque fructu suo ducunt; quo in genere est gloria, **dignitas**, amplitudo, amicitia. Gloria est frequens de aliquo fama cum laude; **dignitas est alicuius honesta et cultu et honore et verecundia digna auctoritas**; amplitudo potentiae aut maiestatis aut aliquarum copiarum magna abundantia; amicitia voluntas erga aliquem rerum bonarum illius ipsius causa quem diligit cum eius pari voluntate. (167) Hic, quia de civilibus causis loquimur, fructus ad amicitiam adiungimus ut eorum quoque causa petenda videatur; ne forte qui nos de omni amicitia dicere existimant, reprendere incipiant. Quamquam sunt qui propter utilitatem modo petendam putant amicitiam; sunt qui propter se solum; sunt qui propter se et utilitatem. Quorum quid verissime constituatur, alius locus erit considerandi. Nunc hoc sic ad usum oratorium relinquatur, utramque propter rem amicitiam esse expetendam. (168) Amicitiarum autem ratio, quoniam partim sunt religionibus iunctae, partim non sunt, et quia partim veteres sunt, partim novae, partim ab illorum, partim ab nostro beneficio profectae, partim utiliores, partim minus utiles, ex causarum dignitatibus, ex

LV. Now I think I should speak of that which is also coupled with advantage; which, nevertheless, we call honourable. There are then many things that attract us not only by their intrinsic **worth** but also by the advantage to be derived from them; this class includes glory, **rank**, influence, and friendship. Glory consists in a person's having a widespread reputation accompanied by praise. **Rank is the possession of a distinguished office, which merits respect, honour, and reverence.** Influence is a fullness of power, dignity, or resources of some sort. Friendship is a desire to do good to some one simply for the benefit of the person whom one loves, with a requital of the feeling on his part. Since we are here discussing speeches about public issues, we associate friendship with benefits to be derived from it, so that it may seem desirable because of these as well as for its own sake. I say this that I may not perhaps be taken to task by those who think I am speaking of every kind of friendship. As a matter of fact there are some who think that friendship is to be sought solely for advantage, others for itself alone and others for itself and for advantage. Which opinion has the best foundation is a matter to be considered at another time. For the present let it be left thus as far as oratorical practice is concerned, that friendship is to be sought

temporum opportunitatibus, ex officiis, ex religionibus, ex vetustatibus habebitur.

for both reasons. In as much as some friendships are related to religious scruples, and some not, and some are old and some new, some arise from a kindness done to us by others, and some from our own services to them, some are more advantageous and some less, an examination of their nature will involve a consideration of the value of causes, the suitableness of times and occasion, moral obligation, religious duties, and length of time.

LVI. Utilitas autem aut in corpore posita est aut in extrariis rebus; quarum tamen rerum multo maxima pars ad corporis commodum revertitur, ut in re publica quaedam sunt quae, ut sic dicam, ad corpus pertinent civitatis, ut agri, portus, pecunia, classis, nautae, milites, socii, quibus rebus incolumitatem ac libertatem retinent civitates, aliae vero, quae iam quiddam magis amplum et minus necessarium conficiunt, ut urbis egregia exornatio atque amplitudo, ut quaedam excellens pecuniae magnitudo, amicitiarum ac societatum multitudo. (169) Quibus rebus non illud solum conficitur ut salvae et incolumes, verum etiam ut amplae atque potentes sint civitates. Quare utilitatis duae partes videntur esse, incolumitas et potentia. Incolumitas est salutis rata atque integra conservatio; potentia est ad sua conservanda et alterius attenuanda idonearum rerum facultas.

LVI. Advantage lies either in the body or in things outside the body. By far the largest part of external advantages, however, results in advantage of the body. For example, in the state there are some things that, so to speak, pertain to the body politic, such as fields, harbours, money, a fleet, sailors, soldiers and allies – the means by which states preserve their safety and liberty – and other things contribute something grander and less necessary, such as the great size and surpassing beauty of a city, an extraordinary amount of money and a multitude of friendships and alliances. These things not only make States safe and secure, but also important and powerful. Therefore, there seem to be two parts to advantage – security and power. Security is a reasoned and unbroken maintenance of safety. Power is the possession of resources sufficient for preserving one's self and weakening another.

Cap. LIX (177)

Dignity is, for Cicero, not only to be considered an *honourable advantage* in bodily and spiritual terms. It also is a bodily *virtue*, like health, force and speed, which is manifest in stately appearance. Commanding office

and appearance both render dignity visible. They therefore constitute the obvious standards for respect and justice. *Decorum* is the basic rule of Roman ethics, and dignity can well be said to be the essence of the decorous. Dignity, founding justice as the object of respect, is also simply visible in the physical attributes of a stately person. Thus stateliness, to Cicero, is virtuous, meritorious, and deserving of respect.

LIX. Laudes autem et vituperationes ex eis locis sumentur qui loci personis sunt attributi, de quibus ante dictum est. Sin distributius tractare qui volet, partiatur in animum et corpus et extraneas res licebit. Animi est virtus cuius de partibus paulo ante dictum est, corporis valetudo, **dignitas**, vires, velocitas; extraneae honos, pecunia, affinitas, genus, amici, patria, potentia, cetera quae simili esse in genere intellegentur.

LIX. Praise and censure will be derived from the topics that are employed with respect to the attributes of persons; these have been discussed above. If one wishes to treat the subject more methodically, these may be divided into mind, body and external circumstances. The virtue of the mind is that whose parts we discussed only recently. The virtues of the body are health, **beauty**, strength, speed. Extraneous virtues are public office, money, connexions by marriage, high birth, friends, country, power, and all the other things that are understood to be in this class.

De Oratore

Book III, Cap. XLV–XLVI (178–80)

The use of dignity in *De Inventione* is further developed in the later *De Oratore*. From this passage, it becomes clear that nature and law are in concert to favour the coincidence of the most dignified and the most useful. The necessity of all parts of the body and organs in animals demonstrates the economy with which a great artwork is made; an economy that we call dignity. The roof of a temple likewise is so indispensible to its integrity and therefore to its dignity, that even a temple in heaven would not lack a roof. Dignity, here, is a kind of super-utility or super-importance. The body and

natural things in general all have this super-utility to an eminent degree as far as they strike the perfect balance between necessity and economy. It is aesthetically and morally pleasing and perfectly fitted to its function or use. Dignity, we must admit from this perspective, is a kind of perfection, which promises that the honourable and the useful do not stand in a relationship of eternal conflict.

(178) Sed ut in plerisque rebus incredibiliter hoc natura est ipsa fabricata, sic in oratione, ut ea quae maximam utilitatem in se continerent eadem haberent plurimum vel **dignitatis** vel saepe etiam venustatis. Incolumitatis ac salutis omnium causa videmus hunc statum esse huius totius mundi atque naturae, rotundum ut caelum terraque ut media sit aeque sua vi nutuque teneatur; sol ut eam circum feratur, ut accedat ad brumale signum et inde sensim ascendat in diversam partem; ut luna accessu et recusso [suo] solis lumen accipiat; ut eadem spatia quinque stellae dispari motu cursuque conficiant. (179) Haec tantam habent vim ut paulum immutata cohaerere non possint, tantam pulchritudinem ut nulla species ne excogitari quidem possit ornatior. Referte nunc animum ad hominum vel etiam ceterorum animantium formam et figuram: nullam partem corporis sine aliqua necessitate afficatam totamque formam quasi perfectam reperietis arte, non casu.

But in oratory as in most matters nature has contrived with incredible skill that the things possessing most utility also have the greatest amount of **dignity**, and indeed frequently of beauty also. We observe that for the safety and security of the universe this whole ordered world of nature is so constituted that the sky is a round vault, with the earth at its centre, held stationary by its own force and stress; and the sun travels round it, approaching towards the constellation of mid-winter and then gradually rising towards the opposite direction; while the moon receives the sun's light as it advances and retires; and five stars accomplish the same courses with different motion and on a different route. This system is so powerful that a slight modification of it would make it impossible for it to hold together, and it is so beautiful that no lovelier vision is even imaginable. Now carry your mind to the form and figure of human beings or even of the other living creatures: you will discover that the body has no part added to its structure that is superfluous, and that its whole shape has the perfection of a work of art and not of an accident.

XLVI. Quid in arboribus? in quibus non truncus, non rami, non folia sunt denique nisi ad suam retinendam conservandamque naturam; nusquam tamen est ulla pars nisi venusta. (180) Linquamus naturam,

XLVI. Take trees: in these the trunk, the branches and lastly the leaves are all without exception designed so as to keep and to preserve their own nature, yet nowhere is there any part which is not beautiful.

artesque videamus: quid tam in navigio
necessarium quam latera, quam cavernae,
quam prora, quam puppis, quam antennae,
quam vela, quam mali? quae tamen hanc
habent in specie venustatem ut non solum
salutis sed etiam voluptatis causa inventa
esse videantur. Columnae et templa et por-
ticus sustinent, tamen habent non plus utilitatis quam **dignitatis**. Capitoli fastigium
illud et ceterarum aedium non venustas sed
necessitas ipsa fabricata est; nam cum esset
habita ratio quemadmodum ex utraque
tecti parte aqua delaberetur, utilitatem
fastigii templi **dignitas** consecuta est, ut
etiamsi in caelo Capitolium statueretur ubi
imber non esse posset, nullam sine fastigio
dignitatem habiturum fuisse videatur.

Let us leave nature and contemplate the
arts: in a ship, what is so indispensable as
the sides, the hold, the bow, the stern, the
yards, the sails and the masts? yet they all
have such a graceful appearance that they
appear to have been invented not only for
the purpose of safety but also for the sake of
giving pleasure. In temples and colonnades,
the pillars are to support the structure, yet
they are as **dignified** in appearance as they
are useful. Yonder pediment of the Capitol
and those of the other temples are the product not of beauty but of actual necessity; for
it was in calculating how to make the rain-
water fall off two sides of the roof that the
dignified design of the gables resulted as a
by-product of the needs of the structure –
with the consequence that even if one were
erecting a citadel in heaven, where no rain
could fall, it would be thought certain to
be entirely lacking in **dignity** without a
pediment.

De Re Publica

Book I, Cap. XXVII (43) and XXXIV (52–3)

Only political and artistic virtuosity combined with luck realises the balance of dignity. Most of the time, the struggle to govern and do things
well is hard work and produces a variety of different results in terms of
value. By observing experiments in different forms of government both
at a distance and close at hand, Cicero comes to advocate in *The Republic*
a mixture of the three good forms of government – kingship, aristocracy
and democracy. Scipio, Cicero's mouthpiece, maintains that aristocratic
distinctions in dignity, whether implying rank or office, should be based

on both moral superiority and excellence, and not on riches. The people have to, or at least seem to have to, appoint someone or some people to be in charge. They consequently invest these with greater dignity, such that absolute political equality would not only be an injustice in relation to leaders and subjects, but it would also be a political failure. Athens, Cicero claims, did not last as a state because it did not have a fixed *cursus honorum* to maintain distinctinctions in dignity, that is, maintain its functionality as a state. Neither monarchy nor democracy gives full justice to dignity, when, as Cicero maintains, it is respected in moral and intellectual excellence alone. His utopian vision therefore is an egalitarian 'meritocracy', where dignity is recognised in those who deserve it for ethical and political reasons. Dignity emerges here as a moral concept – it is not only what commands respect, or what is super-important, it is what *ought* to command respect, what *ought* to be taken to be important. Just like Aristotle's axioms.

XXVII. (43) Sed et in regnis nimis expertes sunt ceteri communis iuris et consilii, et in optimatium dominatu vix particeps libertatis potest esse multitudo, cum omni consilio communi ac potestate careat, et cum omnia per populum geruntur quamvis iustum atque moderatum, tamen ipsa aequabilitas est iniqua, cum habet nullos **gradus dignitatis.** Itaque si Cyrus ille Perses iustissimus fuit sapientissimusque rex, tamen mihi populi res (ea enim est, ut dixi antea, publica) non maxime expetenda fuisse illa videtur, cum regeretur unius nutu ac modo. Si Massilienses, nostri clientes, per delectos et principes cives summa iustitia reguntur, inest tamen in ea condicione populi similitudo quaedam servitutis. Si Athenienses quibusdam temporibus sublato Aeropago nihil nisi populi scitis ac decretis agebant, **quoniam distinctos dignitatis gradus non habebant,** non tenebat ornatum suum civitas. [...]

XXVII: But in kingships the subjects have too small a share in the administration of justice and in deliberation; and in aristocracies the masses can hardly have their share of liberty, since they are entirely excluded from deliberation for the common wealth and from power; and when all the power is in the people's hands, even though they exercise it with justice and moderation, yet the resulting equality itself is inequitable, since it allows no **distinctions in rank.** Therefore, even though the Persian Cyrus was the most just and the wisest of kings, that form of government does not seem to me the most desirable, since 'the property of the people' (for that is what a commonwealth is, as I have said) is administered at the nod and caprice of one man; even though the Massilians, now under our protection, are ruled with the greatest justice by a select number of their leading citizens, such a situation is nevertheless to some extent like slavery for a people; and

even though the Athenians at certain periods, after they had deprived the Areopagus of its power, succeeded in carrying on all their public business by the resolutions and decrees of the people, their State, **because it had no definite distinctions in rank**, could not maintain its fair renown. [...]

(52) Virtute vero gubernante rem publicam quid potest esse praeclarius, cum is, qui inperat aliis, servit ipse nulli cupiditati, cum, quas ad res civis instituit et vocat, eas omnis complexus est ipse nec leges inponit populo, quibus ipse non pareat, sed suam vitam ut legem praefert suis civibus? qui si unus satis omnia consequi posset, nihil opus esset pluribus, si universi videre optimum et in eo consentire possent, nemo delectos principes quaereret. Difficultas ineundi consilii rem a rege ad plures, error et temeritas populorum a multitudine ad paucos transtulit. Sic inter infirmitatem unius temeritatemque multorum medium optimates possederunt locum, quo nihil potest esse moderatius; quibus rem publicam tuentibus beatissimos esse populos necesse est vacuos omni cura et cogitatione aliis permisso otio suo, quibus id tuendum est neque committendum, ut sua commoda populus neglegi a principibus putet. (53) Nam aequabilitas quidem iuris, quam amplexantur liberi populi, neque servari potest (ipsi enim populi, quamvis soluti ecfrenatique sint, praecipueque multis multa tribuunt, et est in ipsis magnus dilectus hominum et **dignitatum**), eaque, quae appellatur aequabilitas, iniquissima est. Cum enim par habetur honos summis et infimis, qui sint in omni populo necesse est, ipsa aequitas iniquissima est; quod in iis civitatibus, quae ab optimis reguntur,

But what can be nobler than the government of the State by virtue? For then the man who rules others is not himself a slave to passion, but has already acquired for himself all those qualities to which he is training and summoning his fellows. Such a man imposes no laws upon the people that he does not obey himself, but puts his own life before his fellow citizens as their law. If a single individual of this character could order all things properly in a State, there would be no need of more than one ruler; or if the citizens as a body could see what was best and agree upon it, no one would desire a selected group of rulers. It has been the difficulty of formulating policies that has transferred the power from a king to a larger number; and the perversity and rashness of popular assemblies that have transferred it from the many to the few. Thus, between the weakness of a single ruler and the rashness of the many, aristocracies have occupied that intermediate position which represents the utmost moderation; and in a State ruled by its best men, the citizens must necessarily enjoy the greatest happiness, being freed from all cares and worries, when once they have entrusted the preservation of their tranquillity to others, whose duty it is to guard it vigilantly and never to allow the people to think that their interests are being neglected by their rulers. For that equality

accidere non potest. Haec fere, Laeli, et quaedam euisdem generis ab iis, qui eam formam rei publicae maxime laudant, disputari solent.

of legal rights of which free peoples are so fond cannot be maintained (for the people themselves, though free and unrestrained, give very many special powers to many individuals, and create great distinctions among men and the **honours** granted to them), and what is called equality is really most inequitable. For when equal honour is given to the highest and the lowest – for men of both types must exist in a nation – then this very 'fairness' is most unfair; but this cannot happen in States ruled by their best citizens. These arguments and others like them, Laelius, are approximately those which are advanced by men who consider this form of government the best.

De Legibus

Book I, Cap. VII (22–3)

In *On the Laws*, Cicero takes part himself in the dialogue, with his friend Atticus and his brother Quintus. Book I develops a theory of natural law according to which human beings have been endowed with intellect and will by the creator God, are equal by virtue of this and by their consequent sense of justice, fairness and equality. They are bound together by nature with a bond of kindness and good will. Cicero explains that the acceptance of divine government, which Atticus has just granted him, implies that all humans are of noble rank. Their dignity reposes on the fact that they are held in favour by the gods. Cicero thus associates natural law with belief in a creator God, on the one hand, and with the recognition of equal dignity in all human beings, on the other. Their equality is founded on the gift of human nature – inclusive of will and intellect – bestowed by and shared with the gods. The customary bestowing of rank based on

nature, generally used to argue for the conservative point of view that the aristocratic families in place have a natural right to rule, is here also understood to play for the benefit of man in general. Common man, like the noble families, has his right in common with the gods because of his noble descent from them. Freedom and reason, hence, is understood to be signs of kinship with the gods. How this exactly squares with the political necessity of having a *cursus honorum* is not dealt with here. Cicero seems to consider this a practical political problem, not a theoretical problem of principle. He probably considered the recognition of human dignity to be included in his utopian meritocracy, such that they in practice would support one another.

This text has been included for its systematic importance for Cicero's thought, despite not making any mention of dignity.

Non faciam longius; huc enim pertinet, animal hoc providum, sagax, multiplex, acutum, memor, plenum rationis et consilii, quem vocamus hominem, praeclara quadam condicione generatum esse a supremo deo; solum est enim ex tot animantium generibus atque naturis particeps rationis et cogitationis, cum cetera sint omnia expertia. Quid est autem non dicam in homine, sed in omni caelo atque terra ratione divinius? Quae cum adolevit atque perfecta est, nominatur rite sapientia. (23) Est igitur, quoniam nihil est ratione melius eaque est et in homine et in deo, prima homini cum deo rationis societas; inter quos autem ratio, inter eosdem etiam recta ratio communis est; quae cum sit lex, lege quoque consociati homines cum dis putandi sumus. Inter quos porro est communio legis, inter eos communio iuris est; quibus autem haec sunt inter eos communia, et civitatis eiusdem habendi sunt. Si vero isdem imperiis et potestatibus parent, multo iam magis; parent autem

I will not make the argument long. Your admission leads us to this: that animal which we call man, endowed with foresight and quick intelligence, complex, keen, possessing memory, full of reason and prudence, has been given a certain distinguished status by the supreme God who created him; for he is the only one among so many different kinds and varieties of living beings who has a share in reason and thought, while all the rest are deprived of it. But what is more divine, I will not say in man only, but in all heaven and earth, than reason? And reason, when it is full grown and perfected, is rightly called wisdom. Therefore, since there is nothing better than reason, and since it exists both in man and God, the first common possession of man and God is reason. But those who have reason in common must also have rights in common. And since right reason is Law, we must believe that men have Law also in common with the gods. Further, those who share Law, must also

huic caelaesti descriptioni mentique divinae et praepotenti deo; ut iam universus hic mundus sit una civitas communis deorum atque hominum existimanda.

share Justice; and those who share these are to be regarded as members of the same commonwealth. If indeed they obey the same authorities and powers, this is true in a far greater degree; but as a matter of fact they do obey this celestial system, the divine mind, and the God of transcendent power. Hence we must now conceive of this whole universe as one commonwealth of which both gods and men are members.

Et quod in civitatibus ratione quadam, de qua dicetur idoneo loco, agnationibus familiarum distinguuntur status, id in rerum natura tanto est magnificentius tantoque praeclarius, ut homines deorum agnatione et gente teneantur.

And just as in States distinctions in legal status are made on account of the blood relationships of families, according to a system which I shall take up in its proper place, so in the universe the same thing holds true, but on a scale much vaster and more splendid, so that men are grouped with Gods on the basis of blood relationship and descent.

Book I, XXII (59)

Cicero also understands divine favour to have imprinted itself in the soul of the human being, so that it works on the soul as its τέλος, as an expectation to be met within itself. When the challenge is met, the divine spark will give man the satisfaction of knowing that he is good, and that he is happy. This idea is taken up by the Fathers of the Church in the light of the biblical heritage so as to understand man to be created not only *in* the image of God, but also *to it*.

Nam qui se ipse norit, primum aliquid se habere sentiet divinum ingeniumque in se suum sicut simulacrum aliquod dicatum putabit tantoque munere deorum semper **dignum** aliquid et faciet et sentiet et, cum se ipse perspexerit totumque temptarit, intelleget, quem ad modum a

For he who knows himself will realize, in the first place, that he has a divine element within him, and will think of his own inner nature as a kind of consecrated image of God; and so he will always act and think in a way **worthy** of so great a gift of the gods, and, when he has examined and thoroughly

natura subornatus in vitam venerit quan- tested himself, he will understand how
taque instrumenta habeat ad obtinendam nobly equipped by Nature he entered life,
adipiscendamque sapientiam, quoniam and what manifold means he possesses for
principio rerum omnium quasi adumbratas the attainment and acquisition of wisdom.
intelligentias animo ac mente conceperit, For from the very first he began to form in
quibus inlustratis sapientia duce bonum his mind and spirit shadowy concepts, as it
virum et ob eam ipsam causam cernat se were, of all sorts, and when these have been
beatum fore. illuminated under the guidance of wisdom,
he perceives that he will be a good man, and
for that very reason, happy.

Tusculan Disputations

Book II, Cap. V (14) and XII–XIII (28–31)

The second book of the *Tusculan Disputations* concern the art of enduring pain. Written in Cicero's darkest hour, the work as a whole is dedicated to the Stoic attitudes to life, death, anxiety, bitterness, pain and the passions in general. Does the suffering of pain diminish one's dignity? This is the question Cicero tries to answer while criticising the Epicurean position and hinting at the possibility of suicide as the last resort. Suffering is an evil, but it is very much the lesser evil compared to degradation. Degrading (*dedecus*) is it, in turn, to think that pain could not be patiently borne or ignored for the sake of respect for virtue and love of honour. This aspect of Cicero's understanding of dignity is linked to the possible conflict between the moral and physical expression of human dignity. When put in front of the stark choice, it is more honourable to choose the spiritual virtue of the soul above the appearance and pain of the body.

The etymological relationship between *dignitas* and *decorum* is, although some claim it to be obvious, uncertain. Nevertheless, the kinship in meaning makes it proper to pay attention to the use of the expressions derived from *decus*, as if the relationship was certain. Dignity, in fact, is

the ultimate reason and ground for what is decorous or proper, and hence also what stands behind its meaning.

A. is the pupil, M. the master, that is, Cicero.

(14) A. Dolorem existimo maximum malorum omnium. M. Etiamne maius quam **dedecus**? A. Non audeo id quidem dicere et me pudet tam cito de sententia esse deiectum. M. Magis esset pudendum, si in sententia permaneres. Quid est **minus dignum** quam tibi peius quidquam videri **dedecore**, flagitio, turpitudine, quae ut effugias, quis est non modo non recusandus, sed non ultro appetendus, subeundus, excipiendus dolor? [...]

A. I consider pain the greatest of all evils. M. Greater even than **disgrace**? A. I do not venture to go so far as that and I am ashamed of having been dislodged so speedily from my position. M. You should have been still more ashamed had you clung to it. For what is more **unworthy** than for you to regard anything as worse than **disgrace**, crime and baseness? And to escape these, what pain should be, I do not say rejected, but should not rather be voluntarily invited, endured and welcomed? [...]

(28) [M.] Virtutis magistri, philosophi, inventi sunt qui summum malum dolorem dicerent. At tu, adolescens, cum id tibi paullo ante dixisses videri, rogatus a me etiamne maius quam **dedecus**, verbo de sententia *destitisti*. Roga hoc idem Epicurum: maius dicet esse malum mediocrem dolorem quam maximum **dedecus**; in ipso enim **dedecore** mali nihil esse, nisi sequantur dolores. Quis igitur Epicurum sequitur dolor, cum hoc ipsum dicit, summum malum esse dolorem? quo **dedecus** maius a philosopho nullum expecto. Qua re satis mihi dedisti, cum respondisti maius tibi videri malum **dedecus** quam dolorem. Hoc ipsum enim si tenebis, intelliges quam sit obsistendum dolori; nec tam quaerendum est dolor malumne sit quam firmandus animus ad dolorem ferendum. Concludunt ratiunculas Stoici cur non sit malum, quasi de verbo, non de re laboretur. (29) – Quid me decipis, Zeno? Nam cum id, quod mihi horribile videtur, tu

Philosophers, the teachers of virtue, have been found ready to say that pain was the highest evil. But you, young man, after saying a little while ago that you shared this view, when asked by me whether you thought that it was a greater evil even than **disgrace**, at a word abandoned your opinion. Put the same questions to Epicurus: he will say that a moderated degree of pain is worse evil than the deepest **disgrace**, for no evil is involved in **disgrace** alone, unless it should be attended by painful circumstances. What pain then does Epicurus feel when he actually affirms that pain is the greatest evil? And yet I cannot look to find any worse **disgrace** than such a sentiment in the mouth of a philosopher. You therefore gave me all I wanted when you replied that you regarded **disgrace** as a greater evil than pain. For if you hold fast simply to this truth you will realize the resistance which must be offered to pain, and we must not endeavour so much to ask

omnino malum negas esse, capior et scire cupio quod modo id, quod ego miserrimum existimem, ne malum quidem sit. – 'Nihil est,' inquit, 'malum, nisi quod turpe atque vitiosum est.' – Ad ineptias redis. Illud enim, quod me angebat, non eximis. Scio dolorem non esse nequitiam; desine id me docere: hoc doce, doleam necne doleam nihil interesse. – 'Numquam quidquam,' inquit, 'ad beate quidem vivendum, quod est in una virtute positum, sed est tamen reiiciendum.' Cur? 'Asperum est, contra naturam, difficile perpessu, triste, durum.'

whether pain be an evil as to strengthen the soul for the endurance of pain. The Stoics construct foolish syllogisms to prove pain no evil, just as if the difficulty in question were a verbal one and not one of matter of fact. Why deceive me, Zeno? When you say that what is dreadful in my eyes is not an evil at all, I am attracted and long to know how it can be true that the condition I regard as utter wretchedness is not even evil. 'There is nothing evil,' says he, 'except what is base and wicked'. Now you are talking foolishly, for you do not take away the cause of my torment: I know that pain is not villainy; stop teaching me that; tell me that it makes no difference whether I am in pain or not in pain. 'It never makes any difference,' says he, 'to the fact of leading a happy life, which is based on virtue alone; but, all the same, pain is to be shunned.' Why? 'It is unpleasing, against nature, hard to endure, melancholy, cruel.'

(30) XIII: Haec est copia verborum, quod omnes uno verbo malum appellamus, id tot modis posse dicere. Definis tu mihi, non tollis dolorem, cum dicis asperum, contra naturam, vix quod ferri tolerarique possit, nec mentiris, sed re succumbere non oportebat, verbis gloriantem. Nihil bonum nisi quod honestum, nihil malum nisi quod turpe: optare hoc quidem est, non docere. Illud et melius et verius, omnia, quae natura aspernetur, in malis esse: quae asciscat, in bonis. Hoc posito et verborum concertatione sublata tantum tamen excellet illud, quod recte amplexantur isti, quod honestum, quod rectum, quod **decorum** appellamus, quod idem interdum virtutis nomine amplectimur, ut omnia praeterea, quae bona corporis et fortunae putantur,

XIII. Here is a flood of words, all to get a number of different expressions for what we call in a single word 'evil'. You are giving me a definition of pain, you are not removing it, when you say that it is unpleasing, against nature, a thing that can scarcely be borne or endured, and you do not lie. But you should not have really yielded the point under a cloak of vaunting words. 'Nothing good but what is honourable, nothing evil but what is base:' this is mere aspiration, not proof. The better and truer statement is that all such things as nature rejects are counted evils, all such things as nature accepts count as goods. Once determine this and do away with the verbal controversy, and it will be found that what the Stoics are right in clinging to, what we call honourable,

perexigua et minuta videantur, nec malum ullum ne si in unum quidem locum collata omnia sint, cum turpitudinis malo comparandum. Qua re si, ut initio concessisti, turpitudo peius est quam dolor, nihil est plane dolor; nam dum tibi turpe nec **dignum** viro videbitur gemere, eiulare, lamentari, frangi, debilitari dolore, dum honestas, dum **dignitas**, dum **decus** aderit, tuque in ea intuens te continebis, cedet profecto virtuti dolor et animi inductione languescet; aut enim nulla virtus est aut contemnendus omnis dolor.

right, **becoming**, and sometimes comprehend under the name of virtue, – this will still stand out in such pre-eminence that, in comparison, all things which are held to be goods of body and fortune will seem insignificant and paltry, whilst it will also be found that no evil, even if all evils were heaped together, is to be compared with the evil of disgrace. Therefore if, as you admitted at the outset, disgrace is worse than pain, pain is clearly of no account; for whilst you shall hold it base and un**worthy** of a man to groan, shriek aloud, wail, break down and be unnerved; so long as honour, so long as **nobility**, so long as **worth** remain, and so long as you control yourself by keeping your eyes upon them, assuredly pain will lead to virtue and grow fainter by a deliberate effort of will; for either no virtue exists or all pain is to be despised.

De Officiis

Book I, Cap. XXVII – XXX (93–100, 105–7)

In his last work *De Officiis*, which is treating of morals in general, dignity is reserved an important place in the treatment of the fourth cardinal virtue: temperance, but it must be noted that dignity in a sense is what the whole treatise is about. *Officium* is translated by duty, which in contemporary English renders the objective sense of *dignitas* as an office. Cicero investigates those relations of giving and receiving service, which constitute the political world. The central phenomenon of this dynamics is, according to Cicero, *officium*, very like what Aristotle called ἀξία. This illustrates well that both right and duty are two aspects of the same social phenomenon,

one viewed in relation to the giver, the other in relation to the receiver. The relationship between them, however, is a matter of recognition. Duties, as well as rights must be recognised for the social dynamics to work. It is Cicero's aim to instruct in the workings of this dynamism, in order to facilitate recognition of a strategic kind, so that the reader (his son) will be able to benefit from the dynamism, instead of being run over by it. *De Officiis* is a book about *how to recognise*. How to recognise what to do, and how to recognise the good.

The first thing to recognise is that one has the duty to be the master of one's passions. This is not only the essence of temperance, but it is also necessary for moral life as such, for prudence, courage and justice, which all are indispensable political virtues. Without temperance, we could not do what is fitting (*decus*) and thus behave with dignity in all the spheres of life.

There are two kinds of *decorum*, one which is 'that which harmonises with man's superiority in those respects in which his nature differs from that of the rest of the animal creation', and a second, which is a prolongation of the first, which makes of man a gentleman (*homo liberalis*). There is, in other words, a dignity attaching to man, as man, and a dignity depending on the exercise of his humanity. Cicero is here distinguishing between a natural dignity and a dignity to cultivate oneself in the manner of a cultivated person. Nature has assigned to us a character (*persona*) of surpassing dignity, beyond the inventions of the poets, and this obliges us not only to act with temperance, but also to be kind to our fellow humans. Kind we must be, and that not only to the good, but to the bad as well, because they all are equally human and hence are deserving of our respect. The two kinds of dignity are therefore ultimately one. If the dignity of nature does not express itself in kindness and solidarity, it lowers itself to the brutish state and loses the gracious stateliness with which moral integrity adorns the virtuous. One must consequently be and do good or become bad. There is no neutral state.

XXVII. Sequitur, ut de una reliqua parte honestatis dicendum sit, in qua verecundia et quasi quidam ornatus vitae, temperantia et modestia omnisque sedatio perturbationum animi et rerum modus cernitur. Hoc loco continetur id, quod

XXVII. We have next to discuss the one remaining division of moral rectitude. That is the one in which we find considerateness and self-control, which give, as it were, a sort of polish to life; it embraces also temperance, complete subjection of all

dici Latine **decorum** potest; Graece enim πρέπον dicitur. Huius vis ea est, ut ab honesto non queat separari; (94) nam et, quod **decet**, honestum est et, quod honestum est, **decet**; qualis autem differentia sit honesti et **decori**, facilius intellegi quam explanari potest. Quicquid est enim, quod **deceat**, id tum apparet, cum antegressa est honestas. Itaque non solum in hac parte honestatis, de qua hoc loco disserendum est, sed etiam in tribus superioribus quid **deceat** apparet. Nam et ratione uti atque oratione prudenter et agere, quod agas, considerate omnique in re quid sit veri videre et tueri **decet**, contraque falli, errare, labi, decipi tam **dedecet** quam delirare et mente esse captum; et iusta omnia **decora** sunt, iniusta contra, ut turpia, sic **indecora**.

Similis est ratio fortitudinis. Quod enim viriliter animoque magno fit, id **dignum** viro et **decorum** videtur, quod contra, id ut turpe, sic **indecorum**.

(95) Quare pertinet quidem ad omnem honestatem hoc, quod dico, **decorum**, et ita pertinet, ut non recondita quadam ratione cernatur, sed sit in promptu. Est enim quiddam, idque intellegitur in omni virtute, quod **deceat**; quod cogitatione magis a virtute potest quam separari. Ut venustas et pulchritudo corporis secerni non potest a valetudine, sic hoc, de quo

the passions, and moderation in all things. Under this head is further included what, in Latin, may be called *decorum* (propriety); for in Greek it is called πρέπον. Such is its essential nature, that it is inseparable from moral goodness; for what is **proper** is morally right, and what is morally right is **proper**. The nature of the difference between morality and **propriety** can be more easily felt than expressed. For whatever **propriety** may be, it is manifested only when there is pre-existing moral rectitude. And so, not only in this division of moral rectitude which we have now to discuss but also in the three preceding divisions, it is clearly brought out what **propriety** is. For to employ reason and speech rationally, to do with careful consideration whatever one does, and in everything to discern the truth and to uphold it – that is **proper**. To be mistaken, on the other hand, to miss the truth, to fall into error, to be led astray – that is as **improper** as to be deranged and lose one's mind. And all things just are **proper**; all things unjust, like all things immoral, are **improper**.

The relation of **propriety** to fortitude is similar. What is done in a manly and courageous spirit seems **becoming** to a man and **proper**; what is done in a contrary fashion is at once immoral and **improper**.

This **propriety**, therefore, of which I am speaking belongs to each division of moral rectitude; and its relation to the cardinal virtues is so close, that it is perfectly self-evident and does not require any abstruse process of reasoning to see it. For there is a certain element of **propriety** perceptible in every act of moral rectitude; and this can be separated from virtue theoretically better

loquimur, **decorum** totum illud quidem est cum virtute confusum, sed mente et cogitatione distinguitur.

than it can be practically. As comeliness and beauty of person are inseparable from the notion of health, so this **propriety** of which we are speaking, while in fact completely blended with virtue, is mentally and theoretically distinguishable from it.

(96) Est autem eius discriptio duplex; nam et generale quoddam **decorum** intellegimus, quod in omni honestate versatur, et aliud huic subiectum, quod pertinet ad singulas partes honestatis. Atque illud superius sic fere definiri solet: **decorum id esse, quod consentaneum sit hominis excellentiae in eo, in quo natura eius a reliquis animantibus differat. Quae autem pars subiecta generi est, eam sic definiunt, ut id decorum velint esse, quod ita naturae consentaneum sit, ut in eo moderatio et temperantia appareat cum specie quadam liberali.**

The classification of **propriety**, moreover, is twofold: (1) we assume a general sort of **propriety**, which is found in moral goodness as a whole; then (2) there is another **propriety**, subordinate to this, which belongs to the several divisions of moral goodness. The former is usually defined somewhat as follows: '**Propriety is that which harmonizes with man's superiority in those respects in which his nature differs from that of the rest of the animal creation**.' And they so define the special type of propriety which is subordinate to the general notion, that they represent it to be that propriety which harmonizes with nature, in the sense that it manifestly embraces temperance and self-control, together with a certain deportment.

XXVIII (97) Haec ita intellegi possumus existimare ex eo **decoro**, quod poëtae sequuntur; de quo alio loco plura dici solent. Sed tum servare illud poëtas, quod **deceat**, dicimus, cum id, **quod quaque persona dignum est, et fit et dicitur;** ut si Aeacus aut Minos diceret: oderint, dum metuant, aut: natis sepulcro ipse est parens, **indecorum** videretur, quod eos fuisse iustos accepimus; at Atreo dicente plausus excitantur; est enim **digna** persona oratio. Sed poëtae, quid quemque **deceat**, ex persona iudicabunt; **nobis autem personam imposuit ipsa natura magna cum excellentia praestantiaque animantium reliquarum.**

XXVIII That this is the common acceptation of **propriety** we may infer from that **propriety** which poets aim to secure. Concerning that, I have occasion to say more in another connection. Now, we say that the poets observe **propriety, when every word or action is in accord with each individual character.** For example, if Aeacus or Minos said: 'Let them hate, if only they fear', or: 'The father is himself his children's tomb,' that would seem **improper**, because we are told that they were just men. But when Atreus speaks those lines, they call forth applause; for the sentiment is in **keeping with** the character. But it will rest with the poets to decide,

according to the individual characters, what is **proper** for each; **but to us Nature herself has assigned a character of surpassing excellence, far superior to that of all other living creatures, and in accordance with that we shall have to decide what propriety requires.**

(98) Quocirca poëtae in magna varietate personarum, etiam vitiosis quid conveniat et quid **deceat**, videbunt, nobis autem cum a natura constantiae, moderationis, temperantiae, verecundiae partes datae sint, cumque eadem natura doceat non neglegere, quem ad modum nos adversus homines geramus, efficitur, ut et illud, quod ad omnem honestatem pertinet, **decorum** quam late fusum sit, appareat et hoc, quod spectatur in uno quoque genere virtutis. Ut enim pulchritudo corporis apta compositione membrorum movet oculos et delectat hoc ipso, quod inter se omnes partes cum quodam lepore consentiunt, sic hoc **decorum**, quod elucet in vita, movet approbationem eorum, quibuscum vivitur, ordine et cônstantia et moderatione dictorum omnium atque factorum.

The poets will observe, therefore, amid a great variety of characters, what is suitable and **proper** for all – even for the bad. But to us Nature has assigned the roles of steadfastness, temperance, self-control, and considerateness of others; Nature also teaches us not to be careless in our behaviour towards our fellow-men. Hence we may clearly see how wide is the application not only of that **propriety** which is displayed in each particular subdivision of virtue. For, as physical beauty with harmonious symmetry of the limbs engages the attention and delights the eye, for the very reason that all the parts combine in harmony and grace, so this **propriety**, which shines out in our conduct, engages the approbation of our fellow-men by the order, consistency, and self-control it imposes upon every word and deed.

(99) Adhibenda est igitur quaedam reverentia adversus homines et optimi cuiusque et reliquorum. Nam neglegere, quid de se quisque sentiat, non solum arrogantis est, sed etiam omnino dissoluti. Est autem, quod differat in hominum ratione habenda inter iustitiam et verecundiam. Iustitiae partes sunt non violare homines, verecundiae non offendere; in quo maxime vis perspicitur **decori.**

We should, therefore, in our dealings with people show what I may almost call reverence toward all men – not only toward the men who are the best, but toward others as well. For indifference to public opinion implies not merely self-sufficiency, but even total lack of principle. There is, too, a difference between justice and considerateness in one's relations to one's fellow-men. It is the function of justice not to do wrong to one's fellow-men; of considerateness, not to wound their feelings; and in this the essence of **propriety** is best seen.

His igitur expositis, quale sit id, quod decere dicimus, intellectum puto.

With the foregoing exposition, I think it is clear what the nature is of what we term **propriety**.

(100) Officium autem, quod ab eo ducitur, hanc primum habet viam, quae deducit ad convenientiam conservationemque naturae, quam si sequemur ducem, numquam aberrabimus sequemurque et id, quod acutum et perspicax natura est, et id, quod ad hominum consociationem accomodatum, et id, quod vehemens atque forte. Sed maxima vis **decori** in hac inest parte, de qua disputamus; neque enim solum corporis, qui ad naturam apti sunt, sed multo etiam magis animi motus probandi, qui item ad naturam accomodati sunt.

Further, as to the duty, which has its source in propriety, the first road on which it conducts us leads to harmony with Nature and faithful observance of her laws. If we follow Nature as our guide, we shall never go astray, but we shall be pursuing that which is in its nature clear-sighted and penetrating [Wisdom], that which is adapted to promote and strengthen society [Justice], and that which is strong and courageous [Fortitude]. But the very essence of **propriety** is found in the division of virtue which is now under discussion [Temperance]. For it is only when they agree with Nature's laws that we should give our approval to the movements not only of the body, but still more of the spirit.

The following text, which follows on from the previous after a short interval, is the only one in which Cicero comes close to using the literal expression 'human dignity'. Cicero does so to distinguish humanity from brutality in the context, still, of the decorous. We can interpret Cicero to say that it is because we have the dignity of humanity that we must be in command of our passions and exercise self-control. This implies not giving in to inclinations in the same instinctive way as do the animals. So even if we have sensual pleasure in common with animals, giving in to sensuality and its pleasures is not worthy of the dignity of man. Dignity, in contrast, commends self-denial, simplicity and sobriety. Our particular character must, on this account, conform to the universal character, the *telos* of man, in virtue of which he is superior to animals by the faculty of reason. Dignity in its physical expression as stateliness might be more pronounced in some individual characters than in others, but this does not affect the universal character, which, by itself, has a dignity distinct from particular physical endowments.

XXX. (105) Sed pertinet ad omnem officii quaestionem semper in promptu habere, quantum natura hominis pecudibus reliquisque beluis antecedat; illae nihil sentiunt nisi voluptatem ad eamque feruntur omni impetu, hominis autem mens discendo alitur et cogitando, semper aliquid aut anquirit aut agit videndique et audendi delectatione ducitur. Quin etiam, si quis est paulo ad voluptates propensior, modo ne sit ex pecudum genere (sunt enim quidam homines non re, sed nomine), sed si quis est paulo erectior, quamvis voluptate capiatur, occultat et dissimulat appetitum voluptatis propter verecundiam.

XXX. But it is essential to every inquiry about duty that we keep before our eyes how far superior man is by nature to cattle and other beasts: they have no thought except for sensual pleasure and this they are impelled by every instinct to seek; but man's mind is nurtured by study and meditation; he is always either investigating or doing, and he is captivated by the pleasure of seeing and hearing. Nay, even if a man is more than ordinarily inclined to sensual pleasures, provided, of course, that he be not quite on a level with the beasts of the field (for some people are men only in name, not in fact) – if, I say, he is a little too susceptible to the attractions of pleasure, he hides the fact, however much he may be caught in its toils, and for very shame conceals his appetite.

(106) Ex quo intellegitur corporis voluptatem **non satis esse dignam hominis praestantia**, eamque contemni et reici oportere; sin sit quispiam, qui aliquid tribuat voluptati, diligenter ei tenendum esse eius fruendae modum. Itaque victus cultusque corporis ad valetudinem referatur et ad vires, non ad voluptatem. Atque etiam si considerare volumus, quae sit in natura excellentia et **dignitas**, intellegemus, quam sit turpe diffluere luxuria et delicate ac molliter vivere quamque honestum parce, continenter, severe, sobrie.

From this we see that sensual pleasure is **quite unworthy of the dignity of man** and that we ought to despise it and cast it from us; but if some one should be found who sets some value upon sensual gratification, he must keep strictly within the limits of moderate indulgence. One's physical comforts and wants, therefore, should not be ordered according to the calls of pleasure. And if we will only bear in mind the superiority and **dignity** of our nature, we shall realize how wrong it is to abandon ourselves to excess and to live in luxury and voluptuousness, and how right it is to live in thrift, self-denial, simplicity, and sobriety.

(107) Intellegendum etiam est duabus quasi nos a natura indutos esse personis; quarum una communis est ex eo, quod omnes participes sumus rationis praestantiaeque eius, qua antecellimus bestiis, a qua omne honestum **decorum**que trahitur, et ex qua ratio

We must realize also that we are invested by Nature with two characters, as it were: one of these is universal, arising from the fact of our being all alike endowed with reason and with that superiority which lifts us above the brute. From this all morality

inveniendi officii exquiritur, altera autem, quae proprie singulis est tributa. Ut enim in corporibus magnae dissimilitudines sunt (alios videmus velocitate ad cursum, alios viribus ad luctandum valere, itemque in formis aliis **dignitatem** inesse, aliis venustatem), sic in animis existunt maiores etiam varietates.

and **propriety** are derived, and upon it depends the rational method of ascertaining our duty. The other character is the one that is assigned to individuals in particular. In the matter of physical endowment there are great differences: some, we see, excel in speed for the race, others in strength for wrestling; so in point of personal appearance, some have **stateliness**, others comeliness. Diversities of character are greater still.

Cicero thus has an understainding of human dignity in the sense of that which is worthy of the human being, drawing from the same font of meaning as the dignity of office, of appearance and of descent, but quite distinct from it. He considers human dignity to be natural to the general character of man, but he does so in the teleological sense that human dignity must be respected by specific characters conforming to it as best they can.

Book I, XXXVI (130)

Whether it is this distinction between the general and specific character, which leads him to affirm that men have dignity while women are lovely is unclear. What it would entail, if this was so, is that he considers some human beings to be particularly endowed with dignity, and thus in possession of the general character of the species, whereas others are not so, and therefore do not exemplify the general character in possession of human dignity. Women, in accordance with this, would both have and not have the general character of humanity, obliging them to stay superior to the brutes, of course, in Cicero's time, not vote and hold political office and in Cicero's mind dignity *is* such political status, because it is simultaneously responding to duty and having a claim to (public) respect. Had Cicero explicitly accorded dignity to women, he would have argued for their political status as active citizens, and played an entirely different role in history.

Cum autem pulchritudinis duo genera sint, quorum in altero venustas sit, in altero **dignitas**, venustatem muliebrem ducere debemus, **dignitatem virilem**. Ergo et a forma removeatur omnis viro non **dignus** ornatus, et huic simile vitium in gestu motuque caveatur. Nam et palaestrici motus sunt saepe odiosiores, et histrionum non nulli gestus ineptiis non vacant, et in utroque genere quae sunt recta et simplicia, laudantur. Formae autem **dignitas** coloris bonitate tuenda est, color excertitationibus corporis. Adhibenda praeterea munditia est non odiosa neque exquisita nimis, tantum quae fugiat agrestem et inhumanam neglegentiam. Eadem ratio est habenda vestitus, in quo, sicut in plerisque rebus, mediocritas optima est.

Again, there are two orders of beauty: in the one, loveliness predominates; in the other, **dignity**; of these we ought to regard loveliness as the attribute of woman, and **dignity as the attribute of man**. Therefore, let all finery not suitable to a man's **dignity** be kept off from his person, and let him guard against the like fault in gesture and action. The manners taught in the palaestra, for example, are often rather objectionable, and the gestures of actors on the stage are not always free from affectation; but simple, unaffected manners are commendable in both instances. Now **dignity** of mien is also to be enhanced by a good complexion; the complexion is the result of physical exercise. We must besides present an appearance of neatness – not too punctillious or exquisite, but just enough to avoid boorish and illbred slovenliness. We must follow the same principle in regards to dress. In this, as in most things, the best rule is the golden mean.

The text understands dignity as an aesthetic characteristic of the male sex. Is it still understood as dependent on virtue or reason? At any rate, Cicero's rudimentary theory of human dignity is here turned into a theory of the dignity of *man*. No doubt, this dignity of man should be reflected in law, even if it is unclear exactly what such reflection should be (in particular as regards slaves). A double requirement seems to be contemplated by Cicero: on the one hand equality before the law (of all free men) and on the other the possibility of distinguishing oneself through a *cursus honorum*. Cicero probably both believed in the principle of human dignity *and* in the fact that some humans were more human than others. Questioned to this effect, he would, however, possibly have withdrawn. The universal claims inherent in the concept were (and still are?) utopian and Cicero's ability to avoid confrontation looks more like cultural habit or political virtuosity than willfull inconsistency. Nevertheless, the inconsistency remains characteristic of his understanding.

CHAPTER 3

The Dead Sea Scrolls and the Biblical Heritage

The state of Israel has, like (other?) European nation states adopting constitutions after the Second World War, adopted human dignity as a principle
in one of its basic laws (*Basic Law: Human Dignity and Liberty*), but only
quite recently (1992). This situated the State of Israel within the human
rights tradition, at a time when its credibility within the UN was challenged by the Palestinian question. The laws appear in an official English
translation, according to which the Hebrew term translated by human
dignity is כבוד האדם (kvod ha-Adam), the same expression which was used
to translate Pico della Mirandola's *Oration on Human Dignity* into Hebrew
in 1990. The Hebrew Wikipedia article (accessed August 2018) on human
dignity indeed begins with the sentence:

כבוד האדם הוא ערך המתייחס אל תכונתו הייחודית של האדם כאדם; הוא משווה
משמעות מוסרית לעצם היות האדם אנושי.

It translates, in Jeremy Corley's words, as follows: 'The glory of humanity
[= human dignity] is the value relating to the specific quality of the human
being [or humanity] as a human being [or as humanity]. It equates the
ethical significance to the actual essence of the human being.'

'Kvod ha-Adam' is not the only expression used by modern speakers
of Hebrew to translate human dignity. Hershey Friedman, for example,
writes an article on 'human dignity and the Jewish tradition', taking human
dignity to translate 'kvod habriot' (2008). Fred Morgan states that 'the
word kavod is used in a number of compounds found throughout Jewish
literature, each of them imitating the dignity that is due to the divine. These
include "dignity due to [all] creatures" (k'vod habri'ot), "dignity due to the
community" (k'vod hatzibbur), "dignity due to one's parents" (k'vod av
va'eim, found in the Ten Commandments), "dignity due to the majority"

(k'vod harabbim, respecting the majority ruling), even "dignity due to the Rabbi" (k'vod harav)' (Morgan, 2018). He claims that all of these at times can mean what is meant by human dignity. A native speaker suggested that *motar ha-Adam* מותר האדם can also reflect the meaning of human dignity.

The expression *kvod ha-Adam* is not found in the Bible, whether Christian or Jewish, but it is found in the Dead Sea Scrolls, in what Fletcher-Louis (2002, 113) characterises as the 'certainly "sectarian" scrolls' among them; the *Community Rule, the Damascus Document* and the *Hodayot* (the *Thanksgiving Hymns*). It is not surprising that it is translated in this context by 'the glory of Adam', which in English has connotations different from those of human dignity. The documents provide a 'witness to the Essene movement's angelomorphic humanity tradition', which understood 'original, true, redeemed humanity' to be divine, linked with worship in the Temple, as 'a model of the universe', which 'offers its entrants a transfer from earth to heaven, from humanity to divinity and from mortality to immortality' (Fletcher-Louis, 2002, xi). The Essenian theological and liturgical anthropology seems marked by a radical withdrawal into the 'Wilderness' at Qumran, where a true Temple service calls for the *theosis* potentially associated with the Messiah. The glory of Adam is Adam's prelapsarian splendour, which he held from God and lost through sin, but which is promised restored to the sons of 'righteousness', to those God has chosen for his covenant, all of whom are 'in' Adam, in so far as Adam simply means the 'human being'.

Jair Lorberbaum is therefore somewhat correct in affirming that 'the Hebrew counterpart to the expression "human dignity" – kevod ha-adam – hardly exists in classical Jewish sources', if we exclude the Dead Sea Scrolls. It does not seem right, however, that 'this expression entered the Hebrew language and the Jewish-Israeli culture in modern times due to the influence of modern European structures of thought' (Lorberbaum, 2014). Even if one were to regard the Essenes as not contributing to Jewish-Israeli culture, they still wrote in Hebrew. The possibility exists that the Essene tradition and with it the concept of kvod ha-Adam was handed on through rabbinic and/or esoteric traditions. For lack of time, it was not possible to pursue that idea for the present publication; it remains an exiting task.

The connection between the Qumran texts and Pico's treatise, known to be influenced through Flavius Mithridates by the Kabbalah, is, as regards the title, only apparent, as it must be remembered that Pico's treatise only came to bear the name under which it is now known long after its first appearance, in 1557. It remains that the central idea of his oration is shared by the Qumran texts: like the Essenes, Pico believed in the possibility of an ideal humanity, which is angelic (or 'angelomorphic'), that is, divine in nature or status.

The Christians, following Jesus' lead, identified Jesus' body with the true Temple, the Church, and saw, as a consequence, Jesus' passion and resurrection as a key to the restoration of the glory of Adam. To them human dignity was not only created by God, but restored in Christ, and thus the idea of *theosis* was interpreted as relationship with Christ, as being 'in' him and he being in us. Maybe later masonic speculation on the temple, which does not make this identification, but rather identifies the temple with the masonic temple, would arrive at a different conception of human dignity, one that is 'built' in the masonic way, as cities are. It is not difficult to imagine both traditions tracing their ancestry to the liturgical anthropology of Qumran.

The finding among the Qumran scrolls of fragments of *Ecclesiasticus* (the Wisdom of Jesus Ben Sirach) in Hebrew yields a close relative to the expression we investigate: תפארת אדם, the 'splendour of Adam'. The context of the expression allows for an interpretation that lies very close to the meaning of human dignity. The splendour of Adam, as the primal human being, is said to be above the fame of all the kings and prophets of Israel, indicating a universal, fundamental value, which surpasses the importance of all illustrious individuals. Fletcher-Louis makes the case, however, that the Adam referred to must be seen in the light of Simon the High Priest (treated of in the chapter following immediately after), as the human being performing the high-priestly service in the Temple and *thereby* showing forth the splendour of God. However, one interpretation need not exclude the other. The foothold in the Bible may be enough to see that the idea also finds its place in the Christian history of *theosis*, which likewise finds expression in terms of human dignity. We shall look at that in relation to a prayer said over the gifts in the Catholic Mass liturgy in Part II.

Texts from the Community Rule, the Thanksgiving Hymns (Hodayot) and the Damascus Rule (Damascus Document) are taken from *Dead Sea Scrolls Study Edition* by F. Garcia Martinez and E. J. C. Tigchelaar (Leiden: Brill, 2000).

Community Rule (1QS 4.22–23)

כיא בם בחר אל לברית עולמים   For those God has chosen for an everlast-
23 ולהם כול **כבוד**   ing covenant 23 and to them shall belong
אדם   all the **glory of Adam**.

Thanksgiving Hymns (1QH 4.14–15)

ושם [עולם] הקימותה 15   You have raised an [eternal] name, 15 [for-
[לשאת] פשע ולהשליך כול   giving] offence, casting away all their iniq-
עוונותם ולהנחילם בכול **כבוד**   uities, giving them as a legacy all the **glory**
אדם [ו] רוב ימים   **of Adam** [and] abundance of days.

Damascus Rule (CD-A 3.20), p. 555

המחזיקים בו לחיי נצח וכל **כבוד אדם** להם הוא   Those who remained steadfast in it will acquire eternal life, and all the **glory of Adam** is for them.

The Book of Ecclesiasticus (Jesus Sirach), 49, 16

The Hebrew text is taken from *The Hebrew Text of the Book of Ecclesiasticus* ed. Israel Lévy (Leiden: Brill, 1951), p. 69. The Greek text is from *Sapientia Iesu Filii Sirach*, ed. J. Ziegler (Göttingen: Vandenhoeck & Ruprecht, 1965), p. 357. Translations by Jeremy Corley, Saint Patrick's College, Maynooth.

ושם ושת ואנוש נפקדו	And Shem and Seth	Σημ καὶ Σηθ	Shem and Seth were
ועל כל חי תפארת	and Enosh were vis-	ἐν ἀνθρώποις	glorified among
אדם	ited, but above eve-	ἐδοξάσθησαν, καὶ	human beings, and
	ryone living is the	ὑπὲρ πᾶν ζῷον ἐν τῇ	above everything
	splendour of Adam	κτίσει Αδαμ	living in the crea-
			tion was Adam

Were one to pursue the idea of human dignity in the Bible, and not the expression as we do here, key texts frequently referred to are Gen 1:27–8, Psalm 8, and Sir 17:1–7. To have these linked with the glory of Adam, however, and therefore with its loss in sin and restauration through the redemption brought by Christ, is enlightening.

PART II

Medieval Sources

As the Western Roman Empire transformed, some of the structures of impirial administration were incorporated into the adopted religion and with them a legacy of codified law, surviving both as canon law and as a source of secular law. The ideal of dignity as self-control meriting office or responsibility formed part of that legacy. The peoples migrating from the East and the North gradually adopted Christianity, the by now official religion of Rome, as their leaders found in the *mores* of the meek religion an effective justification for their authority. Thus Christianity became synonymous with the customs of a settled, if not a civilised, life. The Church, supported by monasticism and the ideal of Christian marriage, contributed during the centuries lacking strong state power to the creation of a culture that was not dependent on the state but supportive of its emergence. Whereas the gentiles converted, the Jews in Europe kept their own understanding of being the chosen people, and to the extent that the European kingdoms came to rely on tribal and religious loyalty, this proved a recurring social and political problem.

In the patristic and Carolingian sources, we discern two tendencies. One is to criticise the Roman cult of honour, rank and dignity as merely human and therefore prone to typically human deceptions. The other is to claim for the human being the highest dignity since God has both marvellously created the human being in and to his image and still more marvellously restored his human dignity in Christ. The splendour, with which the redeemed human being is decorated as he behaves according to the dignity confided to him, is God's glory, not the glory that comes from other human beings as they accord fame, honour or recognition. His glory is 'the glory of Adam', the prelapsarian dignity restored to its former glory.

Later, in the scholastic sources, the inheritance from Cicero and Aristotle combine to systematically identify the person and dignity, such

that a compatibility with law is achieved, although insignificant due to the weakness of the state. Some testing occurs as to whether this identification applies to women as well as to men. The importance of human dignity for personal comportment is underlined, such that whatever legal implications the notion might have first and foremost concerns the bearer him or herself, and this to the point where, were he to forfeit his dignity by sinning, his life also would lose its inviolability to others.

In the late medieval sources, women affirm aspects of human dignity that were easily forgotten: the dignity of the ill, the pregnant woman and the ordinary layperson. They thus use the notion to vindicate not their own rights exactly, but the rights of all those who are vulnerable. The vindication is subtle, and talking about vindication may seem exaggerated were it not for the trend it were to start, and which must be traced back to here. Women seem to have been advocating for the recognition of human dignity for themselves as much as for others finding themselves in the same twilight situation as them for many generations. The three sources here excerpted enjoyed a very large readership, and it could well be that an important feature of what people learned from them was precisely to vindicate the dignity of the poor in this subtle manner.

CHAPTER 4

Patristic and Carolingian Sources

As the early Christian writers criticised the Roman cult of honour, rank and dignity, they reminded the human being that God raised him to the dignity of being a child, priest, prophet and king in Jesus Christ. The Christian perception that human dignity depends on redemption in Christ had the effect of relativising dignity as the world bestows it, since God is the higher power. Augustine, with St Paul, recalled that the Lord Jesus chose the infirm of this world to confound the strong, and that he did this to reveal the radical newness of status contained in the kingdom of God. Leo the Great affirmed human dignity to be a gracious participation in divine nature, achieved by the Redeemer, whereas Lady Philosophy consoled Boethius to the effect that only the dignity that relies on virtue is real. In this manner, the pagan world marked by the pursuit of worldly power appeared as apparent and another world, in which human dignity manifested itself in justice and righteousness, shone through its cracks.

The use of *dignitas* by Augustine, Leo and Boethius testifies in every case to the transformation of the Roman Empire, and to its transposition into a hierarchical Church. Despite the criticism directed at using dignity to designate an office, it nevertheless often referred to the higher ranks of the priesthood. The dignity of virtue, insisted on by Aristotle and Cicero, morphed into the dignity of the Christian – a dignity received in baptism as a call to holiness. The aristocracy advocated by Cicero crossbred with Germanic customs and grew into feudalism, its *cursus honorum* relative to a military career and tribal loyalty.

With the Carolingian Renaissance, the prayer of St Leo becomes the emblem of the new liturgical order and accordingly promulgates the notion of human dignity throughout the Latin West. It echoes in the *dicta Albini*, in Eriugena, through scholastic times, in the tradition in which

Pico stands, in the early modern forerunners of the Kantian formulation and still into our days.

Augustine of Hippo (354–430)

To Augustine *dignitas* meant, as it did for the Romans, socially recognised importance, a worldly factor, over and against which the moral dignity of the rational soul, believing in Christ and restored by him, ought to be preferred, even to the dignity of an angel. This preference is a matter of right judgement or adequate valuation – it does not happen automatically. In fact, we seem to have a tendency to prefer what is useful to us and value it higher than what is warrented by the created order. Thus, it comes about that we can value a horse or a piece of jewellery higher than a slave. Augustine is not advocating that we should value in this way, on the contrary: according to him we should value in accordance with the natural hierarchy in which the redeemed human being occupies the summit over and above the fallen angel.

Sermon 250

Text from *Patrologia Latina* 38, coll. 1163. Translation is my own.

Dominus Jesus infirma mundi eligens, ut confunderet fortia, et colligens ecclesiam suam de toto orbe terrarum non coepit ab imperatoribus, aut a senatoribus, sed a piscatoribus. Quaecumque enim **dignitates** fuissent prius electae, sibi hoc auderent tribuere, non Dei gratiae.	The Lord Jesus chose the weak of the world to confound the strong, and gathered his church from all the earth. He did not call emperors first, nor senators, but fishermen. This is because any one **important** who had been chosen first, would have attributed this to himself and not to the grace of God.

De civitate Dei

Text from *The City of God against the Pagans*, trans. David E. Wiesen, vol. III, Loeb Classical Library (Cambridge, MA and London: Harvard University Press – William Heinemann, 1968). The translation of the first text is my own.

VIII, 15, 2

Sicut enim fieri potuit ut aeriae volucres terrestribus nobis non solum non praeferantur, verum etiam subiciantur propter rationalis animae quae in nobis est **dignitatem**, ita fieri potuit ut daemones, quamvis magis aerii sint, terrestribus nobis non ideo meliores sint quia est aer quam terra superior; sed ideo eis homines praeferendi sint quoniam spei piorum hominum nequaquam illorum desperatio comparanda est.

For, just as it might and does happen that the birds of the air are not superior to us who dwell on the earth, but are lower than we because of the rational soul which resides in us as our **dignity**, so the demons, although they are in the higher region of the air, are not better than we who are earthly, merely because the air is higher than the earth. On the contrary, men are to be preferred to demons, because their hopelessness is beyond comparison with the hope of human beings who believe.

XI, 16

In his enim quae quoquo modo sunt et non sunt quod Deus est a quo facta sunt, praeponuntur viventia non viventibus, sicut ea quae habent vim gignendi vel etiam appetendi his quae isto motu carent; [...] Sed ista praeponuntur naturae ordine; est autem alius atque alius pro suo cuiusque usu aestimationis modus, quo fit ut quaedam sensu carentia quibusdam sentientibus praeponamus [...]. Quis enim non domui suae panem habere quam mures, nummos quam pulices malit? Sed quid mirum, cum in ipsorum etiam hominum aestimatione, quorum certe natura tantae est **dignitatis**, plerumque carius comparetur equus quam servus, gemma quam famula?

Now among those created things which exist in whatever measure and whose being is not that of God who created them, those that are alive are above those that are not, just as those which have the power of generation or even of aspiration are superior to those which lack such an urge. [...] But these are examples of status according to natural order. There are, however, other standards of value that vary according to the proper use of each created thing, and by this system we rank certain things that lack sensation above certain sentient beings. [...] For who would not rather have bread in his house than mice, or money rather than fleas? When it comes to evaluating men themselves, who surely **rank** very high in

nature, a horse often brings a higher price than a slave, or a jewel more than a servant girl.

Ita libertate iudicandi plurimum distat ratio considerantis a necessitate indigentis seu voluptate cupientis, cum ista quid per se ipsum in rerum gradibus pendat [...]	So in point of freedom of judgement, the rationality of a thoughtful man is poles apart from the necessity felt by a man in want or the calculus of pleasure applied by one who is ruled by desire. Reason weighs a thing according to its intrinsic place in the great scale of being [...]

Leo the Great (400–461)

Leo's sermons plead for the Christian human being to value as recommended by Augustine: value, recognise, respect human dignity! The prayer attributed to him is addressing God in thanksgiving for the gift to count in his eyes, through the merits of his Son, as the summit of the universe.

Latin text from *Corpus Christianorum*, Ser. Lat. vol. CXXXVIII, pp. 88 and 137. English text is adapted from Saint Leo the Great, *Sermons*, The Fathers of the Church, trans. Jane Patricia Freeland C. S. J. B. and Agnes Josephine Conway, S. S. J. (Washington, DC: The Catholic University of America Press, 1996), pp. 79 and 114.

Sermon 21 (25 December 440)

Agnosce, o Christiane, **dignitatem** tuam, *et diuinae consors factus naturae*, noli in ueterem uilitatem degeneri conuersatione recidere.	Realize, o Christian, your **dignity**. Once made a 'partaker in the divine nature,' do not return to your former baseness by a life unworthy [of that dignity].

Sermon 27 (25 December 451)

Expergiscere, o homo, et **dignitatem** tuae agnosce naturae. Recordare te factum *ad imaginem Dei*, quae, etsi in Adam corrupta, in Christo tamen est reformata.

Wake up then, o man, and acknowledge the **dignity** of your nature. Recall that you were made 'according to the image of God.' This nature, although corrupted in Adam, was yet reformed in Christ.

Deus qui humanae substantiae dignitatem

Although it does not seem possible to assign to it a precise date of origin, the prayer referred to by the title *Deus qui humanae substantiae dignitatem* is at least as old as the sixth century. In the so-called Leonine Sacramentary, it opened section XL of the month of December. There it figured as a prayer for the Feast of the Nativity. The similarity of themes between this prayer and the above extracts from Leo's homilies are no doubt reasons, among others, for tracing the Leonine Sacramentary to Leo the Great himself. The insertion in brackets was added, as the prayer was adapted to be said at the offertory as a prayer over the gifts in the liturgical reforms during the Carolingian renaissance, more precisely as the priest pours water into the chalice to begin the sacrifice of the mass. From as early as the thirteenth century it was said at the offertory throughout the Latin Patriarchate until the reforms of the liturgy after the Second Vatican Council. A simplified version of the prayer, where the reference to human dignity has disappeared, is still said today: 'By the mystery of this water and wine may we come to share in the divinity of Christ who humbled himself to share in our humanity.'

For the longer version: *Missale Romanum* ex decreto sacrosancta concilii Tridentini, Urban VII (Dublin: 1804), Ordo Missae, p. 201 and xliv. For the shorter version: *The Roman Missal*, renewed by decree of the most holy second ecumenical council of the Vatican. Promulgated by authority of Pope Paul VI and revised at the direction of Pope John Paul II (English translation according to the third typical edition (Dublin: Veritas, 2011), p. 630). For a detailed history of the prayer see Lebech and McEvoy†, 2019, forthcoming.

Deus qui **humanae substantiae dignitatem**	O God, who wondrously created the **dig-**
Et mirabiliter condidisti et mirabilius	**nity of human nature** and still more won-
reformasti:	drously restored it,
Da nobis [per hujus aquae et vinae	grant, [through the mystery of this water
mysterium]	and wine]
Eius diuinitatis esse consortes	that we may come to share in the divin-
Qui humanitatis nostrae fieri dignatus est	ity of him
particeps	who humbled himself to share in our
	humanity

Although this prayer may at times have been said quietly by the priest, and in Latin, it was said in every mass celebrated in Western Europe for centuries. Considering the number of people affected by this, it constitutes perhaps the most persistent broadcast of the concept in the history of the idea.

Boethius (480–524)

The Consolation of Philosophy

Boethius continues Cicero's critical discussion of offices in relation to moral integrity, and is happy, from his position in captivity, to realise that human beings cannot really *confer* dignity but that it is *due* to the human person of moral integrity. The text illustrates that although dignity was understood to be indispensably restored in Christ, its moral dimension was still understood to be compromised by the sinning of its bearer. The acting in accordance with it, moreover, was understood to preserve it from corruption to the extent that this was in the hands of the individual.

Text from A. Forti Scuto (London: Burns, Oates and Washbourne, 1925); reedited with amendments by G. D. Smith (Hildesheim and New York: Georg Olms Verlag, 1976). Translation from Boethius, *The Consolation of Philosophy*, trans. P. G. Walsh (Oxford: Clarendon Press, 1999).

3, IV

Sed dignitates honorabilem reuerendumque cui prouenerint reddunt. Num uis ea est magistratibus, ut utentium mentibus uirtutes inserant, uitia depellant? Atqui non fugare, sed illustrare potius nequitiam solent; quo fit ut **indignemur** eas saepe nequissimis hominibus contigisse. [...] Videsne quantum malis **dedecus** adiciant **dignitates**? Atqui minus eorum patebit **indignitas**, si nullis honoribus inclarescant. [...] Non enim possumus ob honores reuerentia **dignos** iudicare quos ipsis honoribus iudicamus **indignos**. At si quem sapientia praeditum uideres, num posses eum uel reuerentia, uel ea qua est praeditus sapientia non **dignum** putare? B. Minime. P. Inest enim **dignitas** propria uirtuti, quam protinus in eos quibus fuerit adiuncta transfundit. Quod quia populares facere nequeunt honores, liquet eos propriam **dignitatis** pulchritudinem non habere. [...] nam si eo abiectior est quo magis a pluribus quisque contemnitur, cum reuerendos facere nequeat quos pluribus ostentat, despectiores potius improbos **dignitas** facit. Verum non inpune; reddunt namque improbi parem **dignitatibus** uicem, quas sua contagione commaculant.

Atque ut agnoscas ueram illam reuerentiam per has umbratiles **dignitates** non posse contingere, si qui multiplici

It is true that **public office** bestows honour and respect on incumbents, but do magistracies improve the minds of those who hold them, by inculcating virtues and banishing vices? As a matter of fact, such tenure of offices highlights rather than removes depravity. Hence, the resentment we feel that the most **depraved** individuals have often attained them. [...] Do you observe what deep **disgrace** attaches to the wicked through their tenure of **high positions**? Their **unworthiness** would be less glaring if they did not gain fame through such advancement. [...] The truth is that we cannot regard men as **worthy** of respect because of the offices they hold, if we deem them **unworthy** of such offices. If on the other hand you observe that a man is endowed with wisdom, you could surely not regard him as **unworthy** of respect, or of the wisdom with which he is endowed? 'Of course not,' I replied. 'This is because virtue has a native **worth** which it at once confers on those with whom it is associated. But honours bestowed by the common folk cannot impart such **worth**, so clearly those distinctions do not have the splendour possessed by true **worth**. [...] If a man becomes more contemptible the more he is despised by people at large, tenure of offices makes evil men even more **worthless**, because it cannot win respect for those whom it exposes to the public gaze. And the **offices** themselves suffer thereby, for wicked incumbents make them like themselves, by defiling them with their own pollution.

I would have you realize that the true respect I mentioned cannot be won by these unsubstantial **honours**. So consider

consolatu functus in barbaras nationes forte deuenerit, uenerandumne barbaris honor faciet? Atqui si hoc naturale munus **dignitatibus** foret, ab officio suo quoque gentium nullo modo cessarent; sicut ignis ubique terrarum numquam tamen calere desistit. Sed quoniam id eis non propria uis, sed hominum fallax adnectit opinio, uanescunt ilico, cum ad eos uenerint qui **dignitates** eas esse non aestimant. Sed hoc apud exteras nationes. Inter eos uero apud quos ortae sunt, num perpetuo perdurant? Atqui praetura magna olim potestas, nunc inane nomen et senatorii census grauis sarcina. [...]

Vt enim paulo ante diximus, quod nihil habet proprii decoris, opinione utentium nunc splendorem accipit, nunc amittit. Si igitur reuerendos facere nequeunt **dignitates**, si ultro improborum contagione sordescunt, si mutatione temporum splendere desinunt, si gentium aestimatione uilescunt, quid est quod in se expetendae pulchritudinis habeant, nedum aliis praestent?

this case: suppose a man who had been consul several times chanced to visit uncivilized nations. Would his eminence win him respect there among the barbarians? Yet if **high position** implanted such respect as a law of nature, it would not detract from the tenure of it amongst people anywhere, just as fire does not lose its heat wherever it is. But such respect is not a quality inherent in offices, but rather is attached to them by the delusory beliefs of men; so when they journey abroad among people who do not regard them as **distinctions** of worth, the bubble is pricked there and then. This is the outcome among foreigners, but do those offices endure forever amongst the communities where they originated? Take the praetorship; once it was a powerful office, but nowadays it is an empty title, weighing heavily on the resources of senators. [...]

As I remarked a moment ago, things which have no inherent nobility at one time gain lustre, and at another lose it, according to the views of those who wield them. So if **exalted positions** cannot make men worthy of respect, and if moreover they are tarnished through contagion with worthless men, if they lose their gloss with changes in the times and the world regards them as tawdry, what splendour worth seeking do they possess in themselves, let alone impart to their incumbents?'

Columban (543–615)

Sermon XI

Saint Columban, travelling to the continent and interacting with the Frankish ruling family, and thus not without knowledge of the type of society that had Boethius executed, relates the possibility of achieving moral integrity to the creation of the human being in and to the image of God. Being created in this way is a great honour for the human being, but one one must live up to by a virtuous life, or else fall below the high expectations that accompany this dignity and leave it ruined. It is the love of God that restores the image; grace operating in our actions.

Sancti Columbani Opera, Scriptores Latini Hiberniae, Vol. II, ed. and trans. G. S. M. Walker (Dublin: The Dublin Institute for Advanced Studies, 1957).

Moyses in lege scripsit, *Fecit Deus hominem ad imaginem et similitudinem suam.* Considerate, quaeso, dicti huius **dignitatem**; Deus omnipotens, invisibilis, incomprehensibilis, inenarrabilis, inaestimabilis de limo hominem fingens, imaginis suae **dignitate** nobilitavit. [...] Grandis **dignatio**, quod Deus suae aeternitatis imaginem et morum suorum similitudinem homini donavit. **Magna dignitas homini** Dei similitudo, si conservetur ; sed grandis iterum damnatio Dei imaginis violatio. [...] Quascumque ergo Deus in nobis in prima nostra conditione virtutes seminavit, ipsas ei reddere nos praeceptis docuit. [...] Dei enim dilectio imaginis eius renovatio. [...]

Moses wrote in the law, God made man in His image and likeness. Mark, I beg you, the **distinction** of this saying; God the omnipotent, unseen, unfathomable, ineffable, unsearchable, when making man of clay, ennobled him with the **distinction** of His image. [...] It is a great **dignity** that God bestowed on man the image of His eternity and the likeness of His character. **A grand distinction for man** is the likeness of God, if it be preserved; but again, it is great damnation to defile the image of God. [...] So whatever virtues God sowed in us in our original state, He taught us in the commandments to restore the same to Him. [...] For the love of God is the restoration of his image. [...]

Alcuin? (735–804)

De dignitate conditionis humanae

The little treatise *De dignitate conditionis humanae* was ascribed during the Middle Ages to Saint Ambrose or Saint Augustine, but is possibly by Alcuin and his student Candidus (Lebech and McEvoy, 2009). The different powers of the soul: intellect, will and memory are referred to as '*dignitates*', recalling on the one hand the logical meaning of what is self-evidently important and foundational, and on the other, a given claim to respect. That the human being, or the soul, has a triple dignity in the image of its Creator means that it self-evidently possesses a claim to command respect in a triple way: as intelligence, as will and as memory. The treatise distinguishes between dignity and being in the same way as theology after the first Council of Constantinople made it customary to distinguish between person and being. The speculative dynamic at the origin of both is the theological explanation of the Trinity, and each of them finds its resolution in the understanding of both person and dignity as relation. Conditionality, in fact, is the kind of relation that obtains between a principle and what can be derived from it: the relation of foundation. The human being is related to its dignity, that is, to the fact that the latter is foundational or conditional for it, on condition that God in turn is its condition, that is, is the reason for it. What therefore conditions the human being's unconditional value is his relationship with God: The Christian idea that human dignity is due to being made in the image of God here finds its most speculative expression. *Imago Dei* resides in the ontological relativity of human nature, that is, in its capacity for a spontaneous and autonomous relationship with everything, in intelligence, will and memory, reflecting God's unconditional and founding relationship with everything.

The name of the treatise seems to be echoed in Pope Innocent III's *De miseria humanae conditionis* (c. 1195), which became the background of the Renaissance tradition of treatises on human dignity and human misery (see introduction to Part III).

The text is taken from Migne, *Patrologia Latina*, Garnier, Paris, 1879, vol. 17, cols 1106–8, where it is taken to be a text of Ambrose. As a pseudo-Augustinian text it is reproduced *inter opera Augustini* in *PL* 40, 1213–4 under the title *De creatione primi hominis*, and once again as a text of Albinus (=Alcuin) in *PL* 100, 565–8 with the title *Dicta Albini de imagine Dei*. Trans. James McEvoy and the author. A revised version tracing the treatise to its two parts, is published in Mette Lebech and James McEvoy with John Flood, '*De dignitate conditionis humanae*: Translation, Commentary, and Reception History of the Dicta Albini (Ps.-Alcuin) and the Dicta Candidi', *Viator*, Volume 40, 2 (2009), pp. 1–34. Quotations from Scripture are taken from the Douai Version.

C. I. Faciamus hominem ad imaginem et similitudinem nostram (Gen. I, 26).

Tanta itaque **dignitas humanae conditionis** esse cognoscitur, ut non solo jubentis sermone, sicut alia sex dierum opera, sed consilio sanctae Trinitatis, et opere majestatis divinae creatus sit homo; ut ex primae conditionis honore intelligeret, quantum deberet suo conditori, dum tantum in conditione mox **dignitatis privilegium** praestitit ei conditor; ut tanto ardentius amaret conditorem, quanto mirabilius se ab eo esse conditum intelligeret: nec ob hoc solum quod consilio sanctae Trinitatis sic excellenter a conditore conditus est, sed etiam quod ad imaginem et similitudinem suam ipse creator omnium eum creavit, quod nulli alii ex creaturis donavit.

Ch. 1 'Let us make man to our image and likeness.' (Gen. 1, 26).

It is recognized that the **dignity of the human condition** [or 'of the way man is made'] is so great that it originates, not simply in the word commanding as the other six-day works, but at the counsel of the Holy Trinity, and by the operation of the divine majesty. This was done thus so that, from the honour of being made in this way, man might comprehend how much he owes his Maker, since in the making, the Maker granted him the **privilege of dignity,** so that he would the more ardently love his Maker, the more he understood how astonishingly he was made. This understanding was to derive not only from being made so excellently at the counsel of the Holy Trinity, but also from the fact that the Maker of All created man to His own image and likeness, something which was granted to no other creature.

C.II. Quae imago diligentius ex interioris hominis nobilitate est consideranda. Primo quidem quod sicuti Deus unus semper ubique totus est, omnia vivificans, movens

Ch. II. This image should be more attentively considered in the nobility of the inner man. Firstly, as the one God is always and fully everywhere giving life, movement and

et gubernans, sicut Apostolus confirmat quod: 'In eo vivimus, movemur et sumus' (Act. XVII, 28); sic anima in suo corpore ubique tota viget, vivificans illud, movens et gubernans. Nec enim in majoribus corporis sui membris major, et in minoribus minor: sed in minimis tota, et in maximis tota. Et haec est imago unitatis omnipotentis Dei, quam anima habet in se.

Quae quoque quamdam sanctae Trinitatis habet imaginem. Primo in eo quia sicut Deus est, vivit et sapit; ita anima secundum suum modum est, vivit et sapit. Est quoque et alia trinitas in ea, qua ad imaginem sui conditoris perfectae quidem et summae Trinitatis, quae ex Patre et Filio et Spiritu sancto condita est: et licet unius illa naturae, tres tamen in se **dignitates** habet, id est, intellectum, voluntatem, et memoriam. Quod idem, licet aliis verbis, in Evangelio designatur, cum dicitur: 'Diliges Dominum Deum tuum ex toto corde tuo, et ex tota anima tua, et ex tota mente tua' (Math. XXII, 37), id est, ex toto intellectu, et ex tota voluntate, et ex tota memoria. Nam sicut ex Patre generatur Filius, et ex Patre Filioque procedit Spiritus sanctus; ita ex intellectu generatur voluntas, et ex his item ambobus procedit memoria, sicut facile a sapiente quolibet intelligi potest; nec enim anima perfecta esse sine his tribus, nec horum trium unum aliquod, quantum ad suam pertinet beatitudinem, sine aliis duobus integrum constat: et sicut Deus Pater, Deus Filius, Deus Spiritus sanctus est, non tamen tres dii sunt, sed unus Deus tres habens personas; ita et anima intellectus, anima voluntas, anima memoria, non tamen tres animae in uno corpore, sed una

direction to all, as the Apostle confirms that 'In him we live, and move, and are' (Acts 17, 28); so the soul is alive everywhere in the body, giving life, movement and direction to it. There is no more soul in the important members than there is in the less important; the soul is whole and complete in the least as well as in the greatest part. This is the image the soul has in itself of the unity of the omnipotent God.

It also bears a certain image of the Trinity. Firstly in this that just as God is, has life, and knows, so the soul is, has life, and knows. There is another trinity in it, whereby it was made in the likeness of its Maker, the perfect and highest Trinity of Father and Son and Holy Spirit: though one in nature, it nevertheless has in it three **dignities**, i.e. intellect, will and memory. This is the very same meaning as is found in the Gospel, albeit in different words, when it is said, 'Thou shalt love the Lord thy God with thy whole heart, and with thy whole soul, and with thy whole mind.' (Mt 22, 37): that is to say, with all your intellect, and all your will, and all your memory. Just as the Son is engendered by the Father and the Holy Spirit proceeds from the Father and the Son, so the will is engendered by the intellect and the memory proceeds from them both, as can easily be understood by any wise person. The soul is not perfect without these three, nor can any one of them by itself ensure its happiness. And just as God the Father, God the Son, and God the Holy Spirit are not three gods, but One God having three persons; so the soul is intellect, will, and memory, not three souls in one body, but one soul having three **dignities.** Our interior man bears astonishingly

anima tres habens **dignitates**. Atque in his tribus ejus imaginem mirabiliter gerit in sua natura noster interior homo, ex quibus quasi excellentioribus animae **dignitatibus** jubemur diligere conditorem; ut in quantum intelligitur, diligatur: et quantum diligitur, semper in memoria habeatur. Nec solus sufficit de eo intellectus, nisi fiat in amore ejus voluntas: imo nec haec duo sufficiunt, nisi memoria addatur, qua semper in mente intelligentis et diligentis maneat Deus; ut sicut non potest esse momentum, quo homo non utatur vel fruatur Dei bonitate et misericordia; ita nullum debeat momentum, quo praesentem eum non habeat memoria.

Et ideo, dilectissime fili, juste mihi videtur dictum interiorem hominem imaginem esse Dei; anima enim nominatur totus interior homo, qua vivificatur, regitur, continetur lutea illa massa humectata succis, ne arefacta dissolvatur. Deus dicitur vis illa ineffabiliter magna, et innumerabiliter sapiens, ut scriptum est: 'Magnus Dominus noster, et magna virtus ejus, et sapientiae ejus non est numerus' (Psal. CXLVI); et incomparabiliter suavis, ut alibi dicit: 'Suavis Dominus universis, et miserationes ejus super omnia opera ejus' (Psal. CXLIV, 9). Ex qua, et per quam, et in qua sunt omnia, quae sunt; reguntur omnia, quae sunt; continentur omnia, quae sunt: omnia dico ipsam universitatem, quae est totum, quod aliud est, quam ipse fecit, et non est factus: sed ipse est ex quo, et qui ex eo, et quo (2); quod Deus ex quo est, Pater dicitur a nobis pauperibus sensu, pauperioribus verbis; quod qui ex eo, Filius dicitur: quod quo Spiritus sanctus. Ideo autem dicitur Deus Pater quia ipse est ex quo, et sapientia est, qua

within his nature these three as the image of Him, and is more excellently still in the **dignities** of the soul commanded to love the Maker, so that He may be loved as He is known, and remembered as He is loved. It does not suffice to know Him, unless His will be done in love; still more, these two are not sufficient unless we add the memory in virtue of which God may dwell always in the mind of the one who understands and loves him. Just as there cannot be a single moment in which man is not using or enjoying God's goodness and mercy so there ought to be no moment in which the memory does not keep Him present.

Thus, dearest child, the statement seems true to me that the inner man is the image of God. For by 'soul' is meant the entire inner man; which enlivens, rules and holds together this mass of sap-moistened mud, lest it wither and be dissolved. God is referred to as that power, ineffably great and innumerably wise, of which it is written, 'Great is our Lord, and great is his power; and of his wisdom there is no number' (Ps 146, 5). Incomparably sweet also, as it is said elsewhere, 'The Lord is sweet to all and his tender mercies are over all his works' (Ps 144, 9). From it, and through it, and in it, all things exist, are governed and are contained. By 'all things' I mean the universality, which is the whole. It is other than the One who made it without Himself being made, He is rather that One from Whom, and the One from Him and the One by Whom. That God is the One 'from Whom' we call the Father, in our poverty of wit and even greater poverty of words. That He is the One from Him is called Son, and that

ordinantur omnia: et dilectio, qua se volunt
omnia ita manere, ut ordinata sunt. Ex quo
ergo, et qui ex eo, et quo se diligunt, ipsa
duo tria sunt, et illa tria ideo unum; quia sic
sunt ex uno illa duo, ut tamen ab ipso non
sint separata: sed ex ipso sunt, quia non a se:
et in ipso, quia non separata: et ipsum ipsa
quod ipse, et ipsum ipse quod ipsa; et non
ipsum ipsa qui ipse, et non ipsa ipse quae
ipsa. Vis ista Deus est, et ipse Deus tria est,
et unumquodque horum trium Deus est, et
omnia tria illa non dii, sed Deus est.

He is the One in Whom, the Holy Spirit.
He is called God the Father because He is
the One 'out of Whom' and the Wisdom
by which all things are ordered and the love
by which all things wish to remain in the
way in which they were ordained. Thus the
One out of Whom, the One out of Him
and the One in Whom love each other:
those same Two are Three, and those Three
are One, since those Two come from One
from whom they are not separated, being
not from themselves. The same Two are the
same as the same One; and the same One
is the same as the same Two, yet the same
Two are not the self-same One. God is that
power, and God is three, and each one of
these three is God, and all those three are
not gods but God.

Ad imaginem ergo suam conditor, ut ditum
est, fecit animam hominis, quae tota dicitur anima. Non autem aliud hominis quam
animam significo, cum mentem dico: sed
propter aliud animam, et propter aliud
mentem. Nam totum quod vivit, hominis
anima est: cum autem anima in se agit se, et
ex se, et per se, sola mens dici solet: sensus
vero ad sua ministeria implens, consue-
tius anima dicitur. Mens ergo scire gignit,
et amat scire, quod scit. Non illud scire
dico, quo repente scitur res aliqua, quae
ante nesciri putabatur: sed illud, unde
et aliquod et omne quidquid scitur vel
nescitur, sciri potest. Illud ergo scire mens
gignit, et cum genitum est, scientia potest
dici. Sunt ergo jam duo, mens, et quod ipsa
mens scit: restat tertium utriusque commune. Omnis mens quidquid scit, amat
scire. Amor non minus quam inter duos
est, amantem, et quod amatur. Unus est
ergo amborum amor, qui et tertius est. Non

And so the Maker, as we said above, made
the human soul, all of which is called soul, in
His own image. When I say 'mind' I do not
refer to anything else in man but the soul,
yet the two terms do not mean the same.
For the whole thing that lives is the soul of
man. But when the soul acts on itself, and
from itself and through itself, 'mind' is the
term that is usually employed; whereas the
sense when carrying out its own functions
is more usually referred to as soul. And thus
the mind engenders knowledge and loves to
know what it knows. I do not call knowledge that through which a particular thing
is known which was thought beforehand to
be unknown, but rather that knowing from
which both the particular thing and also
every thing whatsoever that is known or not
known, can be known. That is the knowledge the mind engenders, and which, once
engendered, can be called science. Hence
they are two: the mind, and what the mind

autem potest negari hoc totum unam esse animam, et unam animam haec tria esse; sicut enim haec tria vere una anima sunt, sic non minus vere una anima est hoc unum et hoc alterum et hoc tertium.

knows; there remains a third, which is in common to each of these. Whatever the mind knows, it loves to know. Love is never between less than two: the lover and the beloved. And so the love of both is one – which is also a third. Indeed, it cannot be denied that this whole is one soul and that the one soul is these three; for just as these three really are one soul, so no less is the one soul this one, this other and this third.

Comparet igitur se haec creatura tam eminens Creatori suo supereminenti sibi, excepto hoc, et multum supra se amoto, quod omnis bonitas, et omne bonum, et omnis bonitatis et boni dulcedo Creatoris a se ipso est: creatura vero non solum quod est, sed etiam quod talis est, ab alio est, non a se: et ipse quod est, semper est. Licet et ipsa anima modo quodam suo incommutabilis est; nam semper anima est, postquam esse coeperit, et scit, et scire vult.

Therefore let this very eminent creature compare itself to its Creator who surpasses it super-eminently, except in this super-eminence: that all goodness and every good thing, the sweetness of all goodness and of every good thing, the Creator is himself because of himself. The creature is because of another as regards both that it is and what it is; it is not from itself. What He is, He is forever. Granted, the soul also is somehow immutable; for it is forever, once it has begun to be, and knows and desires to know.

Comparet ergo, ut dixi, se anima eo modo, quo potest, creatori suo; ut dicatur mens Pater, quia gignit scire: dicatur scire Filius, quia ex alio est, et non est aliud, quam ipsum quod ipse est, ex quo est: dicatur amor Spiritus sanctus, quia amborum est eorum, qui se amant. Unde in nostris Scripturis saepius amor, id est, charitas, quae in Deo est erga nos, et quae a nobis in Deum, Spiritus ipse appellatur: et haec de imagine, o dilectissime fili, habeto.

Yes, let the soul compare itself as best it can to its Creator; so that the mind may be called Father, since it engenders knowing; knowing [may be called the] Son since it is from another without being different; and love [may be called the] Holy Spirit, since it is of both who love each other. That is why, in our Scriptures, love, that is, charity, which is in God with regard to us and which is from us in regard to God, is frequently called the Spirit Himself; and these things, dearest child, hold them concerning the image.

C.III. Nunc vero de similitudine aliqua intellige, quae minoribus cernenda est; ut sicut Deus Creator, qui hominem ad similitudinem suam creavit, est charitas, est bonus et justus, patiens atque mitis, mundus et misericors, et caetera virtutum

Ch. III. But now understand of the likeness something that can be learned from lesser things. Just as God, the Creator, who created man to his likeness, is charity, is good and just, patient and mild, pure, merciful and has all the other holy virtues which can

sanctarum insignia, quae de eo leguntur: ita homo creatus est, ut charitatem haberet, ut bonus esset et justus, ut patiens atque mitis, mundus et misericors foret. Quas virtutes quanto plus quisque in seipso habet, tanto propius est Deo, et majorem sui conditoris gerit similitudinem. Si vero, quod absit, aliquis per devia vitiorum, et divortia criminum ab hac nobilissima sui conditoris similitudine degener oberrat, tunc fiet de eo quod scriptum est: 'Et homo cum in honore esset, non intellexit; comparatus est jumentis insipientibus, et similis factus est illis' (Psal. XLVIII, 13).

Qui major honor potuit homini esse, quam ut ad similitudinem sui factoris conderetur, et eisdem virtutum vestimentis ornaretur; quibus et conditor, de quo legitur: 'Dominus regnavit, **decorem** indutus est' (Psal. XCII, 1), id est, omnium virtutum splendore, et totius bonitatis **decore** ornatus? Vel quod majus homini potest esse **dedecus**, aut infelicior miseria, quam ut hac similitudinis gloria sui conditoris amissa, ad informem et irrationabilem brutorum jumentorum delabatur similitudinem?

Quapropter, o dilectissime, quisque diligentius attendat primae conditionis suae excellentiam, et venerandam in seipso sanctae Trinitatis imaginem agnoscat, honoremque similitudinis divinae ad quem creatus est, nobilitate morum, exercitio virtutum, **dignitate** meritorum habere contendat; ut quando appareat qualis sit, tunc similis ei appareat (I Joan. III, 2), qui se mirabiliter ad similitudinem suam in primo Adam condidit, mirabiliusque in secundo reformavit.

be read of him [in the Scriptures], so also man was created to have charity, to be good and just, patient, mild, pure and merciful. The more someone has these virtues in himself the closer he is to God and the greater is the likeness he bears to the Creator. If on the other hand (which would be a terrible thing) someone deviated into vice and strayed criminally from the nobility of his condition of likeness, it will be with him as is written: 'And man when he was in honour did not understand; he is compared to senseless beasts, and is become like to them' (Ps 48, 13).

What greater honour could be bestowed on man than that he should be made to the likeness of his Maker and be beautifully clad in the virtues, like Him of whom we read: 'The Lord hath reigned, he is **clothed** with beauty' (Ps 29, 1), that is, he is decorated with the splendour of all the virtues and with the **beauty** of all goodness? Or what greater **disgrace** could befall him, what more unhappy misery, than that of losing the glory of likeness to his Creator, slipping downwards into crude and irrational likeness with the beasts of burden?

Therefore, dearly beloved, let each one pay attention to the excellence of his condition and acknowledge as something to be venerated in himself the image of the Holy Trinity. Let him struggle by nobility of conduct, exercise of virtues and **dignity** of merits to possess the honour of the divine likeness to which he was created. Then, when he appears, he may appear like Him (cf I Jn 3, 2) who in the first Adam made him astonishingly like Him, and in the Second even more astonishingly reshaped him.

Joannes Scotus Eriugena (c. 815–c. 877)

Periphyseon

Scotus Eriugena adds to the dignity of the creation of the human being that it enfolds in itself all kinds of created being, spiritual and material alike. He thus links human dignity to the microcosmic position of the human being.

Text from Book II, Chapters 4–5 (column 531A-C). Iohannis Scotti seu Eriugenae: *Periphyseon, Liber secundus,* curavit Edvardvs A Jeauneau (Tvrnholti: Typographi Brepols Editores Pontificii, 1997). Translation taken from John the Scot, *Periphyseon. On the Division of Nature,* trans. Myra L. Uhlfelder, with summaries by Jean A Potter, The Library of Liberal Arts (Indianapolis, IN: The Bobbs-Merrill Company, inc., 1976), p. 116–117.

N. Homo [...] in tanta naturae **conditae dignitate** creatus est, ut nulla creatura siue uisibilis siue intelligibilis sit quae in eo repereri non possit. Est enim ex duabus conditae naturae uniuersalibus partibus mirabili quadam adunatione compositus, ex sensibili namque et intelligibili, hoc est ex totius creaturae extremitatibus coniunctus. [...]

A. Plane uideo multumque **nostrae naturae** inter omnia quae facta sunt **dignitatem** admiror, dum in ea ueluti quandam omnium creatarum substantiarum mirabilem compositionem praedictis rationibus suasus perspicio.

T: Man [...] was **made** in such an **honourable position** in created nature that there is no creature, whether visible or invisible, which cannot be found in him. By a marvellous union, he was compounded from the two universal parts of created nature, the sensible and the intelligible; i.e. he was joined from the extremes of all creation. [...]

S: I see this plainly and I marvel greatly at the **dignity of our nature** among all the things which have been made for [...] I perceive in it a kind of remarkable compound of all created substances.

CHAPTER 5

Scholastic Sources

The scholastics explored the Aristotelian and the Ciceronian heritage concerning dignity to the effect of linking the person essentially with dignity, and thus taking a decisive step towards human dignity becoming thinkable as a constitutional principle. This was a genuine and ingenious innovation of an anonymous master leaving behind the *definitio magistralis*: 'a person is a subject defined by a property pertaining to dignity'. The importance accorded to the human person was understood to constitute an appeal to the person himself, to behave in accordance with this dignity, something that was, at least by Abélard and Grosseteste, explicitly understood to concern women as well as men. Is it possible that Hildegard von Bingen (1098–1179), a friend of Bernard, and probably the most successful of her times in shedding light on the paradox of the equal but different dignity of the sexes, did not use the expression *dignitas humana* or even *dignitas* to this end? The nobility of the feminine is powerfully expressed in her poems (Hildegard of Bingen, 1988) and also through the microcosmic idea like in Eriugena, but the expression *dignitas humana* seems not to be employed. If the absence is factual, the innovation of the later medieval sources is all the more important.

Abélard (1079–1142)

Linking dignity with relationship with God solved the problem of recognising dignity to man alone, as distinct from woman, which had been a tendency since Cicero, who regarded dignity also as a quality of appearance

distinct from beauty. Preaching to nuns, Abélard is aware that this tendency needs to be put right in the face of the question of whether there is a dignity specific to man, different from that of woman. He reiterates the fundamentals of the Gospel.

Sermon XIII

Patrologia Latina vol. 178, p. 488, trans. Mary McLaughlin: 'Peter Abélard and the dignity of women: Twelfth century "feminism" in theory and practice' in *Pierre Abélard, Pierre le Vénérable: les courants philosophiques, littéraires et artistiques en occident au milieu du XIIe siècle* (Paris: CNRS, 1975), pp. 287–334.

Quis enim unicus et **dignitate** singularis ita Christus? In quo quoque nec masculum, nec feminam Apostolus esse dicit (*Gal.* III): quia in Christi corpore, quod est Ecclesia, nullam **dignitatem** diversitas sexuum operatur; sed meritorum Christus attendit.	Who is so unique and singular in **dignity** as Christ, in whom, the apostle says, there is 'neither male nor female' (Gal. 3.28)? In the body of Christ, which is the Church, difference of sex, therefore, confers no **dignity**. For Christ looks not to the condition of sex, but to the quality of merits.

Three different evaluations of Abélard's and Héloïse's philosophy of the dignity of man and woman are to be found in Mary McLaughlin (1975), Prudence Allen (1985, 271–292) and Mary Ellen Waithe (1987, II, 67–84). Whereas the first interprets Abélard as a feminist writer, the second regards Héloïse as depreciative of her own dignity for the sake of Abélard, and the third thinks Héloïse reproaches Abélard for undignified behaviour. Héloïse did not use the word *dignitas* to express her philosophy of women's dignity, and, as in the case of Hildegard, this may reflect that the term was still too associated with office for it to be easily associated with women, who much less frequently than men held office.

Bernard of Clairvaux (1090–1153)

The humanist cry of Leo the Great, 'Remember, o man, your own dignity', was repeated by Saint Bernard (*PL* 183, 120 A) and Richard of Saint Victor (*PL* 196, 123 A), and probably by many more throughout the scholastic period. Did women hear it as an exhortation that did not concern them or did they show their dignity by remaining unperturbed by a possible insult? Bernard insists on knowledge and virtue relying on grace, such that if dignity is not recognised as a gift from God, it becomes an obstacle for the one who believes he has it. One can in consequence only vindicate dignity by refraining from sinning.

On Loving God

Text from *Liber de diligendo deo*, in Sancti Bernardii Opera III, *Tractatus et Opuscula*, eds J. Leclercq OSB and H. M. Rochais OSB (Rome: Editiones Cisterciences, 1963). Translation from Bernhard of Clairvaux: *On Loving God* with an analytical commentary by Emero Stiegman, Cistercian Fathers Series: 13 (Rome: Cistercian Publications Inc., 1973/1995). I–II.6.

Multum quippe meruit de nobis, qui et immeritis dedit seipsum nobis. [...] Quibus haec palam sunt, palam arbitror esse et cur Deus diligendus sit, hoc est unde diligi meruerit. [...] Nempe quis alius administrat cibum omni vescenti, cernenti lucem, spiranti flatum? [...] Praecipua dico, non quia excellentiora, sed quia necessariora; sunt quippe corporis. Quaerat enim homo eminentiora bona sua in ea parte sui, qua praeeminet sibi, hoc est anima, quae sunt **dignitas**, scientia, virtus : **dignitatem in homine** liberum dico arbitrium, in quo ei nimirum datum est ceteris non solum praeeminere, sed et praesidere animantibus;

God certainly deserves a lot from us since he gave himself to us when we deserved it least. [...] I think that they to whom this is clear see why God ought to be loved, that is, why he merits to be loved. [...] For who else gives food to all who eat, sight to all who see, and air to all who breathe? [...] I call them the chief gifts, not because they are better but because the body cannot live without them. Man's nobler gifts – **dignity**, knowledge and virtue – are found in the higher part of his being, in his soul. **Man's dignity** is his free will by which he is superior to the beasts and even dominates them. His knowledge is that by which he

scientiam vero, qua eamdem in se **digni-tatem** agnoscat, non a se tamen ; porro virtutem, qua subinde ipsum a quo est, et inquirat non segniter, et teneat fortiter, cum invenerit.

3. Itaque geminum unumquodque trium horum apparet. **Dignitatem** siquidem demonstrat humanam non solum naturae praerogativa, sed et potentia dominatus, quod terror hominis super cuncta animantia terrae imminere decernitur. Scientia quoque duplex erit, si hanc ipsam **dignitatem** vel aliud quodque bonum in nobis, et nobis inesse, et a nobis non esse noverimus. Porro virtus et ipsa aeque bifaria cognoscetur, si auctorem consequenter inquirimus, inventoque inseparabiliter inhaeremus. **Dignitas** ergo sine scientia non prodest; illa vero etiam obest, si virtus defuerit [...]

4. Utrumque ergo scias necesse est, et quid sis, et quod a teipso non sis, ne aut omnino videlicet non glorieris aut inaniter glorieris. Denique si non cognoveris, inquit, teipsam, egredere post greges sodalium tuorum. Revera ita fit : homo factus in honore, cum honorem ipsum non intelligit, talis suae ignorantiae merito comparatur pecoribus, velut quibusdam praesentis suae corruptionis et mortalitatis consortibus. [...] Itaque valde cavenda haec ignorantia, qua de nobis minus nobis forte sentimus ; sed non minus, immo et plus illa, qua plus nobis tribuimus, quod fit si bonum quodcumque in nobis esse, et a nobis, decepti putemus. At vero super utramque ignorantiam declinanda et exsecranda illa praesumptio est, qua sciens et prudens forte audeas de bonis non tuis tuam quaerere gloriam, et quod certus es a te tibi non esse, inde tamen alterius rapere non verearis honorem. [...]

acknowledges that this **dignity** is in him but that it is not of his own making. Virtue is that by which man seeks continuously and eagerly for his Maker and when he finds him, adheres to him with all his might.

3. Each of these three gifts has two aspects. **Dignity** is not only a natural privilege; it is also a power of domination, for the fear of man hangs over all the animals on earth. Knowledge also is twofold, since we understand **this dignity** and other natural qualities are in us, yet we do not create them ourselves. Finally, virtue is seen to be twofold, for by it, we seek our Maker and once we find him, we adhere to him so closely we become unseparable from him. As a result, **dignity** without knowledge is unprofitable, without virtue it can be an obstacle. [...]

4. There are two facts you should know: first, what you are; secondly, that what you are you are not by your own power, lest you fail to boast at all or do so in vain. Finally, if you do not know yourself, do as is written: 'Go follow the flocks of your companions' (Song 1, 6–7). This is really what happens. When a man, promoted to high dignity, does not appreciate the favour received, because of his ignorance he is rightly compared to the animals with whom he shares his present state of corruption and mortality. [...] We should, therefore, fear that ignorance which gives us a too low opinion of ourselves. But we should fear no less, but rather more, that which makes us think ourselves better than we are. This is what happens when we deceive ourselves thinking some good is in us of ourselves. But indeed you should detest and avoid even more than these two forms of ignorance

Quamobrem cum duabus istis, **dignitate** atque scientia, opus est et virtute, quae utriusque fructus est, per qua ille inquiritur ac tenetur, qui omnium auctor et dator merito glorificetur de omnibus. [...]

that presumption by which you, knowingly and on purpose, seek your glory in goods that are not your own and that you are certain are not in you by your own power. [...] For this reason, virtue is as necessary as **dignity** and knowledge, being the fruit of both. By virtue the Maker and Giver of all is sought and adhered to, and rightly glorified in all good things. [...]

Verum homo virtutis, cui nec damnosa scientia, nec infructuosa **dignitas** manet, clamat Deo et ingenue confitetur : Non nobis, inquiens, Domine, non nobis, sed nomini tuo da gloriam ; hoc est : Nil nobis o Domine, de scientia, nil nobis de **dignitate** tribuimus, sed tuo totum, a quo totum est, nomini deputamus. [...] Quis item vel impius putet alium eius, quae in anima splendet, **humanae dignitatis** auctorem, praeter illum ipsum, qui in Genesi loquitur : *Faciamus hominem ad imaginem et similitudinem nostram*? [...] Clamat nempe intus ei innata, et non ignota rationi, iustitia, quia ex toto se illum diligere debeat, cui totum se debere non ignorat.

But the virtuous man, for whom knowledge is not harmful or **dignity** unfruitful, lifts up his voice to God and frankly confesses: 'Not to us, O Lord, not to us, but to your name give glory;' meaning, 'O Lord, we attribute no part of our **dignity** or knowledge to ourselves: we ascribe it all to your name whence all good comes.' [...] Who, again, can be wicked enough to think the author of his **human dignity**, which shines in his soul, is any other than he who says in the book of Genesis: 'Let us make man to our own image and likeness?' [...] For an innate justice, not unknown to reason, cries interiorly to him that he ought to love with his whole being the one to whom he owes all that he is.

Concerning Grace and Free Will

Central to this dignity held from God is freedom, in such a way that the human being is saved by Christ only if he wants to be and is likewise forsaken only if he wants to be.

Text from *De gratia et libero arbitrio* in *Sancti Bernardii Opera III, Tractatus et Opuscula*, eds J. Leclercq OSB and H. M. Rochais OSB (Rome: Editiones Cisterciences, 1963), X, 34 and XI, 36. Trans. from *Concerning Grace and Free Will*, by Watkins W. Williams (London and New York: Society for Promoting Christian Knowledge and The Macmillan Company, 1920).

Sic ergo et liberum arbitrium suo conetur praeesse corpori, ut praeest sapientia orbi, attingens et ipsum a fine usque ad finem fortiter, imperans scilicet singulis sensibus et artubus tam potenter, quatenus non sinat regnare peccatum in suo mortali corpore, nec membra sua det arma iniquitati, sed exhibeat servire iustitiae. Et ita iam non erit homo servus peccati, cum peccatum non fecerit, a quo utique liberatus, iam libertatem recuperare consilii, iam suam vindicare incipiet **dignitatem**, dum divinae in se imagini condignam vestierit similitudinem, immo antiquam reparaverit venustatem.

Hac sane **dignitatis** divinae, ut dictum est, praerogativa rationalem singulariter creaturam Conditor insignivit, quod quemadmodum ipse sui iuris erat suaeque ipsius voluntatis, non necessitatis erat quod bonus erat, ita et illa quoque sui quodammodo iuris in hac parte exsisteret, quatenus nonnisi sua voluntate, aut mala fieret et iuste damnaretur, aut bona maneret et merito salvaretur. Non quod ei propria sufficere posset voluntas ad salutem, sed quod eam nullatenus sine sua voluntate consequeretur. Nemo quippe salvatur invitus.

Therefore let free choice seek to rule its own body, even as Wisdom ruleth the world; itself also reaching 'from one end to another mightily,' to wit, giving its commands to each sense and to each member with such authority that it allow not sin to reign in its mortal body, nor yield its members as weapons to iniquity, but rather present them for the service of righteousness. Thus no longer will the man be the servant of sin, when he doeth not sin; from which indeed set free, he will now begin to recover freedom of council and to vindicate his **dignity**, while he clotheth himself with a likeness befitting the divine image in himself, yea, restoreth his ancient comely state. [...]

Truly, as hath been said, by this prerogative of divine **dignity** the Creator hath singularly honoured the reasonable creature; in such fashion that as He Himself was independent, and was good of his own free will, and by no necessity imposed by another; thus it also should in a manner be so far independent, as neither to become evil and justly to be condemned, nor to remain good and deservedly to be rewarded, save only of its own free will. Not, however, that its own will could suffice unto it for salvation; but that without its own will it could take no step in the direction of salvation. Noone, forsooth, is saved against his will.

Robert Grosseteste (1175–1253)

In the context of his treatise of the Ten Commandments, Robert Grosseteste devices a distinction between the two elements of what was by St Augustine regarded as the tenth commandment, coveting one's

neigbour's goods and coveting his wife, to the point of assigning to each different commandments. He does so because the dignity of the human being (in this case specifically woman) by far exceeds the value of any thing, and therefore makes the desire of taking it (her) from someone (her husband) to be of an entirely different category compared to envying the neighbour for any of his goods.

Grosseteste hands on the platonic idea of man as a microcosm, and links it, like Eriugena and Bernard, to human dignity. He also characteristically stresses the word as an expression of this dignity, since the word proceeds from man as the Word proceeds from God, and thus reflects divine activity *par excellence*. Refraining from calumniating is accordingly of paramount importance for the preservation of human dignity. Grosseteste also exhorts women not to excuse themselves by weakness, since their strength is in the soul. They can, he contends, have the same dignity as men, *if they want*.

On the Ten Commandments

Text from Robert Grosseteste: *De decem mandatis*, eds Richard C. Dales and Edward B. King, Auctores brittannici medii aevi X (Oxford: British Academy and Oxford University Press, 1987). Trans. James McEvoy, 2003.

IX, VI, 6

Tanto autem preciosus est quod furto surripitur, tanto gravius peccat qui surripit. Autem, quanto maior debetur fides et dileccio ei cui aliquid furto surripitur, tanto gravius peccat qui furator; homine autem nulla creatura preciosior vel **dignior** est.

The more precious the thing that is the object of the theft, the more serious is the sin of the thief. And again, the degree in which fidelity and love is due to the person from whom something is stolen, is the same as the degree of seriousness of the sin of that theft; but no creature is of greater price or **dignity** than man.

Treatise on Confession, 'Deus Est'

Text from Siegfried Wenzel: 'Robert Grosseteste's Treatise on Confession, "Deus Est"' in *Franciscan Studies*, Vol. 30 (1970), pp. 218–93, p. 241. Trans. James McEvoy, 2003.

Ultimo namque facturam quandam, hominem scilicet, statuit Altissimus quasi praedictorum omnium exemplar et ex omnibus acceptam ad modum facientis singulas editiones suae sapientiae et in summam unam redigentis. Parificatur quidem angelis per animam, animalibus similiter per sensibilitatem, crescentibus per vegetationem; cum ceteris corporibus in quibusdam corporis partibus habet similitudinem. Secundum corpus ergo vilissimo simile est sicut imperfectissimum, secundum animam aequale optimae creaturae et ita nobilissimum, secundum vero se **totum omnium creaturarum dignissimum**. Haec inquam creatura inter ceteras creaturas creatori est simillima, quia sicut in Deo omnia stant per causam, sic in homine relucent universa per effectum. Et ob hoc est quod homo minor mundus appellatur. Et quoniam inter cuncta optimus est, cum singulis sit impar et omnibus aequatus, obediunt ei naturaliter universa, et sic Dei imago est. Et hoc est quod dixit Dominus: Faciamus hominem ad imaginem et similitudinem nostram. Dedit ei Dominus cunctorum dominium, quorum fuit factus exemplum.

In the last place the Most High set up a certain product, namely man, something like the template of all the aforesaid [creatures] and taken from them all. He did this somewhat in the way of someone making single editions of his wisdom and editing them into a summa. [Man] is indeed made the equal of the angels through his soul, [he is made] similarly to the animals through sensibility and to growing things through vegetation. With the other corporeal things, he has a similarity in some parts of [his] body. Regarding his body, therefore, he is akin to the least worthwhile and is, one might say, the most imperfect thing. Regarding the soul he is equal to the best creature, and so [he is] the most noble thing. Taken in all what he is, however, he has the **greatest dignity of all creatures**. This creature, I say, is among all the other creatures the one which most ressembles the creator, for the reason that just as in God all things stand through the Cause, so in man the whole universe shines again through the effect. And it is on this account that man is called a smaller world. And because he is the best among all, being not equal to each but equated with all, creatures universally obey him by their nature, and so he is the image of God. And this is what the Lord said: 'Let us make man in our image and likeness'. The Lord granted him dominion over all things, of which he was made the programme [exemplar].

Dictum 54

Text and translation from Joseph Goering and Randall Rosenfeld: 'The Tongue is a Pen: Robert Grosseteste's Dictum 54 and Scribal Technology' in *The Journal of Medieval Latin*, Vol. 12 (2002), pp. 114–40.

15

Adde ad hoc quod in interiori verbo sumus Dei similitude; in verbo autem sonante et significante exteriori est expressiua similitude verbi incarnati. Quid igitur tam diligenti custodia observandum ut verbum in quo nostra **summa** consistit **dignitas**, quod qui custodit, ut patet ex iam dictis, custodit animam suam. Et sicut ait Salomon, *Proverbiis* 12: 'Qui custodit os suum custodit animam suam', [*Prov.* 13, 3] in quo 'qui non offendum perfectum est.' [*Iac.* 3, 2] sicut ait Iacobus 3. Et in *Proverbiis* 14: 'Qui moderatur labia sua prudentissimus est' [*Prov.* 10, 19]. Et *Ecclesiasticus*: 'Beatus vir qui non est lapsus verbo ex ore suo' [*Eccles.* 14, 1]. Cum enim verbi nomen aglutinet simul verbum interius cum exteriori, verbumque interius omnis operae sit principium, patet quod qui non offendit in verbo in nullo offendit, quia si offendit in alio, prius offendit in verbo quod est illius operae principium [cf. *Iac.* 3, 2].

Add to this that we are like God in the interior word; in speaking and producing the exterior word, the likeness to the Word incarnate is expressed. What, therefore, ought to be watched with more diligence than the word, in which stands our **highest dignity**, because he who guards his word guards his soul, as is evident from what has already been stated? Solomon says, in Proverbs chapter thirteen: He who offends not [in word] is perfect', [Jac. 3, 2] as James says in chapter three. And in Proverbs fourteen: 'He who guards his tongue is most wise' [Prov. 10, 19]. And Ecclesiasticus: 'Blessed is the man who has not fallen by a word from his mouth.' [Eccles. 14, 1] And since the noun 'word' combines the interior with the exterior word, and the interior word is the origin of every work, it is evident that he who offends not in word offends not, because if he were to offend at all, he must first offend in the word which is the origin of that work [Jac 3, 2].

Hexaëmeron

Text from Robert Grosseteste: *Hexaëmeron*, eds Richard C. Dales and Servus Gieben O. F. M. Cap., Auctores britannici medii aevi VI (Oxford: The British Academy – Oxford University Press, 1982). Trans. from Robert Grosseteste: *On the Six days of Creation*. A Translation of the *Hexaëmeron*

by C. F. J. Martin, Auctores britannici medii aevi VI (2) (Oxford: The
British Academy – Oxford Universtity Press, 1996).

8, XI, 4

Hoc autem consilium, quod in hoc loco
nominant expositores, non est proprie
dictum consilium, quia, ut ait Ioannes
Damascenus: 'Non consiliatur Deus: igno-
rancie enim est consiliari. De eo enim quod
cognoscit, nullus consiliatur. Deus igitur,
omnia noscens simpliciter, non consiliatur'.
Innuitur igitur in hoc loco nomine consilii et modo loquendi consiliativo, cum
dicitur: *Faciamus hominem ad imaginem
nostram*, prerogativa **dignitatis humane
condicionis**, quod videlicet animal hono-
ratissimum in vitam adducitur. Et innuitur
eciam Conditoris cura et providentia specialis faciendi perfectum et preciosissimum
sibi et carissimum opus, et maximum sapi-
entiale et artificiale et ex artificii singulari-
tate maxime inter cetera opera admirabile.
Coniuncta est enim in homine in unitatem
persone suprema creatura, racionalis videlicet et arbitrio libera intelligentia, cum
creatura infima, videlicet terra, et non cum
qualicumque terra, sed cum pulvere sumpto
de terra. Ut enim infra scriptum est secundum translacionem Septuaginta: 'Formavit
Deus hominem pulverem sumens de terra.'
Et quid tam distantium coniunctione arti-
ficialius aut mirabilius potest excogitari?

This consultation, which is the name used
by the expositors on this passage, is not
a consultation in the strict sense, since,
as John Damascene says, 'God does not
consult, since consulting belongs to ignorance. No one consults on something that
he knows. God, then, who knows all things
without qualification, does not consult.'
What is suggested by the word 'consultation' here, and by the consultative way of
talking, when it says: 'Let us make man to
our image' is the privilege of **dignity of the
creation of the human being**, i.e. that the
most honoured of animals is being brought
to life. It also suggests the special care and
providence of the Creator in making this
perfect work of his, that is most precious
and most dear to him, the work that is done
with most wisdom and most craft and is
admirable among all his other works for
the exceptional skill with which it is made.
For in the human being we find joined in
the unity of a person both the supreme
creature – i.e. the rational understanding
that has free will – and the lowest creature,
i.e. earth. And not just any earth, but dust
taken from the earth. As it says lower down
in the translation of the Seventy, 'God
formed man taking dust from the earth'.
What could be conceived of that would
be more wonderful or more skilful than
the union of things that are so distant from
each other?

8, XVIII, 4

Per eandem quoque pluralitatem compellimur intelligere eciam mulierem factam ad Dei imaginem. Oportet enim divisum utriusque copulari, quod homini simpliciter in proximo copultum est, videlicet creari ad imaginem Dei. Unde et Basilius ait: 'Habet itaque mulier fieri ad imaginem Dei sicut et vir. **Sunt enim eiusdem dignitatis eorum nature**, equales eorum virtutes, equales pugne, equales retribuciones. Nec dicat mulier: 'Infirma sum.' Infirmitas enim carnis est, potencia vero in anima est. Quia igitur **eiusdem** est in eis **dignitatis** secundum Deum imago, equalis sit virtus et bonorum operum adieccio'. In omnibus enim que ad veras pertinent virtutes equiparari potest si vult mulier viro.

The same plural means that we have to understand that the woman too was made to the image of God. What is distinguished should be applied to both, since it is applied in the last sentence to the human being without qualification, i.e. being made to the image of God. Hence, Basil says: 'The woman comes to be according to the image of God as much as does the man. For **their natures are of the same dignity**, their virtues are equal, their struggles are equal, and their rewards are equal. The woman should not say 'I am weak'. Weakness is in the flesh, but power is in the soul. Since, then, an image of **the same dignity** is in them, the image of God, their virtue is equal and so is their right to good deeds'. For in all things that have to do with true virtues the woman can be equal to the man, if she wants.

For further discussion of Grosseteste's understanding of human dignity and for the relation to Basil, see Lebech and McEvoy (2013).

Thomas Aquinas (1225–1274)

Aquinas' synthesis of Greek philosophy and Christian faith deeply influenced European culture. His thoughts on dignity and on human dignity in particular are therefore important, even if he, like Cicero, mentions it without having an extensive teaching on the subject. Aquinas in fact incorporates many of Cicero's distinctions, and his notion of dignity owes a great deal to him. As we have seen, Cicero defined justice in terms of dignity, and dignity in terms of the authority to command respect. Thomas accepts these definitions and integrates them into his account of personhood and

of justice. 'Person', having served Christian theology in its efforts to comprehend the Trinity, was defined by Boethius as an *individual substance of rational nature*. This definition was, by Aquinas, combined with the *definitio magistralis*, defining person as a *hypostasis distinguished by dignity*. Dignity hereby comes to characterise the person essentially, and Cicero's understanding of dignity as the origin of rights and duties now slots into place around the person. The person was – in contradistinction from things – already the bearer of rights (the subject of *ius*) in the Roman Law tradition. Since, however, Roman law had allowed for slavery, the possibility existed, that not everyone was to be counted as a person. The status referred to here as 'human dignity' is a rank occupied by the human being *qua* human being, connoting hierarchy, like the rank occupied by superiors 'constituted in dignity', which like all other grades of dignity can be lost by action inappropriate to the status. The hierarchy is established by people occupying ranks according to some constitution (of an order, for example). Some are more qualified than others to occupy various positions, and Aquinas helpfully distinguishes between cause and dignity, such that the dignity should be conferred by reason of this cause. As in Cicero, how the rank of human dignity were to be conjugated with the differences in dignity is left for everyone to think about for themselves. It is to this problem that the late medieval women turn, which we shall treat of in the next chapter.

Texts have been chosen from the *Summa Theologiae* only, because this work is sufficiently representative of Thomas' thought.

Summa Theologiae

Texts are taken from the Marietti printing of the Leonine edition, and translations are from the Blackfriars' edition of the *Summa*.

Whether there is justice in God (Ia q. 21 a. 1)
Thomas often used the definition of distributive justice he inherited from Cicero (who held it from and Aristotle and Plato): *justice is to give everyone according to dignity*. He also referred to Pseudo-Dionysius, who observes justice in God because he gives to all according to their dignity. God as

Creator, Thomas says, has also given humans dignity by endowing them with rational nature, but this can hardly be considered their merit, even if rational nature as such merits respect. Dignity, in fact, is what merits respect as well as goods, so the gift of it cannot be merited in accordance with 'commutative justice'. Once given, however, it can be a ground for merit, so that God's distributive justice is not groundless.

Respondeo dicendum quod duplex est species iustitiae. Una, quae consistit in mutua datione et acceptione: ut puta quae consistit in emptione et venditione, et aliis huiusmodi communicationibus vel commutationibus. Et haec dicitur a Philosopho, in V *Ethic.*, iustitia commutativa, vel directiva commutationum sive communicationum. Et haec non competit Deo: quia, ut dicit Apostolus, *Rom.* 11,35: *quis prior dedit illi, et retribuetur ei?*

Reply: There are two kinds of justice, commutative and distributive. The first consists in mutual giving and receiving, for instance in transactions such as buying and selling and other like shared exchanges. Aristotle calls it 'commutative justice' since it directs dealings on a give-and-take basis. There is no question of this with God; as St Paul asks, *Who has first given to him and recompense shall be made to him?*

Alia, quae consistit in distribuendo: et dicitur distributiva iustitia, secundum quam aliquis gubernator vel dispensator dat unicuique secundum suam **dignitatem**. Sicut igitur ordo congruus familiae, vel cuiuscumque multitudinis gubernatae, demonstrat huiusmodi iustitiam in gubernante; ita ordo universi, qui apparet tam in rebus naturalibus quam in rebus voluntariis, demonstrat Dei iustitiam. Unde dicit Dionysius, 8 cap. de *Div. Nom.*: *Oportet videre in hoc veram Dei esse iustitiam, quod omnibus tribuit propria, secundum uniuscuiusque existentium **dignitatem**; et uniuscuiusque naturam in proprio salvat ordine et virtute.*

The other kind consists in sharing out, and is called 'distributive justice'; this is the rightness of a ruler or steward dispensing to each according to his **worth**. As this justice is displayed in a well-ordered family or community through its head, so the good order of the universe, manifested both in natural and moral beings, sets forth God's justice. That is why Dionysius says, *We ought to see that God is truly just in that he grants what is proper to all existing things according to their **worth**, and maintains the nature of each in its proper place and strength.*

The Divine Persons (Ia q. 29 a.1 and 3)

Thomas' elaboration of the definition of personhood was both common and seminal. He insisted on the individuality of the person, while at the same time retaining the importance of its human – and universal – nature. This

balance is the key to his understanding of the person: whereas the person is of a rational nature, what is ultimately of value is what carries this rational nature, the *hypostasis*. This is how the individual person can remain, true to human experience, undefinable as an individual, yet be something of a certain – namely rational – nature.

At face value, the definition *persona est hypostasis proprietate distincta ad dignitatem pertinente* [the person is a hypostasis distinct by a property pertaining to dignity] sounds paradoxical. Is it not contradictory to attribute to the substrate – which in principle is qualityless – something that distinguishes it *qua* substrate? Yet, *hypostasis* came out of the Trinitarian discussions as a term that no longer simply meant substrate, even if it was still akin to the latter. The modern understanding of *subject* comes closer, connoting as it does the subjective activity of mind. The idea that subjectivity as such is dignified, and that dignity identifies and determines subjectivity to be 'a subject', may be what the anonymous scholastic master had in mind: Dignity is what characterises the person as person. As personhood is what is most perfect in the whole of nature, it must also exist in God, and thus dignity accounts in God for personal individuality in the same way as it does in created rational creatures.

Articulus 1	Article 1:
De definitione personae	The definition of 'person'
Ad primum sic proceditur. Videtur quod incompetens sit definitio personae quam Boethius assignat in libro *de Duabus Naturis*, quae talis est: *Persona est rationalis naturae individua substantia.*	It seems that the definition set out by Boëthius, namely that *person is an individual substance of a rational nature*, is inappropriate.
1. Nullum enim singulare definitur. Sed persona significat quoddam singulare. Ergo persona inconvenienter definitur. [...]	1. No singular thing can be defined. But person signifies something singular. Therefore this definition of person is unsuitable. [...]

Respondeo dicendum quod, licet universale et particulare inveniantur in omnibus generibus, tamen speciali quodam modo individuum invenitur in genere substantiae. Substantia enim individuatur per seipsam, sed accidentia individuantur per subiectum, quod est substantia: dicitur enim haec albedo, inquantum est in hoc subiecto. Unde etiam convenienter individua substantiae habent aliquod speciale nomen prae aliis: dicuntur enim hypostases, vel primae substantiae.

Sed adhuc quodam specialiori et perfectiori modo invenitur particulare et individuum in substantiis rationalibus, quae habent dominium sui actus, et non solum aguntur, sicut alia, sed per se agunt: actiones autem in singularibus sunt. Et ideo etiam inter ceteras substantias quoddam speciale nomen habent singularia rationalis naturae. Et hoc nomen est persona. Et ideo in praedicta definitione personae ponitur substantia individua, inquantum significat singulare in genere substantiae: additur autem rationalis naturae, inquantum significat singulare in rationalibus substantiis.

Ad primum ergo dicendum quod, licet hoc singulare vel illud definiri non possit, tamen id quod pertinet ad communem rationem singularitatis, definiri potest: et sic Philosophus definit substantiam primam. Et hoc modo definit Boethius personam.

Articulus 3
Utrum nomen personae sit ponendum in divinis

Videtur quod nomen personae non sit ponendum in divinis.

Reply: Although we find the universal and the particular in all categories, the individual belongs in a special way to the category of substance. For a substance is individual by itself, whereas accidents are individual through their subject, which is a substance; for we speak of this whiteness inasmuch as it is in this subject. Rightly then and more than others do we call those things individual which are substances; they are given the special names of 'hypostases' or 'first substances'.

However, particularity and individuality are found in a still more special and perfect way in rational substances, which have control over their actions, and are not only acted upon as other beings are, but act of their own initiative. For to act is proper to individuals or singular substances. Hence among all other substances individual beings with rational nature have a special name, and this is 'person'. That is why in this definition of person, the term 'individual substance' is used to mean a singular being in the category of substance; 'rational nature' is added to mean the singular being among rational substances.

Hence: 1. Although this or that singular thing cannot be defined, nevertheless the general character of singularity can be defined, and this is how Aristotle defines 'first substance'. In this way, too, Boëthius defines person.

Article 3:
Whether the word 'person' can be used of God

It seems that the word 'person' should not be used of God.

2. Praeterea, Boethius dicit, in libro *de Duab. Natur. Nomen personae videtur traductum ex his personis quae in comoediis tragoediisque homines repraesentebant; persona enim dicta est a personando, quia concavitate ipsa maior necesse est ut volvatur sonus Graeci vero has personas prosopa vocant, ab eo quod ponantur in facie, atque ante oculos obtegant vultum.* Sed hoc non potest competere in divinis, nisi forte secundum metaphoram. Ergo nomen personae non dicitur de Deo nisi metaphorice.

Respondeo dicendum quod persona significat id quod est perfectissimum in tota natura, scilicet subsistens in rationali natura. Unde, cum omne illud quod est perfectionis, Deo sit attribuendum, eo quod eius essentia continet in se omnem perfectionem; conveniens est ut hoc nomen persona de Deo dicatur, non tamen eodem modo quo dicitur de creaturis, sed excellentiori modo; sicut et alia nomina quae, creaturis a nobis imposita, Deo attribuuntur; sicut supra ostensum est, cum de divinis nominibus ageretur.

Ad secundum dicendum quod, quamvis hoc nomen persona non conveniat Deo quantum ad id a quo impositum est nomen, tamen quantum ad id ad quod significandum imponitur, maxime Deo convenit. Quia enim in comoediis et tragoediis repraesentabantur aliqui homines famosi, impositum est hoc nomen personae ad significandum aliquos **dignitatem** habentes. Unde consueverunt dici personae in ecclesiis, quam habent aliquam **dignitatem.** Propter quod quidam definiunt personam, dicentes quod **persona est** *hypostasis proprietate distincta ad dignitatem pertinente.* Et quia magnae **dignitatis** est in

2. Boethius says, *The word 'person' seems to be derived from those persons who represented characters in comedies and tragedies; it comes from* 'personare' *or* 'to sound through', *since a funnel-shaped mask increases resonance. The Greeks called these persons* προσοπα *since the masks were placed on the face and covered the visage.* Such meaning can apply to God only by metaphor. Therefore the word 'person' is used of God only metaphorically.

Reply: 'Person' means that which is most perfect in the whole of nature, namely what subsists in rational nature. Now since every kind of perfection should be attributed to God, because his nature contains every perfection, it is fitting that the word 'person' should be used of God; nevertheless it is not used in exactly the same sense of God as of creatures but in a higher sense, as are other words by which we name creatures, as was explained elsewhere when we discussed the naming of God.

2. Although we cannot use 'person' of God in its original sense we can extend this perfectly well for our present purpose. Since in comedies and tragedies famous men were represented, the word 'person' came to be used in reference to men of **high rank.** It then became customary in the ecclesiastical world to refer to personages of **rank.** This is why some theologians define person by saying that a person is '**a hypostasis distinguished by dignity**'. To subsist in rational nature is a characteristic implying **dignity** and hence, as already mentioned, every individual with rational nature is called 'person'. Of course the **dignity** of divine

rationali natura subsistere, ideo omne individuum rationalis naturae dicitur persona,
ut dictum est. Sed **dignitas** divinae naturae excedit omnem **dignitatem**: et secundum hoc maxime competit Deo nomen
personae.

nature surpasses all **other**, and so it is completely fitting to use 'person' of God.

*Whether the hypostases still remain when by thought we isolate the relations
from the persons (Ia q. 40 a. 3)*

Thomas makes it plain that there cannot be such a thing as a person without dignity, as dignity is an essential characteristic of the person, so that
not even the subject (the hypostasis) of someone remains if the dignity is
abstracted. From this, we must conclude that dignity is inherent or intrinsic
to the subject and to subjectivity as such, despite the possibility of losing
the immunity to which it entitles by sinning.

Square brackets have been introduced in the translation to bracket
superfluous words, disturbing the meaning relating to the subject under
investigation.

Videtur quod, abstractis per intellectum
proprietatibus seu relationibus a personis,
adhuc remaneant hypostases.

The properties or relations once abstracted
by thought from the persons, it seems that
the hypostases remain.

1. Id enim ad quod aliquid se habet ex additione, potest intelligi remoto eo quod sibi
additur; sicut *homo* se habet ad *animal* ex
additione, et potest intelligi *animal* remoto
rationali. Sed persona se habet ex additione
ad hypostasim: est enim persona hypostasis
proprietate distincta ad **dignitatem** pertinente. Ergo, remota proprietate personali a
persona, intelligitur hypostasis. [...]

1. Wherever B stands as an addition to A,
A can retain its meaning if B is removed,
e.g. 'man' adds something to 'animal' and so
'animal' retains its own meaning if 'man' is
subtracted. Now person adds to hypostasis,
in that person means a hypostasis marked
by a property involving **excellence**. This
property being taken away from the person,
then, hypostasis still keeps its meaning. [...]

Sed contra est quod Hilarius dicit, IV
de Trin. Nihil habet Filius nisi natum.
Nativitate autem est Filius. Ergo, remota
filiatione, non remanet hypostasis Filii. Et
eadem ratio est de aliis personis.

On the other hand there is Hilary's teaching, *The Son has nothing else proper but his
being born.* Now he is Son by his birth.
Thus if this property be taken away, the
hypostasis of the Son would not remain.
And the same argument applies for the
other persons.

Respondeo dicendum quod duplex fit abstractio per intellectum. Una quidem, secundum quod universale abstrahitur a particulari, ut *animal* ab *homine*. Alia vero, secundum quod forma abstrahitur a materia; sicut forma circuli abstrahitur per intellectum ab omni materia sensibilii. Inter has autem abstractiones haec est differentia, quod in abstractione quae fit secundum universale et particulare, non remanet in intellectu *homo*, sed solum *animal*. In abstractione vero quae attenditur secundum formam et materiam, utrumque manet in intellectu: abstrahendo enim formam circuli ab aere, remanet seorsum in intellectu nostro et intellectus circuli et intellectus aeris.

Quamvis autem in divinis non sit universale neque particulare, nec forma et materia, secundum rem; tamen, secundum modum significandi, invenitur aliqua similitudo horum in divinis; secundum quem modum Damascenus dicit quod *commune est substantia, particulare vero hypostasis*. Si igitur loquamur de abstractione quae fit secundum universale et particulare, remotis proprietatibus, remanet in intellectu essentia communis, non autem hypostasis Patris, quae est quasi particulare. Si vero loquamur secundum modum abstractionis formae a materia, remotis proprietatibus non personalibus, remanet intellectus hypostasum et personarum: sicut, remoto per intellectum a Patre quod sit ingenitus vel spirans, remanet hypostasis vel persona Patris. Sed remota proprietate personali per intellectum, tollitur intellectus hypostasis. Non enim

Reply: The mind has two ways of abstracting. In the one it thinks of the universal apart from the particular; e.g. 'animal' apart from 'man'. In the other, it thinks of a form apart from matter; e.g. the mind considers the figure of a circle apart from other perceptible qualities. The difference between the two modes of abstraction is this: in the one regarding the universal and the particular, that from which thought abstracts does not remain; e.g., the difference 'rational' once separated from 'man' there remains in thought not 'man' but just 'animal'. However, in the abstraction that regards form and matter, each remains in thought; e.g. in thinking of the figure of a circle apart from its material, brass, both the thought of circle and the thought of brass remain separately in the mind.

As to the divine, our way of expressing meaning includes something like the universal and the particular, the formal and the material, even though these are not present in the reality. Damascene refers to this, saying that the substance is what is common, the hypostasis is what is particular. Accordingly, we speak of abstraction in its universal-particular mode, the properties being set apart, the essence as common remains in thought, but as particular the hypostasis, e.g. the Father does not. As to the formal-material mode, if the non-personal properties be considered apart, the thought of the hypostases and persons remains; e.g. if by thought we set aside from the Father his being unbegotten or spirating, the hypostasis or person of the Father remains. But to set personal property aside by thought is to take away the meaning of hypostasis. The reason: we

proprietates personales sic intelliguntur advenire hypostasibus divinis, sicut forma subiecto praeexistenti: sed ferunt secum sua supposita, inquantum sunt ipsae personae subsistentes, sicut paternitas est ipse Pater: hypostases enim significant aliquid distinctum in divinis, cum hypostasis sit substantia individua. Cum igitur relatio sit quae distinguit hypostases et constituit eas, ut dictum est, relinquitur quod, relationibus personalibus remotis per intellectum, non remaneant hypostases.

are not to think of personal properties as though coming to the divine hypostases in the way that forms come to a pre-existent subject; rather the properties include their own supposits in that they themselves are the subsisting persons, e.g. fatherhood is the Father. For a hypostasis means something distinct in God, since a hypostasis is an individual substance. The conclusion, then, is that because, as shown, relation is what sets apart and constitutes the hypostases, if thought separates personal relations the hypostases do not remain.

Sed, sicut dictum est, aliqui dicunt quod hypostases in divinis non distinguuntur per relationes, sed per solam originem; ut intelligatur Pater esse hypostasis quaedam per hoc, quod non est ab alio; Filius autem per hoc, quod est ab alio per generationem. Sed relationes advenientes quasi proprietates ad **dignitatem** pertinentes, constituunt rationem personae: unde et personalitates dicuntur. Unde, remotis huiusmodi relationibus per intellectum, remanent quidem hypostases, sed non personae.

There is another opinion: as noted some authors maintain that the hypostases in the divinity are distinct not by relation but by origin – the Father is one hypostasis by reason of his not being from another; the Son, by his being from another through generation. Relations, however, being added as properties involving [a difference in] **excellence,** are constitutive of person as such and hence some call them 'personalities'. Accordingly, such relations being set aside in thought, the hypostases, though not the persons, remain.

Sed hoc non potest esse, propter duo. Primo, quia relationes distinguunt et constituunt hypostases, ut ostensum est. – Secundo, quia omnis hypostasis naturae rationalis est persona, ut patet per definitionem Boethii, dicentis quod *persona est rationalis naturae individua substantia*. Unde, ad hoc quod esset hypostasis et non persona, oporteret abstrahi ex parte naturae rationalitatem; non autem ex parte personae proprietatem.

There are, however, two reasons why that cannot be the case. First, relations, as shown, distinguish and constitute the hypostases. Secondly, every hypostasis in an intellectual nature is a person, as Boëtius' definition clearly states, a person is an *individual substance in rational nature*. 'Hypostasis' without person, then, would mean an abstraction of intelligence from the nature, not simply of property from person.

Ad primum ergo dicendum quod persona non addit supra hypostasim proprietatem distinguentem absolute, sed proprietatem distinguentem ad **dignitatem** pertinentem:

Hence: 1. What person adds to hypostasis is not simply a distinguishing property but a distinguishing property denoting **excellence**; this whole phrase has to be taken

totum enim hoc est accipiendum loco unius differentiae. Ad **dignitatem** autem pertinet proprietas distinguens, secundum quod intelligitur subsistens in natura rationali. Unde, remota proprietate distinguente a persona, non remanet hypostasis: sed remaneret, si tolleretur rationalitas naturae. Tam enim persona quam hypostasis est substantia individua: unde in divinis de ratione utriusque est relatio distinguens.

as standing for the one difference. Now a distinctive property includes **excellence** in that it means a reality subsisting in an intelligent nature. Hence such a property being removed from the person, no hypostasis remains; it would remain only by taking away intelligence from the nature. For both person and hypostasis mean an individual substance and in God the distinctive relation makes up the definition of both.

Whether Natural Law contains several precepts or only one (IaIIae q. 94 a. 2)
Dignity also means what is important in itself, self-evident, or, in Thomas' words, *per se notum*. This it is, of course, only in relation to what is relative; the fundamental always being what is fundamental to something even if in relation to itself as first or ultimate. Accordingly, *dignitas* is the term used throughout the Scholastic period to translate the Greek *axioma*, first principle, as we have already noted in Chapter 1. In this text Thomas explicitly extends *dignitas* beyond first principles of logic (such as the principle of non-contradiction) to practical first principles (such as 'the good is what every agent seeks').

Videtur quod lex naturalis non contineat plura precepta, sed unum tantum. [...]

It seems that natural law does not contain several precepts but only one. [...]

Respondeo dicendum quod, sicut supra dictum est, praecepta legis naturae hoc modo se habent ad rationem practicam, sicut principia prima demonstrationum se habent ad rationem speculativam: utraque enim sunt quaedam principia per se nota. Dicitur autem aliquid per se notum dupliciter: uno modo, secundum se; alio modo, quoad nos. Secundum se quidem quaelibet propositio dicitur per se nota, cuius praedicatum est de ratione subiecti: contingit tamen quod ignoranti definitionem subiecti, talis propositio non erit per se nota. Sicut ista propositio,

Reply: We have drawn a parallel between the precepts of the natural law for the practical reason and the axioms of science for the theoretical reason: both are kinds of self-evident beginnings. Now a truth is self-evident at two stages, one, in itself, two, in our minds. A proposition is self-evident in itself when the predicate is of the essence of the subject. At the same time the proposition may not be self-evident to a man who does not know the definition of the subject. For instance, 'man is a rational animal', is a self-evident proposition of its nature, since to say 'man' is to say 'rational'.

Homo est rationale, est per se nota secundum sui naturam, quia qui dicit hominem, dicit rationale: et tamen ignoranti quid sit homo, haec propositio non est per se nota. Et inde est quod, sicut dicit Boethius, in libro *de Hebdomad.*, quaedam sunt **dignitates** vel propositiones per se notae communiter omnibus: et huiusmodi sunt illae propositiones quarum termini sunt omnibus noti, ut, *Omne totum est maius sua parte*, et *Quae uni et eidem sunt aequalia, sibi invicem sunt aequalia.* Quaedam vero propositiones sunt per se notae solis sapientibus, qui terminos propositionum intelligunt quid significent: sicut intelligenti quod angelus non est corpus, per se notum est quod non est circumscriptive in loco, quod non est manifestum rudibus, qui hoc non capiunt.

In his autem quae in apprehensione omnium cadunt, quidam ordo invenitur. Nam illud quod primo cadit in apprehensione, est ens, cuius intellectus includitur in omnibus quaecumquae quis apprehendit. Et ideo primum principium indemonstrabile est quod non est simul affirmare et negare, quod fundatur supra rationem entis et non entis: et super hoc principio omnia alia fundantur, ut dicitur in IV *Metaphys.* Sicut autem ens est primum quod cadit in apprehensione simpliciter, ita bonum est primum quod cadit in apprehensione practicae rationis, quae ordinatur ad opus: omne enim agens agit propter finem, qui habet rationem boni. Et ideo primum principium in ratione practica est quod fundatur supra rationem boni, quae est, *Bonum est quod omnia appetunt.* Hoc est ergo primum praeceptum legis, quod bonum est faciendum et prosequendum, et malum vitandum. Et

Yet to somebody who does not grasp what man really is, the proposition is not self-evident. That is why Boethius says, *there are some **axioms** or self-evident propositions generally known to all*; such are the propositions the terms of which everybody recognizes, such as, 'the whole is greater than the part', or, 'things equal to a third thing are equal to one another'. Sometimes, however, propositions are self-evident only to the well-informed, who know what the terms of the proposition mean. Thus to one who appreciates that an angel is not a bodily substance it is self-evident that an angel is not circumscribed in place. This, however, is not manifest to those who are uninstructed and do not grasp what is meant.

Now we discover that the things which enter into our apprehension are ranged in a certain order. That which first appears is the real, and some insight into this is included in whatsoever is apprehended. This first indemonstrable principle, 'there is no affirming and denying the same simultaneously', is based on the very nature of the real and the non-real: on this principle, as Aristotle notes, all other propositions are based. To apply an analogy: as to be real enters into human apprehending as such, so to be good first enters the practical reason's apprehending when it is bent on doing something. For every agent acts on account of an end, and to be an end carries the meaning of to be good. Consequently, the first principle for the practical reason is based on the meaning of the good, namely that it is what all things seek after. And so this is the first command of law, 'that good

super hoc fundantur omnia alia praecepta
legis naturae: ut scilicet omnia illa facienda
vel vitanda pertineant ad praecepta legis
naturae, quae ratio practica naturaliter
apprehendit esse bona humana.

is to be sought and done, evil to be avoided';
all other commands of natural law are based
on this. Accordingly, then, natural-law
commands extend to all doing or avoiding
of things recognized by the practical reason
of itself as being human goods.

Unfair discrimination IIaIIae (q. 63, a. 1–3)

'Respect for persons' can mean what we today call 'unfair discrimination'. Someone who does not 'accept persons' is someone to whom social
status does not count, and God is thus (*Eph.* 6, 9) because he is just. This
understanding makes of God's absolute justice, that is, his Love, a coun-
terargument against the traditional definition of justice – to give everyone
according to dignity – at least in so far as dignity is understood as social
standing and is determined by social construction. To safeguard some sense
of the proportionality of human justice, Aquinas therefore introduces a
distinction between *dignitas* and *causa* (translated by *reason*) and justifies discrimination for *good* reason, such as competence. That *dignus* here
is translated with *being qualified* goes to illustrate that what was called
dignity then, is now understood to be 'qualifications'. Qualifications, like
dignity, raise a claim for recognition, and entitle one to something in particular. Hence, the distinction Aquinas makes between *dignitas* and *causa*
is a distinction between person and qualification, both entitling to have
claims met, but the mere fact of being a person not entitling one to some
particular office.

1. Videtur quod personarum acceptio non
sit peccatum. In nomine enim personae
intelligitur **personae dignitas**. Sed considerare **dignitates personarum** pertinet
ad distributivam justiam: Ergo personarum
acceptio non est peccatum.

1. It would seem that discrimination is not
a sin. For the term 'person' suggests a **person's station**. But taking a **person's station**
into account is part of distributive justice.
Therefore, discrimination is not a sin.

2. Praeterea, in rebus humanis personae sunt principaliores quam res, quia res sunt propter personas, et non e converso. Sed rerum acceptio non est peccatum. Ergo multo minus acceptio personarum.

Responsio: Dicendum quod personarum acceptio opponitur distributivae justitiae. Consistit enim aequalitas distributivae justitiae in hoc quod diversis personis diversa tribuuntur secundum proportionem ad **dignitates personarum**. Si ergo aliquis consideret illam proprietatem personae propter quam id quod ei confertur est ei debitum, non erit acceptio personae, sed causae; unde glossa, super illud *ad Ephes., Non est personarum acceptio apud Deum,* dicit quod *judex justus causas discernit, non personas.* Puta si aliquis promoveat aliquem ad magisterium propter sufficientiam scientiae, hic attenditur causa debita, non persona; si autem aliquis consideret in eo cui aliquid confert, non id propter quod id quod ei datur, esset ei proportionatum vel debitum, sed solum hoc quod est iste homo (puta Petrus vel Martinus), est hic acceptio personae quia non attribuitur ei aliquid propter aliquam causam qua faciat eum **dignum**, sed simpliciter attribuitur personae. Ad personam autem refertur quaecumque conditio non faciens ad causam propter quam sit **dignus** hoc dono; puta si aliquis promoveat aliquem ad praelationem vel magisterium quia est dives, vel quia est consanguineus suus, est acceptio personae. Contingit tamen aliquam conditionem personae facere eam **dignam** respectu unius rei, et non respectu alterius; sicut consanguinitas facit aliquem **dignum** ad hoc quod instituatur haeres patrimonii, non autem ad

2. In human affairs people are more important than things, since things are for people and not the other way round. But it is not a sin to discriminate as to things. There is, therefore, even less reason for discrimination as to persons being a sin.

Reply: Unfair discrimination is opposed to distributive justice. This is because the equitable nature of distributive justice consists in different people receiving different things according to their **social worth**, so that for one person to receive something on the basis of what gives him that social worth is respect not of the person but of the reason. This is why a gloss on the passage in *Ephesians* about there *being no partiality with God* is to this effect, *The just judge scrutinizes causes, not appearances.* Therefore if one person appoints another to a teaching post on the basis of his professional competence, he is paying regard to a due cause and not to the person, whereas if what he takes into account is not his qualification for the position but the fact that he is the particular individual he is, say Peter or Martin, he is practising unfair discrimination; for in this case he is giving him something not because he has any **proper title** to it, but only because of personal considerations. And what acting on the basis of such personal considerations means is taking into account factors which are irrelevant to the candidate's **qualification** for the particular position, as for instance, when somebody promotes another to an ecclesiastical or academic preferment because he is rich or a relative. It may, of course, happen that a person is **qualified** in one respect without thereby being qualified in another, in the way in which blood-relationship gives a

hoc quod conferatur ei praelatio ecclesias-
tica. Et ideo eadem conditio personae in
uno negotio considerata facit acceptionem
personae, in alio autem non facit.

person a claim to the inheritance of property, though not to ecclesiastical preferment. Accordingly, to take into account
the same personal condition gives rise to
unfair discrimination in the one case and
not in the other.

Sic ergo patet quod personarum acceptio
opponitur justitiae distributivae in hoc
quod praeter proportionem agitur. Nihil
autem opponitur virtuti nisi peccatum.
Unde consequens est quod personarum
acceptio sit peccatum.

It is, therefore, clear that unfair discrimination is opposed to distributive justice in
so far as it offends against the principle of
apportionment according to social worth.
But nothing is opposed to virtue except sin.
Therefore, unfair discrimination is a sin.

I. Ad primum ergo dicendum quod in distributiva justitia considerantur conditiones
personarum quae faciunt ad causam **dignitatis** vel debiti; sed in acceptione personarum considerantur conditiones quae
non faciunt ad causam, ut dictum est.

Hence: I. The exercise of distributive justice involves taking into consideration such
qualities of people as give them a **title** or
qualification, whereas unfair discrimination is a matter of taking into consideration
factors extraneous thereto, as shown.

2. Ad secundum dicendum quod personae
proportionantur et **dignae** redduntur aliquibus quae eis distribuuntur propter aliquas res
quae pertinent ad conditionem personae; et
ideo hujusmodi conditiones sunt attenden-
dae, tanquam propriae causae. Cum autem
considerantur ipsae personae, attenditur non
causa ut causa; et ideo patet quod quamvis
personae sint **digniores** simpliciter, non
tamen sunt **digniores** quoad hoc.

2. People become **qualified** to receive what
they are allocated in virtue of the things
that go to make up their situation, and this
is why such situations count as due grounds.
But when the mere person is taken into
account, what is not a cause is counted as
a cause. From which it is clear that although
persons as such are **more important** than
things, their being persons is not of itself a
qualification for any sort of office.

Discrimination is most likely to happen in the distribution of lucrative
tasks (offices) and honours. It can therefore also occur in the distribution
of ecclesiastical (spiritual) titles and offices, in which case the sin involved
is graver. However, a person's dignity can be seen in itself (relying exclu-
sively on virtue), and in relation to the common good (in which case connections may contribute as well). Someone better connected (wealthier,
more powerful) may in fact be able to contribute more to the common
good than a more virtuous person with less power and influence may. That
a 'dignitary' here is a translation from *praelatus* illustrates that dignitary has

come to mean someone of importance and consequence because dignity is something that has things follow from it and is of consequence.

1. Videtur quod in dispensatione spiritualium locum non habeat personarum acceptio. Conferre enim **dignitatem** ecclesiasticam seu beneficium alicui propter consanguinitatem videtur ad acceptionem personarum pertinere, quia consanguinitas non est causa faciens hominem **dignum** ecclesiastico beneficio. Sed hoc non videtur esse peccatum, cum hoc ex consuetudine **praelati** Ecclesiae faciant. Ergo peccatum personarum acceptionis non videtur locum habere in dispensatione spiritualium. [...]

Responsio: Dicendum quod, sicut dictum est, acceptio personarum est peccatum inquantum conmtrariatur justitiae. Quanto autem in majoribus aliquis justitiam transgreditur, tanto gravius peccat. Unde cum spiritualia sint temporalibus potiora, gravius peccatum est personas accipere in dispensatione spiritualium quam in dispensatione temporalium.

Et quia personarum acceptio est cum aliquid personae attribuitur praeter proportionem **dignitatis** ipsius, considerare oportet quod **dignitas** alicujus personae potest attendi dupliciter: uno modo simpliciter et secundum se, et sic majoris **dignitatis** est ille qui magis abundat in spiritualibus gratiae donis; alio modo per comparationem ad bonum commune; contingit enim quandoque quod ille qui est minus sanctus et minus sciens potest magis conferre ad bonum commune propter potentiam vel industriam saecularem, vel propter aliquid hujusmodi. Et quia dispensationes spiritualium principalius ordinantur ad

1. It would seem that unfair discrimination does not occur in granting spiritual rights and benefits. Conferring an ecclesiastical **preferment** or benefice on somebody on the grounds of relationship would seem to be an instance of unfair discrimination, since relationship does not **qualify** a person for such a benefit. Yet such a practice would not seem to amount to a sin since **dignitaries** of the Church are accustomed to do this. The sin of unfair discrimination would, therefore, not seem to arise in the granting of spiritual rights and benefits. [...]

Reply: As we have already seen, discrimination is a sin to the extent that it thwarts justice. But the more momentous the matters in which justice is thwarted, the graver the sin. It follows that since spiritual matters are more important than temporal ones, it is a graver sin to practise unfair discrimination in granting spiritual rights and benefits than in dispensing temporal ones.

Now since unfair discrimination occurs where a person is given more than his **social worth** warrants, we should note that a person's **social worth** can be seen in two ways. Firstly, simply in itself – here the person who has greater spiritual gifts of grace **stands higher**; secondly, however, in relation to the common good – for it does happen that somebody who is less holy and less learned can contribute more to the common good, because he has more worldly influence or wisdom, or something of the sort. And because spiritual benefits are dispensed above all for the common good, as St Paul tells us: *To each is given the*

utilitatem communem, secundum illud I *Cor., Unicuique datur manifestatio spiritus ad utilitatem,* ideo quandoque absque acceptione personarum in dispensatione spiritualium illi qui sunt simpliciter minus boni melioribus praeferuntur, sicut etiam et Deus gratias gratis datas quandoque concedit minus bonis.

Ad primum ergo dicendum quod circa consanguineos praelati distinguendum est. Quia quandoque sunt minus **digni** et simpliciter et per respectum ad bonum commune; et sic si **dignioribus** praeferantur, est peccatum personarum acceptionis in dispensatione spiritualium; quorum praelatus ecclesiasticus non est dominus, ut possit ea dare pro libito, sed dispensator, secundum illud I *Cor., Sic nos existimet homo ut ministros Christi, et dispensatores mysteriorum Dei.* Quandoque vero consanguinei praelati ecclesiastici sunt aeque **digni** ut alii: et sic licite potest absque personarum acceptione consanguineos suos praeferre; quia saltem in hoc praeeminent quod de ipsis magis confidere potest ut unanimiter secum negotia Ecclesiae tractent. Esset tamen hoc propter scandalum dimittendum, si ex hoc aliqui exemplum sumerent etiam praeter **dignitatem** bona Ecclesiae consanguineis dandi.

manifestation of the spirit for the common good those who are less truly good may be preferred to the better without this being unfair discrimination – just as even God sometimes gives charismatic grace to the less good.

Hence: 1. We have to make a distinction in relation to a dignitary's relations. For sometimes they are less well **qualified** both in themselves and in relation to the common good, in which case there is a sin of unfair discrimination if they are given spiritual benefits in preference to more **worthy** people; for a dignitary is, after all, a steward of spiritual benefits, and not an absolute owner who can do with them what he wills, as St Paul says, *This is how one should regard us, as servants of Christ and stewards of the mysteries of God.* Relatives of dignitaries may, however, also be as **well qualified** as others, and in such a case it is legitimate to prefer one's relatives without thereby practising unfair discrimination; for they do at least have this advantage over the others that they are more likely to work well together for the Church. This advantage should, however, be set to one side if it begins to give scandal and to encourage the fashion of distributing ecclesiastical benefits regardless of **merit.**

However, the dignity of a dignitary is worthy of respect, even when it does not repose on virtue (which is nevertheless the best), because the dignitary personifies God and the community he rules in his office. Rank, thus, for Aquinas, is divinely instituted, and must be respected. Such theory, of course, relies on it being necessary and useful in relation to the common good to have ranks at all, an idea that was also found in Cicero.

Responsio: Dicendum quod honor est quoddam testimonium de virtute ejus qui honoratur; et ideo sola virtus est debita causa honoris. Sciendum tamen quod aliquis potest honorari non solum propter virtutem propriam, sed etiam propter virtutem alterius, sicut principes et praelati honorantur, etiamsi sint mali, inquantum gerunt personam Dei et communitatis cui praeficiuntur, secundum illud *Prov., Sicut qui immittit lapides in acervum Mercurii, ita qui tribuit insipienti honorem.* Quia gentiles rationem attribuebant Mercurio, acervus Mercurii dicitur cumulus ratiocinii, in quo mercator quandoque mittit unum lapillum loco centum marcarum. Ita etiam honoratur insipiens quia ponitur loco Dei et loco totius communitatis. Et eadem ratione parentes et domini sunt honorandi propter participationem divinae **dignitatis**, qui est omnium pater et dominus. Senes autem sunt honorandi propter signum virtutis, quod est senectus, licet hoc signum quandoque deficiat. Unde, ut dicitur *Sap., senectus vere honoranda est, non diuturna, neque annorum numero computata; cani autem sunt sensus hominis, et aetas senectutis vita est immaculata.*

Reply: Honour consists in the acknowledgement of the virtue of the person honoured. Only virtue, therefore, entitles a person to honour. We should however remark that somebody may be honoured on account not only of his own virtue but of somebody else's too. This is the principle on which prelates and leaders are to be honoured even if they are bad, in so far as they personify God and the community they rule. *Proverbs* makes the point, *Like one who adds chips to Mercury's pile is he who gives honour to a fool.* The pagans thought of the god Mercury as the patron of commerce, so that the sum of cash or even tokens which merchants might include in lieu of actual coins was termed 'Mercury's Pile'. And thus even a fool as he stands for God or the community shares in the honour due to them in the way in which whatever stood for Mercury shared in the honour due to him. And by the same token parents and masters are to be honoured since they have something of the **dignity** of God who is the father and master of all. Old people too deserve honour since their age is a sign of honour – albeit a sign that is occasionally somewhat hollow. And this is of course the reason why *Wisdom* says, *For old age is not honoured for length of time, nor measured by number of years, but understanding is grey hair for men, and a blameless life is ripe old age.*

Whether it is licit to kill sinners (IIaIIae q. 64 a. 2)

Human dignity is, according to Thomas, the dignity of human beings that makes them important in themselves, and therefore of absolute importance for everything else, including other human beings. This importance can, however, be lost by sinning, and cancelled by human acts deviating from the rational order. In this case, it no longer commands the universal respect

due to rational animals. In fact, a human being without his native human dignity, who has himself undone his importance as a human being through his irrational acts, is no more dignified than a beast and may be killed. This doctrine does not compromise the idea that a person is essentially characterised by dignity, since it arises from the idea that the subject determines itself through actions and therefore can cancel the claim to respect stemming from his or her rational nature. When Adam sinned, that in fact was what happened; he came to deserve death. It is on this background that the restoration of human dignity in Christ can be understood as the cancelling of the death penalty incurred by sin. It does contrast with the idea of inalienable human rights even if these cannot entitle to anything that is against the rights of others (see Chapter 12).

3. Praeterea, illud quod est secundum se malum nullo bono fine fieri licet: ut patet per Augustinum, in libro *Contra Mendacium*, et per Philosophum in *Ethic.* Sed occidere hominem secundum se est malum: quia ad omnes homines debemus caritatem habere; *amicos autem volumus vivere et esse*, ut dicitur in IX *Ethic.* Ergo nullo modo licet hominem peccatorem interficere.

Ad tertium dicendum quod homo peccando ab ordine rationis recedit: et ideo decidit a **dignitate humana**, prout scilicet homo est naturaliter liber et propter seipsum existens, et incidit quodammodo in servitutem bestiarum, ut scilicet de ipso ordinetur secundum quod est utile aliis; secundum illud *Psalm.* (48,21): *Homo cum in honore esset, non intellexit: comparatus est iumentis insipientibus, et similis factus est illis*; et *Prov.* 11,29 dicitur: *Qui stultus est serviet sapienti.* Et ideo quamvis hominem in sua **dignitate** manentem occidere sit secundum se malum, tamen hominem peccatorem occidere potest esse bonum, sicut

3. What is intrinsically evil cannot be rendered good by any good end, as both Augustine and Aristotle make clear. But killing a man is intrinsically evil, since we must have the friendship of charity towards all men, and we want *our friends to live and to be*, as the *Ethics* has it. Nothing can therefore make it legitimate to kill a sinner.

Ad 3: A man who sins deviates from the rational order, and so loses his **human dignity** in so far as a man is naturally free and an end unto himself. To that extent, then, he lapses into the subjection of the beasts and their exploitation by others, as Scripture puts it well, *Man cannot abide in his pomp, he is like to the beasts that perish*; and, *The fool will be servant to the wise.* Therefore, to kill a man who retains his natural **dignity** is intrinsically evil, although it may be justifiable to kill a sinner just as it is to kill a beast, for, as Aristotle points out, an evil man is worse than a beast, and more harmful.

occidere bestiam: peior enim est malus
homo bestia, et plus nocet, ut Philosophus
dicit, in I *Polit.* (1253a 32–3) et in VII *Ethic.*
(1150a7–8).

On respect (*IIaIIae q. 102 a. 1–3*)

Cicero's distinctions serve, with only a few adaptations, as the pattern
according to which the moral virtues are treated in the IIaIIae, the virtue
of respect (observantia) included. Thomas endorses its characterisation as
'the virtue by which persons eminent in any position of dignity receive the
deference of a certain service and honour' (*observantia est quam homines
aliqua dignitate antecedentes quodam cultu et honore dignantur*). He thus
not only thinks that human dignity, being a certain rank in the universal
hierarchy of all creatures under God, can be lost, but also that some people
rightly possess eminence of position, according to which they should receive
respect, obedience and service. However, the reason for this respect is
properly speaking that it supports the common good. Thomas therefore
regards respect towards one's superiors rather as a kind of patriotism, akin
to piety, that is, an attitude taken out of love for one's community. When
Aquinas therefore joins the ranks of Aristotle and Cicero in accepting and
advocating a form of meritocracy, he does so because he considers it to be
for the common good.

Circa observantiam autem quaeruntur tria. Primo: utrum observantia sit specialis virtus ab aliis distincta. Secundo: quid observantia exhibeat. Tertio: de comparatione eius ad pietatem.

There are three points of enquiry: 1. whether respect is a special virtue, distinct from others; 2. marks of respect; 3. respect compared to piety.

Articulus 1
Utrum observantia sit specialis virtus ab aliis distincta

Article 1.
Whether respect is a specific kind of virtue, different from others

Videtur quod observantia non sit specialis virtus ab aliis distincta.

It seems that respect is not a specific kind of virtue, different from others.

1. Virtutes enim distinguuntur secundum obiecta. Sed obiectum observantiae non distinguitur ab obiecto pietatis. Dicit enim Tullius, in sua *Rhetorica* (1,II, c. 53), quod *observantia est per quam homines aliqua dignitate antecedentes quodam cultu et honore dignantur.* Sed cultum et honorem etiam pietas exhibet parentibus, qui **dignitate** antecedunt. Ergo observantia non est virtus distincta a pietate.

2. Praeterea, sicut hominibus in **dignitate** constitutis debetur honor et cultus, ita etiam eis qui excellunt in scientia et virtute. Sed non est aliqua specialis virtus per quam honorem et cultum exhibeamus hominibus qui scientiae vel virtutis excellentiam habent. Ergo etiam observantia, per quam cultum et honorem exhibemus his qui nos in **dignitate** antecedunt, non est specialis virtus ab aliis distincta.

3. Praeterea, hominibus in **dignitate** constitutis multa debentur ad quae solvenda lex cogit: secundum illud *Rom.* 13,7: *Reddite omnibus debita: cui tributum, tributum,* etc. Ea vero ad quae per legem compellimur, pertinent ad iustitiam legalem, seu etiam ad iustitiam specialem. Ergo observantia non est per se specialis virtus ab aliis distincta.

Sed contra est quod Tullius condividit observantiam aliis iustitiae partibus, quae sunt speciales virtutes.

Respondeo dicendum quod, sicut ex dictis (q. 101 a. 1) patet, necesse est ut eo modo per quendam ordinatum descensum distinguantur virtutes, sicut et excellentia personarum quibus est aliquid reddendum. Sicut autem carnalis pater particulariter

1. Respect gives not evidence of being a virtue differing specifically from others. Virtues differ where their objectives differ and there is not such distinction between respect and piety. Cicero says, *It is the virtue of respect by which persons eminent in any position of* **dignity** *receive the* **deference** *of a certain service and honour;* and it is also the place of piety to offer service and honour to those superior in **dignity**, namely parents. The two, then, are not different virtues.

2. Further, even as honour and homage are the just due of those in **authority**, so also of those pre-eminent in learning or virtue. Yet there is no special virtue to deal with the second sort of people. Neither, then, is respect, with its concern for showing homage and honour to **authority**, a virtue specifically distinct from others.

3. Further, as the text, *render therefore to all men their dues; tribute to whom tribute is due,* etc. indicates, law binds us to fulfil our many obligations towards persons in **authority**. A specific form of justice, i.e. legal justice, has as its concern all duties under law. Thus, respect does not have anything about it to make it a specific virtue distinct from others.

On the other hand, Cicero divides respect against other parts of justice, themselves all specific virtues.

Reply: I have already made it clear that there is no need to trace a hierarchy of virtues to correspond to the hierarchy of persons to whom we are indebted. In the gradation of such persons, parents share the status of being a particular source of

participat rationem principii, quae universaliter invenitur in Deo; ita etiam persona quae quantum ad aliquid providentiam circa nos gerit, particulariter participat proprietatem patris: quia pater est principium generationis et educationis et disciplinae, et omnium quae ad perfectionem humanae vitae pertinent. Persona autem in **dignitate** constituta est sicut principium gubernationis respectu aliquarum rerum: sicut princeps civitatis in rebus civilibus, dux autem exercitus in rebus bellicis, magister autem in disciplinis, et simile est in aliis. Et inde est quod omnes tales personae patres appellantur, propter similitudinem curae: sicut IV Reg. 5,13, servi Namaan dixerunt ad eum: *Pater, etsi rem grandem dixisset tibi propheta*, etc. Et ideo, sicut sub religione, per quam cultus tribuitur Deo, quodam ordine invenitur pietas, per quam coluntur parentes; ita sub pietate invenitur observantia, per quam cultus et honor exhibetur personis in **dignitate** constitutis.

Ad primum ergo dicendum quod sicut supra (q. 101, a. 3 ad 2) dictum est quod religio per quandam supereminentiam pietas dicitur, et tamen pietas proprie dicta a religione distinguitur; ita etiam pietas per quandam excellentiam potest dici observantia, et tamen observantia proprie dicta a pietate distinguitur.

Ad secundum dicendum quod aliquis ex hoc quod est **in dignitate constitutus**, non solum quandam status excellentiam habet, sed etiam quandam potestatem gubernandi subditos. Unde competit sibi ratio principii, prout est aliorum gubernator. Ex hoc autem quod aliquis habet perfectionem scientiae vel virtutis, non sortitur rationem principii quantum ad alios, sed

life as God is its universal source; so also anyone who exercises care over us in any line, to that extent shares the character of a parent, i.e. one who is the source of birth, upbringing, education and all that contributes to progress in life. Now a person who has some **authority** stands as a source of guidance in regard to some special endeavour – in civil matters, the head of the state, in warfare, the army commander, in education, the teacher, etc. And – as in the text where the servants of Naaman say to him, *Father, if the prophet had bid thee do some great thing*, etc – all such people can be called fathers because of a resemblance in the way they care for us. Therefore, as piety with its homage to parents is derived in a way from the virtue of religion with its homage to God, so also the virtue of respect through which homage and honour are shown to those in **authority** stands in similar relation to piety.

Hence: 1. As has been said, religion is given the name *pietas* in an eminent sense; but in its strict sense, piety differs from religion. In turn, piety could be called respect par excellence, but strictly speaking, the two are different virtues.

2. When a person is in a **position of authority**, he has not only eminence of rank but also some particular power to rule over those subject to him. It is as one who governs others, then, that he stands as a giver of life. Endowments of learning or virtue on the other hand do not give a person this distinction but simply go to make up personal worth. This is why there is a special virtue

solum quandam excellentiam in seipso. Et ideo specialiter quaedam virtus determinatur ad exhibendum honorem et cultum his qui sunt in **dignitate** constituti. – Verum quia per scientiam et virtutem, et omnia alia huiusmodi, aliquis idoneus redditur ad **dignitatis statum**, reverentia quae propter quamcumquae excellentiam aliquibus exhibetur, ad eandem virtutem pertinet.

Ad tertium dicendum quod ad iustitiam specialem proprie sumptam pertinet reddere aequale ei cui aliquid debetur. Quod quidem non potest fieri ad virtuosos, et ad eos qui bene statu **dignitatis** utuntur: sicut nec ad Deum, nec ad parentes. Et ideo ad quandam virtutem adiunctam hoc pertinet: non autem ad iustitiam specialem, quae est principalis virtus. – Iustitia vero legalis se extendit ad actus omnium virtutum, ut supra (q. 58, a. 5,6) dictum est.

Articulus 2
Utrum ad observantiam pertineat exhibere cultum et honorem his qui sunt in dignitate constituti

Videtur quod ad observantiam non pertinet exhibere cultum et honorem his qui sunt in **dignitate** constituti.

1. Quia ut Augustinus dicit, in X *de Civ. Dei*, colere dicimur illas personas quas in quodam honore habemus: et sic idem videtur esse cultus quod honor. Inconvenienter igitur determinatur quod observantia exhibet **in dignitate constitutis** cultum et honorem.

2. Praeterea, ad iustitiam pertinet reddere debitum. Unde et ad observantiam, quae ponitur iustitiae pars. Sed cultum et honorem non debemus omnibus in **dignitate** constitutis, sed solum his qui super nos

bent upon offering honour and homage only to those in **authority**. Still it is true that one becomes fit for a **position of rank** through learning, virtue and the like; so the deference which is shown to others because of superiority of any sort engages this same virtue.

3. The function of particular justice in its strict sense is the exact acquittal of a debt. There is no such possibility with regard to the virtuous, to those who exercise **authority** for our welfare, nor to God or parents. In each of these cases, there is no place for particular justice, a principal virtue, but for one of the allied virtues. General justice, as has been said, ranges over the acts of all virtues.

Article 2.
Whether it is part of respect to offer homage and honour to those in authority

It does not appear to be the business of respect to pay homage and honour to **authority**.

1. As Augustine says, we are said to pay homage to the people we hold in honour, so that homage and honour seem the same. Therefore, there is no point to maintaining that homage and honour are the tributes of respect to those in **authority**.

2. In another way, since satisfying obligations is a work of justice, it is also the concern of respect, a part of justice. There is no obligation, however, to pay honour and homage to all who are in positions

praelationem habent. Ergo inconvenienter determinatur quod eis observantia exhibet cultum et honorem.

3. Praeterea, superioribus nostris in **dignitate** constitutis non solum debemus honorem, sed etiam timorem, et aliquam munerum largitionem: secundum illud *ad Rom.* 13,7: *Reddite omnibus debita: et cui tributum, tributum; cui vectigal, vectigal; timorem, timorem; cui honorem, honorem.* Debemus etiam eis reverentiam et subiectionem: secundum illud *Heb.* 13, 17: *Obedite praepositis vestris, et subiacete eis.* Non ergo convenienter determinatur quod observantia exhibet cultum et honorem.

Sed contra est quod Tullius dicit (*de Inv. Rhet.* 1. II, c. 53), quod *observantia est per quam homines aliqua* **dignitate** *antecedentes quodam cultu et honore* **dignantur.**

Respondeo dicendum quod ad eos qui sunt in **dignitate** constituti pertinet gubernare subditos. Gubernare autem est movere aliquos in debitum finem: sicut nauta gubernat navem ducendo eam ad portum. Omne autem movens habet excellentiam quandam et virtutem supra id quod movetur. Unde oportet quod in eo qui est in **dignitate** constitutus, primo consideretur excellentia status, cum quadam potestate in subditos; secundo, ipsum gubernationis officium. Ratione igitur excellentiae, debetur eis honor, qui est quaedam recognitio excellentiae alicuius. Ratione autem officii gubernationis, debetur eis cultus, cui in quodam obsequio consistit, dum scilicet aliquis eorum

of **authority**, but only to those who have authority over us. Consequently, there is no proper basis for asserting without qualification that respect pays its tribute to those in authority.

3. Moreover, we owe to **superiors** not merely honour, but fear as well, and even the bestowal of gifts – *Render therefore to all men their dues. Tribute, to whom tribute is due; custom, to whom custom; fear to whom fear, honour, to whom honour;* reverence and submission as well – *Obey your prelates and be subject to them.* The restriction of the virtue of respect, then, to offering homage and honour is unfounded.

On the other hand there is Cicero's description that *it is through the virtue of respect that persons* **eminent in some position of authority** *receive the* **deference** *of a certain homage and honour.*

Reply: it is the charge of those placed in a position of **authority** to govern their subjects. And 'to govern' means to guide others to an appointed goal, somewhat as the sailor 'governs' his ship in steering it to harbour. Now everything exercising influence upon another has an eminence and a form of power higher than that of the recipient. In the instance of one holding **authority** we should take into consideration, first, his superior status with power over subjects; and secondly, the actual duty of governing them. On grounds of superiority, he has a right to honour, which means in fact the acknowledgement of another's eminence. On grounds of the task of governing he has a right to homage, which

obedit imperio, et vicem beneficiis eorum pro suo modo rependit.

consists in a definite service, namely that his commands be obeyed and his good offices be recompensed in due measure.

Ad primum ergo dicendum quod in cultu non solum intelligitur honor, sed etiam quaecumque alia pertinent ad decentes actus quibus homo ad alium ordinatur.

Hence 1. 'Homage' embraces not only honour but also anything else implied in those actions appropriate to one person's subordination to another.

Ad secundum dicendum quod, sicut supra dictum est (q. 80), duplex est debitum. Unum quidem legale, ad quod reddendum homo lege compellitur. Et sic debet homo honorem et cultum his qui sunt in dignitate constituti praelationem super ipsum habentes. – Aliud autem est debitum morale, quod ex quadam honestate debetur. Et hoc modo debemus cultum et honorem his qui sunt in dignitate constituti, etiam si non simus eis subiecti.

2. As previously made clear, there are two kinds of debt. The first is termed 'legal', in the sense that a person is held by positive law to pay it; and it is in this way that a person is indebted as to honour and pay homage to those authorities who have actual power over him. The other kind of debt is called 'moral', in the sense that it is owed on the grounds of plain decency. This is the sort of indebtedness obliging us to pay homage and honour to all in authority, even when we are not actually their subjects.

Ad tertium dicendum quod excellentiae eorum qui sunt in dignitate constituti debetur honor ratione sublimioris gradus; timor autem ratione potestatis quam habent ad coercendum. Officio vero gubernationis ipsorum debetur obedientia, per quam subditi moventur ad imperium praesidentium; et tributa, quae sunt quaedam stipendia laboris ipsorum.

3. Honour is owed to the eminence of those in authority, on the grounds of their superior rank; fear, on the basis of their power of sanctions. Their task of governing gives them a claim of obedience – the response of subjects to the command of those over them – and to tribute, as a kind of remuneration for their labours.

Articulus 3
Utrum observantia sit potior virtus quam pietas

Article 3
Whether respect has higher standing as a virtue than piety

Videtur quod observantia sit potior virtus quam pietas.

It seems that respect is a more important virtue than piety.

2. Praeterea, illi qui sunt in dignitate constituti curam gerunt boni communis. Consanguinei autem pertinent ad bonum privatum, quod est propter bonum commune contemnendum: unde laudabiliter

2. Further, while people in authority are engaged upon the public welfare, relatives form part of our personal well-being. This is to be set aside in favour of the public good; so much so that some men laudably

aliqui seipsos pro bono communi periculis mortis exponunt. Ergo observantia, per quam exhibetur cultus his qui sunt in **dignitate** constituti, est potior virtus quam pietas, quae exhibet cultum personis sanguine coniunctis.

endanger their own lives for it. Respect, with its concern for serving those in **authority**, is, consequently, a more important virtue than piety, with its concern for relatives.

3. Praeterea, honor et reverentia maxime debetur virtuosis, post Deum. Sed virtuosis exhibetur honor et reverentia per observantiae virtutem, ut dictum est (q. 80). Ergo observantia est praecipua post religionem.

3. Moreover, under God the virtuous have chief claim to honour and reverence. Since, as noted above, the virtue of respect looks to this, it is, after religion, the chief virtue.

Sed contra est quod praecepta legis dantur de actibus virtutum. Immediate autem post praecepta religionis, quae pertinent ad primam tabulam, subditur praeceptum de honoratione parentum, quod pertinet ad pietatem. Ergo pietas immediate sequitur religionem ordine **dignitatis.**

On the other hand, acts of the virtues are laid down in the commandments of the Law, and right after the precepts regarding religion, which form the first tablet, comes that of honouring parents, the concern of piety. In order of **rank**, then, piety comes right after religion.

Respondeo dicendum quod personis in **dignitate** constitutis potest aliquid exhiberi dupliciter. Uno modo, in ordine ad bonum commune: puta cum aliquis ei servit in administratione reipublicae. Et hoc iam non pertinet ad observantiam, sed ad pietatem, quae cultum exhibet non solum patri, sed etiam patriae. – Alio modo exhibetur aliquid personis in **dignitate** constitutis pertinens specialiter ad personalem eorum utilitatem vel gloriam. Et hoc proprie pertinet ad observantiam secundum quod a pietate distinguitur.

Reply: There are two possible ways to render service to those in **authority**. First with a view to the public good; an example is assistance given to their civil administration. When this is the case, it is not respect that is engaged but rather piety itself, the bearing of which is not solely towards parents but towards country as well. In another way, those in **authority** can be the recipients of a particular homage towards their personal well-being and glory. Here respect as distinct from piety comes into play.

Et ideo comparatio observantiae ad pietatem necesse est quod attendatur secundum diversas habitudines diversarum personarum ad nos, quas respicit utraque virtus. Manifestum est autem quod personae parentum, et eorum qui sunt nobis sanguine iuncti, substantialius nobis coniunguntur quam personae quae sunt in

Consequently any comparison between respect and piety has necessarily to look to the various relationships which the different people encompassed by each virtue have to us. Clearly the bond uniting us to parents and relatives is more deeply rooted than the one relating us to people in **authority**; birth and upbringing, which have their source in

dignitate constitutae: magis enim ad substantiam pertinet generatio et educatio,
cuius principium est pater, quam exterior
gubernatio, cuius principium sunt illi qui in
dignitate constituuntur. Et secundum hoc,
pietas observantiae praeeminet, inquantum
cultum reddit personis magis coniunctis,
quibus magis obligamur.

Ad secundum dicendum quod ex ea parte
qua personae in dignitate constitutae ordinantur ad bonum commune, non pertinet
earum cultus ad observantiam, sed ad pietatem, ut dictum est.

Ad tertium dicendum quod exhibitio
honoris vel cultus non solum est proportio-
nanda personae cui exhibitur secundum se
considerate, sed etiam secundum quod ad
exhibentes comparatur. Quamvis ergo vir-
tuosi, secundum se considerati, sint magis
digni honore quam personae parentum:
tamen filii magis obligantur, propter benefi-
cia suscepta et coniunctionem naturalem,
ad exhibendum cultum et honorem parentibus quam extraneis virtuosis.

our parents, form more of a part of our very
being than does the direction of our life in
the community, of which those in authority are the source. Herein is the reason why
piety has precedence over respect – it pays
homage to those closer to us, who by that
fact have a more pressing claim on us.

2. In so far as those in authority are involved
with the public good, homage to them, as
has been pointed out, is the province, not
of respect, but of patriotism.

3. Honour and homage ought to be measured not only to the personal worth of the
recipient, but also to his relationship to
those offering them. While, then, the virtuous may be personally more worthy of
honour than our parents, still children are
more obliged to pay homage and honour
to parents than to the virtuous stranger, on
the basis of benefits received and of ties of
flesh and blood.

Late Medieval Sources

The idea that authority is bestowed by God is parallel to the idea that it is God who, in creating human beings, bestows human dignity on them as an ontological claim to respect from everybody else, backed by God's image and likeness. If combined, the claim to respect (the value of human dignity) makes of all human beings superiors in Christ, similar in their claims to each other. Since this similarity is *visible* to all, consisting in the *image* and likeness of God, human dignity is far from being merely subjective, it is objective and open to inter-subjective inspection. This objectivism is inherited from the naturalism of the ancients, but it adds a dimension to it, in so far as the claim to respect for human dignity is a claim on everybody, not only on the subject in relation to himself. Thus is tweaked into place the idea of human rights, as the claims raised by all constituted in dignity in relation to each other, and human dignity emerges as a status laying a claim also on others.

Maybe women did this tweaking. Since women rarely were 'constituted in dignity' by holding office, in relation to men and correspondingly were very familiar with what Aquinas called respect, and regarded as a special virtue, they also were very much in need of respect, since women's specific vulnerabilities related to love and fertility are easily used to imprison and oppress. This fact may have conditioned them to find ways of arguing for respect for human dignity without being able to enforce it, something for which Nietzsche resented them very much. Here we shall see three strategies for the affirmation of human dignity: women celebrating the human dignity of those who suffer, of those who love and of those who are under the authority of someone else.

Gertrude the Great insists that dignity can be recognised beyond weakness and illness in the humble acceptance of suffering. Every creature, whether animal or human, well or ill, is dignified in Christ, in particular

when they submit to serve others with humility and realism. Then the suffering can become a means to keep out what is destructive of the person and increase personal dignity. The praise of the dignity of Mary, the Mother of God, as Birgitta of Sweden contemplates it, becomes an opportunity to affirm the dignity of women, of motherhood and of faithful love, all the more credible for Bridgit herself being a widow and no stranger to the dangers of childbirth and the visceral love of one's offspring. Catherine of Siena addresses the tension between 'ordinary' and 'extraordinary' dignity and asks how it can be that all have the dignity of being made in the image and likeness of God, when some have the specific dignity of priesthood. The answer given is dialectical: The dignity of the priest depends on the dignity of the people to whom he ministers. For their sake, his conferred dignity cannot be lost absolutely, although it can as regards himself. His higher dignity, thus, is relative to the prior dignity of those to whom he ministers.

Gertrude of Helfta (1256–1302)

Gertrud relishes – it seems a feature of her particular genius – the active verbal form of *dignitas, dignare*, to deign, expressing itself in *dignatione*, here translated with 'graciousness', or indeed with 'loving-kindness'. God, who is supremely dignified, deigns to dignify graciously with respect the speck of dust that the human being is in comparison to him. Human dignity relies on God's 'dignation', his gracious goodness, his loving-kindness, which is of such magnitude that confounded humility and gratitude is the only adequate personal response. Although undeserved, the respect God thus shows us, makes us respectable, raises us to a dignity unrivalled by any politically conferred status, the dignity of the Spouse.

The first book of the *Legatus* is an (auto)biography of Gertrud, in which she (or her editing sisters) refers to herself in the third person. The attitudes portrayed are exemplary: attitudes to the fact of being created and redeemed by the intimately Loved One, alive and overwhelmed in his company, overcome by his graciousness, wounded by love for his 'little ones'.

The second book is written in the first person and lets us hear the experience of the protagonist from within her own perspective. The question of illness and suffering is never far, and it is clear that a kind of solution to the problem posed by severe bodily or mental pain is found in its possibility of rendring able to share the life of Christ in a worthy manner. The story told is one of the discovery of dignity through suffering. The fifth book again resumes the third person perspective, and is probably composed by Gertrud's sisters after her death.

Legatus

Text from *Gertrud von Helfta Botschaft von Gottes Güte*, Bd. 1–4, lateinisch-deutsch (Heiligenkreuz: BeundBe Verlag, 2013). Translation of Book I–II from *The Herald of Divine Love*, trans. and ed. Margeret Winkworth, introduced by Sr M. Marnau, Classics of Western Spirituality (New York and Mahwah, NJ: Paulist Press, 1993). Translation from Book V with the help of Helle Gjellerup.

I, 8

Cum zelo quoque justitiae de quo praedictum est, exierat illi etiam tantus compassivae charitatis affectus, ut quemcumque videret rationabiliter perturbatum, seu etiam longe positum intelligeret gravatum, statim omnimodo satagebat ipsum aut verbis relevare aut scriptis animare; et hoc tanto intendebat affectu quod velut infirmus qui magnis febribus aestuans, de die in diem ab infirmitate sperat liberari vel alleviari, sic ipsa de hora in horam illos quos sciebat gravatos a Domino exoptabat consolari: non solum autem erga homines, verumetiam erga omnem creaturam tanto afficiebatur pietatis affectu, ut

Along with this ardent zeal for justice, she also possessed the gift of tender and compassionate charity. If she saw that anyone was in distress for a good reason, or if she had heard that someone, even at a distance, was in trouble, she at once tried to help them in any way she could, by word of mouth or in writing. Like a sick man with a high fever who hopes for relief from his sickness day after day, so hour after hour she besought the Lord to console those whose afflictions were known to her. Her tender-hearted compassion was aroused not only by human sufferings, but by those of every creature. When she saw little birds or other

quamcumque creaturarum, sive volatilium, sive pecudum, aliquod incommodum ex esurie vel siti vel frigore videret perpeti, mox facturae Domini sui compatiens ex intimo cordis affectu, illud incommodum irrationabilis creaturae Domino devote studebat offerre in laudem aeternam, in unione illius **dignitatis** qua omnis creatura in ipso est summe perfecta et nobilitata, desiderans ut Dominus misertus creaturae suae, defectus ipsius **dignaretur** relevare.

animals suffering from hunger or thirst or cold, she was moved to pity for the works of the Lord, devoutly and eagerly, to his eternal praise, in union with that **dignity** by which every creature is supremely perfected and **ennobled** in him.

II, 7

Hinc in festo sacrosanctae Purificationis, dum post gravem infirmitatem lecto decumberem et mane circa ortum diei moesta intra me querularer quod divina visitatione, qua frequentius fueram tali die consolata, corporali infirmitate detenta deberem frustrari, a mediatrice mediatoris Dei et hominum talibus sum verbis consolata: 'Sicut non recolis te acerbiorem dolorem infirmitatum in corpore pertulisse, ita scias te nobilius donum a Filio meo nunquam percepisse, ad quod **digne** percipiendum spiritum tuum roboravit infirmitas corporis praecedens.'

On the most holy feast of the Purification, after a serious illness, I was obliged to stay in bed. Toward daybreak, I was filled with sadness. I complained within myself of being deprived, through bodily infirmity, of that divine visitation which had so often consoled me on this feast day. She who is our mediatrix, the mother of him who is mediator between God and humankind (1 Tim. 2, 5) comforted me with these words: 'Just as you do not remember ever having suffered any greater bodily pain, know that you have never received from my son a nobler gift than the one this bodily weakness has given your soul the strength to receive **worthily**.'

II, 9, 2–3

O **dignitatem** minutissimi illius pulveris, quem illa principalis gemma coelestium nobilitatum de luto palearum sibi ad superponendum assumit! O excellentiam exigui illius flosculi, quem ipse etiam solaris radius de locis palustribus sibi attrahit quasi ad collucendum! O beatitudinem beatae illius et benedictae animae quam Dominus majestatis tantae **dignitatis** aestimat,

Oh, the **dignity** of this minutest speck of dust that has been drawn up out of the mud and taken as a setting for the noblest gem of heaven! Oh, the excellence of this tiny flower which has been drawn up out of the mire by the sun's rays, so that it might shine with the sun's light! Oh, the beatitude of that blissful and blessed soul whom the Lord's Majesty esteems so **highly**! For

quod quamvis sit omnipotens creando, tamen fecit animam, animam, inquam, licet imagine et similitudine ipsius decoratam, tantum tamen distantem a se quantum distat Creator a creatura ! [...] Hoc donum, Domine Deus, quod electis tuis dare posses ex praevalentia omnipotentiae tuae omnino confido, et etiam quod mihi hoc idem dare velles ex amorosa benignitate tua minime diffido. Quomodo autem dare scires prae **indignitate** mea, inscrutabilem sapientiam tuam nequaquam valeo investigare. Sed nunc glorifico et magnifico sapientiam et benignam omnipotentiam tuam. Laudo et adoro omnipotentem et benignam sapientiam tuam. Benedico et gratias ago omnipotenti et sapienti benignitati tuae, Deus meus, quia quidquid mihi unquam impendi potuit, a largitate tua recipe semper inaestimabiliter longe supra **condignum**.

although he exercises his omnipotence in the act of creation, yet the soul which he has made (although it is beautiful in his image and likeness) is as far distant from him as is the creator from the creature. [...] I am entirely confident, Lord God, that you can do everything, and that you can bestow this gift on all your elect. I do not doubt for a moment that you wanted to give it to me in your loving kindness. How, in your inscrutable wisdom, you were able to bestow it on my **unworthy** self, I am unable to discover. All the more, rather, I glorify and magnify the wisdom and goodness of your infinite power. I praise and adore the infinite power and goodness of your wisdom. I bless and give you thanks for your infinite power and wisdom and goodness, Lord, because I have always received of your generosity all the graces that could be accorded to me, always immesuarably surpassing that which I could **deserve**.

II, 13

Item confiteor pietati tuae, benignissime Deus, quod adhuc alio modo adjecisti inertiam meam provocare et, quamvis per interpositam personam initiaveris, per teipsum tamen non minus misericorditer quam etiam **dignanter** consummasti.

Once again I give you thanks for your merciful love, kindest Lord, for having found another way of arousing me from my inertia. Although it was first through the intervention of another person, you yourself completed what you had begun with no less mercy than **goodness**.

II, 19, 1–2

*De laude **dignationis** divinae*

Praise of the Divine **Graciousness**

Gratias ago benignae misericordiae et misericordi benignitati tuae, amantissime Deus, pro revelato testimonio **dignantissimae** pietatis tuae, quo fluctuantem et vacillantem animum meum solidasti [...]

I give you thanks, most loving God, for your kind mercy and for your merciful kindness and for revealing to me the proof of your most **gracious** tenderness, confirming my irresolute and vacillating soul [...]

II, 20, 1

Cor meum et anima mea, cum tota substantia carnis meae omnibusque viribus et sensibus corporis et spiritus mei, cum universitate totius creaturae, laudes et gratiarum actiones dicant tibi, dulcissime Deus, fidelissime amator humanae salutis, pro **dignantissima** misericordia qua non suffecit pietati tuae dissimulare quod toties indecenter parata accedere non vereor ad tui sanctissimi corporis et sanguinis superexcellentissimum convivium, nisi etiam abyssalis supereffluentia tua mihi, instrumentorum tuorum vilissimo et inutilissimo, hunc colorem dono tuo superaddere **dignata** sit: quod gratia tua certitudinem accepi, quod omnis qui ad tuum sacramentum accedere desiderans, sed habens timorem conscientiae, trepidans retrahitur, si humilitate ductus a me famularum tuarum minima quaerit confortari, pro hac ipsius humilitate, tua incontinens pietas **dignum** ipsum judicat tantis sacramentis, quae vere percipiet in fructum salutis aeternae; adjungens quod si quem justitia tua non permitteret **dignum** judicari, nunquam permitteres ad meum consilium humiliari. O Dominator excelse qui in altis habitas et humilia respicis, quid divina dictavit miseratio tua cum videres toties **indigne** accedentem, justitia librante, judicium promereri, tu volens alios **dignos** efficere per virtutem humilitatis, quamvis sine me hoc melius posses, indigentiae tamen meae consulens pietas tua hoc per me perficere decrevit, ut vel sic participari possem meritis ipsorum, qui monitis meis fructu salutis potirentur.

May my heart and soul with all my fleshly being and all the powers and senses of my body and spirit, together with the whole of creation, give praise and thanks to you, sweetest Lord, most faithful Lover of man's salvation, for the **loving kindness** of your mercy, which could not have succeeded in hiding from your love the fact that over and over again I was not afraid to approach the most excellent banquet of your sacred body and blood without due preparation, had not the ineffable abyss of your generosity toward me, the most worthless and useless of your instruments, **deigned** to grant me, in addition to all your other gifts, the following. That is, that through your grace, I learned with certainty that if anyone desires to approach your sacrament, but having a timid conscience is kept back by fear, and is led to seek comfort with me, the least of your servants, you will, in your overflowing love, reward this humility of his by judging him **worthy** of the sacrament. When he then receives it, it will bear fruit for him for his eternal salvation. You added that you would not grant to those whom you in your justice deemed **unworthy** of frequenting this sacrament the humility to seek council with me. O my supreme Lord and Master, you who inhabit the heavens and look down on our lowliness (Ps. 112, 5,6), what were your merciful designs when you saw me so often approaching your sacrament **unworthily** and meriting in this your just condemnation? As you wish to make others **worthy** by the virtue of humility – although the same result might have been obtained better without me – you had mercy of my great poverty and decreed in your goodness

to do it through me, that at least in this manner I might share in the merits of those who have obtained the fruits of salvation through my advice.

V, 1,1

Vere **digna** et Spiritu Sancto plena, venerabilis memoriae, sinceraeque caritatis brachiis amplectenda, veneranda Domina G., benignissima et omni laude et honore **digna** abbatissa.

Yes, she was truly **dignified** and filled by the Holy Spirit, we must venerate her memory and hold her in the arms of pure charity, this reverend Lady G., this highly good abbess, **worthy** of all honor and praise.

V, 1,8

Item dum propter infirmitatem, quia nullam videbatur sibi utilitatem posse perficere in officio, abbatiam desiderat resignare, et super hoc etiam ab ista divinam perquireret voluntatem, his verbis a Domino est instructa: 'Ego per infirmitatem istam sanctifico electam meam mihimetipsi ad inhabitandum, sicut per consecrationem pontificis sanctificatur ecclesia. Item, sicut ecclesia seris obfirmatur ne intrent **indigni**, sic istam etiam per infirmitatem obsero ne sensus ejus exteriora tam diversa possint capere, in quibus quandoque non est magna utilitas, et tamen cor inquietant, et etiam mihi quandoque minus intendere faciunt. [...]'

As the abbess wanted to resign, since she due to illness thought herself incapable of serving in office, and thus inquired as to the divine will as regards her, she was instructed by the Lord in the following words: 'By this illness I sanctify the one I have chosen, in order to live in her, just as by the consecration the pontiff sanctifies a church. Just as the church is closed by locks so that those who are not **worthy** may not enter, so, due to the locks of the illness, her senses cannot perceive the host of external things in which there is seldom great utility and which nevertheless distracts the heart even from me. [...]'

Birgitta of Sweden (1302/1303–1372/1373)

Birgitta turns to Our Lady to see in her the model of the Church, the one whose dignity is spousal and therefore both overwhelming with God's own graciousness and self-effacing with his acceptance of the Cross. In front

of it, Birgitta behaves a little like St Peter at Our Lord's transfiguration, endearingly willing to accept hellfire rather than that any little bit of Our Lady's dignity should be lacking. And for good reason: Our Lady's dignity as Mother of God is the clearest sign of God's plan to embrace humanity fully, and thus of his lover's love for us. To gain this love, to accept it as a given, it would be rational, indeed normal, to be willing to go through hell.

Revelations

Revelaciones, critically edited in the original Latin in *Samlinger utgivne av svenska fornskriftsällskapet, andra serien latinska skrifter*, of Birger Bergh (Uppsala: Almquist och Wiksells, 1967). Translations from Birgitta of Sweden: *Life and Selected Revelations, Classics of Western Spirituality* (New York: Paulist Press, 1990). VII, I, 2–3.

Domina mea regina celi, in tantum gaudet cor meum ex eo, quod altissimus Deus te preeligit in matrem et tantam **dignitatem** tibi conferre **dignatus** est, quod magis ego michi eligerem in inferno eternaliter cruciari, quam quod tu uno minimo puncto de tanta excellenti gloria tua celesti **dignitate** careres.	O my Lady, Queen of Heaven, my heart so rejoices over the fact that the most high God forechose you as his mother and **deigned** to confer upon you so great a **dignity** that I would rather choose for myself eternal excruciation in hell than that you should lack one smallest point of this surpassing glory of your heavenly **dignity**.

Catherine of Siena (1347–1380)

Catherine has accepted this love and has in consequence engaged in a dialogue with God the Father about all the things of the world and all the things she does not understand, confident that his love provides answers surpassing her own imagination. The sections that concern us most are those where Catherine discusses the status or dignity of the clergy – possibly prompted by mixed experiences with their sanctity. It is here their

superior dignity is explained from their ministry to the spousal people, whose unsurpassable dignity is due to God's incarnation as one of us. The magnificence of this existential solution, so politically resilient that its pattern can be applied to everyone to whom one owes respect despite them lacking trustworthyness, also draws attention to the fact that dignity to the person possessing it self-destructs to the extent its privileges are abused by him. With this, Catherine solved a conundrum for many under the authority of someone else. With the assistance of Aquinas, we could say that for her superior dignity is respectable to the extent it serves the common good.

Il dialogo

Il dialogo has undergone a wealth of editions, some of which have divided the work into sections for various purposes. Text from Guiliana Cavallini (ed.), *Il Dialogo della Divina Provvidenza ovvero Libro della Divina Dottrina* (Roma: Edizioni Cateriniane, 1968). Cavallini's edition reveals the structure of the work as it is divided by sequences of petition, answer and thanksgiving. 'The Mystical Body of Holy Church', from which our extracts are taken, contains Chapters 110–35 and is the sixth such sequence in the work. Cavallini is followed by Suzanne Noffke O. P. in her translation *Catherine of Siena: the Dialogue*, Classics of Western Spirituality (New York and Mahwah, NJ: Paulist Press, 1980), from which translations are taken. A history of the different editions of *Il Dialogo* can be found in Cornelia Wolfskeel: 'Catherine of Siena' in *A History of Women Philosophers*, vol. II, pp. 239–52. The argument Catherine is pursuing involves the use of several more references to dignity so that the following are but representative selections. See Noffke pp. 231–9 and Cavallini p. 301–9 for more.

110

Ora ti rispondo di quello che m'ài adimandato sopra i ministri della santa Chiesa. E acciò che tu meglio possa cognoscere la verità, apre l'occhio de l'intelletto tuo e raguarda la eccellenzia loro, e in quanta **dignità** Io gli ò posti. E perchè meglio si cognosce l'uno contrario per l'altro, voglioti mostrare la **dignità** di coloro che esercitarono in virtú il tesoro che Io lo' missi nelle mani [...] unde veniste in tanta eccellenzia, per l'unione ch'Io feci della deità mia nella natura umana, che in questo avete maggiore eccellenzia e **dignità** voi che l'angelo [101a] perch'Io presi la natura vostra e non quella del'angelo.

Now I will answer what you asked me concerning the ministers of holy Church: First so that you may better come to know the truth, open your mind's eye and consider their excellence and the great **dignity** in which I have placed them. But because things can be better known by looking at their opposites, I want to show you the **dignity** of those who use virtuously the treasure I have put into their hands [the faithful] [...] You attained such excellence because of the union I effected between my Godhead and human nature that your excellence and **dignity** is greater than that of the angels. For it was your nature I assumed, and not that of the angels.

113

O carissima figliuola, tutto questo t'ò detto acciò che tu meglio cognosca la **dignità** dove Io ò posti i miei ministri, acciò che piú ti doglia delle miserie loro. Se essi medesimi reguardassero la loro **dignità**, non giacerebbero nella tenebre del peccato mortale nè lordarebbero la facia de l'anima loro. E non tanto che essi offendessero me e la loro **dignità**, ma se dessero il corpo loro ad ardere, non lo' parrebbe potere satisfare a tanta grazia e a tanto benefizio quanto ànno ricevuto, però che a maggiore **dignità** in questa vita non possono venire.

O dearest daughter, I have told you all this so that you may better know how I have **dignified** my ministers, and thus grieve the more over their wickedness: If they themselves had considered their **dignity**, they would not have fallen into the darkness of deadly sin nor muddied the face of their souls. Not only have they sinned against me and against their own **dignity**, but even had they given their bodies to be burned they would not have been able to repay me for the tremendous grace and blessing they have received, for it is impossible to have greater **dignity** than theirs in this life.

120

[...] e 'l giudicio lassate me, e Io, con le vostre orazioni, volendo essi ricevere lo' farò misericordia. E non correggendosi la vita loro, la **dignità** che essi ànno lo' sarà in ruina [...].

Leave the judging to me, and I, because of your prayers and my own desire, will be merciful to them. If they will not change their ways, the **dignity** they have will be their destruction.

PART III

Early Modern Sources

The beginning of Modernity marks the increasing importance of the state and of positive law. As a result, the thinking about constitutional law, foundational for the making of positive law, becomes a theme along with international law, rendered necessary with the expansion of the known world. Both constitutional and international law are increasingly deployed through Modernity to address large-scale social problems, such as the political status of Jews, different Christian denominations, other nationalities, indigenous peoples, peasants, slaves, workers and women. The idea that human dignity could serve as a check on law was not new, but it occurs for the first time making use of those terms in Las Casas' intervention on behalf of the American Indians. What was innovative in his approach was that he spoke for the rights of people not to be enslaved, citing their dignity as the reason. Pufendorf and Grotius, both familiar with the Ciceronian tradition, attempted to adapt it to contemporary conditions in the light of the controversies to which Las Casas' intervention gave rise. They nevertheless came up against the problem that slavery existed throughout the Modern period on an industrial scale, which made it too unrealistic to insist on regarding human dignity as a constitutional principle.

During the early modern period, we find two parallel streams of literature harking back to the medieval tradition, one ridiculing or lamenting the human condition, and the other extolling the dignity of human nature. All the texts presented here belong to the second type, except Hobbes', which is an example of the first. As this stream of early modern sources leads up to the Enlightenment and the French Revolution, we see several tendencies unfold. The Christian tradition splits into various strands, which despite the vehemence of the Reformation leave surprisingly little trace in the texts that interest us. Jewish elements contribute to an esoteric strand, which is neither Christian nor non-Christian, but neo-Platonist.

Moreover, a claim for women's equality in dignity, in particular for access to university education and the professions, is timidly gaining momentum while the political nature of status is increasingly justified as independent of ontological features. This last trait is probably the most recognisably modern one; the political sphere is affirming independence as secular and with this development, the groundwork is laid for the implementation of the idea of human dignity as a legal principle.

Renaissance, Reformation and the New World

City-states and kingdoms rarely possessed constitutions in the sense of a single document listing and defining a set of basic principles. They had, however, a body of laws and ordinances, together with a strong tradition instantiated in their founding institutions. This meant that lawyers could study what constituted these states in the light of the interests they sought to defend. As the body grew, so did the caste of lawyers, while political forces continuously redrafted the map of world. The meeting of constitutional law with the idea of human dignity happens during the Renaissance in Las Casas' desire to have the human dignity of the American Indians respected. This political use is in turn prepared by the women's advocacy for the dignity of the weak as well as Pico's understanding of human dignity as independent of the practice of Christian rites, to which the Indians had no indigenous access. Erasmus' insistence on the opposition between sin and human dignity both complicates and illuminates the issue: redemption is required for the restoration of human dignity since the human being had fallen into sin, according to this understanding, not only of Erasmus, but also of most of his contemporaries. Thus it was presumed that those who went to the new world went as missionaries, to aid in the restoration of human dignity. By the violence being reported at home, however, it came reluctantly to be believed that the conquistadores often fell into worse sin than that from which they were sent to deliver.

Pico della Mirandola (1463–1494)

Oration on the Dignity of Man (1486–1557)

Oration on the Dignity of Man was by Pico called simply *Oration*. Its 1557 publishers gave it the title it now bears and thereby placed it in the genre of responses to Innocent III's *De miseria humane conditionis* (c. 1195), which included Manetti's *De dignitate et excellentia hominis* (1451/1532), Facio's *De dignitate et praestantia hominis* (1447/1448/1611) and Perez de Oliva's *Diálogo del dignidad del hombre* (1545). This was justified by the fact that these, like Pico's oration, underline freedom as the sign of human dignity and celebrate the human being's divine potential although they do so in a manner not quite as innovative as regards the Christian heritage as Pico's does. This may or may not reinforce Pico's text as an authority on human dignity, given that the only mention of the expression 'human dignity' is in the title. Pico may defend ontological mobility up and down the ladder of being by means of freedom, but to him it is only the upward stride to the angelic state, which makes divine and hence gives dignity to the human being; the downward trend leads to brutishness. The interpretation that Pico defends human dignity as autonomy is therefore not quite correct by the contemporary meaning of autonomy – he defends human dignity as the freedom to become divine like the angels through what he calls 'philosophy', whether Chaldean, Judaic, Greek or Latin. It is hard to avoid the impression that the dignity advocated is acquired by this means, not sacramentally received, except if one regards philosophy as sacramental, and there is some evidence, also in our text, that Pico does. At any rate, Pico claims human dignity to be woundrous beyond belief, relying on the idea that man is a creature of indeterminate nature, himself choosing his status. In this, Pico appears to be somewhat at odds, not only with the Christian, but also with the classical tradition, not only because both rely on the idea that the human being, like any other being, has a determinate nature, but also because the cross and resurrection of Christ seems to play no role in the redemption he enviseages. Pico's teachings seem more related to the Hebrew sources explored in Chapter 3 even if he can also be interpreted

to represent a radicalisation of both the Christian and the classical traditions' emphasis on the need to conform to rationality in one's actions to
preserve human dignity in oneself.

The Latin text is taken from the Pico-project website: <https://www.
brown.edu/Departments/Italian_Studies/pico/oratio.html> (last accessed
September 2018). The English translation is by Elisabeth Livermore Forbes,
as published in *The Renaissance Philosophy of Man*, eds E. Cassirer, P. O.
Kristeller and J. H. Randall (Chicago: University of Chicago Press, 1948).
Observations in square brackets are my own.

§ 1–20

§ 1. [132r] Legi, Patres colendissimi, in Arabum monumentis, interrogatum Abdalam sarracenum, quid in hac quasi mundana scena admirandum maxime spectaretur, nihil spectari homine admirabilius respondisse. Cui sententiae illud Mercurii adstipulatur: 'Magnum, o Asclepi, miraculum est homo'.

1. I have read in the records of the Arabians, reverend Fathers, that Abdala the Saracen, when questioned as to what on this stage of the world, as it were, could be seen most worthy of wonder, replied: 'There is nothing to be seen more wonderful than man.' In agreement with this opinion is the saying of Hermes Trismegistus: 'A great miracle, Asclepius, is man.'

§ 2. Horum dictorum rationem cogitanti mihi non satis illa faciebant, quae multa de humanae naturae praestantia afferuntur a multis: esse hominem creaturarum internuntium, superis familiarem, regem inferiorum; sensuum perspicacia, rationis indagine, intelligentiae lumine, naturae interpretem; stabilis evi et fluxi temporis interstitium, et (quod Persae dicunt) mundi copulam, immo hymeneum, ab angelis, teste Davide, paulo deminutum.

But when I weighed the reason for these maxims, the many grounds for the excellence of human nature reported by many men failed to satisfy me that man is the intermediary between creatures, the intimate of the gods, the king of the lower beings, by the acuteness of his senses, by the discernment of his reason, and by the light of his intelligence the interpreter of nature, the interval between fixed eternity and fleeting time, and (as the Persians say) the bond, nay, rather, the marriage song of the world, on David's testimony but little lower than the angels.

§ 3. Magna haec quidem, sed non principalia, idest quae summae admirationis privilegium sibi iure vendicent. Cur enim non ipsos angelos et beatissimos caeli choros magis admiremur? Tandem

Admittedly great though these reasons be, they are not the principal grounds, that is, those which may rightfully claim for themselves the privilege of the highest admiration. For why should we not admire more

intellexisse mihi sum visus, cur felicissi-
mum proindeque **dignum** omni admira-
tione animal sit homo, et quae sit demum
illa conditio quam in universi serie sortitus
sit, non brutis modo, sed astris, sed ultra-
mundanis mentibus invidiosam. Res supra
fidem et mira. Quidni? Nam et propterea
magnum miraculum et admirandum profecto animal iure homo et dicitur et existi-
matur. Sed quae nam ea sit audite, Patres,
et benignis auribus pro vestra humanitate
hanc mihi operam condonate.

§ 4. Iam sum[m]us Pater architectus Deus
hanc quam videmus mundanam domum,
divinitatis templum augustissimum,
archanae legibus sapientiae fabrefecerat.
Supercelestem regionem mentibus deco-
rarat; ethereos globos aeternis animis
vegetarat; excrementarias ac feculentas
inferioris mundi partes omnigena ani-
malium turba complerat. Sed, opere con-
sumato, desiderabat artifex esse aliquem
qui tanti operis rationem perpenderet,
pulchritudinem amaret, magnitudinem
admiraretur. Idcirco iam rebus omnibus (ut
Moses Timeusque testantur) absolutis, de
producendo homine postremo cogitavit.
Verum nec erat in archetipis unde novam
sobolem effingeret, nec in thesauris quod
novo filio hereditarium largiretur, nec in
subselli[i]s totius orbis, ubi universi contemplator iste sederet. Iam plena omnia;
omnia summis, mediis infimisque ordini-
bus fuerant distributa. Sed non erat pater-
nae potestatis in extrema faetura quasi
effeta defecisse; non erat sapientiae, consilii

the angels themselves and the blessed choirs
of heaven? At last it seems to me I have
come to understand why man is the most
fortunate of creatures and consequently
worthy of all admiration and what precisely
is that rank which is his lot in the universal
chain of Being – a rank to be envied not
only by brutes but even by the stars and by
minds beyond this world. It is a matter past
faith and a wondrous one. Why should it
not be? For it is on this very account that
man is rightly called and judged a great
miracle and a wonderful creature indeed.
2. But hear, Fathers, exactly what this rank
is and, as friendly auditors, conformably to
your kindness, do me this favor.

God the Father, the supreme Architect, had
already built this cosmic home we behold,
the most sacred temple of His godhead, by
the laws of His mysterious wisdom. The
region above the heavens He had adorned
with Intelligences, the heavenly spheres He
had quickened with eternal souls, and the
excrementary and filthy parts of the lower
world He had filled with a multitude of
animals of every kind. But, when the work
was finished, the Crafts-man kept wishing
that there were someone to ponder the plan
of so great a work, to love its beauty, and to
wonder at its vastness. Therefore, when everything was done (as Moses and Timaeus
bear witness), He finally took thought
concerning the creation of man. But there
was not among His archetypes that from
which He could fashion a new offspring,
nor was there in His treasure-houses anything which He might bestow on His new
son as an inheritance, nor was there in the
seats of all the world a place where the latter
might sit to contemplate the universe. All

inopia in re necessaria fluctuasse; non erat benefici amoris, ut qui in aliis esset divinam liberalitatem laudaturus in se illam damnare cogeretur.

§ 5. Statuit tandem optimus opifex, ut cui dari nihil proprium poterat commune esset quicquid privatum singulis fuerat. Igitur hominem accepit indiscretae opus imaginis atque in mundi positum meditullio sic est alloquutus: 'Nec certam sedem, nec propriam faciem, nec munus ullum peculiare tibi dedimus, o Adam, ut quam sedem, quam faciem, quae munera tute optaveris, ea, pro voto, pro tua sententia, habeas et possideas. Definita caeteris natura intra praescriptas a nobis leges cohercetur. Tu, nullis angustiis cohercitus, pro tuo arbitrio, in cuius manu te posui, tibi illam prefinies. Medium te mundi posui, ut circumspiceres inde comodius quicquid est in mundo. Nec te celestem neque terrenum, neque mortalem neque immortalem fecimus, ut tui ipsius quasi arbitrarius honorariusque plastes et fictor, in quam/132v/ malueris tute formam effingas. Poteris in inferiora quae sunt bruta degenerare; poteris in superiora quae sunt divina ex tui animi sententia regenerari'.

was now complete; all things had been assigned to the highest, the middle, and the lowest orders. But in its final creation it was not the part of the Father's power to fail as though exhausted. It was not the part of His wisdom to waver in a needful matter through poverty of counsel. It was not the part of His kindly love that he who was to praise God's divine generosity in regard to others should be compelled to condemn it in regard to himself.

3. At last, the best of artisans ordained that that creature to whom He had been able to give nothing proper to himself should have joint possession of whatever had been peculiar to each of the different kinds of being. He therefore took man as a creature of indeterminate nature and, assigning him a place in the middle of the world, addressed him thus: 'Neither a fixed abode nor a form that is thine alone nor any function peculiar to thyself have we given thee, Adam, to the end that according to thy longing; and according to thy judgment thou mayest have and possess what abode, what form, and what functions thou thyself shalt desire. The nature of all other beings is limited and constrained within the bounds of laws prescribed by us. Thou, constrained by no limits, in accordance with thine own free will, in whose hand We have placed thee, shalt ordain for thyself the limits of thy nature. We have set thee at the world's center that thou mayest from thence more easily observe whatever is in the world. We have made thee neither of heaven nor of earth, neither mortal nor immortal, so that with freedom of choice and with honor, as though the maker and molder of thyself, thou mayest fashion thyself in whatever

shape thou shalt prefer. Thou shalt have the power to degenerate into the lower forms of life, which are brutish. Thou shalt have the power, out of thy soul's judgment, to be reborn into the higher forms, which are divine.'

§ 6. O summam Dei patris liberalitatem, summam et admirandam hominis foelicitatem! Cui datum id habere quod optat, id esse quod velit. Bruta simul atque nascuntur id secum afferunt (ut ait Lucilius) e bulga matris quod possessura sunt. Supremi spiritus aut ab initio aut paulo mox id fuerunt, quod sunt futuri in perpetuas aeternitates. Nascenti homini omnifaria semina et omnigenae vitae germina indidit Pater. Quae quisque excoluerit illa adolescent, et fructus suos ferent in illo. Si vegetalia planta fiet, si sensualia obrutescet, si rationalia caeleste evadet animal, si intellectualia angelus erit et Dei filius. Et si nulla creaturarum sorte contentus in unitatis centrum suae se receperit, unus cum Deo spiritus factus, in solitaria Patris caligine qui est super omnia constitutus omnibus antestabit.

4. O supreme generosity of God the Father, O highest and most marvellous felicity of man! To him it is granted to have whatever he chooses, to be whatever he wills. Beasts as soon as they are born (so says Lucilius) bring with them from their mother's womb all they will ever possess. Spiritual beings, either from the beginning or soon thereafter, become what they are to be for ever and ever. On man when he came into life the Father conferred the seeds of all kinds and the germs of every way of life. Whatever seeds each man cultivates will grow to maturity and bear in him their own fruit. If they be vegetative, he will be like a plant. If sensitive, he will become brutish. If rational, he will grow into a heavenly being. If intellectual, he will be an angel and the son of God. And if, happy in the lot of no created thing, he withdraws into the center of his own unity, his spirit, made one with God, in the solitary darkness of God, who is set above all things, shall surpass them all.

§ 7. Quis hunc nostrum chamaeleonta non admiretur? Aut omnino quis aliud quicquam admiretur magis? Quem non immerito Asclepius Atheniensis versipellis huius et se ipsam transformantis naturae argumento per Protheum in mysteriis significari dixit. Hinc illae apud Hebreos et Pythagoricos methamorphoses celebratae.

Who would not admire this our chameleon? Or who could more greatly admire aught else whatever? It is man who Asclepius of Athens, arguing from his mutability of character and from his self-transforming nature, on just grounds says was symbolized by Proteus in the mysteries. Hence those metamorphoses renowned among the Hebrews and the Pythagoreans.

§ 8. Nam et Hebreorum theologia secretior nunc Enoch sanctum in angelum divinitatis, quem vocant מלאך השכינה nunc in alia alios numina reformant. Et Pythagorici scelestos homines in bruta deformant et, si Empedocli creditur, etiam in plantas. Quos imitatus Maumeth illud frequens habebat in ore, qui a divina lege recesserit brutum evadere, et merito quidem. Neque enim plantam cortex, sed stupida et nihil sentiens natura; neque iumenta corium, sed bruta anima et sensualis; nec caelum orbiculatum corpus, sed recta ratio; nec sequestratio corporis, sed spiritalis intelligentia angelum facit. Si quem enim videris deditum ventri, humi serpentem hominem, frutex est, non homo, quem vides; si quem in fantasiae quasi Calipsus vanis praestigiis cecucientem et subscalpenti delinitum illecebra sensibus mancipatum, brutum est, non homo, quem vides. Si recta philosophum ratione omnia discernentem, hunc venereris; caeleste est animal, non terrenum. Si purum contemplatorem corporis nescium, in penetralia mentis relegatum, hic non terrenum, non caeleste animal: hic augustius est numen humana carne circumvestitum.

5. For the occult theology of the Hebrews sometimes transforms the holy Enoch into an angel of divinity whom they call 'Mal'akh Adonay Shebaoth,' [this does not transliterate the Hebrew, which reads: 'mal'akh haššekinah': 'Angel of the Presence'. Book of Enoch 40, 8, see footnote 34 of Pico, 2012, p. 127] and sometimes transforms others into other divinities. The Pythagoreans degrade impious men into brutes and, if one is to believe Empedocles, even into plants. Mohammed, in imitation, often had this saying on his tongue: 'They who have deviated from divine law become beasts,' and surely he spoke justly. For it is not the bark that makes the plant but its senseless and insentient nature; neither is it the hide that makes the beast of burden but its irrational, sensitive soul; neither is it the orbed form that makes the heavens but their undeviating order; nor is it the sundering from body but his spiritual intelligence that makes the angel. For if you see one abandoned to his appetites crawling on the ground, it is a plant and not a man you see; if you see one blinded by the vain illusions of imagery, as it were of Calypso, and, softened by their gnawing allurement; delivered over to his senses, it is a beast and not a man you see. If you see a philosopher determining all things by means of right reason, him you shall reverence: he is a heavenly being and not of this earth. If you see a pure contemplator, one unaware of the body and confined to the inner reaches of the mind, he is neither an earthly nor a heavenly being; he is a more reverend divinity vested with human flesh.

§ 9. Ecquis hominem non admiretur? Qui non immerito in sacris litteris Mosaicis et Christianis, nunc omnis carnis, nunc omnis creaturae appellatione designatur, quando se ipsum ipse in omnis carnis faciem, in omnis creaturae ingenium effingit, fabricat et transformat. Idcirco scribit Evantes Persa, ubi Chaldaicam theologiam enarrat, non esse homini suam ullam et nativam imaginem, extrarias multas et adventitias. Hinc illud Chaldeorum a אנוש הוא שנוים ובמה טבעות בעלחי idest homo variae ac multiformis et desultoriae naturae animal.

6. Is there any who would not admire man, who is, in the sacred writings of Moses and the Christians, not without reason described sometimes by the name of 'all flesh,' sometimes by that of 'every creature,' inasmuch as he himself molds, fashions, and changes himself into the form of all flesh and into the character of every creature? For this reason the Persian Euanthes, in describing the Chaldaean theology, writes that man has no semblance that is inborn and his very own but many that are external and foreign to him; whence this saying of the Chaldaeans: 'Hanorish tharah sharinas,' that is, 'Man is a being of varied, manifold, and inconstant nature.' [See footnote 43, Pico, 2012, 133.]

§ 10. Sed quorsum haec? Ut intelligamus, postquam hac nati sumus conditione, ut id simus quod esse volumus, curare hoc potissimum debere nos, ut illud quidem in nos non dicatur, cum in honore essemus non cognovisse similes factos brutis et iumentis insipientibus. Sed illud potius Asaph prophetae: 'Dii estis et filii Excelsi omnes', ne, abutentes indulgentissima Patris liberalitate, quam dedit ille liberam optionem, e salutari noxiam faciamus nobis. Invadat animum sacra quaedam ambitio ut mediocribus non contenti anhelemus ad summa, adque illa (quando possumus si volumus) consequenda totis viribus enitamur. Dedignemur terre/133r/stria, caelestia contemnamus, et quicquid mundi est denique posthabentes, ultramundanam curiam eminentissimae divinitati proximam advolemus. Ibi, ut sacra tradunt mysteria, Seraphin, Cherubin et Throni primas possident; horum nos iam cedere nescii et secundarum impatientes et **dignitatem** et

But why do we emphasize this? To the end that after we have been born to this condition – that we can become what we will – we should understand that we ought to have especial care to this, that it should never be said against us that, although born to a privileged position, we failed to recognize it and became like unto wild animals and senseless beasts of burden, but that rather the saying of Asaph the prophet should apply: 'Ye are all angels and sons of the Most High,' (Ps. 81, 6) and that we may not, by abusing the most indulgent generosity of the Father, make for ourselves that freedom of choice He has given into something harmful instead of salutary. Let a certain holy ambition invade our souls, so that, not content with the mediocre, we shall pant after the highest and (since we may if we wish) toil with all our strength to obtain it. 7. Let us disdain earthly things, despise heavenly things, and, finally, esteeming less whatever is of the world, hasten to

gloriam emulemur. Erimus illis, cum volu-
erimus, nihilo inferiores.

§ 11. Sed qua ratione, aut quid tandem agentes? Videamus quid illi agant, quam vivant
vitam. Eam si et nos vixerimus (possumus
enim) illorum sortem iam equaverimus.
Ardet Saraph charitatis igne; fulget Cherub
intelligentiae splendore; stat Thronus
iudicii firmitate. Igitur si actuosae ad[d]icti
vitae inferiorum curam recto examine susce-
perimus, Thronorum stata soliditate firma-
bimur. Si ab actionibus feriati, in opificio
opificem, in opifice opificium meditantes,
in contemplandi ocio negociabimur, luce
Cherubica undique corruscabimus. Si
charitate ipsum opificem solum ardebimus,
illius igne, qui edax est, in Saraphicam effi-
giem repente flammabimur. Super Throno,
idest iusto iudice, sedet Deus iudex seculo-
rum. Super Cherub, idest contemplatore,
volat atque eum quasi incubando fovet.
Spiritus enim Domini fertur super aquas,
has, inquam quae super caelos sunt, quae
apud Iob Dominum laudant antelucanis
hymnis. Qui Saraph, idest amator est, in
Deo est, et Deus in eo, immo et Deus et ipse
unum sunt. Magna Thronorum potestas,
quam iudicando; summa Saraphinorum
sublimitas, quam amando assequimur.

that court which is beyond the world and
nearest to the Godhead. There, as the sacred
mysteries relate, Seraphim, Cherubim, and
Thrones hold the first places; let us, incapable of yielding to them, and intolerant
of a lower place, emulate their **dignity** and
their glory. If we have willed it, we shall be
second to them in nothing.

8. But how shall we go about it, and what
in the end shall we do? Let us consider
what they do, what sort of life they lead. If
we also come to lead that life (for we have
the power), we shall then equal their good
fortune. The Seraph burns with the fire of
love. The Cherub glows with the splendor
of intelligence. The Throne stands by the
steadfastness of judgment. Therefore if, in
giving ourselves over to the active life, we
have after due consideration undertaken
the care of the lower beings, we shall be
strengthened with the firm stability of
Thrones. If, unoccupied by deeds, we pass
our time in the leisure of contemplation,
considering the Creator in the creature and
the creature in the Creator, we shall be all
ablaze with Cherubic light. If we long with
love for the Creator himself alone, we shall
speedily flame up with His consuming fire
into a Seraphic likeness. Above the Throne,
that is, above the just judge, God sits as
Judge of the ages. Above the Cherub, that
is, above him who contemplates, God flies,
and cherishes him, as it were, in watching
over him. For the spirit of the Lord moves
upon the waters, the waters, I say, which
are above the firmament and which in Job
praise the Lord with hymns before dawn.
Whoso is a Seraph, that is, a lover, is in God
and God in him, nay, rather, God and himself are one. Great is the power of Thrones,

which we attain in using judgment, and
most high the exaltation of Seraphs, which
we attain in loving.

§ 12. Sed quonam pacto vel iudicare quis-
quam vel amare potest incognita? Amavit
Moses Deum quem vidit, et administravit
iudex in populo quae vidit prius contemplator in monte. Ergo medius Cherub sua
luce et Saraphico igni nos praeparat et ad
Thronorum iudicium pariter illuminat.
Hic est nodus primarum mentium, ordo
Palladicus, philosophiae contemplativae
preses; hic nobis et emulandus primo et
ambiendus, atque adeo comprehendendus
est, unde et ad amoris rapiamur fastigia et ad
munera actionum bene instructi paratique
descendamus. At vero operae precium, si
ad exemplar vitae Cherubicae vita nostra
formanda est, quae illa et qualis sit, quae
actiones, quae illorum opera, pre oculis et
in numerato habere. Quod cum nobis per
nos, qui caro sumus et quae humi sunt sapi-
mus, consequi non liceat, adeamus antiquos
patres, qui de his rebus utpote sibi domes-
ticis et cognatis locupletissimam nobis et
certam fidem facere possunt. Consulamus
Paulum apostolum vas electionis, quid ipse
cum ad tertium sublimatus est caelum,
agentes Cherubinorum exercitus viderit.
Respondebit utique Dyonisio interprete:
purgari illos, tum illuminari, postremo
perfici.

9. But by what means is one able either to
judge or to love things unknown? Moses
loved a God whom he saw and, as judge,
administered among the people what he
had first beheld in contemplation upon the
mountain. Therefore, the Cherub as intermediary by his own light makes us ready for
the Seraphic fire and equally lights the way
to the judgment of the Thrones. This is the
bond of the first minds, the Palladian order,
the chief of contemplative philosophy. This
is the one for us first to emulate, to court,
and to understand; the one from whence
we may be rapt to the heights of love and
descend, well taught and well prepared, to
the functions of active life. But truly it is
worthwhile, if our life is to be modelled on
the example of the Cherubic life, to have
before our eyes and clearly understood
both its nature and its quality and those
things which are the deeds and the labor
of Cherubs. But since it is not permitted us
to attain this through our own efforts, we
who are but flesh and know of the things of
earth, let us go to the ancient fathers who,
inasmuch as they were familiar and conver-
sant with these matters, can give sure and
altogether trustworthy testimony. Let us
consult the Apostle Paul, the chosen vessel,
as to what he saw the hosts of Cherubim
doing when he was himself exalted to the
third heaven. He will answer, according to
the interpretation of Dionysius, that he
saw them being purified, then being illuminated, and at last being made perfect.

§ 13. Ergo et nos Cherubicam in terris vitam emulantes, per moralem scientiam affectuum impetus cohercentes, per dialecticam rationis caliginem discutientes, quasi ignorantiae et vitiorum eluentes sordes animam purgemus, ne aut affectus temere debac[c]hentur aut ratio imprudens quandoque deliret. Tum bene compositam ac expiatam animam naturalis philosophiae lumine perfundamus, ut postremo divinarum rerum eam cognitione perficiamus.

Let us also, therefore, by emulating the Cherubic way of life on earth, by taming the impulses of our passions with moral science, by dispelling the darkness of reason with dialectic, and by, so to speak, washing away the filth of ignorance and vice, cleanse our soul, so that her passions may not rave at random nor her reason through heedlessness ever be deranged. 10. Then let us fill our well-prepared and purified soul with the light of natural philosophy, so that we may at last perfect her in the knowledge of things divine.

§ 14. Et ne nobis nostri sufficiant consulamus Iacob patriarcham cuius imago in sede gloriae sculpta corruscat. Admonebit nos pater sapientissimus in inferno dormiens, mundo in superno vigilans. Sed admonebit per figuram (ita eis omnia contingebant) esse scalas ab imo solo ad caeli summa protensas multorum graduum serie distinctas; fastigio Dominum insidere, contemplatores angelos per eas vicibus alternantes ascendere et descendere.

And lest we be satisfied with those of our faith, let us consult the patriarch Jacob, whose form gleams carved on the throne of glory. Sleeping in the lower world but keeping watch in the upper, the wisest of fathers will advise us. But he will advise us through a figure (in this way everything was wont to come to those men) that there is a ladder extending from the lowest earth to the highest heaven, divided in a series of many steps, with the Lord seated at the top, and angels in contemplation ascending and descending over them alternately by turns.

§ 15. Quod si hoc idem nobis angelicam /133v/ affectantibus vitam factitandum est, queso, quis Domini scalas vel sordidato pede, vel male mundis manibus attinget? Impuro, ut habent mysteria, purum attingere nephas. Sed qui hi pedes? Quae manus? Profecto pes animae illa est portio despicatissima, qua ipsa materiae tanquam terrae solo innititur, altrix inquam potestas et cibaria, fomes libidinis et voluptariae mollitudinis magistra. Manus animae cur irascentiam non dixerimus, quae appetentiae propugnatrix pro ea decertat et sub pulvere ac sole p[r]edatrix rapit, quae

11. If this is what we must practice in our aspiration to the angelic way of life, I ask: 'Who will touch the ladder of the Lord either with fouled foot or with unclean hands?' As the sacred mysteries have it, it is impious for the impure to touch the pure. But what are these feet? What these hands? Surely, the foot of the soul is that most contemptible part by which the soul rests on matter as on the soil of the earth, I mean the nourishing and feeding power, the tinder of lust, and the teacher of pleasurable weakness. Why should we not call the hands of the soul its irascible power, which struggles

illa sub umbra dormitans helluetur? Has manus, hos pedes, idest totam sensualem partem in qua sedet corporis illecebra quae animam obtorto (ut aiunt) detinet collo, ne a scalis tamquam prophani pollutique reiciamur, morali philosophia quasi vivo flumine abluamus. At nec satis hoc erit, si per Iacob scalam discursantibus angelis comites esse volumus, nisi et a gradu in gradum rite promoveri, et a scalarum tramite deorbitare nusquam, et reciprocos obire excursus bene apti prius instructique fuerimus. Quod cum per artem sermocinalem sive rationariam erimus consequuti, iam Cherubico spiritu animati, per scalarum, idest naturae gradus philosophantes, a centro ad centrum omnia pervadentes, nunc unum quasi Osyrim in multitudinem vi titanica dis[c]erpentes descendemus, nunc multitudinem quasi Osyridis membra in unum vi Phebea colligentes ascendemus, donec in sinu Patris qui super scalas est tandem quiescentes, theologica foelicitate consumabimur.

§ 16. Percontemur et iustum Iob, qui fedus iniit cum Deo vitae prius quam ipse ederetur in vitam quid summus Deus in decem illis centenis millibus qui assistunt ei, potissimum desideret: pacem utique respondebit, iuxta id quod apud eum legitur: 'Qui facit pacem in excelsis'. Et quoniam supremi ordinis monita medius ordo inferioribus interpretatur, interpretetur nobis Iob theologi verba Empedocles philosophus. Hic

on its behalf as the champion of desire and as plunderer seizes in the dust and sun what desire will devour slumbering in the shade? These hands, these feet, that is, all the sentient part whereon resides the attraction of the body which, as they say, by wrenching the neck holds the soul in check, lest we be hurled down from the ladder as impious and unclean, let us bathe in moral philosophy as if in a living river. Yet this will not be enough if we wish to be companions of the angels going up and down on Jacob's ladder, unless we have first been well fitted and instructed to be promoted duly from step to step, to stray nowhere from the stairway, and to engage in the alternate comings and goings. Once we have achieved this by the art of discourse or reasoning, then, inspired by the Cherubic spirit, using philosophy through the steps of the ladder, that is, of nature, and penetrating all things from center to center, we shall sometimes descend, with titanic force rending the unity like Osiris into many parts, and we shall sometimes ascend, with the force of Phoebus collecting the parts like the limbs of Osiris into a unity, until, resting at last in the bosom of the Father who is above the ladder, we shall be made perfect with the felicity of theology.

12. Let us also inquire of the just Job, who entered into a life-covenant with God before he himself was brought forth into life, what the most high God requires above all in those tens of hundreds of thousands who attend him. He will answer that it is peace, in accord with what we read in him: 'He maketh peace in his high places.' And since the middle order expounds to the lower orders the counsel of the

duplicem naturam in nostris animis sitam, quarum altera sursum tollimur ad celestia, altera deorsum trudimur ad inferna, per litem et amicitiam, sive bellum et pacem, ut sua testantur carmina, nobis significat. In quibus se lite et discordia actum, furenti similem profugum a diis, in altum iactari conqueritur.

§ 17. Multiplex profecto, Patres, in nobis discordia; gravia et intestina domi habemus et plusquam civilia bella. Quae si noluerimus, si illam affectaverimus pacem, quae in sublime ita nos tollat ut inter excelsos Domini statuamur, sola in nobis compescet prorsus et sedabit philosophia: moralis primum, si noster homo ab hostibus indutias tantum quesierit, multiplicis bruti effrenes excursiones et leonis iurgia, iras animosque contundet. Tum si rectius consulentes nobis perpetuae pacis securitatem desideraverimus, aderit illa et vota nostra liberaliter implebit, quippe quae cesa utraque bestia, quasi icta porca, inviolabile inter carnem et spiritum foedus sanctissimae pacis sanciet. Sedabit dyalectica rationis turbas inter orationum pugnantias et sillogismo captiones anxie tumultuantis. Sedabit naturalis philosophia opinionis lites et dis[s]idia, quae inquietam hinc inde animam vexant, distrahunt et lacerant. Sed ita sedabit, ut meminisse nos iubeat esse naturam iuxta Heraclytum ex bello genitam, ob id ab Homero contentionem vocitatam. Idcirco in ea veram quietem et solidam pacem se nobis prestare non posse,

highest order, let Empedocles the philosopher expound to us the words of Job the theologian. He indicates to us a twofold nature present in our souls, by one side of which we are raised on high to the heavenly regions, and by the other side plunged downward into the lower, through strife and friendship or through war and peace, as he witnesses in the verses in which he makes complaint that he is being driven into the sea, himself goaded by strife and discord into the semblance of a madman and a fugitive from the gods.

13. Surely, Fathers, there is in us a discord many times as great; we have at hand wars grievous and more than civil, wars of the spirit which, if we dislike them, if we aspire to that peace which may so raise us to the sublime that we shall be established among the exalted of the Lord, only philosophy will entirely allay and subdue in us. In the first place, if our man but ask a truce of his enemies, moral philosophy will check the unbridled inroads of the many-sided beast and the leonine passions of wrath and violence. If we then take wiser counsel with ourselves and learn to desire the security of everlasting peace, it will be at hand and will generously fulfil our prayers. After both beasts are felled like a sacrificed sow, it will confirm an inviolable compact of holiest peace between flesh and spirit. Dialectic will appease the tumults of reason made confused and anxious by inconsistencies of statement and sophisms of syllogisms. Natural philosophy will allay the strife and differences of opinion which vex, distract, and wound the spirit from all sides. But she will so assuage them as to compel us to remember that, according to Heraclitus,

esse hoc dominae suae, idest sanctissimae th[e]ologiae, munus et privilegium. Ad illam ipsa et viam monstrabit et comes ducet, quae procul nos videns properantes: 'Venite', inclamavit, 'ad me qui laborastis; venite et ego reficiam vos; venite ad /134r/ me et dabo vobis pacem quam mundus et natura vobis dare non possunt'.

§ 18. Tam blande vocati, tam benigniter invitati, alatis pedibus quasi terrestres Mercurii, in beatissimae amplexus matris evolantes, optata pace perfruemur: pace sanctissima, individua copula, unianimi amicitia, qua omnes animi in una mente, quae est super omnem mentem, non concordent adeo, sed ineffabili quodammodo unum penitus evadant. Haec est illa amicitia quam totius philosophiae finem esse Pythagorici dicunt, haec illa pax quam facit Deus in excelsis suis, quam angeli in terram descendentes annuntiarunt hominibus bonae voluntatis, ut per eam ipsi homines ascendentes in caelum angeli fierent. Hanc pacem amicis, hanc nostro optemus seculo, optemus unicuique domui quam ingredimur, optemus animae nostrae, ut per eam ipsa Dei domus fiat; ut, postquam per moralem et dyalecticam suas sordes excusserit, multiplici philosophia quasi aulico apparatu se exornarit, portarum fastigia theologicis sertis coronarit, descendat Rex gloriae et cum Patre veniens mansionem faciat apud eam. Quo tanto hospite si se **dignam** praestiterit, qua est illius immensa clementia, deaurato vestitu quasi toga

nature was begotten from war, that it was on this account repeatedly called 'strife' by Homer, and that it is not, therefore, in the power of natural philosophy to give us in nature a quiet and unshaken peace but that this is the function and privilege of her mistress, that is, of holiest theology. She will show us the way and as comrade lead us to her who, seeing us hastening from afar, will exclaim 'Come to me, ye who have labored. Come and I will restore you. Come to me, and I will give you peace, which the world and nature cannot give you.'

14. When we have been so soothingly called, so kindly urged, we shall fly up with winged feet, like earthly Mercuries, to the embraces of our blessed mother and enjoy that wished-for peace, most holy peace, indivisible bond, of one accord in the friendship through which all rational souls not only shall come into harmony in the one mind which is above all minds but shall in some ineffable way become altogether one. This is that friendship which the Pythagoreans say is the end of all philosophy. This is that peace which God creates in his heavens, which the angels descending to earth proclaimed to men of good will, that through it men might ascend to heaven and become angels. Let us wish this peace for our friends, for our century. Let us wish it for every home into which we go; let us wish it for our own soul, that through it she shall herself be made the house of God, and to the end that as soon as she has cast out her uncleanness through moral philosophy and dialectic, adorned herself with manifold philosophy as with the splendor of a courtier, and crowned the pediments of her doors with

nuptiali multiplici scientiarum circumdata varietate, speciosum hospitem, non ut hospitem iam, sed ut sponsum excipiet, a quo ne unquam dissolvatur dissolvi cupiet a populo suo et domum patris sui, immo se ipsam oblita, in se ipsa cupiet mori ut vivat in sponso, in cuius conspectu preciosa profecto mors sanctorum eius, mors, inquam, illa, si dici mors debet plenitudo vitae cuius meditationem esse studium philosophiae dixerunt sapientes.

§ 19. Citemus et Mosem ipsum a sacrosanctae et ineffabilis intelligentiae fontana plenitudine, unde angeli suo nectare inebriantur, paulo deminutum. Audiemus venerandum iudicem nobis in deserta huius corporis solitudine habitantibus leges sic edicentem: 'Qui polluti adhuc morali indigent, cum plebe habitent extra tabernaculum sub divo, quasi Thessali sacerdotes interim se expiantes. Qui mores iam composuerunt, in sanctuarium recepti, nondum quidem sacra attractent, sed prius dyaletico famulatu seduli levitae philosophiae sacris ministrent. Tum ad ea et ipsi admissi, nunc superioris Dei regiae multicolorem, idest sydereum aulicum ornatum, nunc caeleste candelabrum septem luminibus distinctum, nunc pellicea elementa, in philosophiae sacerdotio contemplentur, ut postremo per theologicae sublimitatis merita in templi adita recepti, nullo imaginis intercedente velo, divinitatis gloria perfruantur'. Haec

the garlands of theology, the King of Glory may descend and, coming with his Father, make his stay with her. If she show herself worthy of so great a guest, she shall, by the boundless mercy which is his, in golden raiment like a wedding gown, and surrounded by a varied throng of sciences, receive her beautiful guest not merely as a guest but as a spouse from whom she will never be parted. She will desire rather to be parted from her own people and, forgetting her father's house and herself, will desire to die in herself in order to live in her spouse, in whose sight surely the death of his saints is precious – death, I say, if we must call death that fullness of life, the consideration of which wise men have asserted to be the aim of philosophy.

15. Let us also cite Moses himself, but little removed from the springing abundance of the holy and unspeakable wisdom by whose nectar the angels are made drunk. Let us hearken to the venerable judge in these words proclaiming laws to us who are dwellers in the desert loneliness of this body: 'Let those who, as yet unclean, still need moral philosophy, live with the people outside the tabernacle under the sky, meanwhile purifying themselves like the priests of Thessaly. Let those who have already ordered their conduct be received into the sanctuary but not quite yet touch the holy vessels; let them first like zealous Levites in the service of dialectic minister to the holy things of philosophy. Then when they have been admitted even to these, let them now behold the many-colored robe of the higher palace of the Lord, that is to say, the stars; let them now behold the heavenly candlestick divided into seven lights;

nobis profecto Moses et imperat et impe-
rando admonet, excitat, inhortatur, ut per
philosophiam ad futuram caelestem gloriam, dum possumus iter paremus nobis.

§ 20. Verum enimvero, nec Mosayca tantum
aut Christiana mysteria, sed priscorum
quoque theologia harum, de quibus dispu-
taturus accessi, liberalium artium et emolu-
menta nobis et **dignitatem** ostendit. Quid
enim aliud sibi volunt in Graecorum archa-
nis observati initiatorum gradus, quibus
primo per illas quas diximus quasi febru-
ales artes, moralem et dialeticam, purifi-
catis, contingebat mysteriorum susceptio?
Quae quid aliud esse potest quam secretio-
ris per philosophiam naturae interpretatio?
Tum demum ita dispositis illa adveniebat,
ἐποπτεία idest rerum divinarum per theologiae lumen inspectio. Quis talibus sacris
initiari non appetat? Quis humana /134v/
omnia posthabens, fortunae contemnens
bona, corporis negligens, deorum conviva
adhuc degens in terris fieri non cupiat,
et aeternitatis nectare madidus mortale
animal immortalitatis munere donari? Quis
non Socraticis illis furoribus, a Platone in
Fedro decantatis, sic afflari non velit ut
alarum pedumque remigio hinc, idest ex
mundo, qui est positus in maligno, propere
aufugiens, ad caelestem Hierusalem con-
citatissimo cursu feratur? Agemur, Patres,
agemur Socraticis furoribus, qui extra

let them now behold the fur tent, that is,
the elements, in the priesthood of philosophy, so that when they are in the end,
through the favor of theological sublimity, granted entrance into the inner part of
the temple, they may rejoice in the glory
of the Godhead with no veil before his
image.' This of a surety Moses commands
us and, in commanding, summons, urges,
and encourages us by means of philosophy
to prepare ourselves a way, while we can, to
the heavenly glory to come.

16. But indeed not only the Mosaic and
Christian mysteries but also the theology
of the ancients show us the benefits and
value of the liberal arts, the discussion of
which I am about to undertake. For what
else did the degrees of the initiates observed
in the mysteries of the Greeks mean? For
they arrived at a perception of the mysteries
when they had first been purified through
those expiatory sciences, as it were, moral
philosophy and dialectic. What else can
that perception possibly be than an interpretation of occult nature by means of
philosophy? Then at length to those who
were so disposed came that EPOPTEIA
[initiation in the greater Eleusinian myster-
ies] that is to say, the observation of things
divine by the light of theology. Who would
not long to be initiated into such sacred
rites? Who would not desire, by neglect-
ing all human concerns, by despising the
goods of fortune, and by disregarding those
of the body, to become the guest of the gods
while yet living on earth, and, made drunk
by the nectar of eternity, to be endowed
with the gifts of immortality though still
a mortal being? Who would not wish to
be so inflamed with those Socratic frenzies

mentem ita nos ponant, ut mentem nostram et nos ponant in Deo. Agemur ab illis utique, si quid est in nobis ipsi prius egerimus; nam si et per moralem affectuum vires ita per debitas competentias ad modulos fuerint intentae, ut immota invicem consonent concinentia, et per dyalecticam ratio ad numerum se progrediendo moverit, Musarum perciti furore celestem armoniam intimis auribus combibemus. Tum Musarum dux Bacchus in suis mysteriis, idest visibilius naturae signis invisibilia Dei philosophantibus nobis ostendens, inebriabit nos ab ubertate domus Dei, in qua tota si uti Moses erimus fideles, accedens sacratissima theologia duplici furore nos animabit. Nam in illius eminentissimam sublimati speculam, inde et quae sunt, quae erunt quaeque fuerint insectili metientes evo, et primevam pulchritudinem suspicientes, illorum Phebei vates, huius alati erimus amatores et ineffabili demum charitate, quasi aestro perciti, quasi Saraphini ardentes extra nos positi, numine pleni, iam non ipsi nos, sed ille erimus ipse qui fecit nos.

sung by Plato in the *Phaedrus*, that, by the oarage of feet and wings escaping speedily from hence, that is, from a world set on evil, he might be borne on the fastest of courses to the heavenly Jerusalem? Let us be driven, Fathers, let us be driven by the frenzies of Socrates, that they may so throw us into ecstasy as to put our mind and ourselves in God. Let us be driven by them, if we have first done what is in our power. For if through moral philosophy the forces of our passions have by a fitting agreement become so intent on harmony that they can sing together in undisturbed concord, and if through dialectic our reason has moved progressively in a rhythmical measure, then we shall be stirred by the frenzy of the Muses and drink the heavenly harmony with our inmost hearing. Thereupon Bacchus, the leader of the Muses, by showing in his mysteries, that is, in the visible signs of nature, the invisible things of God to us who study philosophy, will intoxicate us with the fullness of God's house, in which, if we prove faithful, like Moses, hallowed theology shall come and inspire us with a doubled frenzy. For, exalted to her lofty height, we shall measure therefrom all things that are and shall be and have been in indivisible eternity; and, admiring their original beauty, like the seers of Phoebus, we shall become her own winged lovers. And at last, roused by ineffable love as by a sting, like burning Seraphim rapt from ourselves, full of divine power we shall no longer be ourselves but shall become He Himself Who made us.

Erasmus of Rotterdam (1466–1536)

In contrast to Pico, Erasmus presents a plainly Christian understanding of human dignity as marred by the fall and redeemed in Christ. He is emphasising how the awareness of this dignity underlines the gravity of sin. The appeal to human dignity obliging the person holding it to morally upright conduct is the most common way human dignity is believed to have consequences at the time of Erasmus.

Handbook of a Christian Soldier

Text from *Erasmus von Rotterdam Ausgewählte Schriften*, Acht Bände Lateinisch und Deutsch, Bd. 1., trans. and ed. Werner Welzig (Darmstadt: Wissenschaftliche Buchgesellschaft, 1995), pp. 322–4. Translation from *Erasmus, Enchiridion militis christiani. An English Version*, Early English Texts Society, no. 282, ed. Anne M. O'Donnell, S. N. D. (Oxford: Oxford University Press, 1981). The old translation is presented here to illustrate the influence the text had at the time.

Rule 18

Atque hoc quidem remedii quamquam unum omnium longe praesentissimum est iis, qui mediocriter in via vitae processerunt, tamen infirmioribus nonnihil profuerint et illa, si sollicitante ad impietatem affectu statim ob oculos mentis revocent, quam foeda, quam execranda, quam exitialis res sit peccatum, contra quanta **hominis dignitas**. In futtilibus etiam negotiis paulisper apud nos ipsos consultamus, in hac re omnium maxima priusquam nosmet assensu veluti chirographo diabolo astringimus, non nostro cum animo reputabimus, a quanto opifice simus conditi, in quam excellenti statu constituti, quam immenso

And veryly this maner of remedye / though it alone of all remedyes be most present and redy, moste sure and quicke in werkynge to them whiche be meanly entered in the waye of lyuyng: neuer the lesse to the weaker sorte these thynges also shall somwhat profyte. If whan affectyon moueth vnto iniquyte / than atones they call before the eyen of the mynde howe filthy, howe abhomynable, howe mischeuous a thynge synne is: on the other syde howe great is the **dignyte of man**. In tryfles and maters suche as skylleth not if all the worlde knewe / we take some delyberacyon and aduysement with our selfe. In this mater of all maters

pretio redempti, ad quantam felicitatem vocati? Hominem generosum illud esse animal, cuius unius gratia mirabilem hanc mundi machinam fabricates est deus, concivem angelorum, filium dei, haeredem immortalitatis, membrum Christi, membrum ecclesiae, corpora nostra templa esse spiritussancti, mentes simulacra simul et adyta divinitatis. At e reginone peccatum esse pestem taeterrimam ac tabem tum animi tum corporis. Utrumque enim in nativam speciem reflorescit innocentia, peccati vero contagio marcescit utrumque etiam in hoc saeculo. Peccatum est letale virus spurcissimi serpentis, auctoramentum diaboli ac servitutis non turpissimae modo, verum etiam miserrimae. Haec atque huiusmodi ubi tecum expenderis, etiam atque etiam delibera, num satis consultum, sit obfucatam momentaneam, venenatam peccati delectatiunculam a tanta **dignitate** in tantam excidere **indignitatem**, unde te per teipsum non queas asserere.

most weyghty and worthy to be pondered / before y^t with consent as with our owne hande writyng we bynde our selfe to the fende / shall we not reken and accompte with our mynde of how noble a craftes man we were made / in howe excellent estate were are set / with howe excedynge great pryce we are bought / vnto howe great felycyte we are called? and that man is that gentle and noble creature for whose sake only god hath forged the meruaylous buyldyng of this worlde / that he is of the company of aungels, the sonne of god, the heyre of immortalyte, a membre of Christe, a membre of the churche / that our bodyes be ye temple of the holy goost / our myndes the ymages and also ye secret habytacions of the deite. And on the other syde y^t synne is the most filthy pestylence and consumpcyon bothe of the mynde and of the body also / for bothe of them through innocencye springeth anewe into their owne naturall kynde / and through contagyon of synne bothe putrifye and rotte euen in this worlde. Synne is that deedly poyson of the moste filthy serpent / the prest wages of the dyuell / and of that seruyce whiche is not most filthy only, but also moste myserable. After thou hast concydred this and suche lyke with thy selfe / pondre wysely and take sure aduysement and delyberacion whether it should be wysely done or no, for an apparaunt momentanye and poysoned lytell short pleasure of synne / to fall from so great **dignyte**, in to so vyle and **wretched** estate / from whence thou cannest not rydde and delyuer thy selfe by thyne owne power and helpe.

Bartholomé de Las Casas (1484–1566)

Reacting against the kind of colonisation he witnessed in the Americas, Las Casas enlists all the authorities he can think of to encourage a more gentle attitude towards the native inhabitants. Las Casas had no doubts that his people had forced themselves on the Indians, but he also thought they had a message that would have conferred them with credibility even in the eyes of the Indians, had they only conducted themselves with dignity. The occasion had been ruined, however. Because of the excessive violence, the Indians would now have only justified fear of and disdain for the Christians. For this betrayal of trust, the Spaniards would have to pay; they would have to restitute to the Indians what they unlawfully took from them because such are the claims of Natural Justice. His countrymen were not easily convinced, and when he admonishes them it is gently and in images from the New Testament. Las Casas also shows himself aware in his correspondence with the emperor, that an absolute ruler cannot consider himself obliged without losing dignity and that the emperor therefore cannot admit wrongdoing. The *Conquistadores*, in contrast, had no qualms committing the 'great crime of not trusting the Supreme Prince, the Christian Emperor of the Holy Roman Empire' if it would serve their interest. In order to avoid the anarchical situation of their open disobedience towards the emperor, Las Casas advised an action within the limits of affordable politics: sending worthy people to govern the colonies instead of those who were in charge there at the time, manifestly not worthy of the Indians. The pragmatic 'solution' was to be black slavery. Despite his final rejection of this, as late as in 1544 Las Casas himself owned several Negro slaves (Hanke, 1959, 9). Opposition to Negro slavery all through the sixteenth century was very weak.

Texts from Bartolomé de las Casas: *Obras Completas* (Madrid: Alianza Editorial, 1988–98), vol. 2 (*De unico vocationis modo*) and 13 (Letters). Translations from Bartolomé de Las Casas: *The Only Way (to Draw all People to a Living Faith)*, ed. Helen Rand Parish, trans. Francis Patrick Sullivan S. J., Sources of American Spirituality (Mahwah, NJ: Paulist Press, 1992) and with the help of Elena Garcia.

De unico vocationis modo No. 16 (manuscript p. 61) (1537)

Docuit discipulos Dominus, secundum Remigium, *in introitu offerre pacem, ut salutatione pacis eligeretur domus vel hospes, ac si patenter diceret: Omnibus offerte pacem, quia aut accipiendo* dignos *aut non accipiendo* indignos *se manifestabunt. Quamvis in fama populi* dignus *electus sit hospes, tamen salutandus est, ut magis sua* dignitate *praedicatores vocentur, quam ultro se ingerere videantur.* El Señor, según Remigio, instruyó a sus discípulos para que el entrar ofrecieran la paz, para que mediante el saludo de la paz averiguaran la casa o huespéd; como si con toda claridad dijera: ofreced a todos la paz, porque aceptándola, se manifestarán **dignos**; e **indignos**, si la rechazan. Y aunque, fundados en la opinión del pueblo hubieran elegido ya un huésped **digno**, habían de saludar, sin embargo, para que los predicadores fueran invitados más por su **dignidad**, que por paracer que se entrometían (p. 173).

Remigius says, 'The Lord taught His disciples to say "peace" when they arrived somewhere, to choose a house or a host by a greeting of peace, as if the Lord said it in so many words: "Greet everyone with peace". So those who accepted would be **worthy** hosts, those who did not, **unworthy** [of being a host]. Though a host might be chosen because of his **public reputation**, still he must be greeted with peace, so [that] the preachers may be invited in because of their own **dignity** and not force themselves on him for another reason' (p. 75).

Letter to the Emperor, IX (1542)

El 2.º inconveniente es que cuanto a los indios que han tenido encomendados y el oro que con ellos han habido, de las minas sacado o dado de tributos, como éste sea beneficio y merced hecha por V. M., que es supremo Príncipe, debe de ser perpetuo y permanecedero, porque de otra manera es derogar a la **dignidad** real de V. M., y por tanto, si V. M. se lo revocase, cosa **indecente** a V. M. sería, y a ellos sería perjudicial, y en alguna manera parecería que por V. M.

The second inconvenience [about restitution] is that the Indians under the command of your officers, and the gold that has been taken from the mines and given as a tribute, has been of both profit and benefit to you, Supreme Prince. It should therefore be lasting, lest it should diminish the royal **dignity** of Your Majesty. If Your Majesty chose to restitute it, it would be **indecent** and they [the Conquistadores] would be damaged. They would think they

eran defraudados y engañados por hacer confianza y tener seguridad de sus cartas y poderes reales: que todas estas cosas, de príncipe cristiano y sapientísimo decirlas y aun sentirlas es gran crimen. [...]

Y manderá Vuestra Majestad poner en ella personas muy egregias y de mucha virtud y justicia, porque las que agora en ella están no son personas **dignas** de estar en ella.

were being deceived by you by trusting you and having faith in your letters and royal powers. Thinking and feeling these things about a Christian and wise King is a great crime. [...]

Your Majesty must send responsible people to her [the Americas] of much virtue and justice. The ones that are there now are not **worthy** of her.

CHAPTER 8

Absolutism and Counterreformation

That dignity now becomes talked about in a politically realist manner as a means to affirm political power is a sign that its political relevance is making itself felt. This furthermore testifies to the affirmation of state power and the increasing importance of the political sphere. Aristotle and Cicero studied the political status of dignitaries but their insights could point in different directions in the new environment of the modern state. Was it the case that the Christian affirmation of human (i.e. universal) dignity now inspired enough confidence to make the idea that dignity is a prerogative of the nobility lack credibility? If this certainly plays a role, so does its shadow or twin: the atheist, secular insistence on the independence of politics from any foundation outside human invention, which, in contrast to the Christian ethics of humility, finds it easy to use political means to vindicate dignity. In the following texts from the Baroque era one senses a certain expectation that the middle classes were about to step forward to affirm their dignity, probably because the writers of these texts, and most writers of the period, themselves belonged to the middle class.

Hugo Grotius (1583–1645)

Grotius maintained, like Cicero, Aristotle and Aquinas, that right (*ius*) is the relationship between a rational being and that which is due to his dignity. That such a right could be renounced as slaves and subjects of the absolute ruler were presumed to have done according to social contract theory, contributed to a modern insistence on autonomy as the centre of human dignity.

To Grotius, as to the ancients, there could be no right without dignity. In this sense, dignity was – also to the moderns – a prerequisite for right and a foundation of it. To dignity, however, Grotius adds that *ius* can also be due to property. Cicero seems to have felt no need to make the distinction made here by Grotius, and the explanation quite likely is that dignity to him included property so that property was simply one of the expressions *dignitas* could take. Rights only meaningfully follow from dignity when the person has certain needs, whether of a biological or a spiritual kind, which give rise to socially recognised claims and corresponding obligations. Questions of property are, on that account, quite naturally the first questions of any theory of rights. In such a theory, human dignity plays the role of rooting the legitimacy of claims in the human person. Grotius, however, by this distinction also plainly recognises the privileges of the propertied classes and grants them the right to have political importance according to their means.

The Jurisprudence of Holland

Text from *Inleidinghe tot de Hollandsche Rechts-gheleertheyd* (Arnheim: P. Gouda Quint, 1895). Translation from *The Jurisprudence of Holland*, I, ed. and trans. R. W. Lee (Oxford: Clarendon Press, 1926), pp. 2–3. Translation adapted.

Eng genomen recht is het opzicht dat daer is tusschen een redelick wezen ende yet dat op het zelve past, door **waerdigheid** ofte tobehooren. **Waerdigheid** is de bequamheid van een redelick wezen tot yet dat begeert werd. Toebehoeren is waer door yet het onze werd genoemt, ende bestaet (als hier nae zal werden verklaert) in begering (L. Jus reale) ende in inschuld (L. Jus personale) [...] Van de rechtvaerdigheid die op 't eng genomen recht zie werd die soorte die op de **waerdigheid** acht neemt ghenoemt begevende (L. Justitia distributiva): de andere die op het tobehoeren let, de vergeldende (L. Justitia commutativa): waer van die, de evenredigheid, deze, de slechte evenheid meest gebruickt.

Right, narrowly understood, is the relation, which exists between a reasonable being and something appropriate to him by **dignity** or property. **Dignity** is the fitness of a reasonable being for any object of desire. Property means that something is called ours; it consists, as will be seen, in real rights (*jus reale*) and in personal rights (*jus personale*). [...] Of the justice which has regards to right, narrowly understood, the kind which takes account of **dignity** is called 'distributative justice'; the other kind which gives heed to property is called 'commutative justice'; the first commonly employs the rule of proportion, the second the rule of simple equality.

Thomas Hobbes (1588–1679)

Thomas Hobbes educated young men destined for power and position in public life. The education of civil servants and courtiers was still mostly a matter of private tutoring in the practical art of court life, administration of property and political thought even if law could be studied at the university. The text displays a radical conservative's understanding of how to bring about, preserve and uphold social order. It is radical because Hobbes in it invents a new theory of absolute monarchy, which in fact relies upon a radical egalitarianism, in turn libertarian at its core. It is conservative because Hobbes in it attempts to think anew the justification of the king as the sole principle of social organisation while preserving the nobility's dependence on the king for its privileges. Hobbes manages in this way to argue both for men's equality and for the absolute power of the state in a way that does not involve a theory of kingship by divine right, nor entices the aristocracy to break faith. In this order, he understands the worth of a man to be the price set on him by others, in contrast with his dignity, which is his value to the Commonwealth. The subjects, however, are all useful in one important respect; they are all contractors in the original social contract. The dignity of a man, on these terms, is the privilege or status accorded by the sovereign state to all the members of the commonwealth in exchange for their usefulness as parties to the social contract. In contrast to the Christian tradition, Hobbes is not interested in the ontological connection between dignity and humanity. Humanity counts to the precise extent that it is a power factor. In cutting loose and setting adrift human dignity from the subject whose dignity it is, and making it rest entirely with the state, Hobbes inverts the Ciceronian tradition such that he must count, following Macchiavelli, as an exact opposite of Grotius and the natural law tradition he interprets. In this Hobbes initiates the politically realist natural law tradition, not to be confused with the former. He also firmly establishes the idea that human dignity could be a status granted by the state for the purpose of its preservation of power, possibly remotely linked to common utility or the good of the commonwealth.

Leviathan

Text according to Thomas Hobbes: *Leviathan*, ed. R. Tuck (Cambridge: Cambridge University Press, 1997). The original edition is available electronically at: <https://books.google.ie/books/about/Leviathan_Or_The_Matter_Form_and_Power_o.html?id=L3FgBpvIWRkC&printsec=frontcover&source=kp_read_button&redir_esc=y#v=onepage&q&f=false> (accessed January 2019).

Chapter X. Of Power, Worth, **Dignity**, Honour, and Worthinesse
The Power *of a Man*, (to take it universally,) is his present means, to obtain some future apparent Good. And is either *Originall*, or *Instrumentall*.
Natural Power is the eminence of the Faculties of Body, or Mind: as extraordinary Strength, Forme, Prudence, Arts, Eloquence, Liberality, Nobility. Instrumental are those Powers, which acquired by these, or by fortune, are means and Instruments to acquire more: as Riches, Reputation, Friends, and the secret working of God, which men call Good Luck. For the nature of Power, is in this point, like to Fame, increasing as it proceeds; or like the motion of heavy bodies, which the further they go, make still the more haste.
The greatest of humane Powers, is that which is compounded of the powers of most men, united by consent, in one person, Naturall, or Civill, that has the use of all their Powers depending on his will; such as is the Power of a Common-wealth: Or depending on the wills of each particular; such as is the Power of a Faction, or of divers factions leagued. Therefore to have servants, is Power; to have friends, is Power: for they are strengths united.
Also Riches joined with liberality, is Power; because it procureth friends, and servants: without liberality, not so; because in this case they defend not; but expose men to Envy, as a Prey.
Reputation of power, is Power; because it draweth with it the adherence of those that need protection. So is reputation of love of man's Country, (called Popularity,) for the same Reason. Also, what quality soever maketh a man beloved, or feared of many; or the reputation of such quality, is Power; because it is a means to have the assistance, and service of many.
Good successe is Power; because it maketh reputation of Wisdom, or good fortune; which makes men either feare him, or rely on him.
Affability of men already in power, is increase of power; because it gaineth love.
Reputation of Prudence in the conduct of Peace or War, is power; because to prudent men, we commit the government of our selves, more willingly than to others.
Nobility is Power, not in all places, but only in those Commonwealths, where it has Priviledges: for in such priviledges consisteth their Power.

Eloquence is power; because it is seeming prudence.

Forme is Power; because being a promise of Good, it recommendeth men to the favour of women and strangers.

The Sciences, are small power; because not eminent; and therefore, not acknowledged in any man; nor are at all, but in a few; and in them, but of few things. For Science is of that nature, as none can understand it to be, but such as in a good measure have attayned it.

Arts of publique use, as Fortification, making of Engines, and other Instruments of War [...] are Power: And though the true mother of them, be Science, namely the Mathematiques; yet, because they are brought into the Light, by the hand of the Artificer, they be esteemed (the Midwife passing with the vulgar for Mother,) as his issue.

The value, or WORTH of a man, is as of all other things, his price; that is to say, so much as would be given for the use of his Power: and therefore is not absolute; but a thing dependant on the need and judgement of another. An able conductor of Soldiers is of great Price in time of War present, or imminent; but in Peace not so. A learned and incorrupt Judge, is much Worth in time of Peace; but not so much in War. And as in other things, so in men, not the seller, but the buyer determines the Price. For let a man (as most men do,) rate themselves at the highest value they can; yet their true value is no more than it is esteemed by others.

The manifestation of the Value we set on one another, is that which is commonly called Honouring, and Dishonouring. To Value a man at a high rate, is to *Honour* him; at a low rate, is to *Dishonour* him. But high, and low, in this case, is to be understood by comparison to the rate that each man setteth on himselfe.

The publique worth of a man, which is the Value set on him by the Commonwealth, is that which men commonly call DIGNITY. And this Value of him by the Common-wealth, is understood, by offices of Command, Judicature, publike Employment; or by Names and Titles, introduced for distinction of such Value.

To pray to another, for ayde of any kind, is to HONOUR; because a signe we have an opinion he has power to help; and the more difficult the ayde is, the more is the Honour.

To obey, is to Honour; because no man obeyes them, whom they think have no power to help, or hurt them. And consequently to disobey, is to Dishonour.

To give great gifts to a man, is to Honour him; because 'tis buying of Protection, and acknowledging of Power. To give little gifts, is to Dishonour; because it is but almes, and signifies an opinion of the need of small helps.

To be sedulous in promoting another's good; also to flatter, is to Honour; as a signe we seek his protection or ayde. To neglect, is to Dishonour.

To give way, or place to another, in any Commodity, is to Honour; being a confession of greater power. To arrogate, is to Dishonour.

To shew any signe of love, or feare of another, is to Honour, for both to love, and
to feare, is to value. To contemne, or lesse to love or feare, then he expects, is to
Dishonour; for 'tis undervaluing.

To praise, magnifie, or call happy, is to Honour; because nothing but goodnesse,
power and felicity is valued. To revile, mock, or pity, is to Dishonour.

To speak to another with consideration, to appear before him with decency, and
humility, is to Honour him; as signes of fear to offend. To speak to him rashly, to do
any thing before him obscenely, slovenly, impudently, is to Dishonour.

To believe, to trust, to rely on another, is to Honour him; signe of opinion of his
vertue and power. To distrust, or not to believe, is to Dishonour.

To hearken to a man's counsell, or discourse of what kind soever, is to Honour; as
a signe we think him wise, or eloquent, or witty. To sleep, or go forth, or talk the
while is to Dishonour.

To do those things to another, which he takes for signes of Honour, or which the
law or Custome makes so, is to Honour; because in approving the Honour done
by others, he acknowledgeth the power which others acknowledge. To refuse to do
them, is to Dishonour.

To agree with in opinion, is to Honour; as being a signe of approving his judgement,
and wisdome. To dissent, is a Dishonour, and an upbraiding of errour; and (if the
dissent be in many things) of folly.

To imitate, is to Honour; for it is vehemently to approve. To imitate one's Enemy,
is to Dishonour.

To honour those another honours, is to Honour him; as a signe of approbation of
his judgement. To honour his Enemies, is to Dishonour him.

To employ in counsell, or in actions of difficulty, is to Honour; as a signe of opinion
of his wisdome, or other power. To deny employment in the same cases, to those
that seek it, is to Dishonour.

All these ways of Honouring, are naturall; and as well within, as without Common-
wealths. But in Common-wealths, where he, or they that have the supreme Authority,
can make whatever they please, to stand for signes of Honour, there be other Honours.
A Sovereigne doth Honour a Subject, with whatsoever Title, or Office, or Employment,
or Action, that he himselfe will have taken for a signe of his will to Honour him. [...]

Honourable is whatsoever possession, action, or quality, is an argument and signe
of Power.

And therefore To be Honoured, loved, or feared of many, is Honourable; as arguments of power. To be Honoured of few or none, *Dishonourable*.

Dominion, and victory is Honourable; because acquired by Power; and servitude,
for need, or feare, is Dishonourable.

Blaise Pascal (1623–1662)

Pascal, in contrast with Hobbes, is only interested in the ontological anchorage of human dignity. It does not come from the outside, is not a physical force, but consists in our ability to think, to disregard all pressures from without, such as political pressures or expectations, and everything not worthy of attention. It has nothing to do with the state, with political power or with any means to excert it. It has everything to do with the ability to prevent unimportant things dominating the human being and impeding its command of itself. The centring of importance on the interiority of the human subject affiliates Pascal to the modern project, on which Descartes also worked, of founding philosophy in the subject.

Pensées

The French text is taken from Pascal: *Œuvres Complètes*, Gallimard, Paris, 2000. Translations are my own.

104 (348 (Brunschweig), 113 (Lafume) and 145 (Sellier)).

Roseau pensant.
Ce n'est point de l'espace que je dois chercher ma **dignité**, mais c'est du règlement de ma pensée. Je n'aurais point d'avantage en possédant des terres. Par l'espace, l'univers me comprend et m'engloutit comme un point; par la pensée, je le comprends.

Thinking reed.
It is not from space that I must seek my **dignity**, but in the ruling of my thought. I should not have more dignity if I possessed lands. By means of space, the universe contains me and engulfs me like a point; by means of thought, I comprehend the universe.

186 (347 (Brunschweig), 200 (Lafume) and 231 (Sellier)).

L'homme n'est qu'un roseau, le plus faible de la nature, mais c'est un roseau pensant. Il ne faut pas que l'univers entier s'arme pour l'écraser: une vapeur, une goutte d'eau suffit pour le tuer. Mais quand l'univers l'écraserait, l'homme serait encore plus noble que ce qui le tue puisqu'il sait qu'il meurt et l'avantage que l'univers a sur lui, l'univers n'en sait rien.

Man is only a reed, the feeblest thing in nature; but a thinking reed. It is not necessary for the whole universe to arm itself to crush him: a vapour, a drop of water is sufficient to kill him. Even if the universe crushed him, man would still be nobler than the thing that destroys him, since he knows that he is dying. The advantage that the universe has over him is unknown to it.

Toute notre **dignité** consiste donc en la pensée. C'est de là qu'il faut nous relever et non de l'espace et de la durée, que nous ne saurions remplir.

All our **dignity** therefore lies in thought. It is by means of thought that we must raise ourselves and not by means of space or time, which we can never fill.

Travaillons donc à bien penser: voilà le principe de la morale.

Let us therefore work to think well: this is the first principle of morality.

527(146 (Brunschweig), 620 (Lafume) and 513 (Sellier)).

L'homme est visiblement fait pour penser. C'est toute sa **dignité** et tout son mérite; et tout son devoir est de penser comme il faut. Or l'ordre de la pensée est de commencer par soi, et par son auteur et sa fin.

Man is obviously made to think; it is the entirety of his **dignity** and of his merit, and his whole duty is to think the way he should. Now the order of thought is to begin with oneself, and with its author and one's end.

636 (365 (Brunschweig), 756 (Lafume) and 626 (Sellier))

Pensée.
Toute la dignité de l'homme est en la pensée. Mais qu'est-ce que cette pensée? Qu'elle est sotte!
La pensée est donc une chose admirable et incomparable par sa nature. Il fallait qu'elle eût d'étranges défauts pour être méprisable, mais elle en a de tels que rien n'est plus ridicule. Qu'elle est grande par sa nature! Qu'elle est basse par ses défauts!

Thought.
Man's whole dignity resides in thought. But what is this thought? It is so silly!
Thought is therefore, according to its nature, marvellous and incomparable. It would have to have strange faults to be contemptible; but it does indeed have such that nothing is more ridiculous. How great is thought by nature! How base it is in its faults!

Samuel Pufendorf (1632–1694)

How to mediate in practice between the approaches of Hobbes and Pascal, between political realism and anthropological idealism? The legal theorist Pufendorf avoids the theoretical problem by following Grotius' lead and describing the character that accounts for the special dignity normally accorded to all humans. In this, he reaches back to a tradition lying well before the Reformation and the resulting mistrust in religious explanations. What he concludes from his classical understanding of human dignity, however, may be particularly modern, namely that being obliged to conform to positive law is in accordance with human dignity. This is a thought adopted by Kant in such a way as to quasi abolish the difference between positive law and justice and lodge the reason for both in the categorical imperative, in human dignity.

De Jure Naturae et Gentium (1673)

Text from *De Jure naturae et gentium Libro octo*, Publications of the Carnegie Endowment for International Peace, The Classics of International Law, Volume I, Photographic Reproduction of the Edition of 1688, with an Introduction by Simons Walter. Translation from Volume II by Oldfather C. H. and Oldfather W. A. (Oxford: Clarendon Press, 1934).

I, III, 1

Ex hoc igitur **dignitas hominus** prae brutis maxime elucet, quod iste nobilissima praeditus est anima, quae et insigni lumine circa cognoscendas et dijudicandas res, et exquisita mobilitate circa easdem adpetendas aut rejiciendas pollet

Now the **dignity of man** far outshines that of beasts by virtue of the fact that he has been endowed with a most exalted soul, which, by its highly developed understanding, can examine into things and judge between them, and, by its remarkable deftness, can embrace or reject them.

2, I, 5

Enimvero quare Creator ejusmodi exlegem licentiam hominibus noluerit concedere, et quare eadem istis nullo modo conveniat, plures rationes adparent, ex conditione naturae humanae, primigenia aut post superveniente resultantes. Requirebat **humanae naturae dignitas**, et praestantia, quae caeteras animantes eminet, ut certam ad normam ipsus actiones exigeretur, quippe citra quam ordo, décor, aut pulchritudo intelligi nequit. Maxima inde homini **dignatio**, quod animam obtinet immortalem, lumine intellectus, facultate res dijudicandi, et eligendi praeditam, et in plurimas artes solertissimam	Now why the Creator was unwilling to endow man with a lawless liberty of this kind [of the animals], and why such a liberty would be utterly inappropriate to him, is clear for many reasons drawn from the natural or acquired condition of human nature. The **dignity of man's nature**, and that excellence of his, in which he surpasses other creatures, required that his actions should be made to conform to a definite rule without which there can be no recognition of order, seemliness or beauty. And so man has that supreme **dignity**, the possesion of an immortal soul, furnished with the light of intellect and the faculty of judgement and choice, and most highly endowed for many an art.

Anne Finch Conway (1631–1679)

Principles of the Most Ancient and Modern Philosophy

Anne Conway's text authored in close proximity with the Cambridge Platonists recalls Pico della Mirandola's not only in content but also in that it is inspired by the 'ancient wisdom of the Hebrews'. Perhabs the husbandry experience of breeding animals or cultivating plant species lies behind her insistence on every (sub-)species having the opportunity to become perfected as well as the possibility of degeneration. Whatever originates her radical (?) ideas, she admits of only three species of things – God, Christ and creatures. Like Pico, Conway affirms that the dignity of the human being can be forfeited ontologically by the person's own brutish behaviour to the point of species change, but, again like Pico, she does not consider any legal implications, which would be the first the lawyers inspired by

Cicero would think of. Is the species change enviseaged the change into Christ, and hence divinisation (and correspondingly a change away from Christlikeness an embrace of the brutish state)? If so, her theories are less without rapport to the tradition than a superficial glance might entice one to think. There are also eccoes of microcosmism in them which links them with previous thinkers such as Eriugena. Even so, her concept of species remains unusual, since it seems to be applicable on various levels, but ultimately restricted to the three already mentioned. The easiness with which she imagines species change makes her a forerunner for the theories concerning descent later advanced by Goethe, Mendel and Darwin.

Text taken from Karen J. Warren: *An Unconventional History of Western Philosophy. Conversations Between Men and Women Philosophers* (Lanham, MD: Rowman and Littlefield, 2009), pp. 263–76. The whole unedited text is available electronically at <http://digital.library.upenn.edu/women/conway/principles/principles.html> (accessed 14 September 2018).

Chapter 6

§.1. Since all creatures are mutable in respect to their natures, the difference between God and nature, rightly considered, is clearly demonstrated by daily experience. [...]

§.2. Now let us consider the extent of this mutability. First, can one individual be changed into another, either of the same or of a different species? I say that this is impossible [...]

§.3. Furthermore, we must ask whether one species can change into another. [...] species are nothing but individual entities subsumed under one general and common idea of the mind [...]

§.4. [...] we must now determine how many species of things there are which are distinguished from each other in terms of their substance or essence. If we look closely into this, we will discover there are only three, which, as was said above, are God, Christ and creatures; and that these three species are really distinct in terms of their essence has already been proved. [...] Furthermore, since it agrees with sound reason and with the order of things that just as God is one and does not have two or three or more distinct substances in himself, and just as Christ is one simple Christ without further distinct substances in himself [...] so likewise all creatures, or the whole of creation, are also a single species in substance or essence although it includes many individuals gathered into subordinate species and distinguished from each other modally but not substantially or essentially. Thus, what Paul says about human beings

can also be understood about all creatures [...], namely, that God made all tribes and troops of creatures from one blood. [...]

§.5. [...] There are others, moreover, who multiply specific entities into their own distinct essences and attributes almost to infinity. This altogether upsets that exceptional order of things and quite obscures the glory of the divine attributes so that it cannot shine with its due splendour in creatures. For if a creature were entirely limited by its own individuality and totally constrained and confined within the very narrow boundaries of its own species to the point that there was no mediator through which one creature could change into another, then no creature could attain further perfection and greater participation in divine goodness, nor could creatures act and react upon each other in different ways.

§.6. [...] since the divine power, goodness and wisdom has created good creatures so that they may continually and infinitely move toward the good through their own mutability, the glory of their attributes shines more and more. [...] For the highest excellence of a creature is to be infinite only in potentiality, not in actuality. That is, it is always able to become more perfect and more excellent to infinity although it never reaches this infinity. [...] Nevertheless, individual creatures are only finitely good and finitely distant in terms of species. However, they are also potentially infinite, that is, they are always capable of greater perfection without end. [...] In fact, daily experience teaches us that various species change into each other: earth changes into water, water into air, air into fire or ether and, vice versa [...] and these are nevertheless distinct species. [...]

§.7. We already saw how the justice of God shines so gloriously in the transmutation of one species into another. For it is most certain that a kind of justice operates not only in human beings and angels but also in all creatures. [...] This justice appears as much in the ascent of creatures as in their descent, that is, when they change for the better or the worse. [...] Therefore, there is a certain justice in all these things, so that in the very transmutation from one species to another, either by ascending from a lower to a higher or by descending in the opposite way, the same justice appears. [...]

§.8. [...] If it is said that **the dignity and nobility of human nature** is diminished and sullied when it is decreed that the body and the soul is to be turned into the nature of a brute, one may reply according to the common axiom, 'the worst corruption is that of the beast.' For when a human being has so greatly degraded himself by his own wilful wrongdoing and has brought his nature, which had been so noble, to a lower state, and when that nature has demeaned itself in spirit to the level of a most foul brute or animal so that it is wholly ruled by lust and earthly desires and becomes like any beast, indeed, worse than any beast, what injustice is this if God compels him to bear the same image in his body as in that spirit into which he has internally transformed himself? Or which degradation do you think is worse, to have the image of a beast in one's spirit or body?

CHAPTER 9

The Enlightenment and its Discontents

The same trends as are operative during the Renaissance and the Baroque period continue into the age of Rococo, adding a dash of romanticism on the one hand and of fashion and artifice on the other. Beneath the sheen, however, more serious forces coil up and express themselves in the hankering for simplicity and straightforward normality. The lack of opportunity for advancement of women through a university education or the professions, coupled with the aesthetic ideal of coquettish idleness, leads to vindication of women's rights to education and access to the professions. In connection with this, we can observe the 'rights language' being fully in place. We also see the two-streamed Renaissance tradition for alternately depreciating and extolling human dignity now having a resurgence in the English literary world (and later in the German), where it takes the form of satires on human nature on the one hand and critiques of these as an insult against 'the dignity of human nature' (Goldgar, 1965) on the other. Hobbes was classified as a satirist in this regard, and Hume represents the view that it is more advantageous to humankind to praise its dignity than to denigrate it. Wesley's defence of the doctrine of original sin was probably dressed up to take part in the satirist tradition by an anonymous pamphleteer, but Zollikofer's contribution, a two-volume collection of sermons on human dignity, purposefully and elegantly sums up both genres.

Martin Martin (?–1718)

Martin's text forms part of the significant body of travel writings of the seventeenth and eighteenth centuries. An early forerunner of romanticism, he praises the simple life of the islanders with whom he sojourns, as expressive of human dignity.

A voyage to St Kilda (1698)

Text from *A voyage to St Kilda the remotest of all the Hebrides; or, Western Isles of Scotland. Giving an account of the very remarkable inhabitants of that place; their Beauty and singular Chastity: (Fornication and Adultery being unknown among them) their genius for Poetry, Musick, Dancing; their surprising Dexterity in climbing the Rocks and Walls of Houses; Diversions, Habits, Food, Language, Diseases and Methods of Cure; their extensive Charity; their Contempt of Gold and Silver as below the* **Dignity of Human Nature;** *their religious Ceremonies, Notions of Spirits and Visions etc etc.* (London: printed for R. Griffith, at the Dunciad in Ludgate Street, 1749) (3rd edn, 1st edn 1698), available in Eighteenth Century Collections Online (accessed 2 November 2017).

> The inhabitants of St. Kilda are much happier than the Generality of Mankind, as being almost the only People in the World who feel the Sweetness of true Liberty: What the Condition of the People in the golden Age is feigned by the Poets to be, that theirs really is; I mean in Innocency and Simplicity, Purity, mutual Love, and cordial Friendship, free from solicitous Cares and anxious Covetousness; from Envy, Deciet, and Dissimulation; from Ambition and Pride, and the Consequences that attend them. They are altogether ignorant of the vices of Foreigners, and governed by the Dictates of Reason and Christianity, as it was first delivered to them by those heroic Souls, whose Zeal moved them to undergo Danger and Trouble to plant Religion here in one of the remotest Corners of the World.
>
> There is this only wanting to make them the happiest People in this habitable Globe, viz. that they themselves do not know how happy they are, and how much they are above the Avarice and Slavery of the rest of Mankind. Their Way of living makes them contemn Gold and Silver, as below the **Dignity of human Nature**; they live by the munificence of Heaven, and have no Designs upon one another, but such as are purely suggested by Justice and Benevolence.

Sophia (Lady Mary Wortley Montagu 1689–1762 or Lady Sophia Fermor 1724–1745)

Woman not Inferior to Man (1739)

Outside St Kilda, in the world Martin left behind, people certainly had designs upon one another. Sophia demonstrates not only that vindication now had become a political possibility but also that the competition between various traditions of dignity made itself felt particularly in the life of women. She uses the term of dignity realistically, like Hobbes, to mean usefulness to the state. Whereas to Hobbes, the educated son of a clergyman, there were no incompatibility of the dignity of title and the dignity of office, Sophia observes that women have no access to the universities or to the professions and thus no possibility of acceding to office, despite their dignity as members of the aristocracy. Her treatise vindicates women's ability to participate in public life and become doctors, teachers, lawyers and politicians, something which was no doubt at the time felt to be beneath the dignity of many a courtier, especially women. Sophia's 'rights-language' is modern, and her concept of dignity tied to society's esteem for *useful* services, and not to the ancient privileges of nobility. Sophia speaks for those who could not find sufficient recognition of their activities to understand who they were in the tasks assigned to them: in particular the decorative noblewoman, whose house and children were all in order, and whose idleness left her exposed to the temptations of intrigue and stupidity.

Text from Sophia: *Woman not Inferior to Man, or, A short and modest Vindication of the Natural Right of the Fair Sex to a perfect Equality of Power, Dignity and Esteem with the Men* (London: Fowler's Walk, 1739). Electronically available at: <https://digital.library.lse.ac.uk/objects/ lse:huc485foq> (accessed 30 January 2019). A sequence to the text exists, as 'A Gentleman' in 1744 responded to the treatise by publishing 'Man superior to Woman, or, the Natural Right of the Men to Sovereign Authority over Women', prompting Sophia to riposte by disputing six questions: whether women are held in esteem by men; whether they are inferior to men in their intellectual capacity; whether men are better qualified to

govern than women; whether women are fit for public offices; for teaching science, and for military offices. This latter pamphlet, however, makes no use of 'dignity' or etymologically related words.

p. 10

> If, upon mature consideration, it appears that there are no other differences between Men and Us than what their tyranny has created, it will appear how unjust they are in excluding us from that power and **dignity** we have a right to share with them; how ungenerous in denying us the equality of esteem, which is our due; and how little reason they have to triumph in the base possession of an authority, which unnatural violence, and lawless usurpation put into their hands.

Sophia explains that women are considered of so little dignity in society because the services they provide are 'so frequent and so usual' (p. 15). It is in other words a version of 'familiarity breeds contempt' that keeps them underesteemed. They are kept in servitude because of

p. 27–8

> the same sordid selfishness, which urged them [men] to engross all power and **dignity** to themselves, [and] prompted them to shut up from us that knowledge which would have made us their competitors.

Having shown that women have equal capacities with men – yet perhaps less ambition, which she ascribes to their modesty – she concludes that men have no right to arrogate all dignity and all public offices to themselves:

p. 48

> We may easily conclude then that if our sex, as it hitherto appears, have all the talents requisite to learn and teach those sciences, which qualify men for power and **dignity**, they are equally capable of applying their knowledge to practice, in exercising that power and **dignity**.

David Hume (1711–1776)

Hume reflects on the advantage of either magnifying or depreciating human nature and comes down decisively on the side of the former. He thus situates himself in the eighteenth-century debate about the dignity of human nature with satirists on the opposite side. Is his concern political or ontological in nature? Despite rhetorics and appearance, probably, like Hobbes', chief among the satirists, political. They both contribute to the secular tradition, which emphasises political status and the relative independence of the political realm vis-à-vis ontology.

Of the Dignity and Meanness of Human Nature (1758)

Essays. Moral Political and Literary, ed. Eugene Miller' (Indianapolis: Liberty Classics, 1987) pp. 80–6.

Essay XI

There are certain sects, which secretly form themselves in the learned world, as well as factions in the political; and though sometimes they come not to an open rupture, they give a different turn to the ways of thinking of those who have taken part on either side. The most remarkable of this kind are the sects, founded on the different sentiments with regard to the *dignity of human nature*; which is a point that seems to have divided philosophers and poets as well as divines, from the beginning of the world to this day. Some exalt our species to the skies, and represent man as a kind of human demigod [...]. Others insist upon the blind sides of human nature, and can discover nothing, except vanity, in which man surpasses the other animals [...]. If an author possess the talent of rhetoric and declamation, he commonly takes part with the former: if his turn lie towards irony and ridicule, he naturally throws himself into the other extreme.

I am far from thinking, that all those, who have depreciated our species, have been enemies to virtue, and have exposed the frailties of their fellow creatures with any bad intention. [...] I must, however, be of opinion, that the sentiments of those, who are inclined to think favourably of mankind, are more advantageous to virtue, than the contrary principles, which give us a mean opinion of our nature. When a man is prepossessed with a high notion of his rank and character in the creation, he

will naturally endeavour to act up to it, and will scorn to do a base or vicious action, which might sink him below that figure which he makes in his own imagination. [...]

In forming our notions of human nature, we are apt to make a comparison between men and animals, the only creatures endowed with thought that fall under our senses. Certainly, this comparison is favourable to mankind. [...]

There are two means commonly employed to destroy this conclusion: First, by making an unfair representation of the case, and insisting only upon the weakness of human nature. And secondly, by forming a new and secret comparison between man and beings of the most perfect wisdom. Among the other excellencies of man, this is one, that he can form an idea of perfections much beyond what he has experience of in himself; and is not limited in his conception of wisdom and virtue. He can easily exalt his notions and conceive a degree of knowledge, which, when compared with his own, will make the latter appear very contemptible, and will cause the difference between that and the sagacity of animals, in a manner, to disappear and vanish. Now this being a point, in which all the world is agreed, that human understanding falls infinitely short of perfect wisdom; it is proper we should know when this comparison takes place, that we may not dispute where there is no real difference in our sentiments. Man falls much more short of perfect wisdom, and even of his own ideas of perfect wisdom, than animals do of man; yet the latter difference is so considerable, that nothing but a comparison with the former can make it appear of little moment.

John Wesley (1703–1791)

'The Dignity of Human Nature' (1762)

(London, 1762) Eighteenth Century Collections Online (accessed 2 November 2017). Is this an in fact anonymous pamphlet reproducing the first part of Wesley's *The Doctrine of Original Sin* (Bristol, 1757) under an ironic title, as Goldgar suggests (1965, note 12)? Green's bibliography of John and Charles Wesley (1906, no. 210) states the title is given in sarcasm, and that the final sentence here reproduced has been added, but that it has not been possible for him to determine the circumstances leading to the publication. It remains that the publications are identical except for the title and the addition at the end concerning the dignity of human nature (pp. 28 and 58).

From the Israelites to the Indians, over the 'moscovites' and the 'mahometians' to the Christians of various denominations; of human nature only this can be said:

> how amazingly ignorant! How totally devoid of civil and sacred wisdom! How shockingly savage in both their tempers and manners! Their idolatry is of the basest and vilest kind. [...]

> Still, then, sin is the baleful source of affliction. And consequently the flood of miseries, which covers the face of the earth, which overwhelms not only single persons, but whole families, Towns, Cities, Kingdoms, is a demonstrative proof of the overflowing of ungodliness, in every nation under heaven. Such (if we can believe our eyes, ears, or experience) is the present *Dignity of Human Nature*! (pp. 28, 58)

To the extent that the last sentence was added to a justification of the doctrine of original sin, what results may have been intended to ridicule, and in that case, the intent could hardly have been his. Whatever the case may be: Wesley was in fact a strong supporter of the abolition of slavery, something that in the contemporary sense of the expression would entail he had a high regard for human dignity. Abolitionism, in fact, will contribute importantly to the forging of the expression into a constitutional principle.

Georg Joachim Zollikofer (1730–1788)

Zollikofer's sermons must be seen in the same context as the satire on Wesley and Hume's distinction between two tendencies: that of the double stream of literature satirising or extolling the dignity of human nature. However, here we have a full, very carefully structured, treatise length treatment of the subject in homiletic form. The sermons enjoyed great success to judge from Heydenreich's response and Tooke's translation of them. They represent in substance what was probably for the epoch a very common reasoned Christian understanding of human dignity. In contrast with Hobbes and Hume, there is an interest in the ontological or theological foundation of it. There is also an inclusion of an explanation of the misery of the human condition.

The work is in two volumes. Sermon 1–3 of the first volume consist of reflections directly concerned with what human dignity is: the first addresses wherein the dignity of man consists, the second what stands in opposition to human dignity and the third how and by what means Christianity restores human dignity. These three sermons are excerpted below. The remaining sermons treat of the value of various aspects of human life (life, health, wealth, honour, pleasure, etc.), all valuable because of human dignity. Although human dignity is therefore not directly linked to legal aspects, the treatise as a whole provides a foundation for law, since it gives an account of what values ought to be respected by the law that is in conformity with or relying on human dignity.

Towards the end of the extracts, a reference to Leo the Great in combination with the terminology of the outgoing epoch ties the treatise to the earliest beginnings of the Christian tradition for conceptualising human dignity.

Sermons on the Dignity of Man (1783)

Text from *Predigten Über die Würde des Menschen und den Werth der vornehmsten Dinge die zur menschlichen Glückseligkeit gehöhren, oder dazu gerechnet werden*, Bd. 1 (Leipzig, 1788) 1st edn 1783, Nabu public Domain reprints. Translated into English by William Tooke as *Sermons on the Dignity of Man and the value of the objects principally relating to human happiness* (London: printed by A. Strahan for T. N. Longman and O. Rees, 1802). The abreviations in the German text (e.g. M. A. Z.) are remnants of the homiletic form and stands for addresses like 'meine achtete Zuhöhrer'. They have not been included by the translator.

Sermon I–III, extracts

I. Worin besteht die **Würde des Menschen**? Wir können den Menschen von zwo verschiedenen Seiten betrachten, M. A. Z. Von der einen ist er sehr eingeschränkt, schwach, fehlerhaft; scheint wenig vor den

I. Wherein the **Dignity of Man** consists Man may be considered in two different ways. In one way we find him a very limited, feeble, and defective being, little superior, at best, to the beasts of the field

Thieren des Feldes voraus zu haben [...] Von der anderen Seite zeiget er die schönsten, größten Anlagen und Fähigkeiten; äußert Kräfte, die ihn weit über die ganze leblose und thierische Schöpfung erheben [...] Von der einen Seite betrachtet, scheint die menschliche Natur ein Gegenstand des Mitleidens zu seyn, und dem, der sie so betrachtet, allen Mut zu benehmen und alle Ansprüche auf **Würde** und Große für Einbildungen einens sinnlichen Stolzes zu erklären: von der anderen Seite scheint sie die größte Achtung und Ehrerbietung zu verdienen, und denjenigen, der sie aus diesem Gesichtspunkte sich vorstellet, weit über alles, was um ihn her ist, zu erheben, und ihn zu allem was groß und edel ist, fähig und **würdig** zu machen. Und von welcher Seite, M. A. Z, sollen wir uns nun den Menschen vorstellen? Ohne Zweifel müssen wir ihn von beyden kennen lernen, wenn wir ihn und seine Bestimmung richtig beurtheilen, wenn wir weder stolz noch mutlos, weder verwegen noch versagt seyn sollen.

Inzwischen glaube ich doch, daß die menschliche Natur von ihrer schönen und guten Seite nicht oft genug betrachtet wird, und doch öfter von dieser, als von der entgegengesetzten, betrachtet werden sollte. [...] Auch wird gewiß der Mensch, der sich daran gewöhnet, sich mehr von dieser, als von jener Seite zu betrachten, weit richtiger urtheilen, weit edler denken, weit besser und tugendhafter handeln, als derjenige, der das Gefühl seiner Niedrigkeit und Schwäche herrschend bey sich werben läßt. Wohlan, M. A. Z, wir wollen die Vorstellungsart wählen, die uns am meisten nützen und die Seligkeit verspricht. Wir wollen die **Würde des Menschen** betrachten. [...]

[...] Considered in another light, he discovers the fairest dispositions, and the greatest capacities. Look at the effects of his external force; they indicate a being far more elevated than the inanimate or the animal creation. [...] Considered on one side, human nature appears an object of compassion. And they who thus view it, take all possible pains to dismay us by derision, by representing our pretentions to **dignity** as the fancies of a foolish pride. On the other side, man seems to merit the greatest esteem and veneration. And such as regard him in this light, exalt him far above all surrounding creatures, make him capable of every **excellence**, and fitted for the highest grandeur. Now, in which way shall we contemplate man? Doubtless, we should study and understand him in both, if we would judge rightly of the ends for which he is made; if we would neither be rash through pride, nor disheartened by conscious abasement.

It seems to me, however, as if human nature was not frequently enough considered on its fair and advantageous side; though it should oftener be so than the other. [...] the man that accustoms himself to consider human nature rather on this side than the other, will judge far more rightly, think far more nobly, act far better and more virtuously, than he who suffers the sentiment of his meanness and imperfections to ever be before him. Well then; we will chuse the representation that promises us the most advantage and the greatest happiness. We will consider the **dignity of man**. [...]

Durch die **Würde des Menschen** verstehen wir überhaupt alles, was seine Natur, sein Zustand, seine Bestimmung vorzüglich Großes und Ehrwürdiges an sich haben; alles was ihm in der Augen Gottes und aller verständigen Wesen einen vorzüglichen Werth giebt. Eine **Würde,** worauf sich das innere edle Gefühl seiner Kräfte und Vorzüge gründet, und die sich durch die erhabene Sinnes- und Handelnsart äußert, die ihm eigen ist; eine **Würde,** die uns die Lobpreisung des Psalmisten einstimmen heißt, der in unserem Terte Zu Gott saget: *Du hast den Menschen nur auf eine kurze Zeit geringer macht als den Engel; aber mit Ehre und Pracht hast du ihn gekrönet.*

Worin besteht also die **Würde des Menschen?** Oder was giebt ihm den **Werth,** den er hat? Und wie und wodurch äußert sich seine **Würde?** Oder, was bringt sie in ihm und außer ihm hervor? Dies sind die Hauptfragen, die wir hier zu beantworten haben.

Verstand, Freyheit, Thätigkeit, immer zunehmende Vollkommenheit, Unsterblichkeit, das Verhältniß, in welchen er gegen Gott, und gegen seinen Sohn Jesum steht, die Stelle, die er auf dem Erdboden einnimmt, und das, was er in Absicht auf denselben ist und thut; das machet die **Würde des Menschen** aus, das giebt ihm seinen vorzüglichen großen Werth.

Verstand und Vernunft adeln den Menschen. Dies ist der erste und vornehmste Grund seiner **Würde.** Dies erhebt ihn weit über alle andere Geschöpfe des Erdbodens. Dadurch wird er zum Verwandten der Engel; dadurch schwingt er sich bis zur Gottheit empor. Er ist nicht ganz Fleisch, nicht ganz sinnlich, nicht gleich den Thieren des Feldes und diese

By the **dignity of man,** we are, in general, to understand, whatever is eminently great and honourable in his nature, his situation, and his vocation; all that gives him an eminent value in the sight of God and of all rational beings. A **dignity** which is grounded on his intrinsically noble and generous sentiments, his privileges, and his powers, and is displayed in the excellency of intellect and power of action peculiar to him. A **dignity** which forces from us some such exclamations to the deity as those of the Psalmist: 'Thou hast made him a little lower than the angels, and hast crowned him with glory and honour!'

Wherein, then, does the **dignity of man** consist? Or what gives him the **dignity** he has? And how and whereby does he exhibit his **dignity?** – These are the principal questions we have now to answer.

Understanding, freedom, activity, an always progressive perfection, immortality, the relation in which he stands towards God, and towards his son Jesus, the station he fills on the earth, and what he is and does in regards to all these: this composes the **dignity of man;** this gives him his eminently great worth.

Man is ennobled by understanding and reason. These form the first and chief ground of his **dignity.** These exalt him far above all the other creatures of the earth. By these he is related with spiritual beings; by these he takes flight to the regions above and soars to the seat of God. He is neither altogether material nor altogether spirit; not, like the beasts of the field, attached

Erde geheftet, nicht gleich ihnen unfähig, den Eindrücken der äußern Dinge zu wiederstehen. Er kann seine Augen in die Hohe richten, und sich mit seinem Geiste über alles Irdische und Sichtbare erheben: er kann sich besinnen; sich selbst von allem, was außer ihm ist, und seine Gedanken von dem, was in ihm denket, unterscheiden; kann die Vergangenheit, die Gegenwart und die Zukunft in seinen Vorstellungen von einander absondern; hat ein inniges, klares Bewußtseyn seines Daseins und seiner Wirkungen; kann nach den Ursachen und Absichten der Dinge forschen, ihre Verhältnisse gegen einander untersuchen, sie in ihrer Verbindung und in ihrer Folge übersehen, und aus dem, was er kennet und sieht, in tausend Fällen mit Sicherheit auf dasjenige schliessen, was er noch nicht kennet und nicht sieht. [...]

Freyheit, M. A. Z., moralische Freyheit ist ein anderer charakteristischer Zug des Menschen, ein anderer Grund seiner **Würde**. Wenn Sonne, Mond und Sterne, und die ganze Körperwelt, nach mechanischen, ihnen unbekannten Gesetzen wirken und sich bewegen; wenn das Thier blinden, unwiderstehlichen Trieben folget, und ganz von den Eindrücken der außern Dinge abhängt; so ist der Mensch weder jenen Gesetzen, noch diesen Trieben schlecherdings unterworfen. Er kann jene Gesetze in Absicht auf seine Bewegungen und Handlungen auf tausenderlen Art einschränken, verändern, aufheben: er kann diesen Trieben widerstehen und sie gänzlich bezwingen. Er kann überlegen, vergleichen, wählen, Entschlüsse fassen, seine Entschlüsse ausführen, sie wieder fahren lassen und mit andern vertauschen.

to the earth; not incapable, like them, of resisting the impression of external things. He can lift his eyes on high, and roam in the spirit above terrestrial and visible objects: he can investigate himself; distinguish himself from every thing around him, and secern his thoughts from that which thinks within him; he can discriminate the past, the present, and the future in the conceptions of his capacious mind; has an inward and clear consciousness of his existence and his actions; can inquire into the causes and motives of events, investigate their proportion and affinity with each other, view their connections and consequences; and, from what he knows and sees, can judge in a thousand cases of what he knows and sees not yet. [...]

Freedom, moral freedom, is another characteristic of man; another source of his **dignity**. While the sun, the moon, the stars, and all the host of heaven, move and act and revolve in the regions of space by mechanical laws unknown to them; while the animals blindly pursue their irresistible instincts, and are entirely dependent on impressions from without; man is not absolutely subjected to those laws, nor impelled by these instincts. He can control, alter, or decline these laws in a thousand different ways, in regard to his motions and actions: he can withstand, or totally surmount these instincts. He can consider, compare, select, resolve, execute his resolves, or relinquish and change them for others. He distinguishes truth from error, good from bad, and semblance from reality; suffers not himself to be imposed on by every spe-

Er unterscheidet Wahrheit und Irrthum, Gutes und Böses, Schein und Wirklichkeit von einander; läßt sich nicht von jedem vorübergehenden Schimmer, von jedem betrüglichen Glanze, von jeder reizenden oder fürchterlichen Gestalt täuschen; bleibt nicht bey dem gegenwärtigen Augenblicke stehen; sieht auf die entferntern Folgen der Dinge; und darf weder den Aussprüchen seiner Sinne, noch einem dunkeln, innern Gefühle blindlings folgen. Er wählet und thut das, was er für recht und gut, für das Beste im jedem Falle erkennet; er verwirft und flieht das, was er für unrecht und böse, für überwiegend schädlich hält; und richtet sich bey dieser Wahl und bey diesem Verhalten blos nach den Einsichten seines Verstandes, nach dem Lichte seiner Vernunft. Freylich können ihn diese Einsichten oft trügen; dieses Licht kann ihn zuweilen irreführen. Aber auch dann ist ihm der Weg zur Rückkehr nicht verschlossen. Er kann seines Betrugs gewahr werden, seinen Irrthum erkennen, seine Wahl bereuen, sein Verhalten ändern, und durch diese traurigen Erfahrungen noch vorsichtiger und freyer handeln lernen. So leitet, so führet, so beherrschet er sich selbst, und gewissermaßen auch die äußern Dinge, die ihn umgeben. So ist er weder ein blindes Triebrad in dem Weltsysteme, noch ein Sklave seiner eigenen Sinne, noch ein Spiel äußerer Ursachen und Zufälle. So thut er nicht anders als was er will, und nichts kann ihn zwingen, etwas anders zu wollen, als was er jedesmal für das beste hällt. Und welche Vorzüge muß ihm das nicht vor der ganzen leblosen sowohl, als vor der blos empfindenden, aber nicht vernünftig denkenden Schöpfung geben! Welchen Werth, welche **Würde** müssen nicht alle seine

cious outside, every deceitful lustre, every desirable or terrific appearance: he stops not at the present moment; sees to the remotest consequences of things; and is neither necessitated blindly to trust the informations of his senses, nor implicitly to follow his feelings as they arise. He chuses and does that which he finds to be right and good, and best for the occasion; he rejects and avoids that which he holds to be unjust and base, or productive of more harm than good; and directs himself in his choice and his conduct, by the perceptions of his intellect, by the light of his reason. These perceptions indeed may often deceive him; this light may sometimes lead him astray. But then the way is not shut to his return. He can discover the deceit, be aware of his error, repent of his mistake, alter his conduct, and learn by these sad experiences to act more prudently and more cautiously in the future. He thus guides, directs and governs himself according to the circumstances of external things. Thus, he is neither a blind rotatory being in the system of the universe, nor the slave of his own judgement, nor the sport of outward causes and events. Thus, he does nothing but what he wills, and nothing can compel him to will any thing but what he at this time holds for the best. And what a high privilege does this give him over all the inanimate as well as the merely sensitive but irrational creation! What importance, what **dignity** must all his conclusions and actions acquire from hence, that they are peculiarly his own resolutions, his own actions, the principles, aims, consistency, and connection whereof he knows, and can give an account of to himself and to others! How much more valuable must one single good action of a

Entschlüsse und Handlungen dadurch bekommen, daß es recht eigentlich *seine* Entschlüsse und *seine* Handlungen sind, deren Gründe, deren Absichten, deren Entstehung und Verbindung er weiss, von den er sich und anderen Rechenschaft geben kann! Wie viel mehr muß nicht eine einzige gute That des Menschen werth seyn, als der ganze wohlthätige Einfluß, den die Sonne, ihrer selbst, und ihrer Wirkungen unbewußt, über ganze Welten verbreitet!

Thätigkeit, die mannigfaltigste, unermü-deteste Thätigkeit, ist ein dritter charac-teristischer Zug des Menschen, ein dritter Grund seiner **Würde**. Freylich ist alles in der Natur in unaufhörlicher Bewegung und Wirksamkeit; das Leblose wie das Lebendige, die thierische wie die vernünf-tige Welt. Alles ist und hat Kraft, und jede Kraft wirket das, was sie wirken kann und soll. Gänzliche Unthätigkeit, unbeweg-liche Trägheit, völliger Tod scheinen aus der Schöpfung Gottes verbannet zu seyn. Aber wo finden wir größere und mannig-faltigere Thätigkeit als bey den Menschen? Und wo Thätigkeit mit Bewußtseyn, mit Überlegung, mit Absichten, als nur bey ihm? Wann höhret der menschliche Geist auf, zu denken? Und wie schnell, wie zahl-los folgen seine Gedanken nach einander! Wann höhret er auf, Veränderungen in sich und außer sich hervorzubringen? Und wie mannigfaltig, wie groß sind nicht diese Veränderungen! Wie viel Gutes, wie viel Böses, wie viel gemeinnützliches, wie viel Gemeinschädliches, bringt nicht oft Ein Gedanke, Ein Wort, Ein Blik, Eine Miene, Eine Bewegung des Menschen hervor! Und wie weit, wie unermäßlich verbreitet sich nicht der Einfluß dessen, was er thut,

man be, than the whole benign influence of the sun, unconscious of itself and of all its effects, diffused throughout the system.

Activity, the most diversified, the most indefatigable activity, is a third character-istic of man, a third source of his **dignity**. Indeed, everything in nature is incessantly moving; the inanimate as well as the living, the animal no less than the rational world. Every thing has force, and all force effects what it can and must produce. Perfect inac-tivity, immovable sloth, compleat death, seem to be excluded from the creation of God. But where shall we find greater and more diversified activity than in man? And where activity with consciousness, with reflection, with design, but in him? When does the human spirit cease from thinking? And how rapidly, how innumerably do its thoughts succeed to each other! When does it cease from producing revolutions, various and great, within and without! How much good, how much mischief, how much gen-eral advantage, how much general harm is often occasioned by a thought, a word, a look, a gesture, an emotion of man! And how far, how immensely wide is the influ-ence of what he does extended through time and space! – How various, how con-nected, how intricate, how comprehensive, how extensive are often his occupations and enterprizes! [...]

der Zeit und dem Raume nach! – Wie verschieden, wie zusammengesetzt, wie verwickelt, wie viel umfassend, wie weit ausgehend sind nicht seine Geschäfte und Unternehmungen! [...]

Thut viertes die Fähigkeit, immer weiter zu gehen und immer vollkommener zu werden hinzu, so werdet ihr einen neuen Grund seiner vorzüglichen **Würde** entdecken. Schön ist die Sonne, schön der Mond, schön sind die Sterne, schön die Gewächse und Pflanzen, die unsern Erdboden schmücken; jedes vollkommen und unverbesserlich in seiner Art: aber sie bleiben wie sie sind; ihre Gestalt, ihre Schönheit, ihre Bewegung, ihre Wirksamkeit ist und bleibt immer dieselbe. Sie sind ganz das, was sie seyn soll und kann. Nicht so der Mensch, M.Th.Z. Nie ist er ganz das, was er seyn soll und kann. [...] Eine Stufe der Vollkommenheit führet ihn zur andern, und nie steht er so hoch, daß er nicht noch höher steigen könnte. [...]

Ist er nicht unsterblich? Ja, der Mensch, und dies ist der fünfte Grund seiner **Würde**, der Mensch ist zur Unsterblichkeit bestimmt. Er soll ewig fortdauern, ewig leben, ewig als ein vernünftiges, freyes, höchstthätiges, nach Vollkommenheit strebendes Wesen leben! Unsterblichkeit, M. Th. Fr., ewiges Leben, welch ein Vorzug, welch eine **Würde** ist das nicht! Alle Schönheiten der Natur können dahinwelken und verschwinden, Sonnen und Sterne ihren Schein verlieren, die reichsten Lichtquellen versiegen, die ganze sichtbare Welt in Nacht versinken: der Mensch überlebet sie alle und findet in sich, findet in der Geisterwelt, findet in Gott, dem Vater aller Geister, weit mehr, als ihm die ganze sichtbare Welt geben kann. [...]

Add to this, fourthly, the capacity of continually advancing, and constantly acquiring new degrees of perfection; and you will discover a fresh ground of his pre-eminence and **dignity**. The sun is glorious to behold, fair is the moon, fair are the stars, beautiful the vegetables and plants that adorn the surface of the earth; each of them is good and perfect in its kind: but they remain as they are; their figure, their beauty, their motion, their operation is invariably the same. They are absolutely that which they should and can be. Not so is man. He is never absolutely what he should and can be. [...] One degree of perfection leads him on to another: never stands he so high, but he may ascend still higher. [...]

Is he not immortal? Yes; and this is the fifth source of his **dignity**. Man is designed for immortality. He is to continue without end, to live forever, to live eternally as a rational, free, and active being, as a being continually endeavouring at perfection! – Immortality! everlasting life! what a prerogative, what a **dignity** this is! All the beauties of nature shall fade and perish; the sun and the orbs of heaven shall lose their lustre; the richest sources of light shall be exhausted; the whole visible world shall sink into night: but man survives them all, and finds in himself, in the world of spirits, in God, the father of spirits, far more than all the visible world can give. [...]

Auch ist der Mensch, M. Brüder, und dies erhöhet seine **Würde**, dies setzet sie in ihr volles Licht, der Mensch ist ein Ebenbild Gottes [...] So oft er Wahrheit denket; so oft er Gutes will und wirket; so oft er Ordnung und Schönheit empfindet und befördert; so oft er Liebe und Freude und Seligkeit um sich her verbreitet: so oft denket, und will, und wirket, und empfindet, und handelt er auf eine Gott ähnliche Art; so oft treibe er das Werk seines Schöpfers und Vaters; so oft befordert er die Absichten des obersten Wesens; so oft genießt er etwas von reiner göttlicher Glückseligkeit; und je mehr, je öfter er solches thut, desto heller stralet das Bild der Gottheit an ihm, desto weniger kann man seinen höhern Ursprung und seine **Würde** an ihm verkennen. Dann redet und handelt Gott gleichsam sichtbarer Weise in ihm und durch ihn; giebt durch ihn der Wahrheit Zeugniß; unterrichtet und offenbaret sich durch ihn den Menschen; behauptet durch ihn die Sache der Tugend; spricht durch ihn dem Bekümmerten Trost ein; gießt durch ihn Balsam in das verwundete Herz des Betrübten; reicht durch ihn dem Elenden Hälse und Beystand, dem Hungrigen Brot, dem Schwachen Stärke dar; verschönert durch ihn seine Welt, und bringt mehr Leben und Freude in derselben durch ihn hervor. Und ein solches Werkzeug in der Hand Gottes zu seyn; eine solche Ähnlichkeit mit ihm, dem Allervolkommensten, zu haben; sich so Gott zu nähern, und gleichsam seine Stelle auf Erden zu vertreten: das sollte dem Menschen nicht eine große, nicht die größte Würde geben?

Man is likewise, and this adds infinitely to his **dignity**, this sets him in his perfect light, man is the image of God. [...] As often as he thinks of truth; as often as he is inclined to goodness, and brings it to effect; as often as he perceives, admires, and promotes order and harmony; as often as he spreads love, and joy and happiness around him: so often does he think, and will, and perform, and feel, and act in a godlike manner; so often does he pursue the work of his creator and father; so often does he promote the designs of the Sovereign Being; so often does he obtain a taste of pure divine felicity; and the more he does so, the oftener he acts in this manner, the greater is his similitude with God, the brighter does the image of God shine in him, the less are we able to mistake his high descent, and to overlook the **dignity** of his nature. It is then that God visibly acts, as it were in him and though him; by him he gives testimony of truth; he instructs and reveals himself to mankind by him; by him he maintains the cause of virtue; by him he speaks comfort to the afflicted; by him he pours balm into the wounded heart; by him affords help and support to the wretched, distributes bread to the hungry, and gives strength to the weak; his world is improved by him; and through him he spreads life and joy more diffusively around. And to be such an instrument in the hand of God; to have such a similitude with him, the most perfect, the most glorious being; to approach so near to the divinity, and in a manner, to stand in his place upon the earth; must not all this confer a great, or rather the greatest **dignity** on man?

Eben dies bringt ihn ja dem Eingebornen des Vaters, seinem Sohne Jesu, so nahe; dies verbindet ihn so genau, so innig mit dem, an welchem der Vater das größte Wohlgefallen hat, den er zum Herrn über alles gesetzt hat, und der das höchste Muster aller menschlichen Vollkommenheit ist. Und welche **Würde der Menschheit** liegt nicht in ihrem Verhältnisse gegen Jesum, den sie als ihren Widerhersteller, und ihr Haupt verehret! Ihn, dieses vollkommenste Ebenbild des Vaters, diesen Abglanz der göttlichen Herrlichkeit, zum Blutsverwandten, zum Brüder, zum Freunde, zum Anführer und Vorgänger, zum Herrn, zum Mittler zwischen Gott und uns zu haben; mit ihm so genau, so unauflöslich vereiniget zu seyn, wie die Glieder des Leibes mit dem Haupte desselben vereiniget sind; von ihm so geliebet zu werden, wie kein Freund den anderen liebet, noch lieben kann; mit ihm so eines Sinnes zu seyn, und so einerley Geschäfte mit ihm zu treiben, wie er gemeinschaftlich mit dem Vater wirket und mit ihm Eins ist; in mehr als einer Absicht seine Stelle auf Erden unter den Menschen zu vertreten, und sein da angefangenes Werk fortzusetzen; wie sehr muß das nicht die **Menschheit erhöhen!** [...]

Betrachtet endlich den Menschen nach seiner äußern Gestalt, und in seinem Verhältnisse gegen den Erdboden; betrachtet die Stelle, die er auf demselben einnimmt, das, was er in Absicht auf alle übrige Erdbewohner, auf alles, was ihn da umgiebt, ist und thut: so werdet ihr auch in dieser Rücksicht seine **Würde** nicht verkennen können. Seht, wie der Mensch mitten unter allen niedrigen Geschöpfen, die ihn umringen, voll Selbstgefühls da steht; wie ihn

This circumstance it is that brings him so near to the only begotten of the Father, to his son Jesus; this it is that connects him so closely, so intimately with him in whom the Father is well pleased, whom he has constituted Lord of all, and is the highest pattern of all human perfection. And what a **dignity** does man acquire from his relationship to Jesus, whom he reveres as his restorer and chief! To have him, the most complete image of the Father, the reflex beam of divine effulgence, for his relation, his brother, his friend, his captain and leader, his lord; to be as strictly, as indissolubly united with him, as the members of the body are united to the head; to be so beloved of him as no friend ever loved another, or can love him, to be so unanimous with him, and to carry on the same designs, to work with him as he does with the Father; in more than one respect to represent him on earth among mankind, and to forward the purposes he began; how much must this exalt the **dignity of man!** [...]

Lastly, consider man in his outward figure, and his station in the world. Consider the place he fills upon the earth; what he is and does with all its other inhabitants; and in this regard also you cannot mistake his **dignity.** See how he stands, full of consciousness, amidst all inferior creatures; how exalted and eminent he is above them, how all proclaim him the sovereign of the globe and its inhabitants, the substitute of its author, and the priest of nature! With

alles vor denselben auszeichnet und über sie erhebt; wie ihn alles, als den Beherrscher dieses Erdbodens und seiner Bewohner, als den Stellvertreter seines Schöpfers auf demselben, als den Priester der Natur, ankündiget! mit welchem weitreichenden Blicken er alles, was um ihn her ist, überschauet, sondert, ordnet, verbindet, umfasset; bald von der Erde gen Himmel hinauf staunet, und dann wieder von dem Himmel auf die Erde mit Wonnegefühl herabsieht [...].

Wie schön, wie erhaben ist nicht seine Gestalt! Wie bedeutungsvoll jeder Zug seines Antlitzes, jede Stellung, jede Bewegung seines Körpers! Wie mächtig sein Auge spricht! Wie sich da seine ganze Seele zeiget und mit unwiedersteltcher Gewalt bald Ehrfurcht, bald Unterwerfung und Gehorsam, bald Liebe fordert; izt Muth und Entschlossenheit einflößt, dann Vergnügen und Zufriedenheit um sich her verbreitet! Wie es oft mit einem Blicke die Bosheit entwaffnet, alle Anschläge der Ungerechtigkeit zernichtet, den Kummer aus der Brust des Geängstigten verscheucht, und da, wo Finsterniss und Traurigkeit herrschten, Licht und himmlische Freuden schaffet! Wer kann da die Hoheit, die **Würde des Menschen** verkennen? –

Und wer kann es leugnen, daß sich alles auf diesem Erdboden auf den Menschen bezieht, alles durch ihn belebet, verschönert, verbunden, Mittel der menschlichen Glückseligkeit, und der Verherrlichung Gottes wird? [...] Stellet auch den Erdboden ohne Menschen, ohne verständige Geschöpfe vor, was werdet ihr auf demselben erblicken? Freylich noch viele große Schönheiten; aber mehr wilde als sanfte, mehr fürchterliche als reizende

what a comprehensive view does he survey, distribute, order, connect and apprehend; now darting his eye from earth to heaven, and then looking down from heaven upon earth with sentiments of delight; affectionately cherishing every thing that lives and moves; his sentimental heart expands to the innumerable streams of pleasure and joy, which from all sides flow to meet him, till he is lost in the sweetest sentiments of love and adoration! [...]

How beautiful, how elevated his mien! How significant and expressive every feature of his face, every attitude, every movement of his person! How forcible is the language of his eye! How he displays his whole soul by a glance of it, and with an irresistible energy at one time commands reverence, at another submission and obedience, and at another love; now inspiring courage and resolution, then pleasure and satisfaction in all about him! How often does he confound the wicked with a look, defeat the schemes of injustice, drive sorrow from the breast of the mourner, and dart life and heavenly joy where darkness and distress prevailed. Who can here mistake the elevation and the **dignity of man**!

And who can deny, that all things on the earth relate to man, that all are animated, beautified, and connected as the means of human happiness, and for the glory of God? [...] Represent to yourself the earth without mankind, without rational creatures on it, and what do you discover it to contain? Certainly still many great beauties; but more savage than gentle, more tremendous than delightful beauties; still indeed much life, but life without con-

Schönheiten; freylich noch viel Leben, aber Leben ohne Bewußtseyn, ohne Überlegung, ohne eigentlichen Genuß, ohne Rücksicht auf den Urheber desselben. Nein, die Natur ist schön, entzückend schön; aber der Mensch verschönert sie, sammelt alle einzelne, zerstreute Schönheiten um sich her, und sieht, und fühlet, und genießt sie, und freuet sich derselben. Die Natur ist fruchtbar, unerschöpflich fruchtbar; aber der Mensch vervielfältigt, erhöhet, veredelt dieses Leben; und ist selig in dem Genusse desselben. [...]

Und der Mensch, M. A. Z., der dieses alles ist, und thut und hervor bringt; der Mensch, der einen solchen Verstand, eine solche Freyheit, eine solche Thätigkeit besitzt; der einen immer zunehmenden Vollkommenheit fähig, der unsterblich, Gott ähnlich, mit seinem Sohne Jesu Christo so genau vereiniget ist; und diese Stelle auf dem Erdboden einnimmt, und in solchen Verhältnissen gegen alle übrige Geschöpfe desselben steht: der sollte nicht eine große **Würde**, einen vorzüglichen Werth in den Augen Gottes und aller denkenden Wesen haben?

O so beurtheile denn den Menschen, beurtheile dich selbst richtiger, o du, der du vielleicht nur auf seine und deine Schwachheiten und Gebrechen siehst, und das Schönste und Beste an ihm und an dir verkennet! Achte ihn, achte dich selbst, so wie es der Wahrheit gemäß ist. [...] erkenne und fühle deine **Würde**, deine Kräfte, deine Vorzüge, o Mensch, und erkenne, und fühle sie mit frohem und dankbarem Herzen! Es ist nicht Einbildung, nicht Stolz; es ist Selbstgefühl, das sich auf Wahrheit gründet; und stolz kann und wird dich dieses

sciousness, without reflection, without appropriate enjoyment, without recollection of the great author of it. No, nature is beautiful, enchantingly beautiful; but man adorns it, collects about him the scattered and single beauties, and sees and feels, and enjoys them, and delights in them. Nature is fruitful, inexhaustibly fruitful; but man improves her fertility, guides it, and gives it its most generally useful direction. Nature is full of life; but man diversifies, elevates, and ennobles this life, and is happy in the enjoyment of it. [...]

And man, who effects and produces all this; man, who posesses such an understanding, such a freedom, such activity, such capacities for ever tending to perfection; a being immortal; a being in the similitude of God, so intimately connected with his son Jesus Christ; and sustaining such a part upon the globe, and filling such a character in regard to the other creatures; must not man possess great **dignity** in the sight of God, a preeminent dignity in his sight, and in that of all rational existences?

Judge then more justly of mankind, judge more justly of thyself, o thou, who probably only beholdest thyself on the side of weakness and imperfection, and considerest not the superiority and the excellency of thy nature! Treat mankind, and treat thyself conformably with truth. [...] confess and feel thy **dignity**, thy faculties, thy privileges, o man! And feel and confess them with a cheerful and a grateful heart! It is not imagination, it is not pride; it is sentiment founded on truth; and pride can and will undo this sentiment of thy **dignity**, so

Gefühl deiner **Würde** nicht machen, so lange du sie behältst, so lange du dich noch mit deinen Augen, und mit deinem Geiste zu demjenigen erheben kannst, der diese Kräfte, diese Vorzüge, diese Würde, und das Gefühl davon gegeben hat, der sie dir in jedem Augenblicke aufs neue giebt, und zu dessen Verherrlichung du alles seyn und thun sollst, was du bist und thust. Nein, erkenne und fühle den ganzen Werth deiner vernünftigen Natur, den ganzen Werth deiner vorzüglichen Anlagen und Fähigkeiten und Kräfte! Sonst kannst du sie nicht **würdig** gebrauchen, kannst nicht das werden, nicht das thun, nicht das genießen, was du nach deiner Natur und deiner Bestimmung werden, und thun und genießen sollst; sonst kannst du deinem Schöpfer den Dank nicht geben, und deinen Mitgeschöpfen die Dienste nicht leisten, die du ihm und ihnen schuldig bist. [...]

Laß den aber auch die Erkenntniß deiner **Würde** nicht blos Vorstellung deines Verstandes seyn. Laß sie alle deine Gesinnungen beleben, dein ganzes Herz erweitern und durchwarmen, sich in allen deinen Thaten äußern. Denke richtig und groß; handle frey und edel; werde immer thätiger im Recht- und Wohlthun; strebe unabläßig nach höhere Vollkommenheit; lebe als ein Geschöpf, das nie ganz sterben, das ewig leben soll; suche Gott immer ähnlicher zu werden, und seinem Ebenbilde, Jesu Christo immer näher zu kommen; behaupte deine, dir angewiesene Stelle auf Erden, wirke und herrsche damit Weisheit und Güte, und verbreite immer mehr Leben und Freude und Seligkeit um dich her. So wirst du der Menschheit, und Gott,

long as thou restrainest it, so long as thou canst not lift thine eyes and raise thy mind to him who has given thee these abilities, these prerogatives, who gives thee them afresh at every moment, and to whose glory thou shouldst be and do all that thou art and dost. No; feel and acknowledge the whole value of thy reasonable nature, the whole worth of thy superior dispositions and capacities and powers! Else canst thou not use them **worthily**; canst not become, not do, not enjoy, that which thou mayest become and do and enjoy by thy nature and thy appointment; else canst thou not render thy creator the gratitude, nor perform the service to thy fellow-creatures, which thou owest to him and to them. [...]

But let not the knowledge of thy **dignity** be a bare representation of thy mind. Let it animate all thy sentiments, expand and warm thy heart, and display itself in all thy actions. Think justly and greatly; act freely and generously; be constantly more and more active in justice and beneficence; strive unremittedly after higher perfection; live as a creature that is not wholly to die; that is to live for ever; endeavour to acquire daily a nearer resemblance with God, and to approach nearer to the model of his son Jesus Christ; fulfil the functions appointed thee on earth, there act and rule with wisdom and loving kindness, and continually disseminate more life and joy and happiness around thee. So wilt thou do honour to mankind, and to God their

ihrem Schöpfer und Vater, Ehre bringen, und es mit der That beweisen, daß dich Gott mit großer **Würde** und Herrlichkeit gekrönet, und dich nur etwas, und nur auf eine Zeitlang geringer gemacht hat, als die Engel.

II. Was ist der **Würde des Menschen** zuwieder?

Je größer die **Würde des Menschen** ist, M. A.Zuh., desto stärker ist er verpflichtet, dieselbe zu behaupten, und derselben gemäß zu denken und zu handeln. Je größer die **Würde des Menschen** ist, desto mehr erniedriget und beschimpfet ihn alles, was mit derselben streitet, ihn derselben beräubet, oder ihren Glanz verdunkelt. Besser, weit besser ist es, M.Th.Fr., die niedrigste Stelle zu bekleiden, als über andere erhaben zu seyn, und sich durch niedrige Gesinnungen und Thaten zu schanden [...] Ich werde euch [...] zeigen, was der **Würde des Menschen** zuwider ist, oder mit derselben streitet. [...]

Adeln Verstand und Vernunft den Menschen; so handelt er seiner **Würde** zuwider, so erniedriget er sich selbst, wenn er seinen Verstand und seine Vernunft nicht anbauet, wenn er sie nicht dazu gebrauchet, wozu sie ihm der Schöpfer gegeben hat; wenn ihm Wahrheit und Irrtum, Schein und Wirklichkeit gleichgültige Dinge sind [...]. Wo bleibt denn eure **Würde**, wodurch zeiget sich euer Adel, Menschen die ihr das Nachdenken, und die ihm so günstige, oft so unentbehrliche Stille und Einsamkeit scheuet; die ihr in einer immerwährenden, den Geist betäubenden, geräuschvollen Zerstreuung lebet; so selten zu einem klaren innigen Bewußtseyn euer selbst und eures Zustandes gelanget; eure Besonnenheit und eure Überlegungskraft so selten anwendet, und immer weit mehr außer euch, als in

creator and father, and incontrovertibly evince, that God has crowned thee with **glory** and honour, and has made thee only for this period of time lower than the spirits of bliss.

II. What is in opposition to the **Dignity of Man**.

The greater **man's dignity** is, so much the more highly is he engaged to assert it, and to think and act in conformity to it. The greater his **dignity**, the more does everything that is in opposition to it, that lessens and obscures its splendour, debase and degrade him. Better, far better is it to fill the lowest place, than to be exalted above others, and to disgrace one-self by low sentiments and shameful actions [...] I shall show you what is derogatory to the **dignity of man**. [...]

A man acts inconsistently with his high endowment of intelligence and reason; he acts in opposition to his **dignity**, debases and degrades himself, when he neglects to cultivate his understanding and his reason, when he neglects to use them to those purposes for which the creator bestowed them; when truth and error, semblance and reality, are things indifferent to him, [...]. Where is then your **dignity**, how does your nobility appear, you who avoid that retirement and silence which is so favourable, and generally so indispensable to reflection; you who benumb your spirit by an unceasing round of dissipation, distraction, and tumultuous amusement; who seldom attain to any clear and intimate consciousness of yourselves and your condition; who seldom exercise yourselves in consideration or reflection;

euch, weit mehr in der Meinung und dem Urteile anderer, als in dem mit Selbstgefühl verbundenen Gebrauche eurer innern Kräfte existiret und lebet? [...]

Alles ferner, M. A. Z. alles, was mit der Freyheit des Menschen streitet, was ihren Gebrauch einschränket und hindert, das streitet mit der **Würde der Menschheit**, das entehret, erniedriget den Menschen, und machet ihn der Stelle **unwürdig**, die er unter den Geschöpfen Gottes bekleidet [...] Ihr seyd Sklaven, Sklaven der Sinne, Sklaven des Zufalls, Sklaven der Menschen, Sklaven eurer Lüste und Begierden, und so lange ihr das seyd, so lange setzet ihr euch zu den Thieren des Feldes herab, so lange ist die **Würde der Menschheit** kaum an euch zu erkennen; nur selten blikt ein schwacher Strahl ihres Glanzes aus der finstern Hülle hervor, die sie verbirgt. Soll sie wieder heller an euch glänzen, o so zerbrechen die Fesseln der Knechtschaft, womit euch die Sinnlichkeit gefangen hält [...].

Ist ferner die dem Menschen angeschaffene, und stets mehr oder weniger wirksame, nie ganz zerstöhrbare Thätigkeit ein solcher characteristicher Zug seiner **Würde**, so muß drittens alles mit der **Würde der Menschheit** streiten, was diese Thätigkeit schwächet, unterdrücket, fesselt, oder ihr eine verkehrte und schädliche Richtung giebt. [...] Menschen, die ihr so denket und handelt, die ihr euern Thätigkeitstrieb so unterdrücket, oder ihm eine so verkehrte Richtung gebet, erwachet aus euerm Schlummer, schämet euch eurer Trägheit, wenn ihr **die Würde eurer Natur** behaupten wollet. [...] Als Mensch leben heißt wirken, und mit Bewustseyn wirken, und recht viel Gutes wirken. [...]

turn your thoughts constantly more without than within; exist more by the opinions and judgements of others, than live in that self-sentiment which is the necessary concomitant of habitual meditation? [...]

Farther, every thing that opposes the freedom of man, whatever contracts and prevents its use, militates against the **dignity of man**; dishonours, debases him, and renders him **unworthy** of the station he fills among the creatures of God. [...] Ye are slaves, slaves to the senses, slaves to accident, slaves to men, slaves to your lusts and your appetites; and, so long as you are so, you reduce yourselves to the level of beasts in the field, so long is the **dignity of man** scarcely distinguishable in you; and only now and then a feeble ray of your lustre appears through the thick veil which covers it. Would you have it shine forth again in all its splendour? Oh, then break the chains of that bondage by which sensuality holds you captive [...]

If that natural activity, which is constantly more or less operative in man, and can never be entirely destroyed, be another characteristic feature of his **dignity**; then, thirdly, every thing must be contrary to it which enervates, suppresses, enthrals, or gives it a perverse and pernicious direction. [...] Ye who think and act in this manner, who so suppress your propensity to action, or give it so wrong a direction, awake from your slumbers, be ashamed of your sloth, if you would maintain the **dignity of your nature**. [...] To live like a man, means, to use our activity, to be conscious of our actions, and to do as much good as we can. [...]

Ist die Fähigkeit, immer weiter zu gehen, und immer vollkommener zu werden, ein vierter Vorzug des Menschen, so muß alles dasjenige mit seiner **Würde** streiten, was die Entwicklung dieser Fähigkeit verhindert, alles was ihn in seinem Streben nach höhere Vollkommenheit aufhält, zurücksetzet, verdrossen und mutlos machet. [...] heißt das vorwärts streben, heißt das seine Fähigkeit, immer vollkommener zu werden, gehörig entwickeln, und dadurch die Ehre der Menschheit behaupten, wenn man sich scheuet, weiser und besser als andere zu seyn, sich durch richtigere Urtheile, durch edlere Gesinnungen, durch reinere Tugenden vor andern auszuzeichnen; wenn man den algemein betretenen Pfad nie zu verlassen, sich über die herrschenden Vorurtheile und Gewohnheiten nie zu erheben sich getrauet, den Vorwurf der Sonderbarkeit ängstlich fürchtet, und sich blos nach andern, und gemeiniglich nach sehr mittelmässigen Köpfen und schwachen Herzen bildet und richtet? [...] Nein, wollet ihr auch in dieser Absicht die **Würde eurer Natur** behaupten, M.Th.Fr., so lasset euch weder eurer Trägheit, noch das Beyspiel anderer willkürliche Schranken setzen, glaubet nie, weise und tugendhaft und fromm genug zu seyn, nie Gutes genug gethan, und der Welt dienste genug geleistet zu haben [...]

Denn, ihr seyd unsterblich, M.Th.Fr., und auch dies giebt euch eine **Würde**, die euch weit über die ganze leblose, und der Vergänglichkeit unterworfene Schöpfung erhebt! [...] Und doch opferst du so selten das betrügliche Vergnügen des gegenwärtiges Augenblickes der bleibenden Freude des Himmels auf! [...] Nein, willst du deine

If the capacity of ever advancing, and of ever tending to greater excellence, be a fourth prerogative of man, then must every thing be in opposition to his **dignity** that hinders the expansion of that capacity, that checks him, that puts him back, or fatigues or dispirits him in his struggle after higher excellence. [...] Is that to be called stretching forward, always striving for perfection, duly using our faculties, and thereby maintaining the glorious privileges of man, when we are afraid of being wiser and better than others, of shewing our superiority by sounder judgement, nobler sentiments, and a purer virtue? When we will not venture to leave the common, the beaten path, will not rise above prevailing prejudices and customs, from a dread of being charged with affectation and singularity, and are contented to regulate and frame ourselves by others, and commonly by people of moderate talents and feeble hearts? [...] No; would you likewise in this respect maintain the **dignity of your nature**? Then allow neither your sloth nor the example of others to confine you by an arbitrary control. Never think that you are wise and virtuous and pious enough, that you have already done good enough, and have rendered service enough to the world [...]

Then you are immortal. And this likewise gives you a **dignity** which eminently raises you above the whole inanimate and transitory creation. [...] And yet does every loss of earthly things as deeply affect thee as if thou hadst no other and

Würde behaupten, o Mensch, so vergiß nie, daß du zur Unsterblichkeit bestimmt bist [...]. Hänge nicht mit deinem Herzen an Dingen, die du gewiß, die du vielleicht so bald verlieren wirst! Behandle nicht mit Gleichgültigkeit Dinge, die einen so großen, immerwahrenden Einfluß in alle künftigen Schicksale haben können und werden! [...]

Willst du deine **Würde** behaupten, o Mensch, so hüte dich sechstens vor allem, was dem genauen und seligen Verhältnisse zuwieder ist, in welchem du gegen Gott und seinen Sohn Jesum stehest, vor allem, was deine Gottähnlichkeit, deine Christusähnlichkeit schwächet, verdunkelt, zerstöhret. – Achte deine Geisteskräfte, durch welche du nicht nur mit den Engeln verwandt, sondern göttlichen Geschlechts bist, recht hoch, und hüte dich vor allem Mißbrauche derselben, denn es ist Mißbrauch dessen, was dir am glorreichsten ist, was dich der Gottheit am Nächsten bringt. Hüte dich vor dem Irrthume und der Sünde, denn Irrthum und Sünde entfernen Dich von Gott, und machen dich weniger fähig, Gemeinschaft mit ihm zu haben. Hüte dich vor allem, was mit dem Sinne Jesu, dieses Musters aller **menschlichen Würde**, dieses volkommensten Ebenbildes des Vaters, streitet. [...]

Ist endlich, o Mensch, **Würde** und Hoheit auch in deiner äußerlichen Gestalt, o so hüte dich, sie durch niedrige Gesinnungen, durch unzeitigen Kummer und Gram durch unordentliche, heftige Leidenschaften zu verunstalten und zu verzerren. Laß die Schöhnheit und den Adel deines Geistes deine körperliche Schönheit beleben und erhöhen. Laß dein Auge nie Falschheit und Arglist, nie Neid und Hass,

greater satisfactions to expect! [...] No; would thou support thy **dignity**, o, man! Then never forget that thou art appointed to immortality. [...] Let not thy heart be attached to things, which thou must certainly lose, which thou probably must leave so soon! Treat not with indifference things that have and will have such great and everlasting influence on all thy future fortunes! [...]

Wouldst thou maintain thy **dignity**, o man! Then, sixthly, above all beware whatever is in opposition to the close and blessed relation in which thou standest towards God and his son Jesus, of all that may weaken, obscure, or destroy thy resemblance to the deity, thy resemblance to Christ. – Reverence thy spirit, by which thou art not only related to angels, but are the offspring of God; and beware of misusing its faculties, for that is to misuse what is most glorious in thee, what brings thee into affinity with God. Beware of every error, and of every sin; for error and sin remove thee from God, and make thee less capable of communion with him. Beware of everything that is contrary to the mind of Jesus, that pattern of **human dignity**, that perfect image of the Father. [...]

Lastly, o man! There is **dignity** and grandeur in thy outward form; oh then beware of disfiguring it by any degrading sentiments, any unseemly grief and sorrow, any violent inordinate passions. Let the beauty and the nobility of thy spirit animate and enhance the beauty of thy person. Let thine eyes speak neither falsehood nor artifice, neither envy nor hatred; thy lips

deinen Mund nie Betrug und Lügen, sondern jenes und diesen lauter Wahrheit,
lauter Liebe sprechen. Laß deine Blicke
menschenfreundlich, dein Antlitz heiter,
und alle deine Geberden und Stellungen
Ausdrück deines richtigen Verstandes und
deines guten, edlen Herzens seyn!

Bist du der erste, der vornehmste, Bewohner
dieses Erdbodens, o Mensch, herrscht und
regierest du da im Namen deinen höchsten Oberherrn, und willst du die **Würde**
einens Statthalters Gottes in dieser Provinz
seines Reichs behaupten, o so herrsche
und regiere mit Weisheit und Güte! Sei
nicht der Tyrann, sey der Beschützer, der
Versorger, der Führer aller niedrigern Arten
von Geschöpfen; scheuche sie nicht von
dir zurück, sondern nähere dich ihnen mit
Wohlgefallen, mit Mitleiden, mit Hülfe.
Verdirb und zerstöre sie nicht ohne Noth,
und wenn du ihrer bedarfst, wenn du selbst
ihres Lebens nicht schonen kannst, so hüte
dich, ihre Leiden und Schmerzen zu häufen,
quäle sie nicht, um deine wilde Lust zu ver-
längern, oder deinen üppigen Geschmak
zu befriedigen. Verheere und verwüste die
Erde nicht, die du schmücken und ver-
schönern sollst. Verbreite nicht Tod und
Schrecken, sondern Leben und Freude um
dich her. Sey vornehmlich der Wohlthäter
deiner Brüder, von welchem Stande, von
welchem Volke sie seyn, und welche Stelle
sie immer bekleiden mögen. Verachte
keinen; beleidige keinen; laß keinen
deine Macht, oder deine Vorzüge anders
als durch Wohltun fühlen; lege seinem
Fesseln der Knechtschaft auf, da jeder
eben die Ansprüche auf Freiheit hat, die du

neither treachery nor lies; but both they
and these, simple truth, and simple love.
Let thy look be friendly to mankind; let thy
countenance be open; and all thy mien and
gesture express thy cultivated understanding, thy kind and generous heart!

Art thou the principal, the chief inhabit-
ant of the earth? Then rule and govern, o
man! In the name of Thy Great Superior;
and if thou wouldst maintain the **dignity**
of God's viceregent in this province of his
domination, then rule and govern with gen-
tleness and wisdom. Be not the tyrant, be
the guardian, the protector, the leader of
all inferior creatures; drive them not from
thee, but approach them with compla-
cency, with compassion, with succor. Slay
and destroy them not without necessity;
and when thou hast need of them, when
thou canst not even spare their lives, at least
forbear to multiply their sufferings, and to
augment their pain; torment them not, to
prolong thy savage pleasure, or to gratify
thy fastidious appetite. Do not desolate
and ravage the earth, which thou art to
improve and adorn. Spread not death and
destruction, but life and joy around thee. Be
principally the benefactor of thy brethren,
of whatever nation, of whatever condition
they may be. Despise none; injure none; let
none feel thy power or thy pre-eminence,
but as the tokens of thy beneficence and
love; lay not the shackles of bondage on
any, for all have the same pretentions to
freedom as thou; disturb none in their
innocent pleasures; refuse to none that
help which thou art able to afford; hinder
no man in his endeavours after perfection;

hast; störe keinen in seinem unschuldigen Vergnügen; verweigere keinem die Hülfe, die du ihm leisten kannst; hindere keinen in seinem Streben nach Vollkommenheit; und laß dir die Besitzungen, die Rechte, die Freyheiten, die Vorzüge, die Freuden eines jedes heilig seyn!

Bist du der Priester der Natur, und willst du diese **Würde** behaupten, o so sey nicht gleichgültig, nicht unempfindlich gegen die Wunder der höchsten Weisheit und Güte, die dich allenthalben, im Kleinen wie im Großen, umgeben. Höre die Stimme der Natur, vernimm ihren tausendfachen Lobgesang, fühle die Freude aller Lebendigen, und laß dein Herz das empfinden, und deine Mund das aussprechen, was jene weder zu empfinden, noch auszusprechen vermögen, und opfere in ihrem Namen demjenigen Preis und Dank, der sie und dich geschaffen, der dich so weit über sie erhoben hat, und dem allein Ehre und Ruhm gehöhret in Ewigkeit!

3. Predigt. Wie und wodurch stellet das Christenthum die **Würde des Menschen** wieder her?

So gewiß ist es, M. A. Z., daß dem Menschen eine große **Würde** eigen ist, und so wenig der unafmerksame Beobachter dieselbe je ganz an ihm verkennen kann: eben so gewiß ist es auch, daß Irrthum und Laster, Aberglaube und Knechtschaft ihren Glanz sehr verdunkelt haben, und daß es Zeiten gegeben hat, wo man die Vorzüge und den Adel der Menschen, ihre Verwandtschaft mit Gott und ihre Bestimmung zu einer großen Vollkommenheit kaum an ihnen bemerken konnte. In welchem Stand der Schwachheit, der Entkräftung, der schändlichsten Selbsterniedrigung waren

and let the possessions, the wealth, the liberty, the privileges, the comforts of every man be sacred to thee!

Art thou the priest of nature; and wouldst thou maintain this **dignity**; then be not indifferent, be not insensible to the wonders of almighty wisdom and goodness which surround thee on all sides. Hearken to the voice of nature, take up her song of praise; participate in the joy of every living thing, and let thy heart feel and thy tongue express what inferior beings can neither express nor feel, and offer up thanksgiving and praise, in the name of all, to him who made both thee and them, who has exalted thee so highly above them, and to whom alone all glory and praise are due forever.

3. How and by what Means Christianity restores the **Dignity of Man**

Certain as it is, that man possesses a great intrinsic **dignity**, and that the attentive observer cannot fail of perceiving it: yet it is no less certain, that error and vice, superstition and slavery, have greatly obscured its lustre; and that there have been times when the prerogatives and the nobility of man, when his relationship with God, and his destination to a higher perfection, were scarcely discernible. Into what state of weakness, of debility, of degradation, have not many nations formerly been, and are still sunk! And how much deeper yet would not mankind have fallen from that

nicht ehemals, und sind noch itzt manche Völker versunken! Und wie viel tiefer würden nicht die Menschen überhaupt von ihrer **Würde** herabgesunken seyn, wenn sie Gott sich selbst überlassen, wenn er ihrem immer zunehmenden Verderben und Elende keinen Einhalt gethan hätte! [...] Wie viel hat nicht Gott insbesondere durch seinen Sohn Jesum zu Wiederherstellung der **menschlichen Würde** gethan? War die nicht die letzte Absicht seines ganzen großen Werks auf Erden? Wie sehr hat nicht Gott die Menschheit durch ihre genaue Verwandtschaft und Verbindung mit seinem Sohne, dem Erstgeborenen unter aller Creaturen, geehret und erhöhet! [...] Wie und wodurch hat das Christenthum in dem Menschen das Gefühl seiner **Würde** gestärket und ihm die Behauptung derselben erleichtert? [...]

Erstlich, sage ich, setzet das Christenthum unsre Verhältnisse gegen Gott in das helleste Licht; und dadurch läßt er den Menschen seine **Würde** fühlen, und erleichtert ihm die Behauptung derselben. Müßte sich der Mensch für ein Werk des blinden Zufalls, für einen Erdensohn im strengsten Sinne des Wortes halten; dürfte er sich keiner andern Herkunft rühmen, als die er mit den Pflanzen, oder mit dem sonst für Geburten der Fäulniß und der Gährung gehaltenen Insekten gemein hätte; könnte er sich nicht bis zum Gedanken und zum Glauben an eine höchste Gottheit emporschwingen, oder wäre ihm dies Gottheit nicht als Schöpfer der Welt, als der Vater der Menschen bekannt: wie wenig Werth müßte nicht sein Daseyn und seine Natur in seinen eigenen Augen

dignity, if God had left them to themselves; if he had put no check to their progressively increasing corruption and misery!

[...] How much has God in particular done by his son Jesus, for the restoration of **human dignity**! Was not this the ultimate aim of the whole of his great work on earth? How much has not God honoured and exalted man by intimate relationship and connection with his son, the first-born among all creatures! [...] How, and by what means, has Christianity rekindled in man the sentiment of his **dignity**, strengthened and eased him in the maintenance of it? [...]

First, I say, christianity places our relation towards God in the clearest light; thus causing man to feel his **dignity**, and enabling him to maintain it. Is man to imagine himself the work of blind chance, or a son of the earth in the strictest sense of the word; may he boast of no other origin than that of the plants; is he sprung, like the insects, from foulness and corruption? Could he not elevate his mind into the belief and contemplation of a sovereign deity; or were not this deity known to him as the creator of the world, as the father of mankind: of how little value would his existence and his nature be in his own sight! What is more insignificant than a sport of chance, which destroys to-morrow what it produced to-day, which never acts by design and rule, and is perpetually at variance with

haben! Was ist unbedeutender als ein Spiel des Zufalls, der heute schaffet und morgen sein Werk zerstöret, nie nach Absichten und Regeln handelt, und stets im Widerspruche mit sich selbst ist! Was ist [un?]wichtiger und ungewisser, als die Existenz einer so oder anders gebildeten Masse von Staub, die nichts als Staub ist, und früher oder später wieder ganz und auf immer in Staub aufgelöset werden soll! Und waren dies nicht die erniedrigenden Vorstellungen, die sich nur gar zu viele Weise und Nichtweise unter den Heiden von dem Menschen und seinem Ursprunge machten? – Wie ganz anders ist nicht der Unterricht, den uns das Christenthume davon giebt! Gott, rufet es einem jeden seiner Bekenner zu, Gott, der Einzige, der Ewige, der Höchstvollkommene ist den Schöpfer und Vater, so wie er der Schöpfer aller Welten, aller Heere des Himmels, und aller Bewohner des Erdbodens ist! Nicht der Zufall, nicht die Notwendigkeit; nein, die höchste Weisheit und Güte hat dich ins Daseyn gerufen, dir Leben und Odem, und alles gegeben. [...]

[...] Der Mensch, für den Gott so viel gethan hat und noch thut; der Mensch, um dessentwillen Gott selbst seines Sohnes, des Eingebohrnen, nicht geschonet, für den er seinen Sohn, den Geliebten, in den Tod dahin gegeben hat! dieser Mensch sollte ein unbedeutendes, verächtliches Geschöpf seyn? sollte nicht einen großen Werth, eine vorzügliche **Würde** haben? sollte diese **Würde** nicht fühlen, und in dem Gefühle derselben nicht selber selig seyn, so bald er sich daran erinnert, wie sehr Gott seiner achtet, wie gnädig Gott gegen ihn gesinnet ist, und wie väterlich Gott für ihn sorget? [...]

itself! What is more worthless and uncertain, than the existence of a heap of dust in this or the other form; which, being nothing but dust, must sooner or later be wholly decomposed, and fall forever into dust! And were not these the degrading conceptions formed by numbers of the wise and the unwise among the heathens, concerning man and his origin? – How totally different is not the instruction which Christianity gives on it! It proclaims aloud to each of its professors: God, the only, the eternal, the supremely perfect, is thy creator and father, as well as the creator of all worlds, of all the hosts of heaven, and of all the inhabitants of the earth! Neither chance nor fate: no; supreme wisdom and goodness called thee into being, gave thee life and breath, and all things. [...]

[...] shall man, for whom [God] has done and still does so great things; shall man, for whose sake God spared not even his son, the beloved, to suffer death: shall this man be a contemptible, and insignificant creature? not be of great worth; not have pre-eminent **dignity**; not feel this **dignity**; not be happy in the sentiment of it whenever he meditates thereon; when he considers how much he is esteemed of God, how graciously God is disposed towards him, and with what paternal tenderness he cares for him? [...]

Das Christenthum machet uns viertens, die **Würde der Menschheit** in der Person Jesu, ihres Hauptes und Wiederherstellers, in seinem Verhalten und in seinen Schicksalen, recht anschaulich, und lehret uns dadurch auf eine eben so faßliche als unleugbare Weise, wessen die menschliche Natur fähig ist, und zu welcher Stufe der Vollkommenheit sie sich zu erheben vermag. [...] **O Mensch, erkenne hier die Würde deine Natur!** Fühle hier, was du als Mensch zu thun, zu dulden, zu erkämpfen, zu erstreben vermagst, zu welcher Höhe du dich als Mensch emporzuschwingen Kraft und Fähigkeit hast! Fühle den ganzen Werth der Vorzüge, womit Gott die Menschheit in der Person ihres Hauptes und Wiederherstellers geehret hat!

Christianity displays clearly to us, in the fourth place, **the dignity of man** in the person of Jesus, its restorer and chief, in his conduct and the circumstances of his life, and teaches us therein, in a no less comprehensible than incontrovertible manner, what human nature is capable of, and to what height of perfection it may ascend. [...] **Acknowledge, here, o man, the dignity of thy nature!** Here feel what thou, as man, mayest do, what thou mayest endure, what thou mayest withstand; to what height thou has power and capacity to raise thyself, as man! Feel the whole value of the privilege whereby God has honoured man, in the person of his chief and restorer!

PART IV

Modern Sources

From the time of the French Revolution the idea that human dignity could be and perhaps should be a, or *the*, constitutional principle becomes awake to its own dynamism. Although the *Declaration of the Rights of Man* was soon to be denounced as discriminatory of women on the one hand and of workers on the other, the revolutionary pattern set the trend for vindication and organisation with the aim of vindication to be seen as a legitimate means to affirm rights. Abolitionism, backed by the Society of Friends and other Christian communities, spread to France during the revolution. It shared with the revolutionaries the ideal of social justice enshrined in law and envisaged, like the revolutionaries, legal means to socially engineer equality. The violence of the revolution helped to broadcast that political literacy was the means to accomplish this end, and that it was within the reach of the ordinary person, despite it costing many lives and livelihoods.

With the French return to Empire, the organisation of society at local, regional and national levels prepared the ground for industrialisation, marked by wage-earner produced goods and the increased importance of the labour market. In this new environment, democratisation was introduced by constitutional change, and therefore, the principles to govern constitutional law were now widely discussed. Proudhon is responsible for the clearest formulation of the constitutional principle of human dignity as well as for the most conspicuous denial of it to women: a tension probably typical of the nineteenth century.

The United Nations' *Declaration of Human Rights* stands as a monument at the end of the two world wars. Its rights language may have been found to be somewhat hollow, but a consensus seemed to have emerged that its basic principle, human dignity, was not up for

discussion. Women's and workers' organisations had obtained the vote for their constituencies in most of Europe before the wars, but the vote had brought totalitarianism to power, and thus left a question concerning democracy's value that is still alive in postmodern scepticism and anarchism.

The French Revolution

The period of the French Revolution is dominated by Kant with his explicit reference to human dignity as the key stone of ethics and law, but Mary Wollstonecraft, who travelled to experience the revolution first hand, is equally important for her vindications of the rights of man and of woman. Wollstonecraft's last vindication gives voice to the same concern in relation to the French Revolution as Olympe de Gouges did: when women were deprived of their privileges as nobles, their dignity as citizens or human beings was not automatically recognised. Yet, the violent transformations seemed part of an ineluctable process to which both Herder and Humboldt point as they accord to the human being and its humanisation in the light of human dignity a key place in history as its *telos*. As Heydenreich reads Zollikofer in the light of Kant, does he attempt to provide a Deist justification to replace Zollikofer's Christian one, in order to be in line with the spirit of the Revolution? Maybe. It was definitely in order to appeal to a masonic audience. Hannah More is unimpressed by most of these initiatives. She warns against the talk about human dignity being a mere token of fashionable *Ersatz*-Christianity.

Johann Gottfried Herder (1744–1803)

Zollikofer was not the only one to concur with Kant's insistence on according to human dignity a key role in ethics. Herder, who studied with Kant in Königsberg 1762–1765, insisted on humanity being the intrinsic goal of all human development or *Bildung*. The belief that humanity has its goal and

measure in itself, underwritten by God in such a way that its realisation is entirely in our own hands, constitutes human dignity.

Texts from Johann Gottfried Herder: *Ideen zur Philosophie der Geschichte der Menschheit*, Hofenberg Sonderausgabe, ed. von Karl-Maria Guth (Berlin: Verlag der Contumax GmbH et Co., 2017) (according to Heinz Stolpe's Aufbau edition from 1965, vol. II, pp. 214–9, 247), 3. Part (1787), 15. Book I, pp. 375–8 and 395 and *Briefe zur Beförderung der Humanität*, 3rd. Collection, no. 27., ed. Heinz Stolpe, with Hans-Joachim Kruse and Dietrich Simon, 2 vols (Berlin-Weimar: Aufbau, 1971), republished by Michael Holzinger in 2013, pp. 97–8. The text is from the 'third collection' and is dated 1794. Translations are my own.

Ideas on the Philosophy of the History of Humanity (1787)

Humanität ist der Zweck der Menschennatur, und Gott hat unserm Geschlecht mit diesem Zweck sein eigenes Schicksal in die Hände gegeben. [...]

Der Zweck einer Sache, die nicht bloß ein totes Mittel ist, muß in ihr selbst liegen. [...] betrachten wir die Menschheit, wie wir sie kennen, nach den Gesetzen, die in ihr liegen, so kennen wir nichts Höheres als Humanität im Menschen; denn selbst, wenn wir uns Engel oder Götter denken, denken wir sie uns nur als idealische, höhere Menschen. [...] In allen Zuständen und Gesellschaften hat der Mensch durchaus nichts anders im Sinn haben, nichts anders anbauen können als Humanität, wie er sich dieselbe auch dachte. [...] Was also in der Geschichte je Gutes getan ward, ist für die Humanität getan worden; was in ihr Törichtes, Lasterhaftes und Abscheuliches in Schwang kam, ward gegen die Humanität verübet, so daß der Mensch sich durchaus keinen andern Zweck aller seiner Erdanstalten denken kann, als der

Humanity is the goal of human nature and by it, God has delivered the destiny of our race into our own hands. [...]

The goal of something, which is not merely a dead means, must lie in itself. [...] if we look at humanity as we know it, according to the laws that govern it from the inside, we know of nothing higher than humanity in human beings; even when we think of angels or gods, we imagine them as ideal, higher human beings. [...] In all conditions and societies the human being has had nothing else in mind, has been able to cultivate nothing else but humanity, as he understood it. [...] The good that was done through history was done for the sake of humanity. The mad, the vicious and the despicable that was brought about was brought about against humanity so that the human being cannot think of an end to all his undertakings on earth, apart from the one that is in himself, in the weak and strong, low and noble nature, which his God gave him.

in ihm selbst, d.i. in der schwachen und starken, niedrigen und edlen Natur liegt, die ihm sein Gott anschuf. [...] Überall also finden wir die Menschheit im Besitz und Gebrauch des Rechtes, sich zu einer Art von Humanität zu bilden, nachdem es solche erkannte.

So einfach dieses Naturgesetz ist, so **würdig** ist es Gottes, so zusammenstimmend und fruchtbar an Folgen für das Geschlecht der Menschen. [...] Der Mensch konnte nicht leben und sich erhalten, wenn er nicht Vernunft brauchen lernte; sobald er diese brauchte, war ihm freilich die Pforte zu tausend Irrtümern und Fehlversuchen, eben aber auch, und selbst durch diese Irrtümer und Fehlversuche, der Weg zum besseren Gebrauch der Vernunft eröffnet.[...]

Wunderbar-schön versöhnt uns der Grundsatz dieses göttlichen Naturgesetzes nicht nur mit der Gestalt unsres Geschlechts auf der weiten Erde, sondern auch mit den Veränderungen desselben durch alle Zeiten hinunter. Allenthalben ist die Menschheit das, was sie aus sich machen konnte, was sie zu werden Lust und Kraft hatte. [...] Kein Zweifel, aber, daß überhaupt, was auf die Erde noch nicht geschehen ist, künftig geschehen werde; denn unverjährbar sind die Rechte der Menschheit und de Kräfte, die Gott in sie legte, unaustilgbar. [...] Die ganze Geschichte der Völker wird uns in diesem Betracht eine Schule des Wettlaufs zu Erreichung des schönsten Kranzes der Humanität und **Menschenwürde**.

[...] *Es waltet eine weise Güte im Schicksal der Menschen; daher es keine schönere* **Würde***, kein dauerhafteres und reineres Glück gibt, als im Rat derselben zu wirken.*

[...] Everywhere we find the human race in possession of the right and using law to form the kind of humanity according to which it understands itself.

As simple this law of nature is, so **worthy** is it of God, so consistent and fruitful is it for the human race. [...] Man could not live and look after himself if he did not learn to use his reason; as soon as he did, however, he opened the door for thousand errors and mistaken attempts, but also, and through these errors and mistaken attempts, the way to a better use of reason. [...]

Wonderfully the axiom of this divine natural law reconciles us with not only the shape of our race on the entire earth, but also with the changes in it through all times. Everywhere humanity is what it could make of itself, what it wanted to be and had the power to become. [...] There is no doubt, however, that what has not yet taken place on earth, will happen in the future, as the rights of humanity does not date and the powers laid in it by God cannot be eradicated. [...] The entire history of peoples becomes in this light for us a school in which to compete for the loveliest wreath of humanity and **human dignity**.

[...] *A wise goodness rules in the destiny of human beings; therefore, there is no finer* **dignity***, no more enduring and purer happiness, than to be active according to its council.*

Letters for the Advancement of Humanity (1794)

Sie fürchten, daß man dem Wort Humanität einen Fleck anhängen werde; könnten wir nicht das Wort ändern? Menschheit, Menschlichkeit, Menschenrechte, Menschenpflichten, **Menschenwürde,** Menschenliebe? [...] Das Menschengeschlecht, wie es jetzt ist und wahrscheinlich lange noch sein wird, hat seinem größten Teil nach keine **Würde;** man darf es eher bemitleiden, als verehren. Es soll aber zum *Charakter seines Geschlechts,* mithin auch zu dessen *Wert* und *Würde* gebildet werden. Das schöne Wort *Menschenliebe* ist so trivial worden, daß man meistens die Menschen liebt, um keiner unter den Menschen wirksam zu lieben. Alle diese Worte enthalten Teilbegriffe unseres Zwecks, den wir gern mit *einem* Ausdruck bezeichnen möchten.

Also wollen wir bei dem Wort *Humanität* bleiben, an welches unter Alten und Neuern die besten Schriftsteller so würdige Begriffe geknüpft haben. Humanität ist der *Charakter unsres Geschlechts;* er ist uns aber nur in Anlagen angeboren und muß uns eigentlich angebildet werden. Wir bringen ihn nicht fertig auf die Welt mit; auf der Welt aber soll er das Ziel unsres Bestrebens, die Summe unsrer Übungen, unser *Wert* sein; denn eine *Angelität* im Menschen kennen wir nicht, und wenn der Dämon, der uns regiert, kein humaner Dämon ist, werden wir Plagegeister der Menschen. Das Göttliche in unserem Geschlecht ist also *Bildung zur Humanität;* alle großen und guten Menschen, Gesetzgeber, Erfinder, Philosophen, Dichter, Künstler, jeder edle Mensch in seinem Stande, bei der Erziehung

You fear that a stain will be attached to the word humanity; could we not change the word? Humanity, humaneness, human rights, human duties, **human dignity,** love of humans? [...] The human race, as it is and probably will be for a long time, has for its largest part no **dignity;** it should rather be pitied than honoured. It must however be built up in and to its character, and so also to its value and **dignity.** The beautiful word 'charity' has become so trivial that one mostly loves humans in order not to love any one of them in particular. All these words hold something of our goal, which we would like to refer to with one expression.

Thus we will stay by the word *humanity,* to which the best of new and old writers alike have linked so worthy concepts. Humanity is the *character of our lineage;* but it is only bred in us as capacity and must thus be brought out in us. We do not bring it finished into being when we are born to the world; in the world, it must be the goal of our endeavours, the sum of our exercises, our *value.* We do not know of an angelic nature in human beings, and if the *demon* that rules us isn't human, we become instead tormenting spirits of each other. The divine in our lineage is thus *education for humanity;* all great and good human beings, legislators, inventors, philosophers, poets, artists, every noble human being, each in their social position, by the education of their children, by the observance of

seiner Kinder, bei der Beobachtung seiner Pflichten, durch Beispiel, Werk, Institut und Lehre hat dazu mitgeholfen. Humanität ist der Schatz und die Ausbeute aller menschlicher Bemühungen, gleichsam die *Kunst unsres Geschlechtes*. Die Bildung zu ihr ist ein Werk, das unablässig fortgesetzt werden muß, oder wir sinken, höhere und niedere Stände, zur rohen Tierheit, zur *Brutalität* zurück.

their duties, through example, work, institution and teaching has helped towards this goal. Humanity is the treasure and the profit of all human endeavours, and at the same time the *art of our lineage*. The education to it is an ongoing task; Without it, we shall sink down to raw animality, to *brutality*, irrespective of social standing.

Immanuel Kant (1724–1804)

Kant's identification of the categorical imperative with human dignity places him as a defender of the intrinsic link not only between human dignity and ethics but also between human dignity and the state. In this, he is very much the forerunner for our understanding of human dignity as a constitutional principle. In contrast to the Ciceronian tradition, which he inherits through Grotius and Pufendorf, he regards aristocracy to be an obstacle to human dignity, inspired or contaminated by the movement that produced the French Revolution. He nevertheless advocates a distinction between active and passive citizens, justified by the possibility of social mobility, in such a way that apprentices and labourers, women, handicapped and children would not be entitled to vote, except if they advanced to a social position of economic independence. Kant did not advocate a 'liberation movement' for women; he just overlooked their situation, or maybe simply did not regard it as particularly difficult. His teachings in this regard mark the transition for women to a state where their nobility could no longer compensate in their private lives for their lack of opportunity for state sponsored advancement.

The hybrid status of the categorical imperative as a synthetic *a priori* judgement, deliberately estranged from metaphysics, complicates Kant's relation to the various traditions. The closest relative to his position is

probably Pico's emphasis on autonomy as the means to choose dignity. What exactly human dignity is for Kant has captured the attention of many. The fact that the formulations of the *Groundwork of the Metaphysics of Morals* are better known than those of the *Metaphysics of Morals* reflects the problem that the embryonic idea is a significant source of inspiration, but may make more sense than the development of it does.

Groundwork understands (human) dignity to be the material aspect of the categorical imperative, the *synthetic a priori* of practical reason, analogous to the forms, categories and ideas of theoretical reason. Without it, ethics and law would not only be unfounded but also inconceivable. Its form as a judgement, which invests the entire universe with meaning through relationship with it in the human being under God, recalls earlier microcosmic motifs, and subtly founds a new metaphysics, a practical metaphysics based on human dignity. Applied in the *Doctrine of Law*, a tension results between it and the citizenship status, which espouses existing social structures. Applied in the *Doctrine of Virtue* the judgement warns against servility, defamation and ridicule. As the basic principle of the new metaphysics, it also founds 'pragmatic' anthropology, that is, anthropology based on practical reason as first philosophy.

The German texts are from the Meiner *Philosophische Bibliothek*, except *Kritik der Urteilskraft*, which is reproduced after the *Akademie Ausgabe*. In the latter case, the language has been slightly modernised. The Meiner Edition presents some text critical progress compared to the standard work, taken into account by the English translation of the practical works by Mary Gregory (ed.), *The Cambridge Edition of the Works of Immanuel Kant; Practical Philosophy* (Cambridge: Cambridge University Press, 1996), which is the translation used here for the works of practical philosophy. The English translation of texts from *Critique of Pure Reason* is by Werner Pluhar (Immanuel Kant: *Critique of Pure Reason* (Indianapolis, IN and Cambridge: Hackett, 1996)). The translation of texts from *Kritik der Urteilskraft* is by J. C. Meredith: *Kant's Critique of Teleological Judgement* (Oxford: Clarendon Press, 1928). The translation of the text from *Anthropologie in pragmatischer Hinsicht* is by Robert B. Louden and taken from *The Cambridge Edition of the Works of Immanuel Kant. Anthropology, History, and Education*, eds Günter Zöller and Robert B. Louden (Cambridge: Cambridge University Press, 2007). The insertion of references to the Academy-edition figures in square brackets in the translation, but it is approximate.

Critique of Pure Reason (1781)

Kant makes use of the concept of dignity to designate the logical superiority of *a priori* necessity (and the rules or types of knowledge which derive from it) as did Aristotle. See also B175/A135-6 and B375-76/A318-9.

B124/A92

Erscheinungen geben gar wohl Fälle an die Hand, aus denen eine Regel möglich ist, nach der etwas gewöhnlichermaßen geschieht, aber niemals, daß der Erfolg notwendig sei: daher der Synthesis der Ursache und Wirkung auch eine **Dignität** anhängt, die man gar nicht empirisch ausdrücken kann, nämlich, daß die Wirkung nicht bloß zu der Ursache hinzukomme, sondern durch dieselbe gesetzt sei, und aus ihr erfolge. Die strenge Allgemeinheit der Regel ist auch gar keine Eigenschaft empirischer Regeln, die durch Induktion keine andere als komparative Allgemeinheit, d. i. ausgebreitete Brauchbarkeit bekommen können. Nun würde sich aber der Gebrauch der reinen Verstandesbegriffe gänzlich ändern, wenn man sie nur als empirische Produkte behandeln wollte.

Appearances may well offer cases from which a rule is possible in accordance with which something usually happens, but never a rule in accordance with which the succession is necessary; thus to the synthesis of cause and effect there attaches a **dignity** that can never be expressed empirically, namely, that the effect does not merely come along with the cause, but is posited through it and follows from it. The strict universality of the rule is therefore not any property of empirical rules, which cannot acquire anything more through induction than comparative universality, i.e., widespread usefulness. But now the use of the pure concepts of the understanding would be entirely altered if one were to treat them only as empirical products.

Groundwork of the Metaphysics of Morals (1785)

Kant claims to give three versions of the categorical imperative, which in turn should give expression to the same intuition. Are these three: 1) always act so that the maxim of your action could be a universal law; 2) always treat humanity as an end in itself and never only as a means and 3) morality and humanity, in so far as it is capable of morality, is that which alone has human dignity? Or is the last to be replaced by: 4/ autonomy is the ground of the dignity of human nature? Maybe this latter is meant as a kind of summing up of the three. Whatever the number of expressions of

the principle, Kant further claims they all have a form, namely universality, a matter, namely an end, and a complete determination of all maxims by means of that formula, namely that all maxims from one's own lawgiving are to harmonise with a possible kingdom of ends.

The purported unity of the intuition may be compromised by this diversity and in particular by the fact that it contains both *a priori* and *a posteriori* elements. If the identification of dignity (which is *a priori*) with humanity (which is *a posteriori*) is effected by a synthetic *a priori* judgement, an adequate explanation of the content of the intuition underlying this judgement is at any rate postponed to *The Critique of Judgement*, where in fact we do see it explained.

In relation to Zollikofer an important difference is to be observed. Kant regards value as established by law, dignity being the only thing that is beyond the law (AK 4:436). In contrast, Zollikofer regarded everything to be of value because of, or in the light of, human dignity, and therefore as something for which the law should make room.

Section II: Transit from Popular Moral Philosophy to Metaphysics of Morals. AK 4: 420–40, extracts

Wir werden also die Möglichkeit eines *kategorischen* Imperativs gänzlich *a priori* zu untersuchen haben, da uns hier der Vorteil nicht zustattenkommt, daß die Wirklichkeit desselben in der Erfahrung gegeben, und also die Möglichkeit nicht zur Festsetzung, sondern bloß zur Erklärung nötig wäre. [...]	We shall thus have to investigate entirely *a priori* the possibility of a categorical imperative, since [AK 4:420] we do not here have the advantage of its reality being given in experience, so that the possibility would be necessary not to establish it but merely to explain it. [...]
Zweitens ist bei diesem kategorischen Imperativ oder Gesetze der Sittlichkeit der Grund der Schwierigkeit (die Möglichkeit desselben einzusehen) auch sehr groß. Er ist ein synthetisch-praktischer Satz *a priori*, und da die Möglichkeit der Sätze dieser Art einzusehen so viel Schwierigkeit in der theoretischen Erkenntnis hat, so läßt sich leicht abnehmen, daß sie in der praktischen nicht weniger haben werde.	Second, in the case of this categorical imperative or law of morality the ground of the difficulty (of insight into its possibility) is also very great. It is an *a priori* synthetic practical proposition; and since it is so difficult to see the possibility of this kind of proposition in theoretical cognition, it can be readily gathered that the difficulty will be no less in practical cognition.

Bei dieser Aufgabe wollen wir zuerst versuchen, ob nicht vielleicht der bloße Begriff eines kategorischen Imperativs auch die Formel desselben an die Hand gebe, die den Satz enthält, der allein ein kategorischer Imperativ sein kann; denn wie ein solches absolutes Gebot möglich sei, wenn wir auch gleich wissen, wie es lautet, wird noch besondere und schwere Bemühung erfordern, die wir aber zum letzten Abschnitte aussetzen.

Wenn ich mir einen *hypothetischen* Imperativ überhaupt denke, so weiß ich nicht zum Voraus, was er enthalten werde: bis mir die Bedingung gegeben ist. Denke ich mir aber einen *kategorischen* Imperativ, so weiß ich sofort, was er enthalte. Denn da der Imperativ außer dem Gesetze nur die Notwendigkeit der Maxime enthält, diesem Gesetze gemäß zu sein, das Gesetz aber keine Bedingung enthält, auf die es eingeschränkt war, so bleibt nichts als die Allgemeinheit eines Gesetzes überhaupt übrig, welchem die Maxime der Handlung gemäß sein soll, und welche Gemäßheit allein der Imperativ eigentlich als notwendig vorstellt.

Der kategorische Imperativ ist also nur ein einziger und zwar dieser: *handle nur nach derjenigen Maxime, durch die du zugleich wollen kannst, daß sie ein allgemeines Gesetz werde.* [...]

Gesetzt aber, es gäbe etwas, *dessen Dasein an sich selbst* einen absoluten Wert hat, was, *als Zweck an sich selbst,* ein Grund bestimmter Gesetze sein könnte, so würde in ihm, und nur in ihm allein, der Grund eines möglichen kategorischen Imperativs d.i. praktischen Gesetzes, liegen.

In this task we want first to inquire whether the mere concept of a categorical imperative may not also provide its formula containing the proposition which alone can be a categorical imperative. For, how such absolute command is possible, even if we know its tenor, will still require special and difficult toil, which, however, we postpone to the last section.

When I think of a *hypothetical* imperative in general I do not know beforehand what it will contain; I do not know this until I am given the condition. But when I think of a *categorical* imperative I know at once what it contains. For, since the imperative contains, beyond the law, only the necessity that the maxim be in conformity with this law, while the law contains [AK 4:421] no condition to which it would be limited, nothing is left with which the maxim of action is to conform but the universality of a law as such; and this conformity alone is what the imperative properly represents as necessary.

There is, therefore, only a single categorical imperative and it is this: *act only in accordance with that maxim through which you can at the same time will that it become a universal law.* [...]

[AK 4:428] But suppose there were something the *existence of which in itself* has an absolute worth, something which as *an end in itself* could be a ground of determinate laws; then in it, and in it alone, would lie the ground of a possible categorical imperative, that is, of a practical law.

Nun sage ich: der Mensch und überhaupt jedes vernünftige Wesen existiert als Zweck an sich selbst, nicht bloß als Mittel zum beliebigen Gebrauche für diesen oder jenen Willen, sondern muß in allen seinen, sowohl auf sich selbst, als auch auf andere vernünftige Wesen gerichteten Handlungen, jederzeit *zugleich als Zweck* betrachtet werden. [...] Die Wesen, deren Dasein zwar nicht auf unserem Willen, sondern der Natur beruht, haben dennoch, wenn sie vernunftlose Wesen sind, nur einen relativen Wert, als Mittel, und heißen daher *Sachen*, dagegen vernünftige Wesen *Personen* genannt werden, weil ihre Natur sie schon als Zwecke an sich selbst, d.i. als etwas, das nicht bloß als Mittel gebraucht werden darf, auszeichnet, mithin sofern alle Willkür einschränkt (und ein Gegenstand der Achtung ist). Dies sind also nicht bloß subjektive Zwecke, deren Existenz, als Wirkung unserer Handlung, *für uns* einen Wert hat: sondern *objektive Zwecke*, d.i. Dinge, deren Dasein an sich selbst Zweck ist, und zwar ein solcher, an dessen Statt kein anderer Zweck gesetzt werden kann, dem sie *bloß* als Mittel zu Diensten stehen sollten, weil ohne dieses überall gar nichts von *absolutem Werte* würde angetroffen werden; wenn aber aller Wert bedingt, mithin zufällig wäre, so könnte für die Vernunft überall kein oberstes praktisches Prinzip angetroffen werden.

Wenn es denn also ein oberstes praktisches Prinzip und, in Ansehung des menschlichen Willens, einen kategorischen Imperativ geben soll, so muß es ein solches sein, daß aus der Vorstellung dessen, was notwendig für jedermann *Zweck* ist, weil es *Zweck an sich selbst* ist, ein *objektives* Prinzip

Now I say that the human being and in general every rational being exists as an end in itself, not merely as a means to be used by this or that will at its discretion; instead he must in all his actions, whether directed to himself or also to other rational beings, always be regarded at the same time as an end. [...] Beings the existence of which rests not on our will but on nature, if they are beings without reason, still have only a relative worth, as means, and are therefore called things, whereas rational beings are called persons because their nature already marks them out as an end in itself, that is, as something that may not be used merely as a means, and hence so far limits all choice (and is an object of respect). These, therefore, are not merely subjective ends, the existence of which as an effect of our action has a worth for us, but rather objective ends, that is, beings the existence of which is in itself an end, and indeed one such that no other end, to which they would serve *merely* as means, can be put in its place, since without it nothing of absolute worth would be found anywhere; but if all worth were conditional and therefore contingent, then no supreme practical principle for reason could be found anywhere.

If, then, there is to be a supreme practical principle and, with respect to the human will, a categorical imperative, it must be one such that, from the representation of what is necessarily an end for everyone because it is end in itself, it constitutes an *objective* principle of the will and thus can serve as a

des Willens ausmacht, mithin zum allgemeinen praktischen Gesetz dienen kann. Der Grund dieses Prinzips ist: *die vernünftige Natur existiert als Zweck an sich selbst.* So stellt sich notwendig der Mensch sein eigenes Dasein vor; sofern ist es also ein *subjektives* Prinzip menschlicher Handlungen. So stellt sich aber auch jedes andere vernünftige Wesen sein Dasein, zufolge ebendesselben Vernunftsgrundes, der auch für mich gilt, vor; also ist es zugleich ein *objektives* Prinzip, woraus als einem obersten praktischen Grunde alle Gesetze des Willens müssen abgeleitet werden können. Der praktische Imperativ wird also folgender sein: *Handle so, daß du die Menschheit, sowohl in deiner Person als in der Person eines jeden anderen, jederzeit zugleich als Zweck, niemals bloß als Mittel brauchest.* [...]

Die praktische Notwendigkeit, nach diesem Prinzip zu handeln, d.i. die Pflicht, beruht gar nicht auf Gefühlen, Antrieben und Neigungen, sondern bloß auf dem Verhältnisse vernünftiger Wesen zueinander, in welchem der Wille eines vernünftigen Wesens jederzeit zugleich als *gesetzgebend* betrachtet werden muß, weil es sie sonst nicht als *Zweck an sich selbst* denken könnte. Die Vernunft bezieht also jede Maxime des Willens als allgemein gesetzgebend auf jeden anderen Willen und auch auf jede Handlung gegen sich selbst, und dies zwar nicht um irgendeines anderen praktischen Bewegungsgrundes oder künftigen Vorteils willen, sondern aus der Idee der *Würde* eines vernünftigen Wesens, das keinem Gesetze gehorcht als dem, das es zugleich selbst gibt.

universal practical law. The ground of this principle is: *rational nature exists as an end in itself.* The human being necessarily [AK 4:429] represents his existence in this way; so far it is thus a *subjective* principle of human actions. But every other rational being also represents his existence in this way consequent on just the same rational ground that also holds for me; thus it is at the same time an *objective* principle from which, as a supreme practical ground, it must be possible to derive all laws of the will. The practical imperative will therefore be the following: *So act that you use humanity, whether in your own person or in the person of any other, always at the same time as an end, never merely as a means.* [...]

[AK 4:434] The practical necessity of acting in accordance with this principle, that is, duty, does not rest at all on feelings, impulses, and inclinations but merely on the relation of rational beings to one another, in which the will of a rational being must always be regarded as at the same time *lawgiving*, since otherwise it could not be thought as an *end in itself.* Reason accordingly refers every maxim of the will as giving universal law to every other will and also to every action toward oneself, and does so not for the sake of any other practical motive or any future advantage but from the idea of the *dignity* of a rational being, who obeys no law other than that which he himself at the same time gives.

Im Reiche der Zwecke hat alles entweder einen *Preis* oder eine **Würde**. Was einen Preis hat, an dessen Stelle kann auch etwas anderes, als *Äquivalent*, gesetzt werden; was dagegen über allen Preis erhaben ist, mithin kein Äquivalent erstattet, das hat eine **Würde**.

Was sich auf die allgemeinen menschlichen Neigungen und Bedürfnisse bezieht, hat einen *Marktpreis*; das, was auch ohne ein Bedürfnis vorauszusetzen einem gewissen Geschmacke, d.i. einem Wohlgefallen am bloßen zwecklosen Spiel unserer Gemütskräfte, gemäß ist, einen *Affektionspreis*; das aber, was die Bedingung ausmacht, unter der allein etwas Zweck an sich selbst sein kann, hat nicht bloß einen relativen Wert, d.i. einen Preis, sondern einen inneren Wert, d.i. **Würde**.

Nun ist Moralität die Bedingung, unter der allein ein vernünftiges Wesen Zweck an sich selbst sein kann; weil nur durch sie es möglich ist, ein gesetzgebendes Glied im Reiche der Zwecke zu sein. **Also ist die Sittlichkeit und die Menschheit, sofern sie derselben fähig ist, dasjenige, was allein Würde hat.** Geschicklichkeit und Fleiß im Arbeiten haben einen Marktpreis; Witz, lebhafte Einbildungskraft und Launen einen Affektionspreis; dagegen Treue im Versprechen, Wohlwollen aus Grundsätzen (nicht aus Instinkt) haben einen inneren Wert. Die Natur sowohl als Kunst enthalten nichts, was sie, in den Ermangelung derselben, an ihre Stelle setzen könnten; denn ihr Wert besteht nicht in Wirkungen, die daraus entspringen, im Vorteil und Nutzen, den sie schaffen, sondern in den Gesinnungen, d.i. den Maximen des Willens, die sich auf diese Art in Handlungen zu offenbaren bereit

In the kingdom of ends, everything has either a *price* or a **dignity**. What has a price can be replaced by something else as its *equivalent;* what on the other hand is raised above all price and therefore admits of no equivalent, has a **dignity**.

What is related to general human inclinations and needs has a *market price*, that which, even without presupposing a need, conforms with a certain taste, that is, with a delight in the mere [AK 4:435] purposeless play of our mental powers, has a *fancy price*, but that which constitutes the condition under which alone something can be an end in itself has not merely a relative worth, that is, a price, but an inner worth, that is, **dignity**.

Now, morality is the condition under which alone a rational being can be an end in itself, since only through this is it possible to be a lawgiving member in the kingdom of ends. **Hence, morality, and humanity in so far as it is capable of morality, is that which alone has dignity.** Skill and diligence in work have a market price; wit, lively imagination and humour have a fancy price; on the other hand, fidelity in promises and benevolence from basic principles (not from instinct) have an inner worth. Nature, as well as art, contains nothing that, lacking these, it could put in their place; for their worth does not consist in the effects arising from them, in the advantage and use they provide, but in dispositions, that is, in maxims of the will that in this way are ready to manifest themselves through actions, even if success does not favour them. Such actions

sind, obgleich auch der Erfolg sie nicht begünstigte. Diese Handlungen bedürfen auch keiner Empfehlung von irgendeiner subjektiven Disposition oder Geschmack, sie mit unmittelbarer Gunst und Wohlgefallen anzusehen, keines unmittelbaren Hanges oder Gefühles für dieselben: sie stellen den Willen, der sie ausübt, als Gegenstand einer unmittelbaren Achtung dar, dazu nichts als Vernunft gefordert wird, um sie dem Willen *aufzuerlegen*, nicht von ihm zu *erschmeicheln*, welches letztere bei Pflichten ohnedem ein Widerspruch wäre. Diese Schätzung gibt also den Wert einer solchen Denkungsart als **Würde** zu erkennen und setzt sie über allen Preis unendlich weg, mit dem sie gar nicht in Anschlag und Vergleichung gebracht werden kann, ohne sich gleichsam an der Heiligkeit derselben zu vergreifen.

Und was ist es denn nun, was die sittlich gute Gesinnung oder die Tugend berechtigt, so hohe Ansprüche zu machen? [...] es hat nichts einen Wert als den, welchen ihm das Gesetz bestimmt. Die Gesetzgebung selbst aber, die allen Wert bestimmt, muß ebendarum eine Würde d.i. unbedingten, unvergleichbaren Wert haben, für welchen das Wort *Achtung* allein den geziemenden Ausdruck der Schätzung abgibt, die ein vernünftiges Wesen über sie anzustellen hat. *Autonomie* **ist also der Grund der Würde der menschlichen und jeder vernünftigen Natur.**

Die angeführten drei Arten, das Prinzip der Sittlichkeit vorzustellen, sind aber im Grunde nur so viele Formeln ebendesselben Gesetzes, deren die eine die anderen zwei von selbst in sich vereinigt. [...] Alle Maximen haben nähmlich

also need no recommendation from any subjective disposition or taste, so as to be looked upon with immediate favour and delight, nor do they need any immediate propensity or feeling for them; they present the will that practices them as the object of an immediate respect, and nothing but reason is required to *impose* them upon the will, not to *coax* them from it, which latter would in any case be a contradiction in the case of duties. This estimation therefore lets the worth of such a cast of mind be cognized as **dignity** and puts it infinitely above all price, with which it cannot be brought into comparison or competition at all without assaulting its holiness.

And what is it, then, that justifies a morally good disposition, or virtue, making such high claims? [...] nothing can [AK 4:436] have a worth other than that which the law determines for it. But the lawgiving itself, which determines all worth, must for that very reason have a **dignity,** that is, an unconditional, incomparable worth; and the word *respect* alone provides a becoming expression for the estimate of it that a rational being must give. *Autonomy* **is therefore the ground of the dignity of human nature and of every rational nature.**

The above three ways of representing the principle of morality are at bottom only so many formulae of the very same law, and anyone of them of itself unites the other two in it. [...] All maxims have, namely,

1. eine *Form*, welche in der Allgemeinheit besteht, und da ist die Formel des sittlichen Imperativs so ausgedrückt: daß die Maximen so müssen gewählt werden, als ob sie wie allgemeine Naturgesetze gelten sollten;

2. eine *Materie*, nähmlich einen Zweck, und da sagt die Formel: daß das vernünftige Wesen, als Zweck seiner Natur nach, mithin als Zweck an sich selbst, jeder Maxime zur einschränkenden Bedingung aller bloß relativen und willkürlichen Zwecke dienen müsse;

3. *eine vollständige Bestimmung* aller Maximen durch jene Formel, nämlich: daß alle Maximen aus eigener Gesetzgebung zu einem möglichen Reiche der Zwecke, als einem Reiche der Natur, zusammenstimmen sollen. [...]

Und hierin liegt eben das Paradoxon, daß bloß die **Würde der Menschheit als vernünftiger Natur**, ohne irgend einen anderen dadurch zu erreichenden Zweck oder Vorteil, mithin die Achtung für eine bloße Idee, dennoch zur unnachlaßlichen Vorschrift des Willens dienen sollte, und daß gerade in dieser Unabhängigkeit der Maxime von allen solchen Triebfedern die Erhabenheit derselben bestehe und die **Würdigkeit** eines jeden vernünftigen Subjekts, ein gesetzgebendes Glied im Reiche der Zwecke zu sein; denn sonst würde es nur als dem Naturgesetze seiner Bedürfnisse unterworfen vorgestellt werden müssen. [...]

Man kann aus dem kurz vorhergehenden sich es jetzt leicht erklären, wie es zugehe: daß, ob wir gleich unter dem Begriffe von Pflicht uns eine Unterwürfigkeit unter dem Gesetze denken, wir uns dadurch doch

1. a *form*, which consists in universality; and in this respect the formula of the moral imperative is expressed thus: that maxims must be chosen as if they were to hold as universal laws of nature;

2. a *matter*, namely an end, and in this respect the formula says that a rational being, as an end by its nature and hence as an end in itself, must in every maxim serve as the limiting condition of all merely relative and arbitrary ends;

3. *a complete determination* of all maxims by means of that formula, namely that all maxims from one's own lawgiving are to harmonize with a possible kingdom of ends as with a kingdom of nature. [...]

[AK 4:439] And just in this lies the paradox that the mere **dignity of humanity as rational nature**, without any other end or advantage to be attained by it – hence respect for a mere idea – is yet to serve as an inflexible precept of the will, and that it is just in this independence of maxims from all such incentives that their sublimity consists, and the **worthiness** of every rational subject to be a lawgiving member in the kingdom of ends; for otherwise he would have to be represented only as subject to the natural law of his needs. [...]

From what has just been said it is now easy to explain how it happens that, although in thinking the concept of duty we think of subjection to the law, [AK 4:440] yet at the same time we thereby represent a certain

zugleich eine gewisse Erhabenheit und Würde an derjenigen Person vorstellen, die alle ihre Pflichten erfüllt. Denn sofern ist zwar keine Erhabenheit an ihr, als sie dem moralischen Gesetze *unterworfen* ist, wohl aber, sofern sie in Ansehung eben desselben zugleich *gesetzgebend* und nur darum ihm untergeordnet ist.

sublimity and *dignity* in the person who fulfils all his duties. For there is indeed no sublimity in him in so far as he is *subject* to the moral law, but there certainly is in so far as he is at the same time *lawgiving* with respect to it and only for that reason subordinated to it.

Critique of Practical Reason (1788)

Again, like in *Critique of Pure Reason*, dignity refers to *a priori* priority.

AK 5:24–5

Alsdann allein ist Vernunft nur, sofern sie für sich selbst den Willen bestimmt (nicht im Dienste der Neigungen ist), ein wahres oberes Begehrungsvermögen, dem das pathologisch bestimmbare untergeordnet ist, und wirklich, ja spezifisch von diesem unterschieden, sodaß sogar die mindeste Beimischung von den Antrieben der letzteren ihrer Stärke und Vorzuge Abbruch tut, sowie das mindeste Empirische, als Bedingung in einer mathematischen Demonstration, ihre **Würde** und Nachdruck herabsetzt und vernichtet. Die Vernunft bestimmt in einem praktischen Gesetze unmittelbar den Willen, nicht vermittelst eines dazwischenkommenden Gefühls der Lust und Unlust, selbst nicht an diesem Gesetze, und nur, daß sie als reine Vernunft praktisch sein kann, macht es ihr möglich, gesetzgebend zu sein.

Then only, in so far as reason of itself (not in the service of the inclinations) determines the will, is reason a true *higher* faculty of desire, to which the pathologically determinable is subordinate, and then only is reason really, and indeed *specifically*, distinct from the latter, so that even the least admixture of the latter's impulses infringes upon its strength and superiority, just as anything at all empirical as a condition in a mathematical demonstration degrades and destroys its **dignity** and force. In a practical law reason determines the will immediately, not by means of an intervening feeling of pleasure or displeasure, not even in this law; and that it can as pure reason be practical is what alone makes it possible for it to *be lawgiving.*

Acting with respect for such priority makes us worthy of happiness, and it confers dignity on us by our conformity with it.

AK 5:130

Daher ist auch die Moral nicht eigentlich die Lehre, wie wir uns glücklich machen, sondern wie wir der Glückseligkeit **würdig** werden sollen. Nur dann, wenn Religion dazu kommt, tritt auch die Hoffnung ein, der Glückseligkeit dereinst in dem Maße teilhaftig zu werden, als wir darauf bedacht gewesen, ihrer nicht **unwürdig** zu sein.

Würdig ist jemand des Besitzes einer Sache oder eines Zustandes, wenn, daß er in diesem Besitze sei, mit dem höchsten Gute zusammenstimmt. Man kann jetzt leicht einsehen, daß alle **Würdigkeit** auf das sittliche Verhalten ankomme, weil dieses im Begriffe des höchsten Guts die Bedingung des übrigen (was zum Zustande gehört), nämlich des Anteils an Glückseligkeit, ausmacht. Nun folgt hieraus: daß man die Moral an sich niemals als Glückseligkeitslehre behandeln müsse, d.i. als eine Anweisung der Glückseligkeit teilhaftig zu werden; denn sie hat es lediglich mit der Vernunftbedingung *(conditio sine qua non)* der letzteren, nicht mit einem Erwerbmittel derselben zu tun. [...]

Auch kann man hieraus ersehen: daß, wenn man nach dem letzten Zwecke Gottes in Schöpfung der Welt fragt, man nicht die Glückseligkeit der vernünftigen Wesen in ihr, sondern das höchste Gut nennen müsse, welches jenem Wunsche dieser Wesen noch eine Bedingung, nämlich die der Glückseligkeit **würdig** zu sein, d.i. die Sittlichkeit eben derselben vernünftigen Wesen, hinzufügt, die allein den Maßstab enthält, nach welchem sie allein der ersteren durch die Hand eines weisen Urhebers teilhaftig zu werden hoffen können. [...] Selbst Menschen können sich durch

For this reason, again, morals is not properly the doctrine of how we are to make ourselves happy but of how we are to become *worthy of* happiness. Only if religion is added to it does there also enter the hope of some day participating in happiness to the degree that we have been intent upon not being **unworthy** of it.

Someone is *worthy* of possessing a thing or a state when it harmonizes with the highest good that he is in possession of it. It can now be readily seen that all **worthiness** depends upon moral conduct, since in the concept of the highest good this constitutes the condition of the rest (which belongs to one's state), namely, of one's share of happiness. Now, from this it follows that *morals* in itself must never be treated as a *doctrine of happiness*, that is, as instruction in how to become happy; for morals has to do solely with the rational condition *(conditio sine qua non) of* happiness and not with the means of acquiring it. [...]

From this it can also be seen that if one asks about *God's final end* in creating the world, one must not name the *happiness* of the rational beings in it but *the highest good*, which adds a condition to that wish of such beings, namely the condition of being **worthy** of happiness, that is, the *morality* of these same rational beings, which condition alone contains the standard in accordance with which they can hope to participate in the former at the hands of a wise author. [...] Human beings themselves can acquire love by beneficence, but by it alone they can never acquire respect, so that the greatest

Wohltun zwar Liebe, aber dadurch allein niemals Achtung erwerben, so daß die größte Wohltätigkeit ihnen nur dadurch Ehre macht, daß sie nach **Würdigkeit** ausgeübt wird.

beneficence procures them honour only when it is exercised in accordance with **worthiness.**

Critique of Judgement (1790)

The following excerpt contains no direct reference to dignity or human dignity, but it does provide an insight into how Kant envisages the relationship between nature and the ideal. Only the acceptance of a moral teleology, establishing a reason for valuing something, will finally give us the intuition we have been looking for all along. Thus, the concept of human dignity relies for its conception and application on an act of self-affirmation in accordance with deep desire. The human being can provide a final end to the universe as a whole through his participation in the categorical imperative, and this alone gives meaning to the universe, under an omniscient and wholly good God.

§ 86–7

Es ist ein Urteil, dessen sich selbst der gemeinste Verstand nicht entschlagen kann, wenn er über das Dasein der Dinge in der Welt und die Existenz der Welt selbst nachdenkt: daß nämlich alle die mannigfaltigen Geschöpfe, [...] zu nichts da sein würden, wenn es in ihnen nicht Menschen (vernünftige Wesen überhaupt) gäbe; d.i. daß ohne den Menschen die ganze Schöpfung eine bloße Wüste, umsonst und ohne Endzweck sein würde. Es ist aber auch nicht das Erkenntnisvermögen desselben (theoretische Vernunft), in Beziehung auf welches das Dasein alles übrigen in der Welt allererst seinen Wert bekommt, etwa damit irgend Jemand da sei, welcher die Welt betrachten könne. Denn wenn diese

[§ 25–6] [AK 5:442] There is a judgement, which even the commonest understanding finds irresistible when it reflects upon the existence of the things in the world and the real existence of the world itself. It is the verdict that all the manifold forms of life, [...] would all exist for nothing, if man, or rational beings of some sort, were not to be found in their midst. Without man, in other words, the whole of creation would be a mere wilderness, a thing in vain, and have no final end. Yet it is not man's cognitive faculty, that is, theoretical reason, that forms the point of reference which alone gives its worth to the existence of all else in the world – as if the meaning of his presence in the world was that there might be

Betrachtung der Welt ihm doch nichts als Dinge ohne Endzweck vorstellig machte, so kann daraus, daß sie erkannt wird, dem Dasein derselben kein Wert erwachsen; und man muß schon einen Endzweck derselben voraussetzen, in Beziehung auf welchen die Weltbetrachtung selbst einen Wert habe. Auch ist es nicht das Gefühl der Lust und der Summe derselben, in Beziehung auf welches wir einen Endzweck der Schöpfung als gegeben denken, d.i. nicht das Wohlsein, der Genuß (er sei körperlich oder geistig), mit einem Worte die Glückseligkeit, wonach wir jenen absoluten Wert schätzen. Denn: daß, wenn der Mensch da ist, er diese ihm selbst zur Endabsicht macht, gibt keinen Begriff, wozu er dann überhaupt da sei, und welchen Wert er dann selbst habe, um ihm seine Existenz angenehm zu machen. Er muß also schon als Endzweck der Schöpfung vorausgesetzt werden, um einen Vernunftgrund zu haben, warum die Natur zu seiner Glückseligkeit zusammenstimmen müsse, wenn sie als ein absolutes Ganze nach Prinzipien der Zwecke betrachtet wird. Also ist es nur das Begehrungsvermögen: aber nicht dasjenige, was ihn von der Natur (durch sinnliche Antriebe) abhängig macht, nicht das, in Ansehung dessen der Wert seines Daseins auf dem, was er empfängt und genießt, beruht: sondern der Wert, welchen er allein sich selbst geben kann, und welchen in dem besteht, was er tut, wie und nach welchem Prinzipien er nicht als Naturglied, sondern in der Freiheit seines Begehrungsvermögens handelt; d. h. ein guter Wille ist dasjenige, wodurch sein Dasein allein einen absoluten Wert und in Beziehung auf welches das Dasein der Welt einen Endzweck haben kann.

some one in it that could make it an object of *contemplation*. For if this contemplation of the world brought to light nothing but things without a final end, the existence of the world could not acquire a worth from the fact of its being known. A final end of the world must be presupposed as that in relation to which the contemplation of the world may itself possess a worth. Neither is it in relation to the feeling of pleasure or the sum of such feelings that we can think that there is a given final end of creation, that is to say, it is not by well-being, nor by enjoyment, whether bodily or mental, not, in a word, by happiness, that we value that absolute worth. For the fact that man, when he does exist, makes happiness his own final purpose, affords us no conception of any reason why he should exist at all, or of any worth he himself possesses, for which his real existence should be made agreeable to him. [AK 5:443] Hence man must already be presupposed to be the final end of creation, in order that we may have a rational ground to explain why nature, when regarded as an absolute whole according to principles of ends, must be in accord with the conditions of his happiness. Accordingly it is only the faculty of desire that can give the required point of reference – yet not that faculty which makes man dependent upon nature (through impulses of sense), that is, not that in respect of which the worth of his existence is dependent on what he receives and enjoys. On the contrary it is the worth which he alone can give to himself, and which consists in what he does in the manner in which and the principles upon which he acts in the freedom of his faculty of desire, and not as a link in the chain of nature. In other words,

a good will is that whereby man's existence can alone possess an absolute worth and in relation to which the existence of the world can have a final end.

Auch stimmt damit das gemeinste Urteil der gesunden Menschenvernunft vollkommen zusammen: nämlich, daß der Mensch nur als moralisches Wesen ein Endzweck der Schöpfung sein könne, wenn man die Beurteilung nur auf diese Frage leitet und veranlasst sie zu versuchen. Was hilft, wird man sagen, daß dieser Mensch so viel Talent hat, daß er damit sogar sehr tätig ist und dadurch einen nützlichen Einfluß auf das gemeine Wesen ausübt und also in Verhältnis sowohl auf seine Glücksumstände, als auch auf Anderer Nutzen einen großen Wert hat, wenn er keinen guten Willen besitzt? Er ist ein verachtungswürdiges Objekt, wenn man ihn nach seinem Inneren betrachtet; und wenn die Schöpfung nicht überall ohne Endzweck sein soll, so muß er, der als Mensch auch dazu gehört, doch als böser Mensch in einer Welt unter moralischen Gesetzen diesen gemäß seines subjektiven Zwecks (der Glückseligkeit) verlustig gehen, als der einzigen Bedingung, unter der seine Existenz mit dem Endzwecke zusammen bestehen kann.

Even the popular verdict of sound human reason, once its reflection is directed to this question and pressed to its consideration, is in complete accord with the judgement that it is only as a moral being that man can be a final end of creation. What, it will be said, does it all avail, that this man has so much talent, that he is even so active in its employment and thus exerts a useful influence upon social and public life, and that he possesses, therefore, considerable alike in relation to his own state of happiness and in relation to what is good for others, if he has not a good will? Looked at from the point of view of his inner self, he is a contemptible object; and, if creation is not to be altogether devoid of a final end, such a man, though as man he is part of creation, must nevertheless, as a bad man dwelling in a world subject to moral laws, forfeit, in accordance with those laws, his own subjective end, that is happiness, as the sole condition under which his real existence can consist with the final end.

Wenn wir nun in der Welt Zweckordnungen antreffen und, wie es die Vernunft unvermeidlich fordert, die Zwecke, die es nur bedingt sind, einem unbedingten obersten, d. i. einem Endzwecke, unterordnen: so sieht man erstlich leicht, daß alsdann nicht von einem Zwecke der Natur (innerhalb derselben), sofern sie existiert, sondern dem Zwecke ihrer Existenz mit allen ihren Einrichtungen, mithin von dem letzten

Now if we find instances in the world of an order adapted to ends, and if, as reason inevitably requires, we subordinate the ends which are only conditionally ends, to one that is unconditioned and supreme, that is to a final end, we readily see, to begin with, that we are then not dealing with an end of nature, included in nature taken as existent, but with the end of the real existence of nature, with all its orderly adaptations

Zwecke der Schöpfung die Rede ist und in diesem auch eigentlich von der obersten Bedingung, unter der allein ein Endzweck (d. i. der Bestimmungs-grund eines höchsten Verstandes zu Hervor-bringung der Weltwesen) Statt finden kann.

Da wir nun den Menschen nur als moralisches Wesen für den Zweck der Schöpfung anerkennen: so haben wir erstlich einen Grund, wenigstens die Hauptbedingung, die Welt als ein nach Zwecken zusammenhängendes Ganze und als System von Endursachen anzusehen; vornehmlich aber für die nach Beschaffenheit unserer Vernunft uns notwendige Beziehung der Naturzwecke auf eine verständige Welturache ein Princip, die Natur und Eigenschaften dieser ersten Ursache als obersten Grundes im Reiche der Zwecke zu denken und so den Begriff derselben zu bestimmen: welches die physische Teleologie nicht vermochte, die nur unbestimmte und eben darum zum theoretischen sowohl als praktischen Gebrauche untaugliche Begriffe von demselben veranlassen konnte.

Aus diesem bestimmten Princip der Causalität des Urwesens werden wir es nicht bloß als Intelligenz und gesetzgebend für die Natur, sondern auch als gesetzgebendes Oberhaupt in einem moralischen Reiche der Zwecke denken müssen. In Beziehung auf das höchste unter seiner Herrschaft allein mögliche Gut, nämlich die Existenz vernünftiger Wesen unter moralischen Gesetzen, werden wir uns dieses Urwesen als *allwissend* denken: damit selbst das Innerste der Gesinnungen (welches den eigentlichen moralischen

included. Consequently, we see that the question is one of the ultimate end of creation, and, more precisely, of the supreme condition under which alone there can be a final end, or, in other words, of the ground that determines a highest intelligence to the production of the beings in the world.

[AK 5:444] It is, then, only as a moral being that we acknowledge man to be the end of creation. Hence, we have, first of all, a reason, or at least the primary condition, for regarding the world as a consistent whole of interconnected ends, and as a system of final causes. Now the structure of our reason is such that we necessarily refer natural ends to an intelligent world-cause. Above all, then, we have one principle applicable to this relation, enabling us to think the nature and attributes of this first cause considered as supreme ground in the kingdom of ends, and to form a definite conception of it. This is what could not be done by physical teleology, which was only able to suggest vague conceptions, which this vagueness made as useless for practical as for theoretical employment.

With such a definite principle as this, of the causality of the original being, we shall not have to regard it merely as an intelligence and as legislating for nature, but as the Sovereign Head legislating in a moral Kingdom of Ends. In relation to the *summum bonum*, which is alone possible under His sovereignty, namely the real existence of rational beings under moral laws, we shall conceive this Original Being to be *omniscient*, so that even our inmost sentiments – wherein lies the distinctive moral value in the actions of rational beings

Wert der Handlungen vernünftiger Weltwesen ausmacht) ihm nicht verborgen sei; als *allmächtig*: damit es die ganze Natur diesem höchsten Zwecke angemessen machen könne; als *allgütig* und zugleich *gerecht*: weil diese beiden Eigenschaften (vereinigt die Weisheit) die Bedingungen der Causalität einer obersten Ursache der Welt als höchsten Guts unter moralischen Gesetzen ausmachen; und so auch alle noch übrigen transzendentalen Eigenschaften, als Ewigkeit, Allgegenwart u. s. w. (denn Güte und Gerechtigkeit sind moralische Eigenschaften), die in Beziehung auf einen solchen Endzweck vorausgesetzt werden, an demselben denken müssen. – Auf solche Weise ergänzt die moralische Teleologie den Mangel der physischen und gründet allererst eine Theologie.

[...] es ein Grundsatz, dem selbst die gemeinste Menschenvernunft unmittelbar Beifall zu geben genötigt ist: daß, wenn überall ein Endzweck, den die Vernunft *a priori* angeben muß, stattfinden soll, dieser kein anderer, als der Mensch (ein jedes vernünftige Weltwesen) unter moralischen Gesetzen sein könne. Denn (so urteilt ein jeder): bestände die Welt aus lauter leblosen, oder zwar zum Teil aus lebenden, aber vernunftlosen Wesen, so würde das Dasein einer solchen Welt gar keinen Wert haben, weil in ihr kein Wesen existierte, das von einem Werte den mindesten Begriff hat. [...] und die Existenz einer solchen Vernunft, die in der Zweckbeziehung ihr selbst das oberste Gesetz sein kann, mit andern Worten die Existenz vernünftiger Wesen unter moralischen Gesetzen, kann also allein als End[zweck] vom Dasein einer Welt gedacht werden. Ist dagegen

in the world – may not be hid from Him. We shall conceive Him as *omnipotent*, so that He may be able to adapt entire nature to this highest end; as both *all-good* and *just*, since these two attributes, which unite to form *wisdom*, constitute the conditions under which a supreme cause of the world can be the source of the greatest good under moral laws. Similarly the other remaining transcendental attributes, such as *eternity, omnipresence*, and so forth (for goodness and justice are moral attributes), all attributes that are presupposed in relation to such a final end, will have to be regarded as belonging to this Original Being. – In this way moral teleology supplements the deficiency of physical teleology, and for the first time establishes a theology.

[...] [AK 5:448] there is a fundamental principle to which even the most ordinary human intelligence is obliged to give immediate assent. It is the principle that if there is to be a final end at all, which reason must assign *a priori*, then it can only be man – or any rational being in the world – subject to moral laws. For – and this is the verdict of everyone – if the world only consisted of lifeless [AK 5:449] beings, or even consisted partly of living, but yet irrational beings, the existence of such a world would have no worth whatever, because there would exist in it no being with the least conception of what worth is. [...] Therefore, the real existence of a reason like this, that in the order of ends can be the supreme law to itself, in other words the real existence of rational beings subject to moral laws, can alone be regarded as the final end of the existence of a world.

dieses nicht so bewandt, so liegt dem Dasein derselben entweder gar kein Zweck in der Ursache, oder es liegen ihm Zwecke ohne Endzweck zum Grunde.	[AK 5:450] But if this is not so, then either no end whatever in the cause underlies the existence of the world, or else only ends without a final end.

The Doctrine of Rights (1797)

The united will of the people is sovereign with the sovereignty of the categorical imperative. Therefore, citizenship status and human dignity should coincide. In the society Kant knows, however, this is not the case. A distinction between passive and active citizenship therefore is brought in to explain why some do not have the vote. Kant, however, puts the explanation forward as seemingly contradictory. His stance on slavery (the extreme case of the various forms of subjection discussed) is that it is impossible to contract yourself into, since no one would want to accept its condition, implying the loss of juridical personality. Is he not implicitly saying that it therefore is in contradiction with human dignity? That women should be able to work their way up from being passive citizens to being active citizens might have sounded comical – Mary Wollstonecraft would have found it insulting, as we shall see from her Vindications – it nevertheless was prophetic in the sense that they, collectively, did. The contradiction between principle and acceptance of practice – the commonest of political occurrences, however regrettable or useful – seems in hindsight to have spurred a development towards the recognition of citizenship to all. When political spokespersons exist, such contradictions in general constitute convincing arguments for eliminating unfounded inequalities. Maybe Kant's text served to bring out this contradiction by stating it.

§ 47	§ 46
Die gesetzgebende Gewalt kann nur dem vereinigten Willen des Volkes zukommen. Denn, da von ihr alles Recht ausgehen soll, so muß sie durch ihr Gesetz schlechterdings niemand Unrecht tun können. Nun ist es, wenn jemand etwas gegen einen	The legislative authority can belong only to the united will of the people. For since all right is to proceed from it, it cannot do anyone wrong by its law. Now when someone makes arrangements about another, it is always possible for him to do the other

Anderen verfügt, immer möglich, daß er ihm dadurch Unrecht tue, nie aber in dem, was er über sich selbst beschließt (denn *volenti non fit injuria*). Also kann nur der übereinstimmende und vereinigte Wille Aller, sofern ein jeder über Alle und Alle über einen jeden ebendasselbe beschließen, mithin nur der allgemeinen vereinigte Volkswille gesetzgebend sein.

Die zur Gesetzgebung vereinigten Glieder einer solchen Gesellschaft (*societas civilis*), d.i. eines Staats, heißen Staatsbürger (*cives*), und die rechtlichen, von ihrem Wesen (als solchem) unabtrennlichen Attribute derselben, sind: gesetzliche Freiheit, keinem anderen Gesetz zu gehorchen, als zu welchem er seine Bestimmung gegeben hat; bürgerliche Gleichheit, keinen Oberen im Volk in Ansehung seiner zu erkennen, als nur einen solchen, den er ebenso rechtlich zu verbinden das moralische Vermögen hat, als dieser ihn verbinden kann; drittens das Attribut der bürgerlichen Selbständigkeit, seine Existenz und Erhaltung nicht der Willkür eines Anderen im Volke, sondern seinen eigenen Rechten und Kräften, als Glied des gemeinen Wesens, verdanken zu können, folglich die bürgerliche Persönlichkeit in Rechtsangelegenheiten durch keinen Anderen vorgestellt werden zu dürfen.

Nur die Fähigkeit der Stimmgebung macht die Qualifikation zum Staatsbürger aus; jene aber setzt die Selbständigkeit dessen im Volke voraus, der nicht bloß Teil des gemeinen Wesens, sondern auch Glied desselben, d.i. aus eigener Willkür in Gemeinschaft mit Anderen handelnder Teil desselben sein will. Die letztere Qualität macht aber die Unterscheidung

wrong; but he can never do wrong in what he decides upon with regard to himself (for *volenti non fit iniuria*). Therefore only [AK 6:314] the concurring and united will of all, in so far as each decides the same thing for all and all for each, and so only the general united will of the people, can be legislative.

The members of such a society who are united for giving law (*societas civilis*), that is, the members of a state, are called *citizens of a state* (*cives*). In terms of rights, the attributes of a citizen, inseparable from his essence (as a citizen), are: lawful freedom, the attribute of obeying no other law than that to which he has given his consent; civil equality, that of not recognizing among the people any superior with the moral capacity to bind him as matter of right in a way that he could not in turn bind the other; and third, the attribute of civil independence, of owing his existence and preservation to his own rights and powers as a member of the commonwealth, not to the choice of another among the people. From his independence follows his civil personality, his attribute of not needing to be represented by another where rights are concerned.

The only qualification for being a citizen is being fit to vote. But being fit to vote presupposes the independence of someone who, as one of the people, wants to be not just a part of the commonwealth but also a member of it, that is, a part of the commonwealth acting from his own choice in community with others. This quality of being independent, however, requires a

des *aktiven* vom *passiven* Staatsbürger notwendig; obgleich der Begriff des letzteren
mit der Erklärung des Begriffs von einem
Staatsbürger überhaupt im Wiederspruch
zu stehen scheint. – Folgende Beispiele
können dazu dienen, diese Schwierigkeit
zu heben: der Geselle bei einem Kaufmann,
oder bei einem Handwerker; der Dienstbote
(nicht der im Dienste der Staat steht), der
Unmündige (*naturaliter vel civiliter*), alles
Frauenzimmer, und überhaupt jedermann,
der nicht nach eigenem Betrieb, sondern
nach der Verfügung Anderer (außer der
des Staats), genötigt ist, seine Existenz
(Nahrung und Schutz) zu erhalten, ent-
behrt der bürgerlichen Persönlichkeit, und
seine Existenz ist gleichsam nur Inhärenz.
– Der Holzhacker, den ich auf meinem
Hofe anstelle, der Schmied in Indien, der
mit seinem Hammer, Ambos und Blasbalg
in die Häuser geht, um da in Eisen zu arbeiten, in Vergleichung mit dem europäischen
Tischler oder Schmied, der die Produkte
aus dieser Arbeit als Ware öffentlich feilstel-
len kann; der Hauslehrer in Vergleichung
mit dem Schulmann, der Zinsbauer in
Vergleichung mit dem Pächter u. dgl., sind
bloß Handlanger des gemeinen Wesens,
weil sie von anderen Individuen befehligt
oder beschützt werden müssen, mithin
keine bürgerliche Selbständigkeit besitzen.

distinction between *active* and *passive* citizens though the concept of a passive citizen
seems to contradict the concept of a citizen as such. – The following examples can
serve to remove this difficulty: an appren-
tice in the service of a merchant or artisan;
a domestic servant (as distinguished from a
civil servant); a minor *(naturaliter vel civiliter); all women and, in general, anyone
whose preservation in existence (his being
fed and protected) depends not on his
management of his own business but on
arrangements made by another (except
the state). All these people lack civil personality and their existence is, as it were,
only inherence. – The woodcutter I hire to
work in my yard; the blacksmith in India,
who goes into people's houses to work on
iron with his hammer, anvil and bellows, as
compared with the European carpenter or
blacksmith who can put the products [AK
6:315] of his work up as goods for sale to
the public; the private tutor, as compared
with the school teacher; the tenant farmer
as compared with the leasehold farmer, and
so forth; these are mere underlings of the
commonwealth because they have to be
under the direction or protection of other
individuals, and so do not possess civil
independence.

Diese Abhängigkeit von dem Willen
Anderer und Ungleichheit ist gleichwohl
keineswegs der Freiheit und Gleichheit
derselben als Menschen, die zusammen
ein Volk ausmachen, entgegen; vielmehr
kann bloß den Bedingungen derselben
gemäß dieses Volk ein Staat werden, und
in eine bürgerliche Verfassung eintreten.

This dependence upon the will of others
and this inequality is however, in no way
opposed to their freedom and equality *as
human beings*, who together make up a
people; on the contrary, it is only in conformity with the conditions of freedom and
equality that this people can become a state
and enter into a civil constitution. But not

In dieser Verfassung aber das Recht der Stimmgebung zu haben, d.i. Staatsbürger, nicht bloß Staatsgenosse zu sein, dazu qualifizieren sich nicht alle mit gleichem Rechte. Denn daraus, daß sie fordern können, von allen Anderen nach Gesetzen der natürlichen Freiheit und Gleichheit als passive Teile des Staats behandelt zu werden, folgt nicht das Recht, auch als aktive Glieder den Staat selbst zu behandeln, zu organisieren oder zu Einführung gewisser Gesetze mitzuwirken; sondern nur daß, welcherlei Art die positiven Gesetze, wozu sie stimmen, auch sein möchten, sie doch den natürlichen der Freiheit und der dieser angemessenen Gleichheit Aller im Volk, sich nämlich aus diesem passiven Zustande zu dem aktiven emporarbeiten zu können, nicht zuwider sein müssen. [...]

D.

Das Recht des obersten Befehlshabers im Staate geht auch 1) auf Verteilung der Ämter, als mit einer Besoldung verbundener Geschäftsführung; 2) der **Würden,** die, als Standeserhöhungen ohne Sold, d.i. Rangerteilung des Oberen (der zum Befehlen) in Ansehung der Niedrigeren (die, obzwar als freie und nur durchs öffentliche Gesetz verbindliche, doch jenen zu gehohrsamen zum voraus bestimmt sind), bloß auf Ehre fundiert sind – und 3) außer diesem (respektiv-wohltätigen) Recht, auch aufs Strafrecht. [...]

Ohne alle **Würde** kann nun wohl kein Mensch im Staate sein, denn er hat wenigstens die des Staatsbürgers; außer wenn er sich durch sein eigenes Verbrechen darum gebracht hat, da er dann zwar im Leben erhalten, aber zum bloßen Werkzeuge der Willkür eines Anderen (entweder des

all persons qualify with equal right to vote within this constitution, that is, to be citizens and not mere associates in the state. For from their being able to demand that all others treat them in accordance with the laws of natural freedom and equality as *passive* parts of the state it does not follow that they also have the right to manage the state itself as *active* members of it, the right to organize it or to cooperate for introducing certain laws. It follows only that, whatever sort of positive laws the citizens might vote for, these laws must still not be contrary to the natural laws of freedom and of the equality of everyone in the people corresponding to this freedom, namely that anyone can work his way up from this passive condition to an active one. [...]

D.

[AK 6:328] The rights of the supreme commander of a state also include: 1) the distribution of offices, which are salaried administrative positions; 2) the distribution of **dignities,** which are eminent estates without pay, based on honour alone, that is, a division of rank into the higher (destined to command) and the lower (which, though free and bound only by public law, is still destined to obey the former); and 3) besides these (relatively beneficent) rights, the right to punish as well. [...]

Certainly no human being in a state can be without any **dignity,** since he at least has the **dignity** of a citizen. The exception is someone who has lost it by his own crime, because [AK 6:330] of which, though he is kept alive, he is made a mere tool of another's choice (either of the state or of

Staates, oder eines anderen Staatsbürgers) gemacht wird. Wer nun das letztere ist (was er nur durch Urteil und Recht werden kann), ist ein Leibeigener (*servus in sensu stricto*) und gehört zum Eigentum (*dominium*) eines Anderen, der daher nicht bloß sein Herr (*herus*), sondern auch sein Eigentümer (*dominus*) ist, der ihn als eine Sache veräußern und nach Belieben (nur nicht zu schandbaren Zwecken) brauchen, und über seine Kräfte, wenngleich nicht über sein Leben und Gliedmaßen verfügen (disponieren) kann. Durch einen Vertrag kann sich niemand zu einer solchen Abhängigkeit verbinden, dadurch er aufhört, eine Person zu sein; denn nur als Person kann er einen Vertrag machen. Nun scheint es zwar, ein Mensch könne sich zu gewissen, der Qualität nach erlaubten, dem Grade nach aber unbestimmten Diensten gegen einen Andern (für Lohn, Kost, oder Schutz) verpflichten, durch einen Verdingungsvertrag (*locatio conductio*), und er werde dadurch bloß Untertan (*subjectus*), nicht Leibeigener (*servus*); allein das ist nur ein falscher Schein. Denn wenn sein Herr befugt ist, die Kräfte seinen Untertan nach Belieben zu benutzen, so kann er sie auch (wie es mit den Negern auf den Zuckerinseln der Fall ist) erschöpfen, bis zum Tode oder der Verzweiflung, und jener hat sich seinem Herrn wirklich als Eigentum weggegeben; welches unmöglich ist. – Er kann sich also nur zu, der Qualität und dem Grade nach bestimmten, Arbeiten verdingen: entweder als Tagelöhner, oder ansässiger Untertan; im letzteren Fall, daß er, teils für den Gebrauch des Bodens seines Herrn, statt des Tageslohns, Dienste auf demselben Boden, teils für die eigene Benutzung desselben bestimmte Abgaben

another). Whoever is another's tool (which he can become only by a verdict and right) is a bondsman (*servus* in *sensu stricto*) and is the property (*dominium*) of another, who is accordingly not merely his master (*herus*) but his owner (*dominus*) and can therefore alienate him as a thing, use him as he pleases (only not for shameful purposes) and dispose of his powers, though not of his life and members. No one can bind himself to this kind of dependence, by which he ceases to be a person, by a contract, since it is only as a person that he can make a contract. Now it might seem that someone could put himself under obligation to another person, by a contract to let and hire (*locatio conductio*), to perform services (in return for wages, board or protection) that are permissible in terms of their quality but indeterminate in terms of their quantity, and that he thereby becomes just a subject (*subjectus*), not a bondsman (*servus*). But this is only a deceptive appearance. For if the master is authorized to use the powers of his subject as he pleases, he can also exhaust them until his subject dies or is driven to despair (as with the Negroes on the Sugar Islands); his subject will in fact have given himself away, as property, to his master, which is impossible. – Someone can therefore hire himself out only for work that is determined as to its kind and its amount, either as a day labourer or as a subject living on his master's property. In the latter case he can make a contract, for a time or indefinitely, to perform services by working on his master's land in exchange for the use of it instead of receiving wages as a day labourer, or to pay rent (a tax) specified by a lease in return for his own use of it, without thereby making himself a serf (*glebae adscriptus*), by which

(einen Zinz) nach einem Pachtvertrage leistet, ohne sich dabei zum Gutsuntertan (*glebae adscriptus*) zu machen, als wodurch er seine Persönlichkeit einbüßen würde, mithin eine Zeit – oder Erbpecht gründen kann. Er mag nun aber auch durch sein Verbrechen ein persönlicher Untertan geworden sein, so kann diese Untertänigkeit ihm doch nicht anerben; weil er sie sich nur durch seine eigene Schuld zugezogen hat, und ebensowenig kann der von einem Leibeigenen erzeugte, wegen der Erziehungskosten, die er gemacht hat, in Anspruch genommen werden, weil Erziehung eine absolute Naturpflicht der Eltern, und, im Falle daß diese Leibeigene waren, der Herren ist, welche mit dem Besitz ihrer Untertanen auch die Pflichten derselben übernommen haben.

he would forfeit his personality. Even if he has become a personal subject by his crime, his subjection cannot be inherited, because he has incurred it only by his own guilt. Nor can a bondsman's offspring be claimed as a bondsman because he has given rise to the expense of being educated; for parents have an absolute natural duty to educate their children and, in case the parents are in bondage, their masters take over this duty along with possession of their subjects.

The Doctrine of Virtue (1797)

In comparison to the 'new' drive towards 'objective' recognition of human dignity in terms of legal personality in all human persons which Kant channels, his insistence on the subjective consequences of human dignity are less ground breaking. However, just as the objective implications of human dignity only in their particulars would have surprised earlier generations, so the subjective implications have an eternal relevance stemming from the radicality of having a basic principle – human dignity – commanding practical living. Acts against the respect due to oneself, subjective acts against human dignity, include submitting to passions, lying, avarice, servility and false humility. Kant's stressing of the duty to respect one's moral dignity in accord with his insistence on objective dignity and when taken in conjunction with it, encourages the individual to claim his rights as a matter of virtue. Ambition, flattery and ridicule are mentioned as acts against the respect due to the dignity of others.

6:420

Was aber die Pflicht des Menschen gegen sich selbst bloß als moralisches Wesen (ohne auf seine Tierheit zu sehen) betrifft, so besteht sie im Formalen, der Übereinstimmung der Maximen seines Willens mit der **Würde der Menschheit** in seiner Person; also im Verbot, daß er sich selbst des Vorzugs eines moralischen Wesens, nämlich nach Prinzipien zu handeln, d.i. der inneren Freiheit, nicht beraube und dadurch zum Spiel bloßer Neigungen, also zur Sache, mache. – Die Laster, welche dieser Pflicht entgegenstehen, sind: die Lüge, der Geiz und die falsche Demut (Kriecherei). [...]

[6:429] Die größte Verletzung der Pflicht des Menschen gegen sich selbst, bloß als moralisches Wesen betrachtet (die Menschheit in seiner Person), ist das Wiederspiel der Wahrhaftigkeit: die Lüge [...] Die Lüge is Wegwerfung und gleichsam Vernichtung seiner **Menschenwürde**. [...] Die Lüge kann eine äußere (*mendacium externum*) oder auch eine innere sein. Durch jene macht er sich in anderer, durch diese aber, was noch mehr ist, in seinen eigenen Augen zum Gegenstande der Verachtung und verletzt die **Würde der Menschheit** in seiner eigenen Person [...]

§ *11*

Der Mensch im System der Natur (*homo phaenomenon, animal rationale*) ist ein Wesen von geringer Bedeutung und hat mit den übrigen Tieren, als Erzeugnissen des Bodens, einen gemeinen Wert (*pretium vulgare*). Selbst daß er vor diesen den Verstand voraus hat und sich selbst Zwecke setzen kann, das gibt ihm doch nur einen äußeren Wert seiner Brauchbarkeit (*pretium usus*),

But a human being's duty to himself as a moral being only (without taking his animality into consideration) consists in what is formal in the consistency of the maxims of his will with the *dignity* **of humanity** in his person. It consists, therefore, in a prohibition against depriving himself of the prerogative of a moral being, that of acting in accordance with principles, that is, inner freedom, and so making himself a plaything of the mere inclinations and hence a thing. – The vices contrary to this duty are lying, avarice, and false humility (servility). [...]

The greatest violation of a human being's duty to himself regarded merely as a moral being (the humanity in his own person) is the contrary of truthfulness, lying [...] – By a lie, a human being throws away and, as it were, annihilates his **dignity as a human being**. [...] A lie can be an external lie (*mendacium externum*) or also an internal lie. – By an external lie, a human being makes himself an object of contempt in the eyes of others; by an internal lie he does what is still worse: he makes himself contemptible in his own eyes and violates the **dignity of humanity** in his own person. [...]

In the system of nature, a human being [AK 6:434] (*homo phaenomenon, animal rationale*) is a being of slight importance and shares with the rest of the animals, as offspring of the earth, an ordinary value (*pretium vulgare*). Although a human being has, in his understanding, something more than the animals and can set himself ends, this gives him only an extrinsic value for

nämlich eines Menschen vor dem anderen, d.i. einen Preis, als einer Ware, in dem Verkehr mit diesen Tieren als Sachen, wo er doch noch einen niedrigeren Wert hat als das allgemeine Tauschmittel, das Geld, dessen Wert daher ausgezeichnet (*pretium eminens*) genannt wird.

Allein der Mensch als Person betrachtet, d.i. als Subjekt einer moralisch-praktischen Vernunft, ist über allen Preis erhaben; denn als ein solcher (*homo noumenon*) ist er nicht bloß als Mittel zu Anderer ihren, ja selbst seinen eigenen Zwecken, sondern als Zweck an sich selbst zu schätzen, d.i. er besitzt eine **Würde (einen absoluten inneren Wert)**, wodurch er allen anderen vernünftigen Weltwesen Achtung für ihn abnötigt, sich mit jedem Anderen dieser Art messen und auf den Fuß der Gleichheit schätzen kann.

Die Menschheit in seiner Person ist das Objekt der Achtung, die er von jedem anderen Menschen fordern kann; deren [er] aber auch sich nicht verlustig machen muß. Er kann und soll sich also, nach einem kleinen sowohl als großen Maßstabe schätzen, nachdem er sich als Sinnenwesen (seiner tierischen Natur nach) oder als intelligibles Wesen (seiner moralischen Anlage nach) betrachtet. Da er sich aber nicht bloß als Person überhaupt, sondern auch als Mensch, d.i. als eine Person, die Pflichten auf sich hat, die ihm seine eigene Vernunft auferlegt, betrachten muß, so kann seine Geringfügigkeit als Tiermensch dem Bewußtseyn seiner **Würde als Vernunftmensch** nicht Abbruch tun, und er soll die moralische Selbstschätzung in Betracht der letzteren nicht verleugnen, d.i. er soll sich um seinen Zweck, der an

his usefulness (*pretium usus*); that is to say, it gives one man a higher value than another, that is a price as of a commodity in exchange with these animals as things, though he still has a lower value than the universal medium of exchange, money, the value of which can therefore be called preeminent (*pretium eminens*).

But a human being regarded as a person, that is, as the subject of a morally practical reason, is exalted above any price; for as a person (*homo noumenon*) he is not to be valued merely as [AK 6:435] a means to the ends of others or even to his own ends, but as an end in itself, that is, he possesses a **dignity (an absolute inner worth)** by which he exacts respect for himself with every other being of this kind and value himself on a footing of equality with them.

Humanity in his person is the object of the respect which he can demand from every other human being, but which he must also not forfeit. Hence he can and should value himself by a low as well as by a high standard, depending on whether he views himself as a sensible being (in terms of his animal nature) or as an intelligible being (in terms of his moral predisposition). Since he must regard himself not only as a person generally but also as a human being, that is as a person who has duties his own reason lays upon him, his insignificance as a human animal may not infringe upon his consciousness of his **dignity as a rational human being**, and he should not disavow the moral self-esteem of such a being, that is, he should pursue his end, which is in itself a duty, not abjectly, not in a servile spirit (*animo servili*) as if he were seeking

sich selbst Pflicht ist, nicht kriechend, nicht knechtisch (*animo servili*), gleich als sich um Gunst bewerbend, bewerben, nicht seine **Würde** verleugnen, sondern immer mit dem Bewußtsein der Erhabenheit seiner moralischen Anlage (welches im Begriff der Tugend schon enthalten ist); und diese Selbstschätzung ist Pflicht des Menschen gegen sich selbst.

a favour, not disavowing his **dignity,** but always with consciousness of his sublime moral predisposition (which is already contained in the concept of virtue). And this self-esteem is a duty of the human being to himself.

Das Bewußtsein und Gefühl der Geringfügigkeit seines moralischen Werts in Vergleichung mit dem Gesetz ist die moralische Demut (*humilitas moralis*). Die Überredung von einer Größe dieses seines Werts, aber nur aus Mangel der Vergleichung mit dem Gesetz, kann der Tugendstolz (*arrogantia moralis*) genannt werden. – Die Entsagung alles Anspruchs auf irgend einen moralischen Wert seiner selbst in der Überredung, sich eben dadurch einen geborgten zu erwerben, ist sittlich-falsche Kriecherei (*humilitas spuria*).

The consciousness and feeling of the insignificance of one's moral worth in comparison with the law is humility (*humilitas moralis*). A conviction of the greatness of one's moral worth, but only from a failure to compare it with the law, can be called moral arrogance (*arrogantia moralis*). – Waiving any claim to moral worth in oneself, in the belief that one will thereby acquire a borrowed worth, is false humility (*humilitas spuria*).

Demut in Vergleichung mit anderen Menschen (ja überhaupt mit irgendeinem endlichen Wesen, und wenn es auch ein Seraph wäre) ist gar keine Pflicht; vielmehr ist die Bestrebung, in diesem Verhältnisse anderen gleichzukommen oder sie zu übertreffen, mit der Überredung, sich dadurch auch einen inneren größeren Wert zu verschaffen, Hochmuth (*ambitio*), welcher der Pflicht gegen andere gerade zuwider ist. Aber die bloß als Mittel zu Erwerbung der Gunst eines Anderen, (wer es auch sei) ausgesonnene Herabsetzung seines eigenen moralischen Werts (Heuchelei und Schmeichelei) ist falsche (erlogene) Demut und, als **Abwürdigung** seiner Persönlichkeit, der Pflicht gegen sich selbst entgegen.

Humility in comparing oneself with other human beings (and indeed with any finite being, even a seraph) is no duty; rather, trying to equal or surpass others in this respect, believing that in this way one will get an even greater inner worth, is ambition (*ambitio*), which is directly contrary to one's duty to others. But belittling one's own moral worth merely as a means to acquiring the [AK 6:436] favour of another, whoever it may be (hypocrisy and flattery) is false (lying) humility, which is contrary to one's duty to oneself since it **degrades** one's personality.

Aus unserer aufrichtigen und genauen Vergleichung mit dem moralischen Gesetz (dessen Heiligkeit und Strenge) muß unvermeidlich wahre Demut folgen: aber daraus, daß wir einer solchen inneren Gesetzgebung fähig sind, daß der (physische) Mensch den (moralischen) Menschen in seiner eigenen Person zu verehren sich gedrungen fühlt, zugleich Erhebung und die höchste Selbstschätzung, als Gefühl seines inneren Werts (*valor*), nach welchem er für keinen Preis (*pretium*) feil ist, und eine **unverlierbare Würde** (*dignitas interna*) besitzt, die ihm Achtung (*reverentia*) gegen sich selbst einflößt.

True humility follows unavoidably from our sincere and exact comparison of ourselves with the moral law (its holiness and strictness). But from our capacity for internal law-giving and from the (natural) human being's feeling himself compelled to revere the (moral) human being within his own person, at the same time there comes an *exaltation* of the highest self-esteem, the feeling of his inner worth (*valor*), in terms of which he is above any price (*pretium*) and possesses an **inalienable dignity** (*dignitas interna*), which instils in him respect for himself (*reverentia*).

§ 12

Mehr oder weniger kann man diese Pflicht, in Beziehung auf die **Würde der Menschheit** in uns, mithin auch gegen uns selbst, in folgenden Beispielen kennbar machen.

This duty with reference to the **dignity of humanity** within us, and so to ourselves, can be recognized, more or less, in the following examples.

Werdet nicht der Menschen Knechte. – Laßt euer Recht nicht ungeahndet von Anderen mit Füßen treten. – Macht keine Schulden, für die ihr nicht volle Sicherheit leistet. – Nehmt nicht Wohltaten an, die ihr entbehren könnt, und seid nicht Schmarotzer oder Schmeichler oder gar (was freilich nur im Grad von dem Vorigen unterschieden ist) Bettler. Daher seid wirtschaftlich, damit ihr nicht bettelarm werdet. – Das Klagen und Winseln, selbst das bloße Schreien bei einem körperlichen Schmerz ist euer schon unwert, am meisten, wenn ihr euch bewußt seid, ihn selbst verschuldet zu haben: daher die Veredelung (Abwendung der Schmach) des Todes eines Delinquenten durch die Standhaftigkeit, mit der er stirbt. – Das Hinknien oder Hinwerfen zur Erde,

Be no man's lackey. – Do not let others tread with impunity on your rights. – Contract no debt for which you cannot give full security. – Do not accept favours you could do without, and do not be a parasite or a flatterer or (what really differs from these only in degree) a beggar. Be thrifty, then, so that you will not become destitute. – Complaining and whining, even crying out in bodily pain, is unworthy of you, especially if you are aware of having deserved it; thus a criminal's death may be ennobled (its disgrace averted) by the resoluteness with which he dies. Kneeling down or prostrating oneself on the ground, even to show your veneration for heavenly objects, is contrary to the **dignity of humanity**, as is invoking them in actual images; for you then humble yourself, not before an *ideal*

selbst um die Verehrung himmlischer
Gegenstände sich dadurch zu versinnli-
chen, ist der **Menschenwürde** zuwider,
sowie die Anrufung derselben in gegenwärtigen Bilder; denn ihr demütigt euch alsdann nicht unter einem Ideal, das euch eure
eigene Vernunft vorstellt, sondern unter
einem Idol, was euer eigenes Gemächsel
ist. [...]

represented to you by your [AK 6:437]
own reason, but before an *idol* of your own
making. [...]

§ *15*

Diese moralische Selbsterkenntnis wird
erstlich die schwärmerische Verachtung
seiner selbst als Mensch (seiner ganzen
Gattung) überhaupt verbannen; denn
sie widerspricht sich selbst. – Es kann ja
nur durch die herrliche in uns befindliche
Anlage zum Guten, welche **den Menschen
achtungswürdig macht**, geschehen, daß er
den Menschen, der dieser zuwiderhandelt
(sich selbst, aber nicht die Menschheit in
sich), **verachtungswürdig** findet. – Dann
aber widersteht sie auch der eigenliebigen
Selbstschätzung, bloße Wünsche, wenn sie
mit noch so großer Sehnsucht geschähen,
da sie an sich doch tatleer sind und bleiben,
für Beweise eines guten Herzens zu halten.
(Gebet ist auch nur ein innerlich vor einem
Herzenskundiger deklarierter Wunsch.)
Unparteilichkeit in Beurteilung unserer
selbst in Vergleichung mit dem Gesetz und
Aufrichtigkeit im Selbstgeständnisse seines
inneren moralischen Werts oder Unwerts
sind Pflichten gegen sich selbst, die aus
jenem ersten Gebot der Selbsterkenntnis
unmittelbar folgen. [...]

[AK 6:441] This moral cognition of oneself will, first, dispel fanatical contempt for
oneself as a human being (for the whole
human race), since this contradicts itself.
It is only through the noble predisposition
to the good in us, which makes **the human
being worthy of respect**, that one can find
one who acts contrary to it contemptible
(the human being himself, but not the
humanity in him). – But such cognition
will also counteract that egotistical self-
esteem which takes mere wishes – wishes
that, however ardent, always remain empty
of deeds – for proof of a good heart. (Prayer
too, is only a wish declared inwardly before
someone who knows hearts). Impartiality
in appraising oneself in comparison with
the law, and sincerity in acknowledging to
oneself one's inner moral worth or lack of
worth [AK 6:442] are duties to oneself that
follow directly from this first command to
cognize oneself. [...]

§ 37

Mäßigung in Ansprüchen überhaupt, d.i. freiwillige Einschränkung der Selbstliebe eines Menschen durch die Selbstliebe Anderer, heißt Bescheidenheit. Der Mangel dieser Mäßigung (Unbescheidenheit) in Ansehung der **Würdigkeit**, von Anderen geliebt zu werden, ist die Eigenliebe (*philautia*). Die Unbescheidenheit der Forderung aber, von Anderen geachtet zu werden, ist der Eigendünkel (*arrogantia*). Achtung, die ich für Andere trage, oder die ein Anderer von mir fordern kann (*observantia aliis praestanda*), ist also die **Anerkennung einer Würde** (*dignitas*) **an anderen Menschen, d.i. eines Werts, der keinen Preis hat, kein Äquivalent**, wogegen das Objekt der Wertschätzung (*aestemii*) ausgetauscht werden könnte. – Die Beurteilung eines Dinges als eines solchen, das keinen Wert hat, ist die Verachtung.

[AK 6:462] *Moderation* in one's demands generally, that is, willing restriction of one's self-love in view of the self-love of others, is called *modesty*. Lack of such moderation (lack of modesty) as regards one's **worthiness** to be *loved* by others is called *egotism* (*philautia*). But lack of modesty in one's claims to be respected by others is *self-conceit* (*arrogantia*). The *respect* that I have for others or that another can require from me (*observantia aliis praestanda*) is therefore **recognition of a dignity** (*dignitas*) **in other human beings, that is, of a worth that has no price, no equivalent** for which the object evaluated (*aestimii*) could be exchanged. – Judging something to be worthless is contempt.

§ 38

Ein jeder Mensch hat rechtmäßigen Anspruch auf Achtung von seinen Nebenmenschen, und wechselseitig ist er dazu auch gegen jeden Anderen verbunden.

Die Menschheit selbst ist eine Würde; denn der Mensch kann von keinem Menschen (weder von Anderen, noch sogar von sich selbst) bloß als Mittel, sondern muß jederzeit zugleich als Zweck gebraucht werden, und darin besteht eben seine **Würde** (die Persönlichkeit), dadurch er sich über alle anderen Weltwesen, die nicht Menschen sind und doch gebraucht werden können, mithin über alle Sachen erhebt. Gleichwie er also sich selbst für keinen Preis weggeben kann (welches der Pflicht der Selbstschätzung widerstreiten

Every human being has a legitimate claim to respect from his fellow human beings and is *in turn* bound to respect every other.

Humanity itself is a dignity; for a human being cannot be used merely as a means by any human being (either by others or by himself) but must always be used at the same time as an end. It is just in this that his **dignity** (personality) consists, by which he raises himself above all other beings in the world that are not human beings and yet can be used, and so over all things. But just as he cannot give himself away at any price (this would conflict with his duty of self-esteem), so neither can he act contrary to the equally necessary self-esteem of

würde), so kann er auch nicht der ebenso
notwendigen Selbstschätzung Anderer
als Menschen entgegen handeln, d.i. er ist
verbunden, die **Würde der Menschheit** an
jedem anderen Menschen praktisch anzu-
erkennen, mithin ruht auf ihm eine Pflicht,
die sich auf die jedem anderen Menschen
notwendig zu erzeigende Achtung bezieht.

others, as human beings, that is, he is under
obligation to acknowledge, in a practical
way, the **dignity of humanity** in every other
human being. Hence, there rests with him
a duty regarding the respect that must be
shown to every other human being.

§ 39

Andere verachten (*contemnere*), i.e. ihnen
die dem Menschen überhaupt schuldige
Achtung weigern, ist auf alle Fälle pflicht-
widrig; denn es sind Menschen. Sie ver-
gleichungsweise mit Anderen innerlich
geringschätzen (*despicatui habere*) ist zwar
bisweilen unvermeidlich, aber die äußere
Bezeigung der Geringschätzung ist doch
Beleidigung. – Was gefährlich ist, ist kein
Gegenstand der Verachtung und so ist es
auch nicht der Lasterhafte; und wenn die
Überlegenheit über die Angriffe desselben
mich berechtigt zu sagen: ich verachte
jenen, so bedeutet das nur so viel als: es ist
keine Gefahr dabei, wenn ich gleich gar
keine Verteidigung gegen ihn veranstaltete,
weil er sich in seiner Verworfenheit selbst
darstellte. Nichtsdestoweniger kann ich
selbst dem Lasterhaften als Menschen nicht
alle Achtung versagen, die ihm wenigstens in der Qualität eines Menschen nicht
entzogen werden kann; ob er zwar durch
seine Tat sich derselben **unwürdig** macht.
So kann es schimpfliche, die Menschheit
selbst entehrende Strafen geben (wie das
Vierteilen, von Hunden zerreißen lassen,
Nasen und Ohren abschneiden), die nicht
bloß dem Ehrliebenden (der auf Achtung
Anderer Anspruch macht, was ein jeder
tun muß) durch diese Entehrung schmerzhafter sind), schmerzhafter sind als der

[AK 6:463] To be *contemptuous* of others
(*contemnere*), that is, to deny them the
respect owed to human beings in general,
is in every case contrary to duty; for they
are human beings. At times one cannot, it is
true, help inwardly *looking down* on some in
comparison with others (*despicatu habere*);
but the outward manifestation of this is
nevertheless an offence. – What is *dangerous* is no object of contempt, and so neither
is a vicious man; and if my superiority to
his attacks justifies my saying that I despise
him, this means only that I am in no danger
from him, even though I have prepared
no defence against him, because he shows
himself in all his depravity. Nonetheless, I
cannot deny all respect to even a vicious
man as a human being; I cannot withdraw
at least the respect that belongs to him in
his quality as a human being, even though
by his deeds he makes himself **unworthy**
of it. So there can be disgraceful punishments that dishonour humanity itself (such
as quartering a man, having him torn by
dogs, cutting off his nose and ears). Not
only are such punishments more painful
than loss of possessions and life to one who
loves honour (who claims the respect of
others as everyone must); they also make
the spectator blush with shame at belonging
to a species that can be treated that way. [...]

Verlust der Güter und des Lebens, sondern auch dem Zuschauer Schamröte abjagen, zu einer Gattung zu gehören, mit der man so verfahren darf. [...]

§ 42

Der Hochmut (*superbia* und, wie dieses Wort es ausdrückt, die Neigung, immer oben zu schwimmen), ist eine Art von Ehrbegierde (*ambitio*), nach welcher wir anderen Menschen ansinnen, sich selbst in Vergleichung mit uns gering zu schätzen, und ist also ein der Achtung, worauf jeder Mensch gesetzmäßigen Anspruch machen kann, widerstreitendes Laster.

Er ist vom Stolz (*animus elatus*), als Ehrliebe, d.i. Sorgfalt, seiner **Menschenwürde** in Vergleichung mit Anderen nichts zu vergeben (der daher auch mit dem Beiwort des edlen belegt zu werden pflegt), unterschieden; denn der Hochmut verlangt von Anderen eine Achtung, die er ihnen doch verweigert. – Aber dieser Stolz selbst wird doch zum Fehler und Beleidigung, wenn er auch bloß ein Ansinnen an Andere ist, sich mit seiner Wichtigkeit zu beschäftigen. [...]

[AK 6:465] *Arrogance* (*superbia* and, as this word expresses it, the inclination to be always on top) is a kind of *ambition* (*ambitio*) in which we demand that others think little of themselves in comparison with us. It is therefore a vice opposed to the respect that every human being can lawfully claim.

It differs from pride proper (*animus elatus*), which is *love of honour*, that is, a concern to yield nothing of one's **human dignity** in comparison with others (so that the adjective '*noble*' is usually added to 'pride' in this sense); for arrogance demands from others a respect it denies them. – But *pride* itself becomes a fault and an offence when it, too, is merely a demand upon others to concern themselves with one's importance. [...]

§ 43

[...] Die geflissentliche Verbreitung (*propalatio*) desjenigen, die Ehre eines Anderen Schmälernden, was auch nicht zur öffentlichen Gerichtsbarkeit gehört, es mag übrigens auch wahr sein, ist Verringerung der Achtung für die Menschheit überhaupt, um endlich auf unsere Gattung selbst den Schatten der **Nichts-würdigkeit** zu werfen und Misanthropie (Menschenscheu) oder Verachtung zur herrschenden Denkungsart zu machen, oder sein moralisches Gefühl durch den öfteren Anblick derselben abzustumpfen und sich daran zu gewöhnen.

[AK 6:467] [...] The intentional *spreading* (*propalatio*) of something that detracts from another's honour – even if it is not a matter of public justice, and even if what is said is true – diminishes respect for humanity as such, so as finally to cast a shadow of **worthlessness** over our race itself, making misanthropy (shying away from human beings) or contempt, the relevant cast of mind, or to dull one's moral feeling by repeatedly exposing one to the sight of such things and accustomising one to it.

Es ist also Tugendpflicht, statt einer hämischen Lust an der Bloßstellung der Fehler Anderer, um sich dadurch die Meinung, gut, wenigstens nicht schlechter als alle anderen Menschen zu sein, zu sichern, den Schleier der Menschenliebe nicht bloß durch Milderung unserer Urteile, sondern auch durch Verschweigung derselben über die Fehler Anderer zu werfen: weil Beispiele der Achtung, welche wir Anderen geben, auch die Bestrebung rege machen können, sie gleichmäßig zu verdienen. – Um deswillen ist die Ausspähungs-sucht der Sitten Anderer (*allotrio-episcopia*) auch für sich selbst schon ein beleidigender Vorwitz der Menschenkunde, welchem jedermann sich mit Recht als einer Verletzung der ihm schuldigen Achtung widersetzen kann.

It is, therefore, a duty of virtue not to take malicious pleasure in exposing the faults of others so that one will be thought as good as, or at least no worse than, others, but rather throw the veil of philanthropy over their faults, not merely by softening our judgements but also by keeping these judgements to ourselves; for examples of respect that we give others can arouse their striving to deserve it. – For this reason, a mania for spying on the morals of others (*allotrio-episcopeia*) is by itself already an offensive inquisitiveness on the part of anthropology, which everyone can resist with right as a violation of the respect due to him.

§ 44

Die leichtfertige Tadelsucht und der Hang, Andere zum Gelächter bloßzustellen, die Spottsucht, um die Fehler eines Anderen zum unmittelbaren Gegenstande seiner Belustigung zu machen, ist Bosheit, [...]

Wanton faultfinding and *mockery*, the propensity to expose others to laughter, to make their faults the immediate object of one's amusement, is a kind of malice. [...]

Hiervon ist doch die scherzhafte, wenngleich spottende Abweisung der beleidigenden Angriffe eines Gegners mit Verachtung (*retorsio iocosa*) unterschieden, wodurch der Spötter (oder überhaupt ein schadenfroher, aber kraftloser Gegner) gleichmäßig verspottet wird, und rechtmäßige Verteidigung der Achtung, die er von jenem fordern kann. Wenn aber der Gegenstand eigentlich kein Gegenstand für den Witz, sondern ein solcher ist, an welchem die Vernunft notwendig ein moralisches Interesse nimmt, so ist es, der Gegner mag noch so viel Spötterei ausgestoßen, hierbei aber

This must be distinguished from a jocular, even if derisive, brushing aside with contempt an insulting attack of an adversary (*retorsio iocosa*), by which the mocker (or, in general, a malicious but ineffectual adversary) is himself made the laughing stock. This is a legitimate defence of the respect one can require from him. But when the object of his mockery is really no object for wit but one in which reason necessarily takes a moral interest, then no matter how much ridicule the adversary may have uttered and thereby left himself open to laughter, it is more befitting the **dignity** of the object and respect for humanity either

auch selbst zugleich noch so viel Blößen zum Belachen gegeben haben, der **Würde** des Gegenstandes und der Achtung für die Menschheit angemessener, dem Angriffe entweder gar keine oder eine mit **Würde** und Ernst geführte Verteidigung entgegenzusetzen.

to put up no defence against the attack or to conduct it with **dignity** and seriousness.

Anmerkung. Man wird wahrnehmen, daß unter dem vorhergehenden Titel nicht sowohl Tugenden angepriesen, als vielmehr die ihnen entgegenstehenden Laster getadelt werden; das liegt aber schon in dem Begriffe der Achtung, sowie wir sie gegen andere Menschen zu beweisen verbunden sind, welche nur eine negative Pflicht ist. – Ich bin nicht verbunden, Andere (bloß als Menschen betrachtet), zu verehren, d.i. ihnen positive Hochachtung zu beweisen. Alle Achtung, zu der ich von Natur verbunden bin, ist die vor dem Gesetz überhaupt (*reverere legem*), und dieses, nicht aber andere Menschen überhaupt zu verehren (*reverentia adversus hominem*) oder hierin ihnen etwas zu leisten, ist allgemeine und unbedingte Menschenpflicht gegen Andere, welche, als die ihnen ursprünglich schuldige Achtung (*observantia debita*), von jedem gefordert werden kann.

Remark. It will be noticed that under the above heading virtues were not so much commended as rather the vices opposed to them censured. But this is already implicit in the concept of the respect we are bound to show other human beings, which is only a negative duty. I am not bound to revere others (regarded merely as human beings), that is, to show them positive high esteem. The only reverence to which I am bound by nature is reverence for the law as such (*revere legem*); [AK 6:468] and to revere the law, but not to revere other human beings in general (*reverentia adversus hominem*) or to perform some act of reverence for them, is a human being's universal and unconditional duty towards others, which each of them can require as the respect originally owed others (*observantia debita*).

Die verschiedene Anderen zu beweisende Achtung nach Verschiedenheit der Beschaffenheit der Menschen oder ihrer zufälligen Verhältnisse, nämlich der des Alters, des Geschlechts, der Abstammung, der Stärke oder Schwäche, oder gar des Standes und der **Würde,** welche zum Teil auf beliebigen Anordnungen beruhen, darf in metaphysischen Anfangsgründen der Tugendlehre nicht ausführlich dargestellt und klassifiziert werden, da es hier nur um die reinen Vernunftprinzipien derselben zu tun ist.

The different forms of respect to be shown to others in accordance with differences in their qualities or contingent relations – differences of age, sex, birth, strength or weakness, or even rank and **dignity,** which depend in part on arbitrary arrangements – cannot be set forth in detail and classified in the metaphysical first principles of a doctrine of virtue, since this has to do only with its pure rational principles.

Anthropology from a Pragmatic Point of View (1798)

§ 1

Daß der Mensch in seiner Vorstellung das Ich haben kann, erhebt ihn unendlich über alle andere auf Erden lebenden Wesen. Dadurch ist er eine Person und vermöge der Einheit des Bewußtseins bei alle Veränderungen, die ihm zugestoßen mögen, eine und dieselbe Person, d.i. ein von Sachen, dergleichen die vernunftlosen Tiere sind, mit denen man nach Belieben schalten und walten kann, durch Rang und **Würde** ganz unterschiedenes Wesen, selbst wenn er das Ich noch nicht sprechen kann, weil er es doch in Gedanken hat: wie es alle Sprachen, wenn sie in der ersten Person reden, doch denken müssen, ob sie zwar diese Ichheit nicht durch ein besonderes Wort ausdrücken.

The fact that the human being can have the 'I' in his representations raises him infinitely above all other living beings on earth. Because of this he is a *person*, and by virtue of the unity of consciousness through all changes that happen to him, one and the same person – i.e. through rank and **dignity** an entirely different being from things, such as irrational animals, with which one can do as one likes. This holds even when he cannot yet say 'I,' because he still has it in his thoughts, just as all languages must think it when they speak in first person, even if they do not have a special word to express this concept of 'I.'

Olympe de Gouges (1748–1793)

Declaration of the rights of woman and of the (woman) citizen (1789)

The French Revolution catalysed the resentment some women had, that they did not have access to what Kant called active citizenship, that is, the opportunity to play an active role in politics. Olympe de Gouges pleaded, like Cicero and Boëthius had done before her, for respect for the dignity of virtue, to replace servile fear of privileges. Her famous 'Declaration of the Rights of Woman and of the (Woman) Citizen' parallels the 'Declaration of the Rights of Man and of the Citizen', and illustrates what the Revolution was not prepared to deal with. Her declaration might have raised some eyebrows, and provoked a thought or two, but women's admission to public

office would take many more years. The utopian universalism that the Revolution brought within striking distance gave women the idea that vindication and political action on their own behalf might succeed in bringing them political status. They no longer had their aristocratic privileges to lose by trying. De Gouges was guillotined under the terror-regime for her Girondin sympathies.

Text from *Oeuvres*. Présentés par Benoite Groult, Collection Mille et une Femmes (Paris: Mercure de France, 1986), pp. 101–12, articles VI and XIII, p. 103 and p. 105. Translations are my own. The first two columns contains the text and translation of the 1789 *Declaration of Man and of the Citizen* taken from <http://mjp.univ-perp.fr/france/ddh1789.htm> (accessed October 2018).

La loi est l'expression de la volonté générale. Tous les citoyens ont droit de concourir personnellement, ou par leurs représentants, à sa formation. Elle doit être la même pour tous, soit qu'elle protège, soit qu'elle punisse. Tous les citoyens étant égaux à ses yeux, sont également admissibles à toutes **dignités,** places et emplois publics, selon leur capacité, et sans autre distinction que celle de leurs vertus et de leurs talents.	The law is the expression of the general will. All citizens have the right to compete personally, or through their representatives, in its formation. It must be the same for everyone, whether it protects or punishes. All citizens being equal in his eyes, are equally eligible for all **dignities,** places and public offices, according to their capacity, and without distinction other than that of their virtues and talents.	La loi doit être l'expression de la volonté générale; toutes les Citoyennes et Citoyens doivent concourir personnellement, ou par leurs représentants, à sa formation; elle doit être la même pour tous: toutes les citoyennes et tous les citoyens, étant égaux à ses yeux, doivent être également admissibles à toutes **dignités,** places et emplois publics, selon leurs capacités, es sans autres distinctions que celles de leurs vertus et de leur talents.	The law should be the expression of the general will. All citizens shall contribute personally, or by their representatives, to its formation; it must be the same for all; and all men and women citizens, equal before the law, must equally be admissible to all **dignities,** places and public offices, according to their capacities, and without any other distinction than that of their virtues and talents.

Pour l'entretien de la force publique, et pour les dépenses d'administration, une contribution commune est indispensable ; elle doit être également répartie entre tous les citoyens, en raison de leurs facultés.	To maintain public power, and for administrative expenses, a joint contribution is indispensable; it must be equally distributed among all citizens, because of their faculties.	Pour l'entretien de la force publique, et pour les dépenses d'administration, les contributions de la femme et de l'homme sont égales; elle a part de toutes les corvées, à toute les tâches pénibles; elle doit donc avoir de même part à la distribution des places, des emplois, des charges, des **dignités** et de l'industrie.	To maintain public power and for administrative expenses, the contributions of women and men are equal; she shares all the yokes and all the difficult tasks; she must therefore have the same share in the distribution of places, public offices, responsibilities, **dignities** and industry.

Olympe de Gouges was also an abolitionist, like many intellectual and/or religious women at the time. In one of her polemical plays against black slavery in the Americas, the Viceroy and slave-owner is a good-hearted Frenchman whose escaped Indian slave saves the life of his daughter. The daughter in turn risks her life to rescue the slave from her father's punishment, which the legal system craves of him as his duty to uphold the interests of the state. The Governor is caught between two senses of dignity, an exterior and an interior, much like Antigone (Kadish and Massardier-Kenny, 1994, 116). The one acquired with public office, to which women did not have access, was of a kind to render the person degradable, either by the system that had conferred the dignity taking it away again or by the base acts the conferring system commanded. Even when confronted with this dilemma intrinsic to public office in an unjust society, Olympe de Gouges sees insufficient advantage in women being held away from it compared to the value of justice and its effects. She remains convinced of a universal right and a universal duty, of men and women, free and slaves alike, to equal rank and equal privilege. She, maybe spurred by the challenge presented by Kant or others like him, argues for equal dignity for all before the law.

Mary Wollstonecraft (1759–1797)

Wollstonecraft's *Vindications* illustrate the kind of political strategy conceived to advance the recognition of the dignity of a particular group of people, which from now on will become common. It encourages the employment of all means to influence the sense of justice, in particular education and religion.

A Vindication of the Rights of Men was written as an answer to Edmund Burke's *Reflections on the Revolution in France* (1790). It is set against the defence of aristocracy presented by Burke, like also for example Thomas Paines' *Rights of Man* (1791), and takes the form of a polemic letter addressed to Burke. She reproaches him for being unable to empathise with the common man and mocks Burke for pretending that the idea of the common man having dignity demands sophisticated metaphysical speculation, reserved for the dreamers among the 'enlightened' philosophers of the age. Burke, in fact, had contended that the common man possesses only the dignity reflected by the aristocrat, and argued, as the conservative he was, that tradition should be left to take care of itself, lest revolution destroy the valuable foundations of the order of society. Wollstonecraft's treatise reads in contrast as a defence not only of the rights of the common man, but also of the rights of the common woman, not to be held in a state of perpetual childhood. It uses the term 'native dignity of man' often to mean the status of human beings and their right to be respected, but it does not even once use the expression 'human dignity'. Phrases like 'dignity of character'; 'dignity of virtue', and 'conscious dignity' are often used, the first two to convey that dignity consists, not in hereditary honours, but in the ability to act virtuously out of a strong character. The last to convey that consciousness of the high status of humans must make them act in consequence thereof, that is, virtuously.

The obstacles to becoming conscious of this dignity are all the things that make people believe they are either more or less than those they ought in reason to recognise as equals. These obstacles are also obstacles to the development of reason. However, reason, in the end, will win, and if the

dialectics of self-respect and respect of others does not assure the victory, the immutability of the will of God shall in the end.

The texts are as reproduced from *Mary Wollstonecraft: A Vindication of the Rights of Men. A Vindication of the Rights of Woman. An Historical and Moral View of the French Revolution*, ed. Janet Todd, Oxford World's Classics (Oxford: Oxford University Press, 1993).

A Vindication of the Rights of Men (1790)

(7) I glow with indignation when I attempt, methodically, to unravel your slavish paradoxes, in which I can find no fixed first principle to refute; I shall not, therefore, condescend to shew where you affirm in one page what you deny in another; and how frequently you draw conclusions without any previous premises: – it would be something like cowardice to fight with a man who had never exercised the weapons with which his opponent chose to combat, and irksome to refute sentence after sentence in which the latent spirit of tyranny appeared. [...]

(8) The civilisation which has taken place in Europe has been very partial, and, like every custom that an arbitrary point of honour has established, refines the manners at the expense of morals, by making sentiments and opinions current in conversation that have no root in the heart, or weight in the cooler resolves of the mind. – And what has stopped its progress? – hereditary property – hereditary honours. The man has been changed into an artificial monster by the station in which he was born, and the consequent homage that benumbed his faculties like the torpedo's touch; – or a being, with a capacity for reasoning, would not have failed to discover, as his faculties unfolded, that true happiness arose from the friendship and intimacy which can only be enjoyed by equals; and that charity is not a condescending distribution of alms, but an intercourse of good offices and mutual benefits, founded on respect for justice and humanity. [...]

(9) Will Mr. Burke be at trouble to inform us, how far we are to go back to discover the rights of men, since the light of reason is such a fallacious guide that none but fools trust to its cold investigation? [...11] Are we to seek for the rights of men in the ages when a few marks were the only penalty imposed for the life of a man, and death for death when the property of the rich was touched? when – I blush to discover the depravity of our nature – when a deer was killed! Are these laws that it is natural to love and sacrilegious to invade? [... 13] There is no end to this implicit submission

to authority – somewhere it must stop, or we return to barbarism; and the capacity of improvement, which gives us a natural sceptre on earth, is a cheat [...].

But on what principle Mr Burke could defend American independence, I cannot conceive: for the whole tenor of his plausible arguments settles slavery on an everlasting foundation. Allowing his servile reverence for antiquity, and prudent attention to self-interest, to have the force which he insists on, the slave trade ought never to be abolished; and because our ignorant forefathers, not understanding **the native dignity of man**, sanctioned a traffic that outrages every suggestion of reason and religion, we are to submit to the inhuman custom, and term an atrocious insult to humanity the love of our country, and a proper submission to the laws by which our property is secured. Security of property! Behold, in a few words, the definition of English liberty. And to this selfish principle every nobler one is sacrificed. [...]

(14) Our penal laws punish with death the thief who steals a few pounds; but to take by violence, or trepan, a man, is no such heinous offence. – For who shall dare to complain of the venerable vestige of the law that rendered the life of a deer more sacred than that of a man? But it was the poor man with only **his native dignity** who was thus oppressed – and only metaphysical sophists and cold mathematicians can discern this insubstantial form; it is a work of abstraction – and a gentleman of lively imagination must borrow some drapery from fancy before he can love or pity a *man*. Misery, to reach your heart, I perceive, must have its caps and bells; your tears are reserved, very naturally considering your character, for the declamation of the theatre, or for the downfall of queens, whose rank alters the nature of folly, and throws a graceful veil over vices that degrade humanity; whilst the distress of many industrious mothers, whose *helpmates* have been torn from them, and the hungry cry of helpless babes, were vulgar sorrows that could not move your commiseration, though they might extort an alms. [...]

(15) It would be straying still further into metaphysics to add, that this is one of the strongest arguments for the natural immortality of the soul. – Everything looks like a means, nothing like an end, or point of rest, when we can say, now let us sit down and enjoy the present moment; our faculties and wishes are proportioned to the present scene; we may return without repining to our sister clod. And, if no **conscious dignity** whisper that we are capable of relishing more refined pleasures, the thirst for truth appears to be allayed: and thought, the faint type of an immaterial energy, no longer bounding it knows not where, is confined to the tenement that affords it sufficient variety. – The rich man may thank his God that he is not like other men – but when is retribution to be made to the miserable, who cry day and night for help, and there is no one at hand to help him? [...]

(23) Property, I do not scruple to aver it, should be fluctuating, which would be the case, if it were more equally divided amongst all children of a family; else it is an everlasting rampart, in consequence of a barbarous feudal institution, that enables the elder son to overpower talents and depress virtue.

Besides, an unmanly servility, most inimical to **true dignity of character** is, by this means, fostered in society. Men of some abilities play on the follies of the rich, and mounting to fortune as they degrade themselves, they stand in the way of men of superior talents, who cannot advance in such crooked paths, or wade through the filth, which parasites never boggle at. Pursuing their way straight forward, their spirit is either bent or broken by the rich man's contumelies, or the difficulties they have to encounter.

The only security of property that nature authorizes and reason sanctions is the right man has to enjoy the acquisitions, which his talents and industry have acquired; and to bequeath them to whom he chooses. [...]

(30) But the cultivation of reason is an arduous task, and men of lively fancy, finding it easier to follow the impulse of passion, endeavour to persuade themselves and others that it is most *natural*. And happy is it for those, who indolently let that heaven-lighted spark rest like the ancient lamps in sepulchres, that some virtuous habits, with which the reason of others shackled them, supplies its place. – Affection for parents, reverence for superiors or antiquity, notions of honour, or that worldly self-interest that shrewdly shews them that honesty is the best policy; all proceed from the reason for which they serve as substitutes; – but it is reason second hand. [...]

(33) This fear of God makes me reverence myself. – Yes, Sir, the regard I have for honest fame, and the friendship of the virtuous, falls short of the respect, which I have for myself. And this, enlightened self-love, if an epithet the meaning of which has been grossly perverted will convey my idea, forces me to see; and if I may venture to borrow a prostituted term, to *feel*, that happiness is reflected, and that, in communicating good, my soul receives its noble ailment. [...]

(42) It is true you lay great stress on the effects produced by the bare idea of liberal descent; but from the conduct of men of rank, men of discernment would rather be led to conclude, that this idea obliterated instead of inspiring **native dignity,** and substituted a factitious pride that disembowelled the man. [...]

(45) Where is the **dignity,** the infallibility of sensibility, in the fair ladies, whom, if the voice of rumour is to be credited, the captive negroes curse in all the agony of bodily pain, for the unheard of tortures they invent? It is probable that some of

them, after the sight of a flagellation, compose their ruffled spirits and exercise their tender feelings by the perusal of the last imported novel. – How true these tears are to nature, I leave you to determine. But these ladies may have read your *Enquiry concerning the Origin of our Ideas of the Sublime and the Beautiful*, and, convinced by your arguments, may have laboured to be pretty, by counterfeiting weakness. [...]

(46) If beautiful weakness be interwoven in a woman's frame, if the chief business of her life be (as you insinuate) to inspire love, and Nature has made an eternal distinction between **the qualities that dignify a rational being** and this animal perfection, her duty and happiness in this life must clash with any preparation for a more exalted state. So that Plato and Milton were grossly mistaken in asserting that human love lead to heavenly, and was only an exaltation of the same affection; for the love of the Deity, which is mixed with the most profound reverence, must be love of perfection, and not compassion for weakness. [...]

(53) The rich and weak will certainly applaud your system, and loudly celebrate your pious reverence for authority and establishments – they find it pleasanter to enjoy than to think; to justify oppression than correct abuses. – *The rights of men* are grating sounds that set their teeth on edge; the impertinent enquiry of philosophic meddling innovation. If the poor are in distress, they will make some benevolent exertions to assist them; they will confer obligations, but not do justice. Benevolence is a very amiable specious quality; yet the aversion, which men feel to accept a right as a favour, should rather be extolled as **a vestige of native dignity**, than stigmatized as the odious offspring of ingratitude. [...]

(59) If society was regulated on a more enlarged plan; if man was contented to be the friend of man, and did not seek to bury the sympathies of humanity in servile appellation of master; if, turning his eyes from ideal regions of taste and elegance, he laboured to give the earth he inhabited all the beauty it is capable of receiving, and was ever on the watch to shed abroad the happiness which human nature can enjoy; – he who, respecting the rights of men, wishes to convince or persuade society that this is the true happiness and **dignity**, is not the cruel *oppressor* of the poor, nor a short-sighted philosopher – HE fears God and loves his fellow-creatures. – Behold the whole duty of man! – the citizen who acts differently is a sophisticated being. [...]

(62) Before I conclude my cursory remarks, it is but just to acknowledge that I coincide with you in your opinion respecting the *sincerity* of many modern philosophers. Your consistency in avowing a veneration for rank and riches deserves praise; but I must own that I have often indignantly observed that some of the enlightened philosophers, who talk most vehemently of the native rights of men, borrow many noble sentiments to adorn their conversation, which have no influence on their conduct.

They bow down to rank, and are careful to secure property; for virtue, without this adventitious drapery, is seldom very respectable in their eyes – nor are they very quick-sighted to discern real **dignity of character** when no sounding name exalts the man above his elbows. – But neither open enmity nor hollow homage destroys the intrinsic value of those principles, which rest on an eternal foundation, and revert for a standard to the immutable attributes of God.

A Vindication of the Rights of Woman (1792)

Wollstonecraft's second vindication was commissioned by her publisher Joseph Johnson to reinforce the success of *A Vindication of the Rights of Men*. Wollstonecraft's interest in the subject was provoked by the lack of debate about the status of women during and in the aftermath of the Revolution, and the work is addressed to one of its protagonists, M. Talleyrand-Perigord, late Bishop of Autun. It provides an explanation of why there should be so little debate of the issue and also reflects on what could be done to improve the situation of women. The recommendations mostly concern education, and in particular education to the conscious dignity of character or virtue, based on the exercise of reason. Respect for oneself as a human being, Wollstonecraft is aware, must begin early and be instilled throughout the formative period. If the opposite is practised, people (whether men or women) will not trust their native dignity and will behave slavishly.

The work undertakes to defend the dignity of women from the position that it is by no means a *fait accompli*. The successful accomplishment of the delicate and difficult task raises the work to the status of a world classic. Women are both regarded and not regarded by society at large as rational by nature, and it is this contradictory situation which Wollstonecraft directs her council to lift as one lifts a ban.

She exposes the cruelty as well as the inconsistency of according contradictory status to some while pretending not to, and hopes by these means to win the reader for her cause. Because the reality displays in her face the utmost political practicability of conferring such contradictory status, she knows that very little is gained by winning sympathy. She must think practically, and with the development over several centuries in mind. Therefore, education remains her focus. Only education can dislodge the

deep-seated prejudices and oppressive ideals she is up against, and change them over time.

(67) Consider, I address you as legislator, whether, when men contend for their freedom, and to be allowed to judge for themselves respecting their own happiness, it be not inconsistent and unjust to subjugate women, even though you firmly believe that you are acting in the manner best calculated to promote their happiness? Who made man the exclusive judge, if women partake with him in the gift of reason? [...]

(73) My own sex, I hope, will excuse me, if I treat them like rational creatures, instead of flattering their fascinating graces, and viewing them as if they were in a state of perpetual childhood, unable to stand alone. I earnestly wish to point out in what **true dignity** and human happiness consists – I wish to persuade women to endeavour to acquire strength, both of mind and of body, and to convince them that the soft phrases, susceptibility of heart, delicacy of sentiment, and refinement of taste, are almost synonymous with epithets of weakness, and that those beings who are only the objects of pity and that kind of love, which has been termed its sister, will soon become objects of contempt. [...]

(75) Women are, in fact, so much degraded by mistaken notions of female excellence, that I do not mean to add a paradox when I assert, that this artificial weakness produces a propensity to tyrannize, and gives birth to cunning, the natural opponent of strength, which leads them to play off those contemptible infantile airs that undermine esteem even whilst they excite desire. Let men become more chaste and modest, and if women do not grow wiser in the same ratio, it will be clear that they have weaker understandings. It seems scarcely necessary to say, that I now speak of the sex in general. Many individuals have more sense than their male relatives; and, as nothing preponderates where there is a constant struggle for an equilibrium, without it has naturally more gravity, some women govern their husbands without degrading themselves, because intellect will always govern. [...]

(78) But if, to crown the whole, there were to be rational creatures produced, allowed to rise in excellence by the exercise of powers implanted for that purpose; if benignity itself thought fit to call into existence a creature above the brutes, who could think and improve himself, why should that inestimable gift, for gift it was, if man was so created as to have a capacity to rise above the state in which sensation produced brutal ease, be called, in direct term, a curse? A curse it might be reckoned, if the whole of our existence were bounded by our continuance in this world; for why should the gracious fountain of life give us passions, and the power of reflecting, only to embitter our days and inspire us with **mistaken notions of dignity**? Why should he lead us from love of ourselves to the sublime emotions, which the discovery of his wisdom

and goodness excites, if these feelings were not set in motion to improve our nature, of which they make a part, and render us capable of enjoying a more godlike portion of happiness? Firmly persuaded that no evil exists in the world that God did not design to take place, I build my belief on the perfection of God. [...]

(86) Consequently, the most perfect education, in my opinion, is such an exercise of the understanding as is best calculated to strengthen the body and form the heart. Or, in other words, to enable the individual to attain such habits of virtue as will render it independent. In fact, it is a farce to call any being virtuous whose virtues do not result from the exercise of its own reason. This was Rousseau's opinion respecting men: I extend it to women, and confidently assert that they have been drawn out of their sphere by false refinement, and not by an endeavour to acquire masculine qualities. Still the regal homage which they receive is so intoxicating, that till the manners of the times are changed, and formed on more reasonable principles, it may be impossible to convince them that the illegitimate power, which they obtain by degrading themselves, is a curse, and that they must return to nature and equality, if they wish to secure the placid satisfaction that unsophisticated affections impart. But for this epoch we must wait – wait, perhaps, till kings and nobles, enlightened by reason, and, preferring **the real dignity of man** to childish state, throw off their gaudy hereditary trappings; and if then women do not resign the arbitrary power of beauty – they will prove that they have less mind than man. [...]

(99) I own it frequently happens that women, who have fostered a romantic unnatural delicacy of feeling, waste their lives in imagining how happy they should have been with a husband who could love them with a fervid increasing affection every day, and all day. But they might as well pine married as single – and would not be a jot more unhappy with a bad husband than longing for a good one. That a proper education; or to speak with more precision, a well stored mind, would enable a woman to support a single life with **dignity**, I grant; but that she should avoid cultivating her taste, lest her husband should occasionally shock it, is quitting a substance for a shadow. [...]

(102) Surely, there can be but one rule of right, if morality has an eternal foundation, and whoever sacrifices virtue, strictly so called, to present convenience, or whose duty it is to act in such a manner, lives only for the passing day, and cannot be an accountable creature.

The poet then should have dropped his sneer when he says, 'if weak women go astray, the stars are more in fault than they'. For that they are bound by the adamantine chain of destiny is most certain, if it be proved that they are never to rise above opinion, or to feel the **dignity of a rational will** that only bows to God, and often forgets that the universe contains any being but itself and the model of perfection to which its

ardent gaze is turned, to adore attributes that, softened into virtues, may be imitated in kind, though the degree overwhelms the enraptured mind.

If, I say, for I would not impress by declamation when reason offers her sober light, if they be really capable of acting like rational creatures, let them not be treated like slaves; or like the brutes who are dependant on the reason of man, when they associate with him; but cultivate their minds, give them the salutary, sublime curb of principle, and let them attain **conscious dignity** by feeling themselves only dependant on God. Teach them, in common with man, to submit to necessity, instead of giving, to render them more pleasing, a sex to morals. [...]

(113) Women, it is true, obtaining power by unjust means, by practising or fostering vice, evidently lose the rank which reason would assign them, and they become either abject slaves or capricious tyrants. They lose all simplicity, all **dignity of mind**, in acquiring power, and act as men are observed to act when they have been exalted by the same means.

It is time to effect a revolution in female manners – time to restore to them their **lost dignity** – and make them, as part of the human species, labour by reforming themselves to reform the world. It is time to separate unchangeable morals from local manners – if men be semi-gods – why let us serve them! And if the **dignity** of the female soul be as disputable as that of animals – if their reason does not afford sufficient light to direct their conduct whilst unerring instinct is denied – they are surely of all creatures the most miserable! and, bent beneath the iron hand of destiny, must submit to be a *fair defect* in creation. But to justify the ways of Providence respecting them, by pointing out some irrefragable reason for thus making such a large portion of mankind accountable and non accountable, would puzzle the subtlest casuist. [...]

(121) That woman is naturally weak, or degraded by a concurrence of circumstances, is, I think, clear. But this position I shall simply contrast with a conclusion, which I have frequently heard fall from sensible men in favour of an aristocracy: that the mass of mankind cannot be anything, or the obsequious slaves, who patiently allow themselves to be driven forward, would feel their own consequence, and spurn their chains. Men, they further observe, submit everywhere to oppression, when they have only to lift up their heads to throw off the yoke; yet, instead of asserting their birth right, they quietly lick the dust, and say, let us eat and drink, for tomorrow we die. Women, I argue from analogy, are degraded by the same propensity to enjoy the present moment; and, at last, despise the freedom, which they have not sufficient virtue to struggle to attain. [...]

(125) Ah! why do women, I write with affectional solicitude, condescend to receive a degree of attention and respect from strangers, different from that reciprocation of civility which the dictates of humanity and the politeness of civilisation authorize between man and man? And, why do they not discover, when 'in the noon of beauty's power', that they are treated like queens only to be deluded by hollow respect, till they are led to resign, or not assume, their natural prerogatives? Confined then in cages like the feathered race, they have nothing to do but to plume themselves, and stalk with mock majesty from perch to perch. It is true they are provided with food and raiment, for which they neither toil nor spin; but health, liberty, and virtue, are given in exchange. But, where, amongst mankind, has been found sufficient strength of mind to enable a being resign these adventitious prerogatives; one who, rising with **the calm dignity of reason** above opinion, dared to be proud of the privileges inherent in man? And it is vain to expect it whilst hereditary power chokes the affections and nips reason in the bud. [...]

(126) A wild wish has just flown from my heart to my head, and I will not stifle it though it may excite a horselaugh. – I do earnestly wish to see the distinction of sex confounded in society, unless where love animates the behaviour. For this distinction is, I am firmly persuaded, the foundation of the weakness of character ascribed to women; is the cause why the understanding is neglected, whilst accomplishments are acquired with sedulous care: and the same cause accounts for their preferring the graceful before the heroic virtues.

(132) I am fully persuaded that we should hear none of these infantine airs, if girls were allowed to take sufficient exercise, and not confined in close rooms till their muscles are relaxed, and their powers of digestion destroyed. To carry the remark still further, if fear in girls, instead of being cherished, perhaps, created, were treated in the same manner as cowardice in boys, we should quickly see women with more **dignified** aspects. It is true, they could not then with equal propriety be termed the sweet flowers that smile in the walk of man; but they would be more respectable members of society, and discharge the important duties of life by the light of their own reason. 'Educate women like men,' says Rousseau, 'and the more they resemble our sex the less power they will have over us.' This is the very point I aim at. I do not wish them to have power over men; but to have power over themselves. [...]

(227) Women then must be considered as only the wanton solace of men, when they become so weak in mind and body, that they cannot exert themselves, unless to pursue some frothy pleasure, or to invent some frivolous fashion. What can be a more melancholy sight to a thinking mind, than to look into the numerous carriages that drive helter-skelter about this metropolis in a morning full of pale-faced creatures who are flying from themselves. I have often wished, with Dr Johnson, to place

some of them in a little shop with half a dozen children looking up to their languid countenances for support. I am much mistaken, if some latent vigour would not soon give health and spirit to their eyes, and some lines drawn by the exercise of reason on the blank cheeks, which before were only undulated by dimples, might restore lost **dignity** to the character, or rather enable it to attain the true **dignity** of its nature.

Wilhelm von Humboldt (1767–1835)

On the Spirit of Humanity (1797)

Humboldt gives voice to thoughts very similar to Kant and Zollikofer, except for his emphasis on spirit.

Text from *Werke in fünf Bänden*. eds Andreas Flitner and Klaus Giel, vol. 1 (Stuttgart: Cotta, 1960), pp. 506–15. Translation is my own.

Der Mensch muß daher etwas aufsuchen, dem er, als einem letzten Ziele, alles unterordnen, und nach dem er, als nach einem absoluten Maßstab, alles beurtheilen kann. Dies kann er nicht anders, als in sich selbst finden, da in dem Inbegriff aller Wesen sich nur auf ihn allein alles bezieht; es kann sich aber weder auf seinen augenblicklichen Genuß, noch auf sein Glück überhaupt beziehen, da es vielmehr ein edler Vorzug seiner Natur ist, den Genuß verschmähen und das Glück entbehren zu können; es kann daher nur in seinem inneren Werth, in seiner höheren Vollkommenheit liegen.

Die Würde des Menschen ist es also, die er aufzusuchen, und die Frage, die er zu beantworten hat, ist die: was ist dasjenige, wonach, als nach einem allgemeinen Maßstabe der Werth der Dinge für den Menschen, und der Werth der Menschen

The human being must therefore find something to which he can subordinate everything as towards a last goal, and according to which he can judge everything as by an absolute standard. This he can find nowhere else but in himself, as all beings relate by their essence only to him; but not to his immediate pleasure or to his happiness in general, as it is a noble prerogative of his nature to be able to forego pleasure and renounce happiness. It can therefore only lie in his inner worth, in his higher perfection.

It is thus **human dignity** that he must seek out, and the question he must answer is: what is that against which the value of things for human beings and the worth of human beings in relation to each other can be determined as against a common

gegen einander bestimmt werden kann? Wie ist es zu erkennen, wo es vorhanden ist? Wie hervorzubringen, wo es noch zu fehlen scheint?

Da es auf Alle Anwendung finden soll, muß es etwas Allgemeines seyn, da es aber niemanden einfallen kann, verschiedene Naturen nach einem einzigen Muster zu Modellen, muß es der Verschiedenheit der Individuen keinen Eintrag thun. Es muß also Etwas seyn, das, immer Eins und eben dasselbe, auf mannigfaltige Weise ausgeführt werden kann. [...]

In beiden Rücksichten schien *Geist* unter allen Wörtern, deren man sich hätte bedienen können, das Schicklichste.

measure? How can we know where it is present? How to make it present where it still seems absent?

As it must be applicable to all, it must be something general. But as no one would model different natures according to a single pattern, it cannot overrule the difference of individuals. It must thus be something that, being always one and the same, can be realised in manifold ways. [...]

On both accounts it seems that spirit is the most appropriate among all the words one could make use of in this regard.

Karl Heinrich Heydenreich (1764–1801)

Reflections on Human Dignity (1803)

Heydenreich concentrates, in his critique of Zollikofer, on the feeling of dignity, convinced of its permanence, as if it was itself responsible for dignity. In the process, he gives voice to the powerless outrage felt for the black slaves being transported to till the land in the Americas by undoubtedly many. Does he consider Kant's Copernican turn better served in this manner? The regret expressed at death and the desire for future achievement and progressive perfection of the human race combine to paint a discretely, but distinctly, secular eschatology, quite different from that of Zollikofer and also from that of Kant, as Kant, despite the horror at slavery, would have found the emphasis on emotion quite alien. It all combines to leave the reader with a sense of puzzlement, possibly shared by the writer, as if the desires expressed were already by himself recognised as being in vain.

Text from *Betrachtungen über die Würde des Menschen, ein Nachtrag zu Zollikofers Reden über diesen Gegenstand im Geiste der Kantischen Sitten- und Religionslehre mit Zollikofers Darstellung über denselben Gegenstand.* Herausgegeben und nach Heydenreichs Grundlinien einer geistigen Redekunst mit einigen Winken zu einer Parallele zwischen Heydenreichs und Zollikofers Ideen begleitet von I. G. Gruger (Leipzig: I. B. Schiegg, 1803) section II, pp. 81–99. Googlebook (accessed July 2018). Translations by myself.

In jeder Menschenseele entwickelt sich mit den Forstschritten ihrer Bildung ein Gefühl, welches in der ganzen thierischen Schöpfung kein Wesen mit uns theilt, das Gefühl der **Würde unsrer Natur.** So bald unser Selbstbewußtseyn sich aufklärt, und unsre geistigen Kräfte sich ihrer Reife zu nähern beginnen, so erwacht auch jenes, und wir können uns dann nicht anders, denn mit inniger tiefer Achtung unsrer selbst und unsres Daseyns denken. Je mehr wir uns von den Zerstreuungen und dem Geräusche der Welt zurückziehen, je angelegentlicher wir uns selbst, das heißt unsrer Vollkommenheit und wahren Zufriedenheit, leben, um so kräftiger wirkt jenes Gefühl, um so mehr beseelt, erhebt, und beseligt es uns. Der edlere Mensch kennt keine schönere Empfindung, als diese; überzeugt, daß sie sich nie, wie alle andre angenehme Gefühle, abstumpft, daß sie ihn unter allen Schicksalen des Lebens, selbst wenn jede Freude ihn verließe, beglei-tet, daß es nichts Schreckliches in der Natur giebt, welches sie nicht überwände, oder doch milderte, arbeitet er unabläs-sig darauf hin, ihr den höchsten Grad des Lebens und der Stärke zu geben. Und da er durch die Gemeinschaft dieses Gefühls, dessen Keim jeder Seele inwohnt, seine nahe Verwandtschaft mit seinen Brüdern auf das interessanteste anerkennt, so ist er auch mit edlem Eifer bestrebt, durch

With the progress of education, an emo-tion develops in every human soul, which none of the animals share with us: the feel-ing of the **dignity of our nature.** As soon as our self-consciousness is enlightened, and our spiritual forces begin to mature, then this [emotion] also awakens, and we cannot then but think of ourselves and of our being with earnest, deep respect. The more we retire from the dissipations and the noise of the world, the more we busy ourselves to live out our perfection and true contentment, the more strongly this feeling acts, the more it inspires and raises us up to be happy. The nobler human being knows of no lovelier feeling than this; convinced that it never, like other feelings, fades, that it in all of life's ups and downs, even if all joy should abandon him, accompanies him, that there is nothing so awful in nature, which it would not overcome, or at least sweeten, he works incessantly to give it the highest degree of life and strength. And as he through the community of this feeling, the seed of which is found in every soul, recognises in the most interesting way his close relatedness to his brothers, he strives with noble eagerness and all the means at his disposal to effect that it awakes around him in general and rules among people as the mightiest drive of their minds, actions and feelings. And it is for him no enthusi-ast's dream that the future age leads to the

alle in seinen Kräften stehende Mittel zu bewirken, daß es rings um ihn her allgemein erwache, und unter den Menschen als die mächtigste Triebfeder, die ihrer Gesinnungen, Handlungen und Gefühle leitet herrsche. Und es ist für ihn kein Traum der Schwärmerey, daß die Zukunft Zeitalter herbey führt, wo es nur in Wenigen noch schlafen, und unmenschliche Beleidigungen desselben, die jetzt noch leider die Jahrbücher unsres Geschlechts ausfüllen, eine seltene Erscheinung seyn werden.

Allein so erhaben auch diese Gefühl ist, und so gewiß jeder Mensch den Saamen desselben in seinem Innern trägt, so giebt es dennoch nur wenige, welche seinen Inhalt zu zergliedern und aufzuklären bestrebt wären; wenige, welche sich über die Vorzüge und Ansprüche Rechenschaft abforderten, die sie zu demselben berichtigten; wenige, die seinen ganzen Umfang deutlich und bestimmt zu übersehen suchten; wenige, die sich von seiner Echtheit, Wahrheit und Heiligkeit durch feste Gründe so überzeugten, daß sie, sicher des Siegs, den Kampf mit der Sophisterey, dem Zweifelgeiste und er Menschenverachtung wagen könnten.

Man kann es als einen untrüglichen Prüfstein der Fortschritte ansehen, deren sich unser Zeitalter in Hinsicht der Kenntnis der sittlichen Natur des Menschen rühmt, zu versuchen, ob sich nach denselben eine reinere, bestimmtere, vollständigere, evidentere Darstellung der **Würde des Menschen** geben lasse, ob es nach denselben vielleicht gelinge, einen Kommentar über dieses Gefühl zu liefern, in welchem jede Seele die getroffene Kopie ihrer erhabensten Vorzüge anerkennen müßte.

point where it will only slumber in a few, and where inhuman infringements of it, which unfortunately still fill the journals of our race, will be a rare occurrence.

However sublime this feeling is, and however certain it is that every human being carry the seeds of it in his innermost, only few have attempted to discern and clarify its content. Only few have accounted for the privileges and claims they attributed to it. Only a few attempted to gain a clear and precise overview of its complete scope. Only a few convinced themselves of its authenticity, truth and sanctity on solid grounds and thus dared to face the battle with sophistry, the spirit of doubt and the contempt for human beings, in the certainty of victory.

One can see it as an unmistakable proof of the progress of which our age boasts in regards to the knowledge of the moral nature of human beings, to research whether it might be possible to give a purer, more determinate and complete description of **human dignity**, and whether it could perhaps be achieved to yield a commentary on this feeling in which every soul would have to recognise its most sublime privileges.

Was sagt jeder Mensch zu sich selbst, wenn er seine **Menschenwürde** fühlt, fühlte er sie auch noch so dunkel? – ganz unstreitig herrscht in ihm die Gedanke: ‚in dir sind von Natur Eigenschaften, die ihrer selbst wegen die höchste unbedingteste Achtung verdienen; du selbst kannst sie dir nicht, deine Mittmenschen, die dir gleich sind, können sie dir nicht, kein höheres Wesen, ja, kein Gott kann sie dir verweigern; niemand kann dich, nach deinem wahren Wesen, als Mittel für irgend einen Theil, ja nicht für das Ganze der Schöpfung ansehen; du kannst nur als ihr Endzweck gedacht werden, und als Mittelpunkt des ganzen Systems der Geschaffenen: eine andre, eine höhere **Würde**, als du, hat keine Art der vernünftigen endlichen Wesen über dir, und die ganze Welt der vernunftlosen lebenden und der leblosen Wesen ist unter dir.

Dies ist der allgemeinste Inhalt alles Gefühls unsrer **Würde**, in welcher Beziehung und unter welchem Verhältnissen immer wir sie empfinden. Frage sich ein jeder, was in allen Fällen, wo er seine **Würde** fühlt, die innigste Gewißheit für ihn ist, und jede seiner geheimsten Regungen, deren er sich dann bewußt ist, wird ihn auf jenen Gedanken zurückführen. Wenn du in hellgesternter Nacht deine staunenden Blicke im Unermeßlichen des Himmels verbreitet, und gestützt auf den größten Reichtum der Sternkund nimmer die Grenzen findest, immer nur stärker und erhabener die Unendlichkeit der Universums fühlst; wenn du dann zu dir selbst zurückkehrst, der Glanz jener zahllosen Welten deine kleine Existenz gleichsam verlöscht hat, und du zweifelst, ob du einen Punkt im All habest, ob auf dich mehr als auf das

What says every human being to himself, when he feels his **human dignity**, however obscurely? – in him rules uncontradicted the thought: 'in you there are naturally properties that deserve the highest and most unconditional respect for their own sakes. You cannot deny it to yourself; your fellow human beings, who are your equals, cannot deny it to you. No higher being, yes, no God can deny it to you; no one can regard you, according to your true nature, as means for any part, or even the whole, of Creation. You can only be regarded as the final goal and centre of the entire system of the created. Another higher **dignity** than yours has no kind of rational finite beings over you, and the entire world of non-rational living and non-living beings is below you.

This is the most general content of the feeling of our **dignity**, in whatever relations and conditions we find it. If one asks what constitutes the innermost certainty of one's **dignity** in all the circumstances where one may feel it, then the most secret sentiments of which one may be conscious will lead one back to that. When you astonished by the clear starry night look out into the immeasurable sky and supported by the greatest riches of astronomy never find the limits, but only ever feels stronger and more sublimely the infinity of the universe; when you then return to yourself, the glory of these worlds without number having drowned you out, and you doubt whether you have a point in it all, whether you shall count more than the smallest particle of sun-dust, whether a higher eye observes you, a higher mind think of you,

kleinste Sonnenstäubchen gerechnet sey, ob ein höheres Auge dich sehe, eine höhere Vernunft dich denke, – erhebt sich dann nicht in deinem Innern kraftvoll und tröstend das Gefühl: ‚Nein, du bist nicht Nichts, du bist Viel, du bist Alles in dem Systeme der geschaffenen Wesen? Wozu jene Welten, die nie ein endlicher Verstand zählt und ermißt, wenn durch sie nichts ausgeführt wird, was du für das Höchste und **Würdigste** unter allem Möglichen erkennst! Sind sie nicht dazu bestimmt, so sind sie, zwar unermeßliche, aber nichtstaugliche und nichtswürdige Staubmassen. Nein, Ocean der Welten, dein Anblick vernichtet mich nicht; nicht durch dich bin ich etwas; du bist ohne mich nichts; bin ich vertilgt, so ist alle Vernunft, alles Gute und Wahre vertilgt, wozu du dann? Wäre ich nicht, so wärst du nicht.‘ – So misst sich der Menschen in seiner **Würde** mit dem unermeßlichen; die Unendlichkeit seiner Bestimmung wird der Maßstab für das, was kein endlicher Verstand ermißt. Das Weltall ist für ihn nicht zu groß, denn er sieht keine Grenzen seiner Kraft und seiner Bestimmung. – Und fühlt er nicht dieselbe Hoheit, wenn er die Menschheit in seinen Brüdern entehrt, wenn er sie geschändet findet? – Dort segelt von den unmenschlichen Küsten Afrika's eine Kauffartenflotte – mit Menschen: – Wesen auf Wesen geschichtet; jedes einen Preis, um den es feil ist, um den es jeder Beutel haben kann, um den Leben und Tod der Willkür des Käufers anheim fällt; tausend Martern sollen ihnen die Vernichtung so werth machen, daß sie auch vor dem tröstenden Glauben der Unsterblichkeit schaudern, daß sie auch für jene Welt keine Hoffnung haben, als, ihre Henker, die Weißen wieder zu finden. – Was empört dich, gefühlvolle Seele, die

– does not then the strong and consoling thought occur to you: ‘No, you are not nothing, you are much, you are everything in the System of created beings? Wherefore all these worlds, which a finite mind shall never count, if through them nothing shall be accomplished, of what you know to be the highest and the most **dignified**! If they should not exist for that purpose, they would be, however immeasurable, but useless and unworthy masses of dust. No, Ocean of the worlds, your gaze does not destroy me; not through you am I something; you are without me nothing. Were I exterminated, then so would be all reason, with everything good and true. Wherefore would you be, then? Were I not, you would not be.’ – Thus the human being measures himself in his **dignity** against the unmeasurable. The infinity of his destiny becomes the measure for that which no finite reason measures. All the world is not too large for him, since he sees no limits to his power and his destiny. – And does he not feel the same height, when he sees his brothers disdained, when he sees them violated? – There a merchant fleet leaves the inhumane shores of Africa – with human beings: – being layered on being, on everyone a price, everyone for sale, someone for every purse, in life and death at the mercy of the buyer. Thousand tortures should so destroy them, that they also would shudder for the consoling faith in immortality, that they also for the world beyond would have no hope other than to find their torturers, the white, again there. – What outrages you, sensitive soul, so that you shrink back? Why does it appear to you as if the end of the world approached, and as if the spirits and beautiful nature itself returned

du zurückbebest? Warum ist dir, als nahe das Ende der Welt, und als kehrten die Geister und die schöne Natur in das formlose Chaos zurück? – Du siehst Menschen schänden, ihrer Brüder, und eben dadurch sich selbst schänden; du siehst Wesen, die die erhabensten der Schöpfung seyn sollten, andre, und noch mehr, sich selbst unter die Thiere erniedrigen; du fühlst die **Würde** deines Geschlechts, und sie wird mit Füßen getreten; kein Wunder, wenn in diesen herzzerreißenden Augenblicken alle Hoffnung, aller Glaube, alle Zuversicht in deiner Seele wankt; – aber du liegst nicht unter; die Menschheit kann nur für kürze Zwischenraume **herabgewürdigt** werden; sie erhebt sich siegreich, wenn auch nach Jahrhunderten erst; das Gefühl deiner Größe und deines Adels bürgt dir für die sittliche Ordnung im Universum, und für die unbestechliche Wage der ewigen Gerechtigkeit. Der Neger soll nicht bluten und im Angstschweiße triefen, damit **nichtswürdige** mit Zucker wuchern; er ist Mensch: seine Drangsale werden sich in Zufriedenheit verwandeln, und die volle Peinigung der Schaam und Selbstverachtung wird auf seine Tyrannen zurückfallen. Diese Unmenschen selbst werden einst den Augenblick ihrer Gräueltat verwünschen, und, geläutert durch Reue und Gewissensquaalen, in den Kreis der Sittlichkeit zurücktreten. – Und was ist unser einziger fester Trost, wenn unverschuldet die Stürme des Schicksals über uns zusammenschlagen, und alle Elemente der Erde gegen uns verschworen scheinen? Nichts kann uns aufrecht halten, als Bewußtseyn der Erhabenheit unsrer Natur und unsres Daseyns: auf ihr ruhen alle Hoffnungen und Aussichten, die wir für die Zukunft fassen können. –

to formless chaos? – You see human beings defile their brothers and thereby themselves; you see beings who should be the most sublime of creatures defile others and still more lower themselves beneath the animals; you feel the **dignity** of your race, and it is trampled upon. No wonder that in such heart-breaking moments all hope, all faith, all confidence within your soul is shaken, – but you are not oppressed; humanity can only for a short interval be **disgraced**, it raises again victorious, even if only after hundreds of years. The feeling of your worth guaranties you the moral order in the universe, and the incorruptible daring of eternal justice. The black man shall not bleed and drip with the sweat of anguish so that the **unworthy** can derive profit from sugar. He is a human being, his troubles will change into contentment and the full trials of shame and self-contempt will fall back on his tyrants. These inhuman beings will themselves at some point wish away their gruesome deed, and be purified, through repentance and bad conscience, and thus re-enter the circle of morality. – And what is our only sure consolation when the storms of destiny undeservedly move in on us, and all the elements of the earth seem to line up against us? Nothing can keep us standing as can the consciousness of the sublimity of our nature and our being: upon it rests all hopes and aspirations we could have for the future. –

Und dieses Gefühl der **Würde der Menschheit** gewinnt immer mehr an Kraft, je tiefer wir in dasselbe eindringen. Andre wenn auch noch so süße Empfindungen verlieren, indem wir sie und ihre Gründe naher betrachten; manche lösen sich ganz in Dunst auf: jenes steigt in dem Verhältnisse, in welchem wir es durch unsre Denkkraft beleuchten; es stammt von der Vernunft her, und fürchtet die Sonne nicht, denn es ist ein Kind der Sonne.

Das Oberste und Heiligste im Menschen ist sein Streben. Und wonach strebt er, wenn er als wahrer, reiner und ganzer Mensch strebt? Welches ist der Zielpunkt, in welchem alle seine gerechten und nothwendigen Wünsche zusammentreffen? Ihnen befriedigt nicht die Dauer und das Wohlseyn des jetzigen Lebens, nicht das Glück und der Grad der Vollkommenheit seines Zeitalters; ihn befriedigen nicht einmal die Fortschritte wenn auch noch so vieler folgenden Jahrhunderte; sein Interesse verbreitet sich über die ganze Unendlichkeit; er fordert eine allgemeine, ewige sittliche Ordnung im Universum. Gerechtigkeit und Weisheit sollen herrschen; jede Kraft, die unendlicher Vervollkommnung fähig ist, soll unendlich vervollkommnet werden, das Reich der vernünftigen Geister in grenzenlosen Fortschritten immer höher und höher steigen; sittliche Güte und beseligender Seelenfriede der guten Wesen sollen sich immer mehr und mehr verbreiten, während zugleich der Unwerth böser Handlungen von seinen rechtmäßigen Folgen begleitet wird. Der Mensch dringt also durch seinen Vernunft zu dem Endzwecke des Weltalls hin; er trägt ihn, eingeprägt

And this feeling of the **dignity of humanity** waxes in power the deeper we penetrate into it. Other, if even just as sweet feelings, wane when we contemplate them and their reasons more closely; many evaporate. The former increases in relation to us throwing light on it by our capacity for thought. It derives from reason and does not fear the sun since it is a child of the sun.

The highest and most sacred in the human being is his striving. And towards what does he strive, when he strives as true, pure and entire human being? What is the end, in which all his just and necessary aspirations meet? They are not satisfied with the length and wellbeing of this life, with the happiness and the level of perfection of the era, not even with the progress of however many coming centuries; his interest extends to all of eternity. He desires a general, eternal moral order in the universe. Justice and wisdom shall rule, every power capable of infinite perfection shall be infinitely perfected. The kingdom of rational spirits shall rise higher and higher in limitless progress; moral Goodness and beatifying peace of soul of the good shall extend further and further, while also the disvalue of bad actions will be accompanied by their just consequences. The human being thus penetrate through his reason to the final goals of the universe, he carries it, naturally, originally in himself, is conserver of the holiest of which a spirit can think and keeps within the limits of his finitude the idea of the infinite, the only possible plan for the world of an unlimited good and powerful God.

durch die Natur, ursprünglich in sich, ist Aufbewahrer des Allerheiligsten, welches ein Geist denken kann, und befaßt in den Schranken seiner Endlichkeit die Idee des Unendlichen, den einzig möglichen Plan für die Welt eines unbeschränkt guten und mächtigen Gottes.

Der Mensch kann die Ausführung dieses Endzwecks nicht blos von dem höchsten Wesen erwarten, ohne sich selbst zur Theilnahme daran verbindlich zu fühlen. Sein Beruf geht wie jener Endzweck, in die Unendlichkeit; auch durch ihn soll der Plan der Welt erreicht werden; seine Wirkungen sollen sich mit den Wirkungen aller vernünftigen Geister für denselben vereinigen. Wenn er sich dieß je verläugnen wollte, so müßte er den edelsten Theil seines Wesens, sein heiligstes Interesse, ja er mußte sich selbst für zwecklos und nichtig erklären. Sein ganzes Seyn ist entweder nichts, oder es ist Wirkung für die Ewigkeit.

Wäre die Überzeugung blos eine erträumte, schmeichlerische Selbsterhöhung des Menschen; wäre sie nichts, als das Werk einer schwärmenden Vernunft, die sie sich in gedichteten Idealen gefällt, so würde sie nicht in jedem unverdorbenen Menschen aus einer wohlgeleiteten Bildung hervorgehen, würde nie ein so mächtiges Interesse gewinnen, nie so feste und tiefe Wurzeln in uns schlagen können. Allein eine einstimmige Erfahrung lehrt, daß, je gebildeter und veredelter ein Mensch ist, es ihm um so weniger möglich sey, sein Interesse und seine Entwürfe auf den Raum des gegenwärtigen Lebens einzuschränken, daß vielmehr sein innigster Wunsch dahin gehe, auch für die Zukunft, für die Vervollkommnung und das Glück der Nachwelt zu wirken. Und

The human being cannot simply wait for the highest Being to carry out this final goal without feeling himself obliged to take part in it. His calling is as all final goals infinite; also through him shall the plan for the world be realised. His effects shall be united with the effects of all rational Spirits for this purpose. If he were to deny this, he would have to regard the noblest part of his being, his holiest interest, yes, himself, as purposeless and void. His entire being is either nothing, or it has effect for eternity.

Were the conviction only a fanciful, flattering self-aggrandisement of human beings, it would be nothing but a product of an enthusiastic reason, pleasing itself with made-up ideals. Then it would not come forth from a well-guided education in every incorrupt human being, it would never gain so much interest and never be able to take so strong and deep roots in us. Already uniform experience teaches us that the more educated and ennobled a human being is, the less is it possible for him to limit his interests and projects to the space of contemporary life. Rather his innermost wish extends also for the future to work for the perfection and the happiness of posterity. And I don't say too much if I claim that the few who attain to the highest grade of true

ich sage nicht zu viel, wenn ich behaupte, daß jene Wenigen, die sich zu dem höchsten Grade der für Menschen möglichen wahren Kultur erheben, so wenig einen Grenzpunkt dieses Verlangens kennen, daß sie vielmehr ihre thätige Theilnahme an den Angelegenheiten des Universums ohne Ende vorsetzen, und immer weiter ausbreiten wollen. Es ist für den weisen und edlen Menschen schrecklich und unerträglich, sich gestehen zu sollen: Es wird eine Zeit seyn, wo du aus der Sphäre des Daseyns getilgt bist; du wirst von deiner Gattung und von dem ganzen Reiche der Geister scheiden müssen; die Schicksale der Menschheit und der ganzen Welt werden sich ins Unendliche fortwinden, du wirst nichts davon wissen; wenn deine Augen brechen, bricht auch auf ewig deine Gemeinschaft mit den Lebenden, und jedes Band ist vernichtet, welches Vernunft und Hoffnung mit der Zukunft knüpften.

Der weise und gute Mensch allein ist der wahre Mensch. – Großes bewundernswürdiges Wesen, welches Gegenwart und Zukunft nicht trennen kann, dessen Blick unaufhaltsam in die Unendlichkeit geht, dessen Theilnahme für das Glück der Welt nie erlischt, welches nicht zu sich sagen kann, ich bin, ohne zugleich zu sagen, ich muß unsterblich seyn!

Der Gedanke der Unsterblichkeit und einer ewigen Wirksamkeit für Welt und Menschheit ist erhaben, aber für die Kräfte des Menschen nicht zu groß, wenn man sie in der Fülle ihres Vermögens und nach ihrem ganzen Umfange betrachtet. Alle streben nach dem unendlichen, und für keine unter ihnen läßt sich ein Grenzpunkt denken, über welchen hinaus sie keiner

culture obtainable for human beings know no limit to this desire, that they in contrast continue their active participation in the affairs of the universe without end, always wanting to extend it. For the wise and noble human being it is terrible and unbearable to have to admit: there will be a time when you will be erased from the sphere of existence, when you will be separated from your kind and from the entire spiritual world. The destinies of humanity and the entire world will unfold infinitely, [but] you will know nothing of it. When your eyes close, your community with the living likewise closes off and every tie reason and hope had tied to the future is destroyed.

The wise and good human being is alone the true human being. – Great, admirable beings, who cannot separate the present from the future, whose gaze constantly turns towards the infinite, whose concern for the happiness of the world is never extinguished, and who cannot say to themselves I am without at the same time saying I must be immortal!

The thought of immortality and an eternal activity for the world and humanity is sublime, but for the powers of humans not too great, if one considers their full potential in its entirety. All strive towards the infinite, and for none of them can a limit be thought beyond which no further cultivation or edification is possible. Who measures the divine, ineffable capacity of

weiteren Kultur und Erhöhung fähig wäre. Wer ermißt das göttliche, unbegreifliche Vermögen der sittlichen Freyheit und Tugendkraft? Ist nicht alle Güte des besten Herzens ein unbegrenztes Streben nach dem bessern, und führt nicht jede Stufe der Veredlung zu einer noch höheren? Kann ein guter Wille je zu viel wirken? Gehört nicht wesentlich zu ihm die Sehnsucht nach Erweiterung seines Wirkungskreises? Ist je ein Tugendhafter so stark, daß er nicht noch stärker werden könnte? Wer setzt unserm Erkenntnisvermögen sein Ziel? Ist je ein menschlicher Sinn an den Schranken gewesen, wo er nichts mehr hätte fassen können? Hat je ein Auge so viel gesehen, daß es nicht mehr hätte sehen können? Ja das Organ kann zerstört werden, die verlöschende Lebenskraft dem Spiele des Sinnes Stillstand für diese Welt gebieten: ist darum die innere Sehkraft erschöpft? Und können nicht wenigstens die edlern Sinnen grenzenlos verfeinert werden? Können nicht die Flügel des Lichts unsre Blicke weiter und weiterführen? Kann unsre Anschauung nicht unendlich an Feinheit, Schärfe und Umfang gewinnen, unser Gehör nicht in entlegnere Fernen dringen, ein zartes Gefühl für Harmonien der Tone bekommen, wovon wir jetzt vielleicht bey den schönsten Werken großer Meister nur eine schwache Ahndung haben? Wer berechnet die Bildungskraft unsrer Phantasie, dieses wundervollen Vermögens, dem jede neue Erscheinung der Welt Stoff zu neuen Schöpfungen ist? Welche große Kräfte sind Verstand und Vernunft, gleichsam die Lichter der Seele, durch welche wir die Umrisse der Wahrheit in voller Klarheit vor uns sehen! Zwar haben sie Grenzen, und werden ewig Grenzen haben; allein

moral freedom and the power of virtues? Is not all goodness of the best hearts an unlimited striving towards the better, and does not every level of cultivation lead to one that is still higher? Can a good will effect too much? Is the yearning for expansion of its scope of work not essential to it? Is a virtuous man ever so strong he could not become stronger still? Who determines the goal of our ability to know? Has human meaning ever been to the limits of where nothing further could be understood? Has an eye seen so much, that it could see no more? Yes, the organ can be destroyed, the waning life power bid the play of the senses die down in this world: is therefore the inner vision exhausted? Cannot at least the noble senses be limitlessly refined? Cannot the wings of light carry our eyes further and further? Can our intuition not infinitely gain in freedom, clarity and breadth, our hearing reach still further away, obtain a tender sense of the harmony of tones whereof we now have only the weakest sense from the most beautiful works of great masters? Who measures the power of our imagination, this wonderful capacity, which every new appearance in the world gives material for new creations? What great powers are reason and intellect, as lights of the soul through which we see in front of us the contours of truth in full clarity! They have certainly limits, and will forever have limits; yet of what ascending perfection are they not capable within these limits? Can the riches of our knowledge be too great? Are they not constantly capable of extension, purification and correction? And our feelings, can they not eternally gain in **dignity** and tenderness? not always move towards a greater harmony with the good and the true?

welcher steigenden Vervollkommnung sind
sie nicht innerhalb dieser Grenzen fähig!
Kann der Reichtum unsre Erkenntnisse je
zu groß seyn? Ist er nicht unaufhörlich der
Erweiterung, Läuterung und Berichtigung
fähig? Und unsre Gefühle, können sie nicht
ewig an **Würde** und Zartheit gewinnen?
Nicht immer in größere Harmonie mit dem
Guten und Wahren treten?

Ja, es ist in dem erhabenen Menschen keine
Kraft, die nicht unendlich machen könnte.
Und dieser Gedanke ist für ihn um so inte-
ressanter, da seine Gattung offenbar zu
einer immer steigenden Vervollkommnung
bestimmt ist. Die Gattungen der vernunftlosen Thiere bleiben sich gleich: die Pferde
unsrer Zeit sind nicht trefflicher, als die
Pferde der Vorwelt; die Hunde haben
nicht an Klugheit und Treue gewonnen,
und weder Affen noch Elephanten sind
dem Menschen näher gerückt, mit dem
sie von Natur so manche Ähnlichkeit
haben. Die Menschheit ist nicht in solche
Grenzen geschlossen: es giebt für sie keine
Vollendung, über die sie sich nicht noch
erheben könnte, keine letzten Grade der
für sie möglichen Kultur in Hinsicht der
Erkenntnisse so wohl, als der Moralität. Ihr
Charakter besteht in der Fähigkeit eines nie
endenden Wachstums, einer immer steigenden Vervollkommnung. Versetze dich im
Geiste über entfernte Jahrhunderte hinaus,
denke die Riesenschritte der Kultur, und
deine Phantasie findet keinen Endpunkt,
wo ein Stillstand der großen und edlen
Kräfte der Menschheit eintreten müßte. In
keinem Zeitalter wird man sagen können:
‚jetzt leben die beste, die aufgeklärtesten,
die einsichtsvollsten Menschen;‘ nie ist die
Menschheit alles, was sie seyn kann. Der

Yes, there is in the sublime human being no
power that could not render infinite. And
this thought is for him so much the more
interesting as his species obviously is made
for an increasing perfection. The species
of animals lacking reason remain equal to
themselves: the horses of our time are not
better than the horses of yesterday; the dogs
have not grown in cleverness and fidelity,
and neither monkeys nor elephants have
moved closer to the human being, with
whom they have by nature such likeness.
Humanity is not enclosed within such
borders: there is for him no perfection,
above which he could not raise himself,
no last grade of possible culture as regards
knowledge as well as morality. Its character
consists in the possibility of never ending
growth, a perpetually increasing perfection. Imagine thyself in distant centuries
and think of the giant steps of culture; your
imagination finds no final point where the
great and noble powers of humanity would
have to come to a standstill. In no age will
one be able to say: 'now live the best, the
most enlightened, the most insightful
human beings;' never is humanity everything she can be. The spirit that animates
our species can incessantly increase in nobility, purity, strength and extended activity;
the amount of knowledge, the degree of

Geist, welcher unter unserer Gattung herrscht, kann unaufhörlich an Adel, Reinheit, Stärke und ausgebreiteter Wirksamkeit gewinnen; die Masse von Kenntnissen, der Grad des Lichtes, welcher dem Ganzen gemeinschaftlich ist, kann immer noch erhöht, und zu einem größern Umfange der wohlthätigen Einflüsse für Glück und Vervollkommnung erweitert werden. Ja, ich erkühne mich zu hoffen, daß die Zukunft Fortschritte der Menschheit herbey führt, von denen die Besten unsrer Zeitgenossen nur eine schwache Ahndung besitzen, und welche für die große Menge unsrer Brüder, wenn sie sie denken könnten, nur ein Gegenstand des Spottes seyn würden.

O gewiß, es sind die seligsten Stunden des weisen und guten Menschen, wenn seine Phantasie in der Stille der Einsamkeit schöneren Jahrhunderten entgegen eilt: er söhnt sich mit seinem Zeitalter aus, wenn er bemerkt, daß die Kräfte der Menschheit jetzt mehr als je thätig sind, die Blüthe der Jugend und die Männliche Reife unsrer Gattung herbey zu führen; wenn er selbst den hohen Beruf in sich fühlt, für diese Bestimmung feurig mitzuwirken, und er im Geiste die schönern Tage der Zukunft auch über Früchten und Denkmälern seines Enthusiasm glänzen sieht. Ohne diese trostvolle und stärkende Aussicht würde er traurig und muthlos, wie vor der Täuschung eines süßen Traumes, zur Gegenwart zurückkehren; der Blick auf eine Welt würde ihn verzweifeln machen, wo noch so wenige ihre erhabensten Kräfte fühlen, wo ihn von allen Seiten Scenen umgeben, welche alle Zuversicht auf die Menschheit in ihn niederdrücken würden, wenn er nicht vom Gefühle ihrer **Würde** so

light, which the whole collectively is, can always be raised further and extend towards a greater expanse of beneficial influences for happiness and perfection. Yes, I dare to hope the future progress of humanity will come about, of which the best of our contemporaries only have a slight premonition, and which for the great mass of our brothers, if they could think of it, would only be an object of disdain.

Oh surely, it is the happiest hours of the wise and good human being, when his imagination in the quiet of loneliness runs towards lovelier centuries: he reconciles himself with his epoch when he notices that the powers of humanity now more than earlier are active to bring about the blooming of youth and the manly maturity of our species; if he feels the high calling in himself, to passionately help bring about this destiny, and he in his vision of the lovelier days of the future also sees it cast its light on the fruits of and monuments to his enthusiasm. Without this consoling and strengthening perspective he would, sad and discouraged, as if disillusioned of a sweet dream, return to reality; the view of a world in which still so few feel their most sublime powers would make him despair; on all sides of him scenes occur which would oppress all confidence in humanity in him if he were not so deeply penetrated by the feeling of his **dignity**. No, he honours humanity also under the pressure of chains, which keeps it

tief und so stark durchdrungen wäre. Nein, er ehrt die Menschheit auch unter dem Drücke der Fesseln, die sie von ihren großen Zwecken entfernen; er sieht sie schon sich ermannen, ihre Lasten abwerfen, und im Gefühle ihrer Macht und Hoheit eine Gestalt gewinnen, die ihrer würdiger ist. Jetzt noch erliegt der Geist der Menschheit unter der Sklaverey, den Bedürfnissen, den Lastern und der Unwissenheit der Einzelnen: diese Hindernisse werden verschwinden; erniedrigende Schranken werden nicht mehr diese verhaßten Trennungen gründen, welche alle nähere Verbrüderung unter Wesen unmöglich machen, die von gleich erhabener Abkunft und durch gleiche **Würde** ihrer Natur verwandt sind, Wesen, die nur durch die ausgebreitete Gemeinschaft und Wechselwirkung unter einander ihre wahre Bildung erlangen können; drückende Nothdurft wird nicht mehr in einer Welt die edelsten Kräfte tödten, in welcher die unermeßlich reiche Natur so wohlthätig für alle Geschöpfe gesorgt hat; Millionen Menschen werden nicht mehr bedauernswürdige Opfer der Dummheit und Barberey bleiben müssen, um nicht zu verhungern oder zu verdursten; kein Mensch wird dem Laster fröhnen müssen, um Speise und Trank zu haben. Nicht Aberglaube und Unduldsamkeit, nicht Nationalvorurtheile nicht selbstsüchtiger nur auf seinen Privatvortheil lauernder Handelsgeist, nicht menschenverachtender Despotism: unter der Maske der Politik, nicht Eifersucht der Völker, die nur eine Geburt ihrer Schwäche und Verwilderung ist, sie alle werden nicht mehr den freyen Gang der allgemeinen Bildung aufhalten, auf gegenseitige Unterdrückung hinwirken,

away from its great goals. He sees it already manning itself up, throwing off its vices, and in the feeling of its power and elevation cutting a figure **worthier** of it. Still the spirit of humanity is subdued by slavery, by needs, vices and the lack of knowledge of the individual: these hindrances will disappear; degrading limits will no longer found these hated separations, that render impossible the closer connections between beings who nevertheless are related through their equally elevated origin and the equal **dignity** of their nature. They can only attain through each other and through the extended community and interaction between them, their true education. Oppressive needs will no longer kill the noblest forces in a world where the immeasurable riches of nature so beneficially look after all; millions of human beings will not have to become pitiful victims of stupidity and barbary, in order not to starve or thirst. No man will need to indulge vices in order to have food and drink. No superstition and intolerance, no national prejudices, no self-serving spirit of commerce lying in wait for its private interest, no despotic despising of humans under the mask of politics, no envy of peoples which only gives birth to their weakness and return to primitivity, none will oppose the free progression of universal education, none act to mutually oppress, none lower the noblest of all species of the beings of the world to the baseness of a ruling egoism. No, these poisons of humanity will then no longer be: they work themselves towards their destruction and wear themselves gradually out. There comes a time where this cosmopolitan spirit, so far for most, only a fantasy inspired by enthusiasm, shall claim the hearts of people

und die edelste von allen Gattungen der Wesen der Erde zu Niedrigkeit eines herrschenden Egoism herabwürdigen. Nein, diese Gifte der Menschheit werden einst nicht mehr seyn; sie wirken selbst zu ihrer Vernichtung, und zehren sich allmählich auf. Es näht eine Zeit wo jene weltbürgerliche Geist, der bisher für die Meisten nur ein schwärmerisches Bild der Phantasie war, seine Herrschaft in den Herzen der Menschen, die ihm ganz gewidmet seyn sollen, behaupten, wo jeder aus freyer menschenliebender Gesinnung sein eigenes Bestes mit dem Gemeinbesten des großen Ganzes vereinigen, wo jeder nicht blos nothgedrungen für sein gegenwärtiges Bedürfnis, sondern auch für Zukunft und Nachwelt selbst unter großen Aufopferungen wirken wird. Die wahre Aufklärung wird dann nicht mehr das Eigenthum einiger wenigen Nationen seyn; die Auswahl der nothwendigen zu einer ächtmenschlichen Kultur: erforderlichen Einsichten und Kenntnisse wird nach und nach in alle Theile der bewohnten Erde übergehen; der früher gebildete Europäer wird das Licht der Vernunft mit den wildesten Stammen Amerika's theilen, und die Frage: ob die Schwarzen von den Küsten Afrika's vielleicht nur verlarvte Bestien, nur Gestalten von Menschen (eine Frage, die jetzt noch Weltweise aufwerfen) wird nicht mehr möglich seyn. Hat unsre Gattung sich einmal zu diesem Grade von Moralität und Geistesvollkommenheit erhoben, so besitzt sie dadurch um so mehr Kraft zu höheren Fortschritten; sie kann nicht in Verwilderung und Sittenlosigkeit zurückfallen. Alle bisherige Revolutionen, wo wir die Menschheit in Hinsicht der Tugend und Aufklärung sinken sehen, waren nur

completely dedicated to it, where everyone out of free humanitarian love shall reconcile his own good with that of the common good of the great all. Then all shall work, even under great sacrifices, not simply as forced by his current need, but also for the sake of future and posterity. True enlightenment will then no longer be the property of some nations; the choice of the necessary for a truly human culture: useful insights and knowledge will little by little spread to all parts of the inhabited world; the earlier educated European will share the light of reason with the wildest tribes of America, and the question: whether the black from Africa's coasts perhaps only are chrysalises of animals, only shapes of humans (a question raised by the worldly wise) will no longer be possible.

Have our species once achieved this level of morality, it will even more have the power to make still higher progress; it cannot return to the wild and to immorality. All previous revolutions, where we have seen humanity sink as regards virtue and enlightenment were only destinies of individual nations, mainly occasioned through

Schicksale einzelner Nationen, größtens-
theils durch andre Einzelne bewirkt: sie
sind nicht mehr möglich, so bald unsre
ganze Gattung jene allgemeine Kultur
besitzt, die ihre männliche Reife ausmacht,
eine Kultur, welche alle Völker unter der
Herrschaft des guten Willens und des
Lichtes der Vernunft zu einem Staate
vereinigt. Alle Menschen sind dann wie
ein Mensch zu betrachten, dessen sämtli-
che Glieder mit harmonischem Eifer für
seine Erhaltung und sein wahres Wohl
zusammenwirken.

other individuals. They are no longer possible as soon as our whole species possesses universal culture, which constitutes
its manly maturity, a culture that brings
all peoples under the rule of the good will
and the light of reason into one state. All
human beings will then be like one, whose
every limb work with harmonious eagerness together to preserve the whole and for
its true good.

Hannah More (1745–1833)

A Blue Stocking Society member, a very practical philanthropist and an
extremely prolific writer, Hannah More's understanding of human dignity is
unsentimental. She understands the awareness of sinfulness as the criterion
for realism, and regards all fashionable condoning of religious languish-
ing, not tempered by this insight, to be sad. Her abolitionist Christianity
does not see the professionalisation of women as the only way to respect
their dignity, and in contrast warns against it leading to the neglect of
their children. Her practical concern for the education of the young and
of teenage girls reflect another type of realism: to change society for the
better you have to start where you are.

An Estimate of the Religion of the Fashionable World (1791)

3rd edn (London: T. Cadell, 1791), pp. 228–33. Eighteenth Century
Collections Online.

But if I were to venture to take my estimate with a view more immediately evangelical; if I presumed to look for that genuine christianity which consists in 'repentance towards God, and faith in our Lord Jesus Christ;' to insist that, whatever *natural* religion and *fashionable* religion may teach, it is the peculiarity of the *christian* religion to humble the sinner and exalt the Saviour; to insist that not only the grossly flagitious, but that *all*, have sinned; that *all* are by nature in a state of condemnation; that all stand in need of mercy, of which there is no hope but on the Gospel terms; that eternal life is promised to those *only* who accept it on the offered conditions of 'faith, repentance, and renewed obedience;' – if I were to insist on such evidences of our christianity as these; if I were to express these doctrines in plain scriptural terms, without lowering, qualifying, disguising, or doing them away; if I were to insist on this belief, and its implied and corresponding practices; I am aware that, with whatever condescending patience this little tract might have been so far perused, many a fashionable reader would here throw it aside, as having now detected the palpable enthusiast, the abettor of 'strange doctrines,' long ago consigned over by the liberal and the polite to bigots and fanatics. And yet, if the Bible be true, this is a simple and faithful description of christianity.

After having, however, just ventured to hint that such are indeed the humbling doctrines of the Gospel, to which alone eternal life is promised; I shall, in deep humility, forbear enlarging on this part of the subject, which has been exhausted by the labours of wise and pious men in all ages. Unhappily, however, the most awakening of these writers are not the favourite guests in the closets of the more fashionable Christians; who, when they happen to be more seriously disposed than ordinary, are fond of finding out some middle kind of reading, which recommends some half-way state, something between paganism and Christianity, suspending the mind, like the position on Mahomet's tomb, between earth and heaven: a kind of reading which, while it quiets the conscience by being on the side of morals, neither awaken their fears, nor alarms their security. [...] It agreeably represents the readers to themselves as amiable persons; guilty indeed of a few faults, but never as condemned sinners under sentence of death. It commonly abounds with high encomiums on the **dignity of human nature**; the good effects of virtue on health, fortune and reputation; the dangers of a blind zeal, the mischiefs of enthusiasm, and the folly of being 'righteous over much:' with various other kindred sentiments, which, if they do not fall in of themselves with the corruptions of our nature, may, by a little warping, be easily accommodated to them.

These are the too successful practices of lukewarm and temporising divines, who have become popular by blunting the edge of that heavenly tempered weapon, whose salutary keenness, but for their 'deceitful handling,' would oftener 'pierce to the dividing asunder of soul and spirit.'

But those severer preachers of righteousness, who disgust by applying too closely to the conscience; who probe the inmost heart, and lay open all its latent peccancies; who treat of principles as the only certain source of manners; who lay the axe to the root, oftener that the pruning knife to the branch; who insist much and often on the great leading truths, that man is a fallen creature, who must be restored, if he be restored at all, by means very little flattering to human pride – such as these will seldom find access to the houses and the hearts of the more modish Christians; unless they happen to owe their admission to some subordinate quality of style; unless they can captivate, with the seducing graces of language, those well-bred readers, who are childishly amusing themselves with the garnish, when they are perishing for want of food; who are searching for polished periods, when they should be in quest of alarming truths; who are looking for elegance of composition, when they should be anxious for eternal life.

Strictures on the Modern System of Female Education (1799)

Strictures on the Modern System of Female Education with a View of the Principles and Conduct Prevalent among Women of Rank and Fortune, two volumes, volume 2, 3rd edn (London: T. Cadell, Jr. and Davies, 1799) pp. 255–60 (extracts). Eighteenth Century Collections Online.

To this doctrine [of original sin] it is important to conciliate the minds, more especially of young persons, who are peculiarly disposed to turn away from it as a morose, unamiable and gloomy idea: they are apt to accuse those who are more strict and serious, of unnecessary severity, and to suspect them of thinking unjustly ill of mankind. [...] The opposition to this doctrine in the young arises partly from ingenuousness of heart, partly from a habit of indulging themselves in favourable suppositions respecting the world, rather than of pursuing truth, which is always the grand thing to be pursued; and partly from the popularity of the tenet, that *everybody is so wonderfully good!* [...] Profane history abundantly confirms this truth: the history of the world being in fact little else than the history of the crimes of the human race. Even though the annals of remote ages lie so involved in obscurity, that some degree of uncertainty attaches itself to many of the events recorded, yet this one melancholy truth is always clear, that most of the miseries which have been brought upon mankind, have proceeded from this general depravity.

The world we now live in furnishes abundant proof of this truth. In a world formed on the deceitful theory of those who assert the innocence and **dignity of man**, almost all the professions, since they would have been rendered useless by such a state

of innocence, would not have existed. Without sin, we may nearly presume there would have been no sickness; so that every medical professor is a standing evidence of this sad truth. [...] Had man persevered in his original integrity, there would have been no litigation, for there would be no contests about property in a world where none would be inclined to attack it. [...] Why in the fairest transaction of business is nothing executed without bonds, receipts, and notes of hand? Why does not a perfect confidence in the *dignity of human nature* abolish all these securities?; if not between enemies, or people indifferent to each other, yet at least between friends and kindred, and the most honourable connections? Why, but because of that universal suspicion between man and man, which, by all we see, and hear, and feel, is become interwoven with our very make?

The Spirit of Prayer (1825)

The Complete Works of Hannah More in seven volumes, Duodecimo, to match Robert's memoirs of the author (New York: Harper and Brothers, Cliff Street, 1835), vol. 7, pp. 299–392, p. 302 (digitised by Google, accessed 29 August 2018).

The self-sufficiency of man arising from his imaginary **dignity**, is a favourite doctrine with the nominal Christian. He feeds his pride with this pernicious aliment. And, as we hear much, so we hear falsely, of the **dignity of human nature**. Prayer, founded on the true principles of scripture, alone teaches us wherein our true **dignity** consists. The **dignity** of a fallen creature is a perfect anomaly. True **dignity**, contrary to the common opinion, that it is an inherent excellence, is actually a sense of the want of it; it consists not in our valuing ourselves, but in a continual feeling of our dependence upon God, and an unceasing aim at conformity to his image.

CHAPTER II

Industrialisation and Democracy

As vindications and organised campaigns for the rights of slaves, women and workers unfold, a tendency to backlash makes itself felt, stemming from competing interests. Nietzsche, voicing a criticism of culture as such, throws his full weight against, so it seems, the idea that human dignity should be a constitutional principle. His motivations, commanding an important following otherwise, seem hard to follow, except as a conservative claim for the resurrection of some form of aristocracy based in the artistic genius. Nonetheless, the pluralism of the many voices itself makes for the consolidation of democracy. Democracy will soon come to constitute an argument by itself, in need of no further justification.

Georg Wilhelm Friedrich Hegel (1770–1831)

Hegel gives a speculative version of the idea that human dignity is dependency on or conformity with the Absolute, thus prolonging a theme of the Classical, the Christian and the Enlightenment understanding.

Lectures on the Philosophy of Religion (1821–1831)

Text from *Vorlesungen über der Philosophie der Religion* I, *Werke*, vol. 16, eds Eva Moldenhauer and Karl Markus Michel (Frankfurt am Main: Suhrkamp, 1969), p. 301. My own translation.

Auch deshalb sollte man meinen, der Mensch, weil er als diese *Macht* so viel gilt, sei hier hoch geehrt und habe das Gefühl seiner *Würde*. Aber im Gegenteil, vollkommenen Unwert hat hier der Mensch – denn **Würde hat der Mensch** nicht dadurch, was er als unmittelbarer Wille ist, sondern nur indem er von einem Anundfürsichseienden, einem Substantiellem weiß und diesem seinen natürlichen Willen unterwirft und gemäß macht. Erst durch das Aufheben der natürlichen Unbändigkeit und durch das Wissen, das ein Allgemeines, Anundfürsichseiendes das Wahre sei, erhält er eine **Würde**, und dann ist erst das Leben selbst auch etwas wert.

Also for that reason, should one think that the human being because he counts so much as this *power*, would here be highly respected and have the feeling of his **dignity**. But in contrast, the human being has here no value at all – since **the human being has dignity** not through what he is as immediate will, but only in that he knows and subjects his natural will to a substantial being-in-and-for-itself by conforming to it. First through the assumption of the natural unruliness and through the knowledge that a universal being-in-and-for-itself is the True, does he acquire his **dignity**, and only then is life itself also valuable.

France

Fifty years after the Revolution slavery is finally abolished throughout the empire.

Decree abolishing slavery throughout the French empire (27 April 1848)

Considérant que l'esclavage est un attentat contre la **dignité humaine**; qu'en détruisant le libre arbitre de l'homme, il supprime le principe naturel du droit et du devoir; qu'il est une violation flagrante du dogme républicain: Liberté, Egalité, Fraternité, [...]

Considering that slavery is an assault against **human dignity**, that in destroying the free will of the human being, it suppresses the natural principle of justice and duty; that it is in flagrant violation of the republican principles of freedom, equality and fraternity, [...]

Pierre-Joseph Proudhon (1809–1865)

For Proudhon human dignity stands at the heart of justice as the feeling of the essence of humanity in the other as well as in oneself. The tying of human dignity to feeling, independent of community or divinity, he may have inherited from Heydenreich, standing in the same masonic tradition as he. But here it has the added meaning of explaining why I (everyone) have an interest in the respect for the human dignity of others: I feel his human dignity violated *in mine*, and is therefore personally concerned by his oppression. In this, and in the formulation of the reliance of justice on human dignity Proudhon is ground-breaking.

Justice in the Revolution and in the Church (1858)

Text from *Oeuvres Complètes* de P. J. Proudhon (Paris: Garnier Frères, 1858) Vol. 8, Part 1 (Vol. I of IV). Translation is my own.

Second Study: Persons

Chapitre VI. Age nouveau: La Révolution.
– Immanence et réalité de la Justice

XXX.

[...] Sentir et affirmer la **dignité humaine**, d'abord dans tout ce qui nous est propre, puis dans la personne du prochain, et cela sans retour d'égoïsme comme sans considération aucune de la divinité or de communauté: voilà le *droit*. [...]

XXXI.

Sentir son être dans les autres, au point de sacrifier à ce sentiment tout autre intérêt, d'exiger pour autrui le même respect que pour soi-même [...] semble au premier abord étrange. [...] Or tout homme tend à déterminer et à faire prévaloir son

Chapter VI. The New Age: The Revolution.
– Immanence and Reality of Justice.

XXX.

[...] To feel and affirm **human dignity**, first in all that is ours and then in the person of my neighbour, and that without the return of egoism and without any consideration of divinity or community: that's what's *right*. [...]

XXXI.

To feel one's being in others, to the point of sacrificing to it all other interests, to claim for the other the same respect as for oneself [...] seems at first strange. [...] All human beings tend to affirm and put forward first their own essence, which is their

essence, qui est sa **dignité** même. [...] Il en résulte que l'essence étant identique et une pour tous les hommes, chacun de nous se sent tout a la fois comme personne et comme espèce (50) ; que l'injure commise est ressentie par les tiers et par l'offenseur lui-même comme par l'offensé ; qu'en conséquence, la protestation est commune, ce qui est précisément la justice.

Pour me servir du langage théologique [...] quand la Justice fait entendre dans notre âme sa voix impérieuse, c'est le VERBE, *Logos*, âme commune de l'humanité, incarné en chacun de nous, qui nous appelle et nous somme de le défendre. [...]

XXXII.

[...] La justice, ne nous lassons pas de le rappeler, est le sentiment de la **dignité humaine**. [...]

XXXIII.

[...] La Révolution seule a conçu et défini le contrat social. [...] Il existe donc un contrat ou constitution de la société, donné *a priori* par les formes de la conscience [...] C'est l'acte par lequel des hommes, se forment en groupe, déclarent, *ipso facto*, l'identité et la solidarité de leurs **dignités** respectives, se reconnaissent réciproquement et au même titre souverains, et se portent l'un pour l'autre garants. [...] La Justice devient ainsi un autre égoïsme. [...]

very **dignity**. [...] From this results that the essence, which is one and the same for all, makes every one of us feel like a person and at the same time as [part of the] species (50). [From this also results] that the injury committed is felt by a third party and by the perpetrator himself as well as by the offended; that as a consequence, the protestation is common [to them], which is precisely [what] justice [is].

To use theological language [...] when justice makes its commanding voice heard in our soul, it is the WORD, the *Logos*, the common soul of humanity, incarnated in every one of us, who calls us and summons us to defend it. [...]

XXXII.

[...] Justice, let us not tire of repeating it, is the feeling of **human dignity**. [...]

XXXIII.

[...] Only the revolution has conceived and defined the social contract. [...] There thus exists a contract or constitution of society, given *a priori* by the forms of conscience [...] It is the act by which human beings form themselves into a group, declaring, *ipso facto*, the identity and solidarity of their respective **dignities**, recognising themselves reciprocally and by the same fact sovereign, guaranteeing [the sovereignty of] each other. [...] In this way, justice becomes another egoism. [...]

Chapitre VII. Définition de la justice	Chapter VII. The Definition of Justice
XXXIV.	XXXIV.
Nous pouvons maintenant donner la défi-nition de la Justice ; plus tard, nous en constaterons la REALITÉ.	We can now proceed to give the definition of justice; later we shall see its REALITY.

1. L'homme, en vertu de la raison dont il est doué, à la faculté de sentir sa dignité dans la personne de son semblable comme dans sa propre personne, de s'affirmer, tout à la fois comme individu et comme espèce.

1. The human being, by virtue of reason with which he is gifted, have the ability to feel his dignity in the person of his neighbour as well as in his own person, and to affirm himself at the same time as individual and as species.

2. La JUSTICE est le produit de cette faculté : c'est *le respect, spontanément éprouvé et réciproquement garanti, de la dignité humaine en quelque personne et dans quelque circonstance qu'elle se trouve compromise et a quelque risque que nous expose sa défense.* [...] Le droit est pour chacun la faculté d'exiger des autres le respect de la dignité humaine dans sa personne ; – le devoir, l'obligation pour chacun de respecter cette dignité en autrui.

2. JUSTICE is the product of this ability: it *is the respect, spontaneously felt and reciprocally guaranteed, for human dignity in whatever person and in whatever circumstance it is found compromised and no matter the risk to which its defence exposes us.* [...] The right is for everyone the ability to claim from others the respect due to human dignity in one's own person; – duty [is] the obligation everyone has to respect this dignity in others.

Henriette (Hortense Wild) (1814–1896)

Peaceful Democracy (1849)

Feminists had to react to Proudhon's contradiction: being so clearly committed to the dignity of the human essence, his denial of humanity to women was outrageously insulting. Henriette's comment is on an earlier writing, but Proudhon was not to change his mind on women's status.

Text from *La Démocratie Pacifique*, journal des fouriéristes, 5 January 1849, as quoted in *Maitron en ligne Dictionnaire Biographique. Mouvement Ouvrier*, <http://maitron-en-ligne.univ-paris1.fr/spip.php?article36613> (accessed 27 August 2018). Translation is my own.

Mauvais chrétien, socialiste haineux, vous poursuivez le monopole sous la sa forme matérielle et particulièrement saisissable, ce qui est bien: mais quand on veut l'attaquer sous sa forme affective, vous vous mettez à la traverse et criez au scandale ! Vous voulez de la **dignité** et de l'égalité des hommes, et vous repoussez la **dignité** et l'égalité des sexes? La femme dites-vous n'a rien à attendre de plus et son devoir est de rester dans la retraite pour laquelle la nature la créée. Pitié de vos sophismes, honte à vos idées de résignation quand même !	A bad Christian, a socialist full of hatred, you pursue the monopoly in its material and particularly comprehensible form, which is good; but when one wants to attack it in its affective form, you baulk and cry 'scandal!' You want **dignity** and equality for human beings, but reject **dignity** and equality for the sexes? The woman, you say, should not expect anything more and her duty is to stay in the retreat nature has created for her. Pity on your sophisms, shame on your ideas of resignation!

Ferdinand Lassalle (Ferdinand Johan Gottlieb Lassal/ Ferdinand Lassalle-Wolfson) (1825–1864)

Socialists take up the now politicised idea and claim the rights to a life more worthy of human dignity. If anarchists like Proudhon could be successful in using this idea, so could socialists. They would also inherit the problem from him as to whether or in what way the idea concerned women.

The Working Man's Programme (1862)

Text from *Reden und Schriften*, ed. Friedrich Jenaczek (München: Deutcher Taschenbuch Verlag, 1970), p. 37–40. Translation from *The Working Man's Programme*, trans. Edward Peeters (London: The Modern Press, 1884). Translation slightly adapted.

So sehr der Arbeiter und der Kleinbürger, mit einem Worte die ganze nicht Kapital besitzende Klasse, berechtigt ist, vom Staate zu verlangen, daß er sein ganzes Sinnen und Trachten darauf richte, wie die kummervolle und notbeladene materielle Lage der arbeitenden Klassen zu verbessern, und wie auch ihnen, durch deren Hände alle die Reichtümer produziert worden, mit denen unsere Zivilisation prunkt, deren Händen alle die Produkte ihre Entstehung verdanken, ohne welche die gesamte Gesellschaft keinen Tag existieren könnte, zu einem reichlicheren und gesicherten Erwerbe und damit wieder zu der Möglichkeit geistiger Bildung und somit erst zu einem wahrhaft **menschenwürdiger** Dasein zu verhelfen sei – wie sehr, sage ich, die arbeitenden Klassen auch berechtigt sind, dies vom Staate zu fordern und dies als seinen wahrhaften Zweck hinzustellen, so darf und wird dennoch der Arbeiter niemals vergessen, daß alles einmal erworbene gesetzliche Eigentum vollständig unantastbar und rechtmäßig ist.

The working man and the poor citizen, in a word, the whole of that class, which is without capital, is fully justified in demanding from the state that it should direct its aim and all its endeavours towards the improvement of the sorrowful and needy condition of the working classes, and to the discovery of the means by which it may help to raise those by whose hands all the riches with which our civilization delights to adorn itself have been produced. To the same hands all those products owe their existence, without which the whole community would perish in a single day; it is therefore the duty of the state to help these to more ample and assured wages, and further to the possibility of a spiritual education, and through this to an existence truly **worthy of man**. Fully as the working classes are justified in demanding this from the state, and in pointing out this as its true aim, so the working man must and will never forget that the right to all property once lawfully earned is thoroughly legitimate and unassailable.

Friedrich Wilhelm Nietzsche (1844–1900)

Nietzsche links the idea of the dignity of the human being with the dignity of work, neither of which he approves of. He rather sees both ideas as slaves' ploys to manipulate the strong and he instead longs for a return to a utopian aristocracy under the genius, who will lead others through their unconscious desires to find their lost dignity in his prerogatives. Is this simply a conservative reaction against the left-wing use of the idea? It seems more than that, in that it rejects the idea of human dignity in its

entirety (also as it might be used by conservatives), a rejection to which
later Nietzscheans, like Hannah Arendt, will refer back as prophetic. One
is tempted by the pathos to look towards that which is denied, and see! –
we get an accurate outline of the effects and the substance of the idea of
human dignity. In fact, it may have been part of what prompted Pope Leo
XIII (and his collaborators) to write *Rerum Novarum* (1891), the encycli-
cal that has since been credited with founding the social doctrine of the
Church, which intervenes to admonish respect for work as an expression of
human dignity.

The Greek State (1871)

Text from *Fünf Vorreden zu fünf ungeschriebene Büchern* (3), *Kritische
Studienausgabe*, vol. 1, eds Giorgio Colli and Mazzino Montinari, vol. 3.
(Berlin – New York: Deutscher Taschenbuch-Verlag – de Gruyter, 1988)
pp. 764–77. Trans. Maximilian A. Mügge, in *Early Greek Philosophy and
Other Essays, The Complete Works of Friedrich Nietzsche*, ed. Oscar Levy,
vol. 2 (New York: The Macmillan Company, 1911).

Wir Neueren haben vor den Griechen zwei Begriffe voraus, die gleichsam als Trostmittel einer durchaus sklavisch sich gebährenden und dabei das Wort 'Sklave' ängstlich scheuenden Welt gegeben sind: wir reden von der ,**Würde des Menschen**' und von der ,**Würde der Arbeit**'. Alles quält sich, um ein elendes Leben elend zu per-petuieren; diese furchtbare Noth zwingt zu verzehrender Arbeit, die nun der vom ,Willen' verführte Mensch – oder richti-ger – menschliche Intellekt gelegentlich als etwas **Würdevolles** anstaunt. Damit aber die Arbeit einen Anspruch auf ehrende Titel habe, wäre es vor allem nöthig, daß das Dasein selbst, zu dem sie doch nur ein

We moderns have an advantage over the Greeks in two ideas, which are given as it were as a compensation to a world behav-ing thoroughly slavishly and yet at the same time anxiously eschewing the word 'slave': we talk of the '**dignity of man**' and of the '**dignity** of labour'. Everybody worries in order miserably to perpetuate a miser-able existence; this awful need compels him to consuming labour; man (or, more exactly, the human intellect) seduced by the 'Will' occasionally marvels at labour as something **dignified**. However, in order that labour might have a claim on titles of honour, it would be necessary above all, that Existence itself, to which labour after

qualvolles Mittel ist, etwas mehr **Würde** und Werth habe, als dies ernst meinenden Philosophien und Religionen bisher erschienen ist. Was durften wir anderes in der Arbeidsnoth aller der Millionen finden als den Trieb um jeden Preis da zu sein, denselben allmächtigen Trieb, durch den verkümmerte Pflanzen ihre Wurzeln in erdloses Gestein strecken! [...]

In der neueren Welt, die, zusammengehalten mit der griechischen, zumeist nur Abnormitäten und Centauren schafft, in der der einzelne Mensch, gleich jenem fabelhaften Wesen im Eingange der horazischen Poetik, aus Stücken bunt zusammengesetzt ist, zeigt sich oft an demselben Menschen zugleich die Gier des Existenz-Kampfes und des Kunstbedürfnisses: aus welcher unnatürlichen Verschmelzung die Noth entstanden ist jene erstere Gier vor dem Kunstbedürfnisse zu entschuldigen und zu weihen. Deshalb glaubt man an die ‚**Würde des Menschen**' und die ‚**Würde der Arbeit**'. [...]

Die Griechen brauchen solchen Begriffs-Hallucinationen nicht, bei ihnen sprichet sich mit erschreckender Offenheit aus, daß die Arbeit eine Schmach sei – und eine verborgener und seltner redender, aber überall lebendige Weisheit fügte hinzu, daß auch das Menschending ein schmähliches und klägliches Nichts und eines ‚Schattens Traum' sei. Die Arbeit ist eine Schmach, weil das Dasein keinen Werth an sich hat [...] Solche Phantome, wie die **Würde des Menschen**, die **Würde der Arbeit**, sind die dürftigen Erzeugnisse des sich vor sich selbst versteckenden Sklaventhums. Unselige Zeit, in der der Sklave solche Begriffe braucht, in der er

all only is a painful means, should have more **dignity** and value than it appears to have had, up to the present, to serious philosophies and religions. What else may we find in the labour-need of all the millions but the impulse to exist at any price, the same all-powerful impulse by which stunted plants stretch their roots through earthless rocks! [...]

In the modern world, which, compared with the Greek, usually produces only abnormalities and centaurs, in which the individual, like that fabulous creature in the beginning of the Horatian Art of Poety, is jumbled together out of pieces, here in the modern world in one and the same man the greed of the struggle for existence and the need for art show themselves at the same time: out of this unnatural amalgamation has originated the dilemma, to excuse and to consecrate that first greed before this need for art. Therefore; we believe in the 'Dignity of man' and the '**Dignity of labour**'. [...]

The Greeks did not require such conceptual hallucinations, for among them the idea that labour is a disgrace is expressed with startling frankness; and another piece of wisdom, more hidden and less articulate, but everywhere alive, added that the human thing also was an ignominious and piteous nothing and the 'dream of a shadow'. Labour is a disgrace, because existence has no value in itself [...] Such phantoms as the **dignity of man**, the **dignity** of labour, are the needy products of slavedom hiding itself from itself. Wo[e]ful time, in which the slave requires such conceptions, in which he is incited to think about and beyond himself! Cursed seducers, who

zum Nachdenken über sich und über sich hinaus aufgereizt wird! Unselige Verführer, die den Unschuldsstand des Sklaven durch die Frucht vom Baume der Erkenntnis vernichtet haben! Jetzt muß dieser sich mit solchen durchsichtigen Lügen von einem Tage zum anderen hinhalten, wie sie in der angeblichen ‚Gleichberechtigung Aller‘ oder in den sogenannten ‚Grundrechten des Menschen‘, des Menschen als solchen, oder in der **Würde** der Arbeit für jeden tiefer Blickenden erkennbar sind. Er darf ja nicht begreifen, auf welcher Stufe und in welcher Höhe erst ungefähr von ‚**Würde**‘ gesprochen werden kann, dort nähmlich wo das Individuum völlig über sich hinausgeht und nicht mehr im Dienste seines individuellen Weiterlebens zeugen und arbeiten muß. [...]

Demgemäß müssen wir uns dazu verstehen, als grausam klingende Wahrheit hinzustellen, daß zum Wesen einer Kultur das Sklaventhum gehöre: eine Wahrheit freilich, die über den absoluten Werth des Daseins keinen Zweifel übrigläßt. [...] Das Elend der mühsam lebenden Menschen muß noch gesteigert werden, um einer geringen Anzahl olympischer Menschen die Produktion der Kunstwelt zu ermöglichen. Hier liegt der Quell jenes Ingrimms, den die Kommunisten und Socialisten und auch ihre blasseren Abkömmlinge, die Weiße Race der ‚Liberalen‘ jeder Zeit gegen die Künste, aber auch gegen das klassische Alterthum genährt haben. [...] Eins nämlich ist nicht zu vergessen: dieselbe Grausamkeit, die wir im Wesen jeder Kultur fanden, liegt auch im Wesen jeder mächtigen Religion und überhaupt in der Natur der Macht, die immer böse ist [...]

have destroyed the slave's state of innocence by the fruit of the tree of knowledge! Now the slave must vainly scrape through from one day to another with transparent lies recognisable to every one of deeper insight, such as the alleged 'equal rights of all' or the so-called 'fundamental rights of man as such,' or the '**dignity** of labour.' Indeed he is not to understand at what stage and at what height **dignity** can first be mentioned – namely, at the point where the individual goes wholly beyond himself and no longer has to work and to produce in order to preserve his individual existence. [...]

Accordingly, we must accept this cruel sounding truth, that slavery is of the essence of Culture; a truth of course, which leaves no doubt as to the absolute value of Existence. [...] The misery of toiling men must still increase in order to make the production of the world of art possible to a small number of Olympian men. Here is to be found the source of that secret wrath nourished by Communists and Socialists of all times, and also by their feebler descendants, the white race of the 'Liberals', not only against the arts, but also against classical antiquity. [...] it is not to be forgotten that the same cruelty, which we found in the essence of every Culture, lies also in the essence of every powerful religion and in general in the essence of *power*, which is always evil [...]

Deshalb dürfen wir auch die herrliche Kultur mit einem bluttriefenden Sieger vergleichen, der bei seinem Triumphzüge die an seinen Wagen gefesselten besiegten als Sklaven mitschleppt: als welchen eine wohlthätige Macht die Augen verblendet hat, so daß sie, von den Rädern des Wagens fast zermalmt, doch noch rufen ‚**Würde der Arbeit!**‘ ‚**Würde des Menschen!**‘ [...]

Ich dächte, der kriegerischer Mensch wäre ein Mittel des militärischen Genius und seine Arbeit wiederum nur ein Mittel desselben Genius; und nicht ihm, als absolutem Menschen und Nicht-genius, sondern ihm als Mittel der Genius – [...] komme ein Grad von **Würde** zu, jener **Würde** nämlich, zum Mittel des Genius **gewürdigt** zu sein. [...] jeder Mensch, mit seiner gesamten Thätigkeit, hat nur soviel **Würde**, als er, bewußt oder unbewußt, Werkzeug des Genius ist; woraus sofort die ethische Consequenz zu erschließen ist, daß der ‚Mensch an sich‘, der absolute Mensch, weder **Würde**, noch Rechte, noch Pflichten besitzt: nur als völlig determiniertes, unbewußten Zwecken dienendes Wesen kann der Mensch seine Existenz entschuldigen.

Therefore we may compare this grand Culture with a bloodstained victor, who in his triumphal procession carries the defeated along as slaves chained to his chariot, slaves whom a beneficent power has so blinded that, almost crushed by the wheels of the chariot, they nevertheless still exclaim: '**Dignity** of labour!' '**Dignity** of **Man!**' [...]

I should like to think the warlike man to be a means of the military genius and his labour again only a tool in the hands of that same genius; and not to him, as absolute man and non-genius, but to him as a means of the genius – [...] is due a degree of **dignity**, of that **dignity** namely, to have been **worthy** of being a means of the genius. [...] every human being, with his total activity, only has **dignity** in so far as he is a tool of the genius, consciously or unconsciously; from this we may immediately deduce the ethical conclusion, that 'man in himself', the absolute man possesses neither **dignity**, nor rights, nor duties; only as a wholly determined being serving unconscious purposes can man excuse his existence.

Thomas Mann (1875–1955)

Split between Nietzschean desire and modern democracy, Mann encapsulates something of the spirit of the bourgeois intelligentsia before and between the world wars. The emphasis on illness recalls Gertrude of Helfta,

and the refusal to let freethinking monopolise the conceptualisation of human dignity highlights the ongoing cultural competition between Christian and secular traditions.

Texts from *Gesammelte Werke in Dreizehn Bände* (Frankfurt a. M. S: Fischer Verlag). 'Goethe und Tolstoi' from vol. IX, 1960, 1974, pp. 79–80; the translation is my own. The extract from *The Magic Mountain* is from vol. III, 1952 pp. 92–3 and pp. 409–10. Trans. H. T. Lowe-Porter (London: Secker and Warburg, 1980), p. 64 and p. 294, adaptation in square brackets.

Goethe and Tolstoi (1921)

Hier ist ein wenig Philosophie der Krankheit am Platz – mit aller gebotenen Beschränkung. Krankheit hat ein doppeltes Gesicht, eine doppelte Beziehung zum **menschlichen und seiner Würde**. Sie ist einerseits dieser **Würde** feindlich, indem sie durch Überbetonung des Körperlichen, durch ein Zurückweisen des Menschen auf seinen Körper entmenschlichend wirkt, den Menschen zum bloßen Körpers **herabwürdigt**. Andererseits aber ist es möglich, Krankheit sogar als etwas höchst **Menschenwürdiges** zu denken und zu empfinden. Denn, wenn es zu weit ginge zu sagen, das Krankheit Geist, oder gar (was sehr tendenziös klänge), daß Geist Krankheit sei, so haben diese Begriffe doch viel miteinander zu tun. Geist nämlich ist stolz, ist emanzipatorische Widersetzlichkeit (dies Wort im rein logischen wie auch im streitbaren Sinn genommen) gegen die Natur, ist Abgelöstheit, Entfernung, Entfremdung von ihr; Geist ist das, was den Menschen, dies von der Natur in hohem Grade gelöste, in hohem Maße sich ihr entgegengesetzt fühlende Wesen, vor allem übrigen organischen

Here a little philosophy of illness is needed – within its own indicated limits. Illness has a double face, a double relationship with **the human and its dignity**. It is on the one hand an enemy of this **dignity**, as far as it, through exaggeration of the bodily and referral of human beings to their body, effects dehumanization, and **debases** the human being by reduction to his body. On the other hand, it is possible to think and feel illness as something in the finest **harmony with human dignity**. Thus, if it would be going too far to say that illness is spirit, or even (which would sound very biased), that spirit is illness, the two concepts have nevertheless much to do with one another. Spirit, in fact, is pride, is emancipatory opposition (this word taken in its purely logical function as well as in its combative meaning) in relation to nature; is separation, removal, alienation from it. Spirit is what characterises human beings, these to a large extent loosened from and feeling themselves in opposition to nature and distinguished above all other organic life. The question, the aristocratic question, is whether they are in fact more human the

Leben auszeichnet, und die Frage, die aristokratische Frage ist, ob er nicht in desto höherem Grade Mensch sei, je gelöster von der Natur, das heißt, je kränker er sei. Denn was wäre Krankheit, wenn nicht Abgetrenntheit von der Natur? [...]

War es nicht Nietzsche, der den Menschen ‚das kranke Tier' genannt hat? Und meinte er nicht damit, daß der Mensch eben nur insofern mehr sei denn Tier, als er krank sei? Im Geist also, in der Krankheit beruht die **Würde des Menschen**, und der Genius der Krankheit ist menschlicher als der der Gesundheit.

more they are loosened from nature, the more ill they are. What would in fact illness be if not isolation from nature? [...]

Was it not Nietzsche who called the human being 'the sick animal'? And did he not thereby mean that the human being is only superior to the animal to the extent that he is ill? In the spirit, thus, in illness, lies **human dignity**, and the genius of illness is more human than the genius of health.

The Magic Mountain (1924)

'Wir Humanisten haben alle eine pädagogische Ader [...] Man soll dem Humanisten das Amt der Erziehung nicht nehmen, – man kann es ihm nicht nehmen, den nur bei ihm ist die Überlieferung von der **Würde** und Schönheit **des Menschen**. Einst löste er den Priester ab, der sich in trüben und menschenfeindlichen Zeiten die Führung der Jugend anmaßen durfte' [...] 'Ich finde, man muß sich klar sein über die verschiedenen Geistesrichtungen oder Geistesstimmungen, wie man wohl richtiger sagen sollte, es gibt die fromme und die freie. Sie haben beide ihre Vorzüge, aber was ich gegen die freie, die Settembrini'sche meine ich, auf dem Herzen habe, ist nur, daß sie die **Menschenwürde** so ganz in Pacht zu haben glaubt, das ist übertrieben. Die andere enthält auch viel **menschliche Würde** in ihrer Art und gibt Veranlassung zu einer Menge Wohlstand und properer

We humanists have all of us a pedagogical itch [...] the office of schoolmaster should not – cannot – be taken from the humanist, for the tradition of the beauty and **dignity of man** rests in his hands. The priest, who in troubled and inhuman times arrogated to himself the office of guide to youth, has been dismissed [...] I find one ought to be clear about these two intellectual trends, or perhaps it would be better to say states of mind: I mean the devout and the free-thinking. They both have their good sides; what I have against Settembrini's – the free-thinking line – is that he seems to imagine it has a corner in **human dignity**. That's exaggerated, I consider, because the other [also contains a good deal of **human dignity** in its own way and occasions a good bit of prosperity,] correct bearing and uplifting ceremony; more, in fact, than the free-thinking when you remember it has our

Haltung und nobler Förmlichkeit, mehr sogar als die 'freie', obgleich sie die menschliche Schwäche und Hinfälligkeit ja besonders im Auge hat und der Gedanke an Tod und Verwesung eine so wichtige Rolle darin spielt. [...]

human infirmity and proneness to err directly in mind, and thoughts of death and decay play such an important role in it. [...]

Edith Stein (1891–1942)

In Stein, we find an attempt to synthesise the traditions, such that the individuality of the human person emphasised in the classical and Christian traditions is fused with the subjectivity of the modern tradition. In consequence, Stein prefers the 'magisterial definition' of the person mentioned by Thomas Aquinas: *persona est hypostasis proprietate distincta ad dignitatem pertinente* (ESGA 11/12, pp. 304–5 and ESGA 15, p. 88). In it, she sees the key to respect for women as well as for men, in so far as they are respected for who and what they are as concrete individual human beings. Women's rights therefore do not *a priori* have to be the *same* as men's, nor do the different classes necessarily have to have the *same* rights, but they must all be in accordance with human dignity. The surest way of offending human dignity is to abdicate one's own responsibility to be in command of oneself by succumbing to an addiction.

Potency and Act (1931)

Text from *Potenz und Akt, Edith Stein Gesamtausgabe* 10 (Freiburg: Herder, 2005), p. 258. Translation from *Potency and Act*, trans. Walter Redmond, *The Collected Works of Edith Stein* XI (Washington, DC: ICS Publications, 2009), pp. 395–6. Translation slightly adapted.

In der natürlichen Auffassung des Menschen, der Auffassung, die wir im unreflektierten Leben von uns und von anderen haben, bedeutet uns Individualität etwas anderes: Wir halten uns selbst und die andern, ohne uns darüber theoretisch klar zu sein, jeden einzelnen für einzig in seiner Art, d.h. für eine eigene Spezies, wie es Thomas für die Engel in Anspruch nimmt. Auch ein Mensch, der theoretisch eine entgegensetzte Auffassung vertritt, fühlt sich in seiner **Menschenwürde** gekränkt, wenn er nur als ‚Nummer‘, als ‚Exemplar eines Typus‘ behandelt wird. Aller Sehnsucht nach ‚Verständnis‘, aller Klage über ‚Nichtverstandenwerden‘ liegt das Verlangen zugrunde, als Individuum, mit seiner spezifischen Eigenart, die eine singuläre ist, erfaßt zu werden. Die Vorstellung eines ‚Doppelgängers‘ hat etwas Entsetzliches, Widernatürliches an sich (was allerdings darauf hindeutet, daß es nicht etwas völlig Unmögliches, Absurdes sein dürfte). Sollte eine solche vor aller Theorie liegende Grundhaltung und -Einstellung des Geistes sich als unberechtigt erweisen lassen?

In our natural view of the human being, the view we have of ourselves and of others in unreflective living, individuality means something else to us: without being theoretically clear about it, we take it that every one of us, every individual, is unique in kind, I mean, each of us is our own species – the claim Thomas made for the angels. Even someone who holds a different view will feel his **human dignity** injured if he is treated as a mere 'number,' a mere 'instance of his type.' Behind all our longing to be 'understood' and all our complaining about 'not being appreciated,' lies the desire to be seen as an individual with our own specific peculiarity, which is unique. There is something dreadful, unnatural, about the idea of a 'double' (though it does suggest that having a double is not completely impossible or absurd). Will this basic outlook and attitude of mind, which is anterior to all theories, prove to be unfounded?

The Problems of Educating Girls Today (1932)

'Probleme der neueren Mädchenbildung', *Edith Stein Gesamtausgabe* 13 (Freiburg: Herder, 2000), pp. 127–208, p. 175. My own translation.

So muß Mädchenbildung zur Ausprägung und Bejahung des eigentümlichen Weiblichen Seins führen, und dazu gehört die gottgewollte Stellung an der Seite des Mannes, nicht an seiner Stelle, aber auch nicht in einer erniedrigenden Rolle, die die personalen Würde des Menschen nicht entspricht.	Thus the education of girls must lead to the highlighting and affirmation of the being that is specifically womanly, and to it belongs the divinely ordained place beside man, not in his place, but also not in a humiliating role, which does not correspond to the personal dignity of human beings.

What is the Human Being? (1933)

Text from *Edith Stein Gesamtausgabe 15* (Freiburg: Herder, 2005), I, C, p. 13. My own translation.

Von einer *Gleichheit der Menschen* kann nur gesprochen werden, sofern alle dieselbe *Menschennatur* haben, zum selben Ziel in der Gotteskindschaft berufen sind und nach demselben Gesetz im *Gericht* Lohn und Strafe erhalten sollen. Dagegen hat der Schöpfer der Natur, ,von dem alle Vaterschaft im Himmel und auf Erden ihren Namen hat', eine *Ungleichheit des Rechtes und der Macht* begründet. Dabei sind Rechte und Pflichten von Obrigkeit und Untertanen so abgegrenzt, daß der Herrschbegierde ein Maß gesetzt ist und der Gehorsam leicht wird, sicher begründet und der **Menschenwürde** durchaus angemessen ist.	Of an equality of human beings can be spoken only as far as all have the same human nature, are called to the same end as children of God, and will be judged and receive reward or punishment according to the same law. In contrast to this the creator of nature, 'from whom all paternity on earth and in heaven has its name' has established an inequality of rights and power. According to it, the rights and duties of civil authority and of subjects are so delimited, that the lust for power is checked and obedience becomes light, well founded and perfectly in accordance with **human dignity**.

Life in a Jewish Family (1933–1935)

Text from *Edith Stein Gesamtausgabe 1* (Freiburg: Herder, 2002) II, 3, p. 49. English translation from *Life in a Jewish Family*, trans. Josephine Koeppel, OCD (Washington, DC: ICS Publications, 1986), pp. 74–5. Translation slightly altered.

Aber in meinem Inneren gab es noch eine verborgene Welt. Was ich am Tage sah und hörte, daß wurde dort verarbeitet. Der Anblick eines Betrunkenen konnte mich tage- und nächtelang verfolgen und quälen. Ich bin später oft dankbar gewesen, daß von meinen Brüdern in diesem Punkte nichts zu befürchten war, und daß ich keinen andern mir nahestehenden Menschen in diesem schauderhaften Zustand sehen mußte. Es blieb mir immer unbegreiflich, wie man über so etwas lachen konnte, und ich habe in meiner Studentenzeit angefangen, ohne Irgendeiner Organisation beizutreten oder ein Gelübde abzulegen, jeden Tropfen Alkohol zu meiden, um nicht durch eigene Schuld etwas von meiner Geistesfreiheit und **Menschenwürde** zu verlieren. [...] Von all diesen Dingen, an denen ich heimlich litt, sagte ich niemandem ein Wort. Es kam mir gar nicht in dem Sinn, daß man über so etwas sprechen könnte. Nur selten verriet sich meinen Angehörigen etwas davon; ich bekam nämlich manchmal ohne erkennbare Ursache plötzlich Fieber, und im Delirium sprach ich dann aus, was mich innerlich beschäftigte. [...] Man nannte das ‚Nervosität‘ und suchte mich nach Möglichkeit vor Überreizung zu schützen.

Within me, however, there was a hidden world. Whatever I saw or heard throughout my days was pondered over there. The sight of a drunkard could haunt and plague me for days and nights on end. Later, I was grateful that as far as my brothers were concerned there was never any danger of their being intoxicated, nor had I ever to see any near relative in such a terrible condition. I could never understand how one could possibly laugh at such a state; and in my student years, without ever joining any organisation or taking any form of pledge, I began to abstain from every drop of alcohol to avoid being personally responsible for losing even the smallest particle of my freedom of spirit and **human dignity**. [...] I never mentioned a word to anyone of these things, which caused me so much hidden suffering. It never occurred to me that one could speak about such matters. Only infrequently did I give my family an inkling of what was happening: for no apparent reason I sometimes developed a fever and in delirium then spoke of the things which were oppressing me inwardly. [...] They called it 'nerves' and tried, as much as possible, to shield me from overexcitement.

The Impact of the Second World War

The world wars marked a progressive but finally complete transition to nation states in Europe. This was probably a function of the ideal of democracy: *demos* means people, and *a* people is a nation. As aristocratic dynasties finally lost their grip on the last of the empires in Europe, the Austro-Hungarian Empire was carved out according to ethnic groups and the Jews were left with no land to claim as their own and no place to go. What followed had no real parallel in European history, and it is still difficult to talk about. It was this that forged the notion of human dignity definitively into a constitutional principle immediately after the wars had ended.

In the aftermath, reflections on human dignity continue to be profoundly marked by the experience of the wars. The idea of untouchability (*Unantastbarkeit*) predominates in the German linguistic sphere, whereas inalienability predominates as an innovation in the English-speaking world. It may be a by-product of the experience of horror to recognise the human dignity of the perpetrator, but it also presents a political necessity since those who had been responsible for the crimes committed were still around and some in high office. To pretend no unspeakable crime had taken place was also impossible. That human dignity was inherent in the violator as well as in the violated could be a kind of compromise that allowed for a new start, in itself setting aright the perpetrator, as it confronted him with his vain attempt and also vindicating the violated by affirming in him the dignity sought eradicated.

The acquisition of the experience upon which relies the conceptualisation of human dignity as a constitutional principle is reflected in all the texts of this chapter. Violations of human dignity recall this traumatic experience, and thus the foundation is always at hand for existential testing.

Otto Karrer (1888–1976)

Karrer is giving voice to this experience first-hand from within a Christian perspective, which, like any perspective would be, is overwhelmed by it. Karrer survived the war and worked then to reconcile Catholic and Protestant Christians.

The Dignity of the Human Person (1940)

Text from *Schicksal und Würde des Menschen. Die Frohbotschaft Christi*, 2nd revised edn (Einsiedeln and Köln: Verlagsanstalt Benzinger et Co., 1941), pp. 89–94. Translation is my own.

Die großen Themen der christlichen Frohbotschaft von der Vaterschaft Gottes und von der Brüderschaft der Menschen rufen nach der Ergänzung im dritten: von der **Würde der menschlichen Person**. Wie in Gottes Dreifaltigkeit das eine Wesen in dreifachem Antlitz aufscheint, der göttliche Vater und Sohn und Geist, so ergibt auch die Selbstoffenbarung Gottes einen Dreiklang von Motiven, die zusammen die christliche Frohbotschaft bilden. Und wie dort der Sohn vom Vater ausgeht und von beiden der Heilige Geist, so ist auch hier ein Zusammenhang geistiger Art: Vom Glauben an die Vaterschaft Gottes ergab sich uns die Brüderschaft der Menschen. Weil Gott der Vater aller ist, darum sind alle Menschen Brüder: die christliche Theologie begründet die christliche Soziologie. Und sie zusammen begründen die christliche Anthropologie, die Lehre vom Menschen: Aus der Vaterschaft Gottes einerseits schöpft der Glaube

The great themes of the Christian gospel, the fatherhood of God and the brotherhood of men, calls for a completion in a third: the **dignity of the human person**. In the same way as in the Trinitarian God the One Being shows itself forth in a threefold Countenance, the divine Father and Son and Spirit, so the revelation of God ushers in an accord of three motives, which together form the Christian gospel. As in the first, the Son proceeds from the Father and the Holy Spirit from both, so we see also here a spiritual connection: from faith in the fatherhood of God we received the brotherhood of men. Because God is father of all, all human beings are siblings: Christian theology founds Christian sociology. Together they found Christian anthropology, that which is taught about the human being: From faith in the fatherhood of God on the one hand is created the consciousness of the value that every human being has, and through the relation

das Bewußtsein des Wertes, den jeder Mensch besitzt, und durch die Beziehung zu seinesgleichen, in der menschlichen Gemeinschaft, erhält die Person ihre nähere Bestimmung, ihre Begrenzung und ihr Recht im Lebensraume.

1. Das Thema ist heute von besonderer Aktualität. Was die Geschichte von je erkennen ließ, ist heute flagrant geworden, nämlich die Tatsache, daß die Trübung oder Leugnung der göttlichen Vaterschaft auch zur Verzerrung und Leugnung der Brüderschaft der Menschen, zur Zerreißung der Menschheit im Zeichen des Klassenkampfes und des Rassenmythus führt, – und in diesem Zeichen wird dann, durch eine innere Konsequenz, der Angriff gegen den Menschen selbst geführt, geschehen die Bestialitäten der Sozialrevolution gegen Angehörige bestimmter Klassen und die Progrome des Hasses gegen Menschen bestimmter Rasse oder auch bestimmten Glaubens. Wer möchte die Zusammenhänge nicht sehen, wie sich eines aus dem anderen ergibt in dieser antichristliche Trinität: Leugnung Gottes das Erste, Leugnung der menschlichen Brüderschaft das Zweite, und schließlich Leugnung des Individuums, Verstümmelung und Vernichtung der Persönlichkeit, der Gewissensfreiheit, ja, des psychischen Daseins selbst!

Gläubige Christen sehen diese Dinge mit Ernst, aber ohne Furcht für die Religion. Denn das Ganze ist ein Beweis Gottes und Seiner Gerichte in der Menschheit, wie sie Christus in Seinen Endreden und der Seher der Geheimen Offenbarung geschaut hat, – Gerichte Gottes, so mächtig und eindringlich, daß nur der sie überhöhren kann, der

ship with his fellow human beings in the human community, the person receives his specific call, his limits and rights in life.

1. The theme is of specific actuality today. What history from of old has taught us has today become obvious, the fact that the clouding or the denial of the divine fatherhood also leads to the distortion and denial of the brotherhood of men, to the tearing apart of humanity in the name of class struggle or racial mythology. In this name is perpetrated, through an inner necessity, the attack against human beings themselves, the bestialities of the social revolution against members of certain classes and the pogroms of hatred against people of a certain race or faith. Who cannot see the connections as they follow from one another in this anti-Christian trinity: denial of God the first, denial of human brotherhood next, and finally denial of the individual, truncation or destruction of the personality, the freedom of conscience and even the existence of the psyche.

Faithful Christians see these things clearly, but without fear for the religion, since it all is proof of God and his judgement among men, as Christ in his final speech and the visionary of the Apocalypse have seen, – the judgement of God, so powerful and urgent that only those who want to ignore it can. The rebellion against God takes revenge

sie überhöhren will. Die Erhebung gegen Gott rächt sich an der Menschheit selbst! Gott lebt und herrscht. Die Erfahrung der Weltwirklichkeit soll uns um so tiefer im Glauben begründen, daß wir um so klarer sehen und um so reiner lieben die erhabene Wahrheit Christi, die Größe seiner Frohbotschaft von der Vaterschaft Gottes, von der Brüderschaft der Menschen und von der **Würde der menschlichen Person.**

2. Worauf beruht diese **Würde**? – Ich spreche von **Menschenwürde** überhaupt, nicht nur des Christen oder des guten Menschen. Sie beruht auf einem dreifachen Wert:

a) daß jeder ein Geschöpf des allmächtigen, liebenden Vaters ist, daß er mit seinem persönlichen Wesen, seinen Eigenschaften, in seiner geistigen Seele das Geheimnis des Gottesverwandten, die Erkenntnis und die Freiheit mit der Verantwortung für sein eigenes Schicksal trägt;

b) daß jeder in seiner Menschlichkeit, seinen Mängeln und Armseligkeiten, durch das Liebesopfer des göttlichen Sohnes, unseres Menschenbruders, erlösungsfähig, durch seinen Anteil an Christi Leiden **ehrwürdig** und zur persönlichen Läuterung und Reinigung befähigt und berufen ist;

c) daß jeder in der inneren Gegenwart des göttlichen Geistes, durch Dessen Wirken im geistigen Seelengrunde, die verborgene Quelle seines Aufstiegs zum Guten, zur sittlichen Reifung und Vollendung hat – mit einer Bedeutung als Glied in der Gemeinschaft und mit einer Bedeutung für das eigene ewige Leben in der Unsterblichkeit.

on humanity itself. God lives and rules. The experience of the reality of the world must root us deeper in faith so that we see more clearly and love more purely the sublime truth of Christ, the greatness of his gospel concerning the fatherhood of God, the brotherhood of human beings and the **dignity of the human person.**

2. Upon what rests this **dignity**? – I speak of **human dignity** simply, not only that of the Christian or that of the good human being. It relies on a threefold value:

a) that everyone is a creature of the almighty, loving Father, that he carries in his personal being, his capacities and in his spiritual soul the mystery of being related to God in knowledge and freedom together with responsibility for his own destiny;

b) that everyone in his humanity, his faults and miseries, through the sacrifice of love of the divine Son, our human brother, is capable of being saved and **worthy**, through his part in Christ's suffering, enabled and called to conversion and purification;

c) that everyone has in the inner presence of the divine Spirit and his working in the depth of the soul the hidden source of his ascent to the good, to moral maturation and perfection – with a meaning as a member of the community and a meaning for one's own eternal life in immortality.

Etwas gewaltig Großes, Ernstes und Frohes ist es um die **Würde des Menschen** im Lichte des christlichen Glaubens. Es begründet Demut und Selbstbewußtsein zugleich, und begründet Ehrfurcht vor jedem, der ein Menschenantlitz trägt. Denn jeder ein Mensch ist wertvoll, auch der geringste, unscheinbarste, und bildet mit seiner Berufung, seiner Freiheit, seiner Verantwortung und Schuld, seiner Auferstehung und Unsterblichkeit das Geheimnis Gottes in der menschlichen Natur: erschütternd durch die Tiefe der Schmerzen, die ein jeder durchleiden muß, um ein reines Bild zu werden, ergreifend durch die Liebe Gottes, die sich jedes erbarmt und ihn erlösen will zur herrlichen Freiheit der Kinder Gottes, beglückend durch den Ausblick auf die unermeßlichen Möglichkeiten des unsterblichen Lebens in der Verklärung.

Es wird nichts davon aufgehoben, wenn der Gemeinschaft bei der konkreten Entfaltung und Gestaltung des Persönlichkeitslebens ein gewisser Einfluß zusteht. Der einzelne lebt ja als Glied in der Gemeinschaft und anders nicht, und also kann er nicht Ansprüche ohne Beziehung auf die Gesamtheit geltend machen. So wird der Anteil an äußeren Gütern, die der einzelne in der Gemeinschaft für sich erwarten kann, von der Gemeinschaft selbst, beziehungsweise ihrer rechtmäßigen Autorität bestimmt. Seine **Menschenwürde** wird davon nicht betroffen. Aber kein Mensch gegenüber dem anderen – infolgedessen auch keine Vielheit von Menschen, keine Majorität etwa gegenüber dem einzelnen – hat ein Recht, sein Leben selbst zu nehmen, zu begrenzen, oder ihm die wesentliche

The **dignity of human beings** is about something powerfully great, serious and joyful in the light of the Christian faith. It constitutes a reason for both humility and self-consciousness as well as for respect for everyone with a human countenance. Every human being is valuable, also the least and the slightest. He holds within his very own calling, freedom, responsibility and guilt, resurrection and immortality the mystery of God in human nature: shattering through the depth of the pain that everyone must suffer to become a pure image, moving through the love of God, who takes pity on everyone and wants to save him to the glorious freedom of being a child of God, delighting through the vision of immeasurable possibilities of the immortal life of the transfiguration.

Nothing is subtracted from this if the community has a certain influence on the concrete unfolding and formation of the personal life. The individual lives as a member of the community, and otherwise not, and he cannot make claims without them having a bearing on the whole. Thus, the part of external goods the individual can expect in the community is determined by the community or by its legitimate authority. His **human dignity** is not touched by this. But no man has the right, and also no group, even a majority, to take a life, to limit it, or to take away the necessary foundation for its existence in accordance with **human dignity**: the right to freely determine [one's actions] from personal conscience, (that is, except if the community is challenged to self-defence by personal crime or misuse

Grundlage für das menschenwürdige
Dasein zu entziehen: das Recht der freien
Selbstbestimmung aus dem persönlichen
Gewissen (es sei denn, er fordere durch
persönliche Verbrechen, durch Mißbrauch
seines Lebensrechtes, die Gemeinschaft zur
Abwehr heraus). Denn das Recht, sich nach
der inneren Einsicht, nach dem Gewissen
zu bestimmen, ist dem Menschen von Gott
gegeben, wie wir gesehen; darin besteht
seine Würde, und er wäre ohne dies nicht
mehr er selbst, ein Mensch.

3. Was für praktische Folgerungen ergeben
sich aus dem Gesagten?

a) Achte dich selbst: Wirf dich nicht
weg an das Gemeine! Denn ‚was nützt es
dem Menschen, wenn er die ganze Welt
gewänne, aber an seiner Seele Schaden
litte?' (Mt. 16, 26). Darum wirf dich
weg an die Masse, denn in der Masse
herrscht das Gemeine, wie bei den Geiern,
nach Jesu Gleichnis, die sich über das Aas
hermachen (Mt. 24, 28). Und wirf dich
nicht weg an einen Menschen, daß du ihm
zuliebe dich selbst, dein Gewissen, preis-
gäbest, denn ‚was könnte ein Mensch zum
Ersatz für die Seele bieten?' (Mt. 16, 16).
Und wirf dich nicht weg an einen Führer,
daß er dir an Stelle deines Gewissens
sei, – niemand kann einem anderen in
diesem Sinne Führer sein. Laß dich bera-
ten, höre auf guten Rat, aber laß dich
nicht beherrschen von einem Menschen!
Gott allein diene, Ihn liebe aus ganzem
Herzen, aus ganzer Seele! Ihm dienen ist
menschenwürdig, heißt seine Seele, seine
Menschenwürde bewahren.

of the right to life). The right to determine
oneself from inner insight in accordance
with one's conscience is given by God to
human beings, as we see; in this consists
his dignity, and he would not be himself,
a human being, without it.

3. What practical consequences arise from
this?

a) Respect yourself: do not throw yourself
away to the vulgar! For 'what use is it to a
human being to gain the whole world, if
he were to suffer the loss of his own soul?'
(Mt. 16, 26). Do not throw yourself away
to the crowd since the vulgar rules the
crowd, like the vultures in Jesus' parable,
who fall upon the carcass (Mt 24, 28). Do
not throw yourself away to a human being
that you for his sake would give up your
conscience, for 'what could a human being
offer in exchange for his soul'? (Mt. 16, 16).
Do not throw yourself away to a leader, who
would take the place of your conscience,
– no one can in this way be the leader of
another. Take counsel and good advice, but
let not yourself be manipulated by a human
being! Serve only God, love him with your
whole heart, your entire soul! To serve him
is worthy of human beings, through it one
preserves one's soul, one's human dignity.

b) Achte jeden: Ehre in jedem Gottes Geschöpf! Jeden hat Er ‚bei seinem Namen gerufen' (Is. 43, 1), jeder trägt ‚auf seiner Stirne', im Geheimnis seiner Seele, ‚einen Namen, den niemand kennt als Er' (Geheime Offenbarung 2, 17); ‚jeder hat seine Gaben von Gott' (1 Kor. 7, 7), der eine eines, der andere zwei, der dritte fünf, ein anderer zehn Talente. Beneide keinen, weil er dir reicher, begnadeter, glücklicher scheint, und wolle mit keinem tauschen: du weißt nicht, welche Last dir zufiele, wenn du, Bettler, die Rolle des Königs im Welttheater zu spielen hättest. Aber verachte auch keinen und richte keinen, und wäre er der ärmste Tropf; denn du siehst nicht in sein Inneres; ‚Gott allein sieht ins Herz', und Sein Geheimnis, wenn auch gebrochen, sieht dich in jedem an, und ‚viele Letzte werden die Ersten, und viele Erste die Letzten sein' (Mt. 10, 31).

c) Liebe die Deinen, und sei gut zu allen! Liebe die, die dir zu lieben gegeben sind und dich wiederlieben! Laß deine Seele nicht frieren in stolzer Einsamkeit! Füreinander und miteinander Leid und Freude teilen: so spendest du ihnen Freude und empfängst auch selber die Freude, die du zum Leben brauchst. Nicht alle kannst du lieben – aber gut, barmherzig kannst du zu jedem sein, der dir in seiner Schwachheit und Not begegnet. Auch der Geringste ist ein Mensch wie du! Und wolltest du einen von diesen Kleinen verachten, würdest du deinen Herrn verachten, und wenn du einen von diesen aufnimmst, so nimmst du Christus auf, Der Sich für ihn wie für dich dahingegeben hat und dem Verlorenen nachgeht, es zu retten und heimzuholen auf den Schultern der Barmherzigkeit.

b) Respect everyone: honour in all God's creature! He has called everyone 'by their name' (Is. 43, 1), everyone carries 'on their forehead', in the secret of his soul, 'a name that no one but He knows' (Apocalypse 2, 17); 'everyone has their gifts from God' (1 Cor. 7, 7), one, one talent, another two, a third five and another ten. Do not envy anyone because he seems to you richer, more graceful or happier. Do not want to exchange conditions with anyone: you do not know what vice would be yours, if you, who are now a beggar, would have to play the role of king on the stage of the world. Neither despise anyone or judge him even if he is the poorest twit because you do not see into his innermost; 'God alone sees the heart', and His mystery faces you in everyone even if in a broken way. 'Many of the last will be the first and many who are first will be the last' (Mt 10, 31).

c) Love your own and be good to all! Love those who it is given to you to love and who love you back! Do not let your soul freeze in proud loneliness! Share suffering and joy with each other and for each other: then you will give them joy and also yourself receive the joy you need to live. You cannot love everyone – but mercy you can show to anyone who meets you in his weakness and necessity. Also the poorest is a human being like yourself! If you were to despise one of these little ones, it is your Lord you would despise, and when you accept one of these, it is Christ you accept, who has given Himself up for him and for you and who seeks out the lost, in order to bring it home on his shoulders of mercy.

Wie eindringlich begründet Jesus die How urgently Jesus backs the respect for
Ehrfurcht von der **Menschenwürde**! Ja, **human dignity**! Yes, Christianity pro-
das Christentum verkündet, schützt, ver- claims, protects, defends **human dignity**,
teidigt die **Menschenwürde**, wie keine like no other worldview. One can only love
Weltanschauung. Man kann es nur lieben, it as a just human being. Those who hate
als rechter Mensch. Und die es hassen, sind it are also those who hate human beings.
auch die Hasser der Menschen. Gott ver- May God forgive them, for they do not
zeihe ihnen, denn sie wissen nicht, was sie know what they do! You, however, should
tun! Du aber kämpfe den guten Kampf fight the good fight as a witness to God's
als Zeuge des Reiches Gottes, als lieben- kingdom as a loving father – take care of
den Vater – pflege die Brüderlichkeit um the brotherliness because of Him – respect
Seinetwillen – achte die **Menschenwürde**! **human dignity**!

The United Nations

It is fitting that the first words solemnly pronounced to celebrate that the
war was over, after the silence imposed by the atrocities, concerned human
dignity. What is new in the declaration is the idea that the rights flowing
from human dignity are conceived to be inalienable. Human dignity is
said to be inherent (not actually inalienable), and in relation to those who
act against the principles of the United Nations or commit non-political
crimes (Art. 14 (2)), it is only the right to asylum that does not apply.
Those who commit crimes against humanity or violates human dignity are
in other words not except from prosecution in the jurisdiction in which
these crimes have been committed. In article 28 it is furthermore stated
that 'in the exercise of his rights and freedoms, everyone shall be subject
only to such limitations as are determined by law solely for the purpose
of securing due recognition and respect for the rights and freedoms of
others and of meeting the just requirements of morality, public order and
the general welfare in a democratic society.' Thus the rights are envisaged
as limited by other human beings' rights. Furthermore: 'These rights and
freedoms may in no case be exercised contrary to the purposes and principles of the United Nations', such that the common good, and in particular

the common good of peace would always have to figure in the exercise of rights. The inalienable rights issuing from inherent human dignity are thus never rights to violate the rights of others. It is left unsaid how inherent dignity fares when atrocities are committed. It is possible that there was no agreement as to whether such dignity was in need of restoration and in what sense. Some might see punishment as restorative; others forgiveness or redemption. By leaving the question open, the legacy of the Third Reich was left for the member states to deal with as they thought best.

The Universal Declaration of Human Rights

Adopted and proclaimed by General Assembly resolution 217 A (III) of 10 December 1948, available at <https://www.ohchr.org/EN/UDHR/ Documents/UDHR_Translations/eng.pdf>.

PREAMBLE
Whereas recognition of the **inherent dignity and of the equal and inalienable rights of all members of the human family** is the foundation of freedom, justice and peace in the world,

Whereas disregard and contempt for human rights have resulted in barbarous acts which have outraged the conscience of mankind, and the advent of a world in which human beings shall enjoy freedom of speech and belief and freedom from fear and want has been proclaimed as the highest aspiration of the common people,

Whereas it is essential, if man is not to be compelled to have recourse, as a last resort, to rebellion against tyranny and oppression, that human rights should be protected by the rule of law,

Whereas it is essential to promote the development of friendly relations between nations,

Whereas the peoples of the United Nations have in the Charter reaffirmed their faith in fundamental human rights, in **the dignity and worth of the human person** and in the equal rights of men and women and have determined to promote social progress and better standards of life in larger freedom,

Whereas Member States have pledged themselves to achieve, in co-operation with the United Nations, the promotion of universal respect for and observance of human rights and fundamental freedoms,

Whereas a common understanding of these rights and freedoms is of the greatest importance for the full realization of this pledge,

Now, Therefore THE GENERAL ASSEMBLY proclaims THIS UNIVERSAL DECLARATION OF HUMAN RIGHTS as a common standard of achievement for all peoples and all nations, to the end that every individual and every organ of society, keeping this Declaration constantly in mind, shall strive by teaching and education to promote respect for these rights and freedoms and by progressive measures, national and international, to secure their universal and effective recognition and observance, both among the peoples of Member States themselves and among the peoples of territories under their jurisdiction.

Article 1.
All human beings are born free and equal in **dignity** and rights. They are endowed with reason and conscience and should act towards one another in a spirit of brotherhood.

Article 2.
Everyone is entitled to all the rights and freedoms set forth in this Declaration, without distinction of any kind, such as race, colour, sex, language, religion, political or other opinion, national or social origin, property, birth or other status. Furthermore, no distinction shall be made on the basis of the political, jurisdictional or international status of the country or territory to which a person belongs, whether it be independent, trust, non-self-governing or under any other limitation of sovereignty.

Article 3.
Everyone has the right to life, liberty and security of person.

Article 4.
No one shall be held in slavery or servitude; slavery and the slave trade shall be prohibited in all their forms.

Article 5.
No one shall be subjected to torture or to cruel, inhuman or degrading treatment or punishment.

Article 6.
Everyone has the right to recognition everywhere as a person before the law.

Article 7.

All are equal before the law and are entitled without any discrimination to equal protection of the law. All are entitled to equal protection against any discrimination in violation of this Declaration and against any incitement to such discrimination.

Article 8.

Everyone has the right to an effective remedy by the competent national tribunals for acts violating the fundamental rights granted him by the constitution or by law.

Article 9.

No one shall be subjected to arbitrary arrest, detention or exile.

Article 10.

Everyone is entitled in full equality to a fair and public hearing by an independent and impartial tribunal, in the determination of his rights and obligations and of any criminal charge against him.

Article 11.

(1) Everyone charged with a penal offence has the right to be presumed innocent until proved guilty according to law in a public trial at which he has had all the guarantees necessary for his defence.

(2) No one shall be held guilty of any penal offence on account of any act or omission which did not constitute a penal offence, under national or international law, at the time when it was committed. Nor shall a heavier penalty be imposed than the one that was applicable at the time the penal offence was committed.

Article 12.

No one shall be subjected to arbitrary interference with his privacy, family, home or correspondence, nor to attacks upon his honour and reputation. Everyone has the right to the protection of the law against such interference or attacks.

Article 13.

(1) Everyone has the right to freedom of movement and residence within the borders of each state.

(2) Everyone has the right to leave any country, including his own, and to return to his country.

Article 14.

(1) Everyone has the right to seek and to enjoy in other countries asylum from persecution.

(2) This right may not be invoked in the case of prosecutions genuinely arising from non-political crimes or from acts contrary to the purposes and principles of the United Nations.

Article 15.
(1) Everyone has the right to a nationality.
(2) No one shall be arbitrarily deprived of his nationality nor denied the right to change his nationality.

Article 16.
(1) Men and women of full age, without any limitation due to race, nationality or religion, have the right to marry and to found a family. They are entitled to equal rights as to marriage, during marriage and at its dissolution.
(2) Marriage shall be entered into only with the free and full consent of the intending spouses.
The family is the natural and fundamental group unit of society and is entitled to protection by society and the State.

Article 17.
(1) Everyone has the right to own property alone as well as in association with others.
(2) No one shall be arbitrarily deprived of his property.

Article 18.
Everyone has the right to freedom of thought, conscience and religion; this right includes freedom to change his religion or belief, and freedom, either alone or in community with others and in public or private, to manifest his religion or belief in teaching, practice, worship and observance.

Article 19.
Everyone has the right to freedom of opinion and expression; this right includes freedom to hold opinions without interference and to seek, receive and impart information and ideas through any media and regardless of frontiers.

Article 20.
(1) Everyone has the right to freedom of peaceful assembly and association.
(2) No one may be compelled to belong to an association.

Article 21.
(1) Everyone has the right to take part in the government of his country, directly or through freely chosen representatives.
(2) Everyone has the right of equal access to public service in his country.

(3) The will of the people shall be the basis of the authority of government; this will shall be expressed in periodic and genuine elections, which shall be by universal and equal suffrage and shall be held by secret vote or by equivalent free voting procedures.

Article 22.

Everyone, as a member of society, has the right to social security and is entitled to realization, through national effort and international co-operation and in accordance with the organization and resources of each State, of the economic, social and cultural rights indispensable for his **dignity** and the free development of his personality.

Article 23.

(1) Everyone has the right to work, to free choice of employment, to just and favourable conditions of work and to protection against unemployment.

(2) Everyone, without any discrimination, has the right to equal pay for equal work.

(3) Everyone who works has the right to just and favourable remuneration ensuring for himself and his family an existence worthy of **human dignity**, and supplemented, if necessary, by other means of social protection.

(4) Everyone has the right to form and to join trade unions for the protection of his interests.

Article 24.

Everyone has the right to rest and leisure, including reasonable limitation of working hours and periodic holidays with pay.

Article 25.

(1) Everyone has the right to a standard of living adequate for the health and well-being of himself and of his family, including food, clothing, housing and medical care and necessary social services, and the right to security in the event of unemployment, sickness, disability, widowhood, old age or other lack of livelihood in circumstances beyond his control.

(2) Motherhood and childhood are entitled to special care and assistance. All children, whether born in or out of wedlock, shall enjoy the same social protection.

Article 26.

(1) Everyone has the right to education. Education shall be free, at least in the elementary and fundamental stages. Elementary education shall be compulsory. Technical and professional education shall be made generally available and higher education shall be equally accessible to all on the basis of merit.

(2) Education shall be directed to the full development of the human personality and to the strengthening of respect for human rights and fundamental freedoms. It

shall promote understanding, tolerance and friendship among all nations, racial or religious groups, and shall further the activities of the United Nations for the maintenance of peace.

(3) Parents have a prior right to choose the kind of education that shall be given to their children.

Article 27.

(1) Everyone has the right freely to participate in the cultural life of the community, to enjoy the arts and to share in scientific advancement and its benefits.

(2) Everyone has the right to the protection of the moral and material interests resulting from any scientific, literary or artistic production of which he is the author.

Article 28.

Everyone is entitled to a social and international order in which the rights and freedoms set forth in this Declaration can be fully realized.

Article 29.

(1) Everyone has duties to the community in which alone the free and full development of his personality is possible.

(2) In the exercise of his rights and freedoms, everyone shall be subject only to such limitations as are determined by law solely for the purpose of securing due recognition and respect for the rights and freedoms of others and of meeting the just requirements of morality, public order and the general welfare in a democratic society.

(3) These rights and freedoms may in no case be exercised contrary to the purposes and principles of the United Nations.

Article 30.

Nothing in this Declaration may be interpreted as implying for any State, group or person any right to engage in any activity or to perform any act aimed at the destruction of any of the rights and freedoms set forth herein.

Ernst Bloch (1885–1977)

As human dignity had now achieved the status of a constitutional principle, might it then be possible also to vindicate economic prosperity by means or in terms of it? Bloch is advocating a rapprochement between social utopianism and natural law theory, claiming they both have a share and a stake in the idea of human dignity.

Natural Law and Human Dignity (1961)

Text from *Naturrecht und menschliche Würde*, Frankfurt, Suhrkamp Verlag, 1961, pp. 12–4, 135–6, 237, 250–1. The translation is taken from *Natural Law and Human Dignity*, trans. Dennis J. Schmidt (Cambridge, MA: MIT Press, 1986), 1st edn 1961, pp. xxviii–xxx, 116, 208, 220–1.

Die Erbitterung war nicht nur moralisch, wenn es Kant als keine Kleinigkeit ansah, daß der Mensch von seinen Herrschern als eine solche behandelt wird, 'indem sie ihn als teils tierisch, als bloßes Werkzeug ihrer Absichten, belasten, teils in ihren Streitigkeiten gegeneinander aufstellen, um ihn schlachten zu lassen'. Und folgende Weisung bei Marx ist nicht nur ökonomisch, wenn er lehrt, ,alle Verhältnisse umzuwerfen, in denen der Mensch ein erniedrigtes, ein geknechtetes, ein verlassenes, ein verächtliches Wesen ist'. Verständlich daher, daß dergleichen ebenso als bloß ,soziologisches' Wesen ausgestaltet oder abgemattet wurde, wie es immer wieder aufhorchen läßt. Altes Eisen also sieht anders aus, das Überalterte steckt mehr in dem, was der Naturrecht angriff, als in ihm selber. Der einfache kritische Spruch: ,Tausend Jahre Unrecht

The exasperation that Kant felt was not only a moral exasperation when he said that he refused to consider it an insignificant matter that man was treated as insignificant by his rulers 'in that they treat him as a beast of burden, or as a mere instrument of their own intentions, or in that they array men against each other in order to solve their quarrels.' And Marx is not merely giving economic advice when he teaches us 'to overthrow all relations in which man is a degraded, enslaved, abandoned, or despised being.' It is therefore quite understandable that this being that is always set aside or reduced to a merely 'sociological' subject continues to command our attention. It does not belong on the scrap heap; what is outdated is not natural law itself but what it attacks. The simple critical saying 'A thousand years of injustice still do not make an hour of justice' and the constructive

machen noch keine Stunde Recht', die kon-
struktive Definition: ,Aufklärung ist der
Ausgang des Menschen aus seiner selbst
verschuldeten Unmündigkeit', beide haben
ihren Lohn noch nicht dahin. Dergestalt
also, daß weder **menschliche Würde**
ohne ökonomische Befreiung möglich ist
noch diese, jenseits von Unternehmern
und Unternommenen jeder Art, ohne
die Sache Menschenrechte. Beides
geschieht nicht automatisch im selben
Akt, sondern ist wechselseitig aufeinan-
der angewiesen, bei ökonomischem Prius,
humanistischem Primat. Keine wirkliche
Installierung der Menschenrechte ohne
Ende der Ausbeutung, kein wirkliches
Ende der Ausbeutung ohne Installierung
der Menschenrechte. [...]

Soziale Utopien und Naturrecht hatten
ein sich ergänzendes Anliegen im gleichen
humanen Raum; getrennt marschierend,
leider nicht vereint schlagend. Obgleich
beide in dem Entscheidenden einig waren,
das menschlichere Gesellschaft heißt, so
bestanden doch zwischen Sozialutopien
und Naturrechtslehren lange wichtige
Unterschiede. [...] Die Sozialutopie ging
auf menschliches Glück, das Naturrecht
auf **menschliche Würde**. [...] Nirgends
fällt Naturrechtliches mit bloßem
Rechtsgefühl zusammen, wohl aber konnte
es sich (in der Stoa, deutlich in der ,guten
Natur' Rousseaus) mit einer sehr alten
Geborgenheit treffen und ihrem Maß: dem
Mutterrecht. [...]

(A)ll diese Ataraxien stammten in der Stoa
bereits aus seiner Entgegensetzung, die als
solche vaterrechtliche Überordnungen vor-
aussetzt und sie verneint. Und dennoch:
es wirkte auch hier der weit stärkere, der

definition 'Enlightenment is man's release
from self-imposed tutelage' both retain
their value, for neither has its worth in
that which natural law once attacked. This
means that **human dignity** is not possible
without economic liberation, and this liberation is not possible without the cause of
human rights, which is beyond all forms of
contracts and contractors. Liberation and
dignity are not automatically born of the
same act; rather they refer to each other
reciprocally – with economic priority, we
find humanistic primacy. There can be no
true installation of human rights without
the end of exploitation, no true end to
exploitation without the installation of
human rights. [...]

Social utopias and natural law had mutually
complementary concerns within the same
human space; they marched separately, but,
sadly, did not strike together. Although
they were in accord on the decisive issue,
a more humane society, there nevertheless
arose important differences between the
doctrines of social utopia and natural law.
[...] Social utopian thought directed its
efforts toward human happiness, natural
law was directed toward **human dignity**.
[...] Natural law never coincided with a
mere sense of justice, but (in the Stoics,
and clearly in Rousseau's 'good nature') it
easily found for itself an ancient place of
security and its measure: maternal law. [...]

All of these forms of ataraxia stem from the
Stoics, from an opposition that presupposes
patriarchal authorities in order to deny
them. And nevertheless, one finds here the
strong effect of the archetype of the great

genuinere Archetyp der Großen Mutter herein: so hat personhafte Ataraxie selber sich mit ihm regulär verbunden. Denn die Macht der **persönlichen Würde** ist hier letzthin eingebaut in die eines hegendes Gattungsbegriff, eines universal erweiterten Bona Dea-Begriffs mit Licht: er wurde humanitas genannt. In der ungebeugten Person galt es, die **Würde der Menschheit** zu wahren; humanitas aber ist von Eirene her auch mit dem milderen Stoltz und Halt des Friedens umgeben. [...]

Die sonach intendierte 'Emanzipation zum Menschen' nimmt weit weniger sogar den philanthropischen Affekt der Sozialutopien auf als den stolzen des Naturrechts. Was aber Glück und **Würde** angeht, die betonten Anliegen der Sozialutopien hier, der Naturrechtslehren dort, so lange getrennt marschierend und leider immer noch nicht vereint schlagend, mit einem Prius menschlicher Versorgung, einem Primat **menschlicher Würde**: so ist mehr als je neben dem konkreten Erbe am sozialutopischen ein ebenso Konkretes am Programm Citoyen fällig. Item: mehr als je ist es an der Zeit, auch die Unterschiede in den sozialutopischen und den naturrechtlichen Intentionsfeldern funktionell endlich verbunden zu sehen und praktisch aufgehoben. Kraft der Gewissheit: es gibt keine **menschliche Würde** ohne Ende der Not, aber auch kein menschgemäßes Glück ohne Ende alter oder neuer Untertänigkeit. [...]

So ist oder war Eigentums-Ursprung (die possessive Willensmacht) der subjektiven Rechte mit jenem zweiten Ursprung verbunden [...] Dieser zweite Ursprung des subjektiven Rechts, als Parole des revolutionären Kampfs, läßt sich

mother, for the ataraxia of the person was regularly associated with her. The power of the **dignity of the person** is here finally built into the power of a generic concept of the protector, of a concept of Bona Dea with light enlarged to a universal dimension: it was called *humanitas*. In the person who does not bow down, it was the **dignity of humanity** that was being saved; but *humanitas* is [by Eirene] given a pride and a firmness softer and milder than peace. [...]

The intended 'emancipation of men' takes far less from the philanthropic affect of social utopias than it does from the pride of natural law. Happiness and **dignity**, the concerns emphasized on the one hand by social utopias and on the other by doctrines of natural law, for so long marched separately and sadly never struck together with the priority of human care and support, and the *primat* of **human dignity**: It is more than ever necessary that along with the concrete heritage of social utopian thought, an equally concrete program of the *citoyen* be recognised. It is more necessary than ever before that even the differences in the intentional fields finally be recognised as functionally related and practically surmounted. This thanks to the certainty that there can be no **human dignity** without the end of misery and need, but also no human happiness without the end of old and new forms of servitude. [...]

Thus, property, as the origin (as the power of the possessive will) of subjective right, is connected with this second origin [...] As the slogan of the revolutionary struggle, this second origin of subjective right no longer can be hung up with the concept

selbstverständlich nicht mehr in Verhakung
mit dem Eigentumsbegriff, mit diesem
Grundbegriff der bisherigen Ökonomie
halten. Aber der Ursprung (die **menschliche Würde**) ist deshalb, weil er außerhalb
der Klassenökonomie liegt, nicht außerhalb
der marxistisch verstandenen Ökonomie.
Marx selber rekurriert (nicht nur in seinen
Jugendschriften) unaufhörlich auf den
zweiten Ursprung: auf das Grundrecht,
sich nicht als Kanaille behandeln zu lassen.

of private property, that basic concept
of all previous economy. But although it
lies outside the class economy, the origin
(**human dignity**) is not therefore outside
the economy understood in a Marxist sense.
Marx himself continually returns (and not
only in his early writings) to this second
origin: to the fundamental right not to be
treated as scum.

Gabriel Marcel (1889–1973)

The revival of the principle is in the interest of all, but can such revival be
accomplished, without any reference to the sacred? Marcel warns against
the sterility of rationalism and against associating dignity with pomp. He
wants instead to focus attention on the dignity of the weak and poor. Their
dignity will not be recognised by a vindication of an abstract equality, but
only by fraternal embrace, nor will it be recognised without acceptance of
congenital condemnation to underline its seriousness.

The Existential Background of Human Dignity (1963)

La dignité humaine et ses assises existentielles (Paris : Aubier, 1964). Translation
from *The Existential Background of Human Dignity* (Cambridge, MA:
Harvard University Press, 1963), slightly adapted.

Il faut bien reconnaître que la phraséologie
courante sur ce qu'on appelle la **dignité de
la personne humaine** est imprégnée d'un
kantisme réduit d'ailleurs à sa plus simple
expression ; je vise ici l'idée d'après laquelle
la valeur inaliénable de la personne réside

We must admit that in current phraseology
what is called the **dignity of the human
being** is described in terms of Kantianism
(here, by the way, reduced to its simplest
expression). I refer to the idea according
to which the inalienable value of man lies

dans le fait qu'elle est un être rationnel : on met d'ailleurs plutôt l'accent sur la faculté de comprendre et de saisir l'ordre intelligible du monde ou plutôt sur celle de se conformer soi-même à certaine maximes reconnues comme universelles. Il ne serait, dans mon esprit, être question de contester la légitimité d'une telle interprétation. Mais en même temps, il me parait difficile de contester que depuis près d'un siècle ce rationalisme, pour respectable qu'il soit, a beaucoup perdu de ce que l'on pourrait appeler sa vitalité, comme si sa prise sur les esprits s'était peu à peu desserrée. Et le développement de la philosophie de l'existence sous ses différents aspects, mais aussi pourrait-on dire de la philosophie de la vie chez Bergson et ses continuateurs, ne serait pas compréhensible sans cette sorte de désaffection de plus en plus générale, pour une pensée exposée à tous les dangers qui guettent le formalisme.

Je crois profondément, en ce qui me concerne, que nous ne pouvons arriver à préserver le principe mystérieux qui est au cœur de la **dignité humaine**, qu'à condition de parvenir à expliciter la qualité proprement sacrale qui lui est propre, et cette qualité apparait d'autant plus clairement que nous nous attacherons davantage à l'être humain considéré dans sa nudité et dans sa faiblesse, à l'être humain désarmé tel que nous le trouvons chez l'enfant, chez le vieillard, ou chez le pauvre. Il convient ici, me semble-t-il, de réfléchir sur un paradoxe qui se présente au premier abord comme singulièrement embarrassant.

in the fact that he is a rational being, that stress is placed on his faculty of understanding and comprehending the intelligible order of the world, or rather on his faculty of conforming to certain maxims considered as universally valid. To my mind, there can be no question of challenging the legitimate value of such an interpretation. Yet, at the same time, it seems to me difficult to deny that during the last hundred years or so this rationalism, respectable as it may be, has lost much of what can be termed its vitality, as if it had gradually loosened its hold on men's minds. And the development of the philosophy of existence in its various aspects, and also, we might add, of the philosophy of life espoused by Bergson and his followers, could not be understood without this increasing lack of interest in a form of thought threatened by the dangers of formalism.

It is my profound belief that we cannot succeed in preserving the mysterious principle at the heart of **human dignity** unless we succeed in making explicit the properly sacral quality peculiar to it, a quality which will appear all the more clearly when we consider the human being in his nudity and weakness – the human being as helpless as the child, the old man, or the pauper. Here we should consider a paradox, which appears at first glance to be extremely embarrassing.

Ne risquons-nous pas en effet communé-
ment de nous laisser tromper par ce que
j'appellerai volontiers une conception
décorative de la **dignité**, celle-ci étant plus
ou moins confondue avec l'apparat dont
s'entoure volontiers la puissance ? [...] Mais
en même temps, il est toujours à craindre
qu'humainement parlant cette pompe ne
recouvre que du vide et du mensonge, –
et en ce cas on peut vraiment dire qu'elle
se retourne en quelque sorte contre elle-
même, et qu'elle devient en fin de compte
aux yeux de l'observateur critique comme
une récusation accablante de soi. [...]

C'est d'ailleurs dans cette ligne de pensée
existentielle qu'apparaissent, me semble-t-il,
les insuffisances du rationaliste, telles que
l'homme d'aujourd'hui ne peut guère man-
quer de les ressentir. C'est comme si nous
étions de plus en plus sensibilisés au fait que
la raison peut devenir grimace ou parodie.
Mais un autre ordre de considération inter-
vient ici dans le même sens ; on peut dire que
notre temps aura vu s'effectuer ce que j'appel-
lerais assez volontiers une sécularisation progressive de la raison, une étude fonctionnelle
tendant de plus en plus à réduire celle-ci à un
ensemble d'opérations techniques relevant
d'une science descriptive qui ne laisse guère
subsister autour d'elle le halo dont s'entourait
encore par exemple le mot *Vernunft*, pour
Kant et ses successeurs. [...]

Comme je l'indiquais il y a un instant, l'égalité est essentiellement revendicative, elle est
au sens le plus fort du mot ego-centrique.
'Je suis ton égal, son égal, ou leur égal.' Et
en creusant davantage on n'aurait aucune
peine à retrouver à la suite de Nietzsche et
de Scheler la présence du ressentiment au
cœur de l'égalité. [...]

Do we not run the risk, as a rule, of let-
ting ourselves be deceived by what I would
like to call a decorative conception of **dignity** – and the word 'dignity' is here significant – which we more or less confuse with
the display of pomp that usually accompanies power? [...] But at the same time there
is always the fear that, *humanly speaking*,
this pomp may conceal only emptiness and
deceit – and if so, it can be truthfully said
it turns against itself, as it were, and finally
in the eyes of the critical observer deals a
crushing blow to its own authority. [...]

It is in this line of existential thought that
rationalism, it seems to me, shows its weakness, a weakness that the men of the present day can hardly fail to notice. It is as
if we had become more and more aware
of the fact that reason may become sham
and parody. But considerations of another
kind point in the same direction: it can be
said that our times will have witnessed what
I might readily term a gradual seculariza-
tion of reason, a functional treatment tending more and more to reduce reason to a
series of technical operations depending
on a descriptive science. Around it there
is hardly anything left of the aura, which
still accompanied the word *Vernunft*, for
example, for Kant and his followers. [...]

As I have already noted, equality is essentially the claiming of something; it is, in
the fullest sense of the word, ego-centric.
I am your equal, his equal, or their equal.
Probing further, we would not have any
difficulty in finding, after Nietzsche and
Scheler, the presence of resentment at the
heart of equality. [...]

Mais c'est ici le lieu de refermer ce qui fut en somme une longue parenthèse : tout ce qui précède nous conduit à penser que si la **dignité humaine** peut être aujourd'hui pleinement reconnue, sans par là on s'engage à nouveau dans les ornières d'un rationalisme abstrait, c'est à condition de se placer dans la perspective de la fraternité et non dans celle de l'égalitarisme [...]

Ici s'oppose – d'une façon qui me semble éclairante pour la pensée que j'ai cherché à exprimer dans cette leçon – à une **dignité** qui parce qu'elle est affectation, se mue en son contraire, la **dignité** inaliénable qui s'attache à la condamnation que tout homme subit de fait même de sa naissance. Il y a d'ailleurs là un paradoxe dont le sens mérite d'être approfondi.

But here I should close what may well be regarded as a long parenthesis: everything we have said leads us to think that if **human dignity** can be fully recognised without our necessarily falling into the old groove of abstract rationalism, it is on condition that we place ourselves in the perspective of fraternity and not of equalitarianism. [...]

Here we have a contrast which I find especially illuminating for the thought I have tried to bring out in this chapter – the contrast between an affected **dignity** which, because of its affectation, becomes the very antithesis of **dignity**, and the inalienable **dignity** inherent in the condemnation which is the fate of every man from the very fact of his birth. And here lies a paradox whose meaning deserves to be clarified.

Hannah Arendt (1906–1975)

Human dignity, apart from its dependence on affirmation by fellow human beings, is a myth to Arendt, albeit the most powerful one we ever created, as indeed Nietzsche before her thought. Human rights only make sense if they include a right *not to be dependent* on an inborn human dignity irrespective of human community, that is, on an abstract, ontological or metaphysical reality. Yet, human dignity is, as it should be, respected in a greeting across the abyss of the world, but disrespected when ignored or overlooked by turning the alterity of the other's teleology into a means in my own. Hence, it is radically particular and resists even becoming a means in the idea of progress. Arendt's paradoxical rejection and employment of metaphysics extends to human dignity: she considers its necessity oppressive but recognises that community is organised around it.

'What is Existenz Philosophy?' (1946)

Essays in Understanding, 1930–54: Formation, Exile and Totalitarianism,
ed. Jerome Kohn (New York: Harcourt, Brace and Co., 1994), p. 187.

> The movement of transcendence in thought, a movement basic to man's nature, and
> the failure of thought inherent in that movement brings us at least to a recognition
> that man as 'master of his thoughts' is not only more than what he thinks – and this
> alone would probably provide basis enough for a new definition of **human dignity**
> – but is also constitutionally a being that is more than a Self and wills more than
> himself. With this understanding, existential philosophy has emerged from its period
> of preoccupation with Self-ness.

The Origins of Totalitarianism (1951)

The Burden of our Time (alias the first edition of the later called *The Origins
of Totalitarianism*) (London: Secker and Warburg, 1951), p. 439. (OBS!
This section does not occur in *The Origins of Totalitarianism*).

> The concept of human rights can again be meaningful only if they are redefined as a
> right to the human condition itself, which depends upon belonging to some human
> community, the right never to be dependent upon some inborn **human dignity**
> which de facto, aside from its guarantee by fellow-men, not only does not exist but
> is the last and possibly most arrogant myth we have invented in all our long history.

The Origins of Totalitarianism (San Diego, CA: Harcourt Brace Jovanovich,
1979), p. 458.

> It is chiefly for the sake of this supersense, for the sake of complete consistency,
> that it is necessary for totalitarianism to destroy every trace of what we commonly
> call **human dignity**. For respect for **human dignity** implies the recognition of my
> fellow men or our fellow nations as subjects, as builders of worlds or co-builders of
> a common world. No ideology, which aims at the explanation of all historical events
> of the past and at mapping out the course of all the events of the future can bear the
> unpredictability which springs from the fact that men are creative, that they can
> bring forward something so new that nobody ever foresaw it.

Letter to Karl Jaspers (1951)

4 March, Hannah Arendt/Karl Jaspers, no. 109, p. 166, in *Hannah Arendt/ Karl Jaspers Correspondence, 1926–69*, eds Lotte Koehler and Hans Saner, trans. Robert and Rita Kimber (New York: Harcourt Brace Jovanovich, 1992).

> What radical evil really is I don't know, but it seems to me it somehow has to do with the following phenomenon: making human beings as human beings superfluous (not using them as means to an end, which leaves their essence as humans untouched and impinges only on their **human dignity**; rather making them superfluous as human beings). This happens as soon as all unpredictability – which, in human beings, is equivalent of spontaneity – is eliminated.

Denktagebuch (1951)

Text from *Denktagebuch: 1950–73*, eds Ursula Ludz and Ingeborg Nodmann, 2 vols (Munich: Piper, 2003), I, Heft V, Juli 1951, 11, p. 109. Translation from John Douglas Macready: *Hannah Arendt and the Fragility of Human Dignity* (Lanham, MD and London: Lexington Books, 2018), pp. 84–5.

Kant, *Selbstzweck*: Mit welcher Konsequenz das eigentümliche *Zwischen* der *Pluralität* übersehen wird! Das absolut isolierte und selbstherrliche Subjekt begegnet einem zweiten in der Welt, gedenkt also sofort, sich dieses zweiten als Mittel zu bedienen; denn wofür sollte es sonst gut sein, da es doch sichtlich aus der Welt her begegnet? In der Begegnung zweier Menschen, zweier Selbstzwecke, öffnet sich die Welt

Kant, self-as-purposeful-end: With what consequence the characteristic *between* *of plurality* is overlooked! The absolutely isolated and autocratic subject encounters a second [subject] in the world, and thus immediately thinks of making use of this second as a means; for what else should it be good for, since it evidently was encountered from within the world? In the encounter of two human beings, of two selves-as-pur-

wie ein Abgrund, der die Zwecke auf ewig voneinander durch die Summe der Mittel, die die Welt *ist*, fernhält. Die Achtung und der Respekt der ‚**Menschenwürde**‘ ist wie ein ohnmächtiger Gruß über den Abgrund hinweg. Das Böse bei Kant ist, dieses ohnmächtigen Grußes aus der absoluten Distanz unfähig zu sein und dadurch, nämlich durch den Willen zur rücksichtslosen Realisierung der Zwecke, nämlich durch die Revolte gegen die eigene Ohnmacht, den Anderen in den Abgrund der Mittel zu reißen, ihn zu verweltlichen, zu ent-subjektivieren, ihn zu einem Objekt des Willens zu machen.

poseful-ends, the world opens itself like an abyss that forever holds the purposes apart from one another by means of the total sum of the means that *is* the world. The attention and respect for '**human dignity**' is like an impotent greeting across the abyss. Evil, according to Kant, is to be incapable of this impotent greeting from the absolute distance, and through this – namely, through the will – to the ruthless realization of purpose, namely through the revolt against its own impotence – dragging the Other into the abyss of means, turning the Other into world, de-subjectivizing [the Other], making him into an object of the will.

Life of the Mind (Appendix: 'Judging') (1970–75)

Text from *The Life of the Mind*, One-volume edition, San Diego, CA, New York and London: Harcourt Brace and Co., 1978, p. 272.

> In Kant himself there is this contradiction: Infinite Progress is the law of the human species; at the same time **man's dignity** demands that he is seen, every single one … in his particularity, reflecting as such, but without any comparison and independent of time, mankind in general. In other words, the very idea of progress – if it is more than a mere change of circumstances and an improvement of the world – contradicts Kant's notion of **man's dignity**.

Second Vatican Council (1962–1965)

Our Lady's gracious acceptance of her indispensable participation in the plan of salvation had been extolled as an example for Christians since early times. That no one could be obliged to accept God's grace was a

consequence everyone had to accept, of more consequence perhaps now, in a world where secularism was becoming dominant. In this world, religious freedom was being claimed as a human right founded in the dignity of the human person, as proclaimed by the human rights tradition of the United Nations. The Council adapts its own perspective and language to this tradition, to show its respect for it, no doubt, and to affirm the right to religious freedom in a secular world for its faithful. It refrains from insisting that the dignity of the human substance is in need of restoration until redeemed in Christ, as had been recalled by the prayer in use since Leo the Great, now quietly omitted.

Dignitatis Humanae (1965)

Declaration on Religious Liberty in *Vatican Council II, The Conciliar and the Post Conciliar Documents*, ed. Austin Flannery O. P. (Northport, NY: Costello Publishing Company, 1975), pp. 799–812. Promulgated by Pope Paul VI, 7 December 1965. <http://www.vatican.va>archive>documents>.

1. A sense of the **dignity of the human person** has been impressing itself more and more deeply on the consciousness of contemporary man, and the demand is increasingly being made that men should act on their own judgement, enjoying and making use of a responsible freedom, not driven by coercion but motivated by a sense of duty. The demand is likewise being made that constitutional limits should be set to the powers of government, in order that there may be no encroachment on the rightful freedom of the person and of associations. The demand for freedom in human society chiefly regards the quest for the values proper to the human spirit. It regards, in the first place, the free exercise of religion in society. This Vatican Council takes careful note of these desires in the minds of men. It proposes to declare them to be greatly in accord with truth and justice. To this end, it searches into the sacred tradition and doctrine of the Church – the treasury out of which the Church continually brings forth new things that are in harmony with the things that are old. [...]
2. This Vatican Council declares that the human person has a right to religious freedom. [...] The Council further declares that the right to religious freedom has its foundation in the very **dignity of the human person** as this **dignity** is known through the revealed word and through reason itself. This right of the

human person to religious freedom is to be recognised in the constitutional law whereby society is governed and thus it is to become a civil right.

It is in accordance with their **dignity as persons** – that is, beings endowed with reason and free will and therefore privileged to bear personal responsibility – that all men should be impelled by nature and also bound by a moral obligation to seek the truth, especially religious truth. They are also bound to adhere to the truth, once it is known, and to order their whole lives in accord with the demands of truth. However, men cannot discharge these obligations in a manner in keeping with their own nature unless they enjoy immunity from external coercion as well as psychological freedom. Therefore, the right to religious freedom has its foundation not in the subjective disposition of the person, but in his very nature. In consequence, the right to this immunity continues to exist even in those who do not live up to their obligation of seeking the truth and adhering to it and the exercise of this right is not to be impeded, provided that just public order be observed. [...]

Truth, however, is to be sought after in a manner proper to the **dignity of the human person** and his social nature. The inquiry is to be free, carried on with the aid of teaching and instruction, communication and dialogue, in the course of which men explain to one another the truth they have discovered, or think they have discovered, in order to assist one another in the quest for truth. [...]

9. The declaration of this Vatican Council on the right of man to religious freedom has its foundation in the **dignity of the person**, whose exigencies have come to be fully known to human reason through centuries of experience. [...] Revelation does not indeed affirm in so many words the rights of man to immunity from external coercion in matters religious. It does, however, disclose the **dignity of the human person** in its full dimensions. [...]

11. [...] God has regard for the **dignity of the human person** whom he himself created and man is to be guided by his own judgement and he is to enjoy freedom. [...]

12. In faithfulness therefore to the truth of the Gospel, the Church is following the way of Christ and the apostles when she recognises and gives support to the principle of religious freedom as befitting the **dignity of man** and as being in accord with divine revelation. [...] Thus the leaven of the Gospel has long been about its quiet work in the minds of men, and to it is due in great measure the fact that in the course of time men have come more widely to recognise their **dignity as persons**, and the conviction has grown stronger that the person in society is to be kept free from all manner of coercion in matters religious.

Conclusion

Having completed this anthology, and thus repeatedly referred back to the intuition of human dignity in and through all the ways in which it has been thought about and discussed in the texts here proposed, it seems to me that it can be expressed in the following way.

It is:

1. The value of human beings motivating respect for them as such;
2. A constitutional principle according to which this value, when respected by government, is established as the status of human beings;
3. A value that can be violated in others by successfully enticing or conditioning them to prefer other values to it;
4. A value I can compromise in myself by preferring other values to it; and
5. A value that can be and has been restored by God's love for us in the redemption brought by Christ.

The fifth feature may be specific to the Christian tradition, but all the other features seem shared by all traditions in such a way that the fifth feature does not have to be considered as contradicting the first four in any way. The lack of substantial theoretical disagreement about what human dignity is, is nevertheless matched by disagreements about the practical implications involved in the respect of human dignity, about what a human being is and about what rights and duties human dignity originates. That human dignity would be something of which intuition can be had, in and through differing traditions for its conceptualisation, presupposes, postulates or hopes for ultimate or at least proximate intelligibility – sustainable enough for us to communicate about it. Making that assumption seems to be part of the cult we owe to human dignity and also of what is owed to the reader of an anthology of texts on human dignity. Some might feel that intuiting human dignity is a private matter, or indeed that human dignity is a useless

or meaningless concept. The credit that must be given to these observations is that there is darkness at the heart of the intelligibility of human dignity: It is unfathomable, ultimately relation to the absolute standing us looking into the interactive unconditional and it does call for privacy what we do when thus faced. It also does seem futile to form any kind of concept of what is facing us then. Nevertheless, our whole being as humans express it, and that allows us to intuit it, if not to conceive of it.

Although it would not be fair to present this as a conclusion in the sense of it following from an argument, since, properly speaking, no argument has been made in this anthology, the account could be seen to conclude it in the sense that an induction follows from many instances of the same thing. It entails an understanding of values as intelligible by their motivating power, as sketched in Edith Stein's value theory, to be further explored on a future occasion.

The story told throughout this anthology is the story of how the expression 'human dignity' was coined to designate first the norm according to which the individual ought to live his life, then the privileged status of the human person underwritten by God and then the status backed by the United Nations to be respected by all its member states in their citizens and in all human beings. In this story, there is a movement from emphasising the duties human dignity lays upon the individual, to emphasise the rights it entails and which should be respected by others. It is paradoxical that we think this movement is one away from a moralising attitude towards a liberal one, since we are as much 'others' as we are subjects of rights. Is it because we understand the human rights tradition to be something other than morality, closer to positive law?

The story told here ends in 1965 since the developments in relation to the notion of human dignity thereafter would need a careful treatment of their own. The reason why many readers will have found and used this anthology, however, will no doubt be the controversies that arose after this cut-off point. I hope the bit of distance provided by the historical perspective will allow the reader to engage again in those debates better informed.

Bibliography

Bibliographies, Dictionary Entries, Handbooks and Anthologies

'Dignitas' in *Lexicon Totus Latinitatis*. A Dictionary of the Latin Language by I. J. G. Scheller, rev. and trans. J. E. Riddle (Oxford: Oxford University Press, 1835).

Dignity, Ethics and Law (Copenhagen: Centre for Ethics and Law, 1999).

Dürig, W., 'Dignitas' in *Real Lexicon für Antike und Christentum*, ed. Klauser (Stuttgart: Anton Hierseman, 1957).

Düwell, Marcus, Jens Braarvig, Roger Brownsword, and Dietmar Mieth, *The Cambridge Handbook of Human Dignity* (Cambridge: Cambridge University Press, 2014).

Haferkamp, Björn, 'The Concept of Human Dignity: an Annotated Bibliography', in K. Bayertz, ed., *Sanctity of Life and Human Dignity* (Dordrecht: Kluwer, 1996), 275–91.

Horstmann, R. P. 'Menschenwürde' in *Historisches Wörterbuch der Philosophie*, ed. Ritter und Gründer, vol. 5 (Basel – Stuttgart: Schwabe und Cie, 1980).

Parker, Philip, *Dignitate. Webster's Timeline History 74 BC – 2005* (San Diego, CA: ICON Group, 2009).

Wetz, Franz Josef, *Texte zur Menschenwürde* (Stuttgart: Reclam, 2011).

Ancient Sources

Aristotle, *Aristoteles Latinus* IV, 2 et 3 edn altera, *Analytica Posteriora. Translationes Iacobi, anonymi sive 'Ioannis', Gerardi et Recensio Guillelmi de Moerbeka*, ed. Laurentius Mino-Paluello and Bernardus G. Dod (Bruges – Paris: Desclée de Brouwer, 1968).

——, *Aristoteles Latinus* XXVI, 1–3, 4: *Ethica Nicomachea Translatio Grosseteste.* Textus recognitus, ed. R. A. Gauthier (Leiden and Bruxelles: Brill and Desclee de Brouwer, 1973).

——, *The Complete Works*, Revised Oxford Translation, Vol. I–II, ed. J. Barnes (Princeton, NJ: Princeton University Press, 1984).

——, in Latin in Thomas Aquinas, *Opera Omnia* iussu Leonis XIII p.m. edita, *Sent. Libri Ethicorum*, vol. 47–8 (Rome – Paris: Commissio Leonina – Vrin, 1969) and in *Expositio Libri Posteriorum*, vol. I* (2) (editio altera retracta) (Rome – Paris: Commissio Leonina – Vrin, 1989).

——, *Nicomachean Ethics*, trans. H. Rackham (Cambridge, MA and London: Harvard University Press (Loeb), 1990).

——, *Posterior Analytics*, trans. H. Tredennick (London and Cambridge, MA: Heineman and Harvard University Press (Loeb), 1976).

Beentjes, Pancratius C., *The Book of Ben Sira in Hebrew, A Text Edition of All Extant Hebrew Manuscripts and a Synopsis of All Parallel Hebrew Ben Sira Texts*, Supplements to *Vetus Testamentum* 68 (Leiden and Atlanta, GA: Brill and Society of Biblical Literature, 2003).

Cicero, *De Inventione, De optimo genere oratorum, Topica*, trans. H. M. Hubbel (London and Cambridge, MA: Heinemann and Harvard University Press (Loeb), 1949).

——, *De Officiis*, trans. W. Miller (London and New York: Heinemann and MacMillan Co. (Loeb), 1913).

——, *De Oratore*, Vol. I–II, trans. Sutton and Rackham (London and Cambridge, MA: Heinemann and Harvard University Press (Loeb), 1958).

——, *De Re Publica, De Legibus*, trans. C. W. Keyes (London: Heinemann and G. P. Putnam's Sons (Loeb), 1928).

——, *Tusculan Disputations*, trans. J. E. King (London and Cambridge, MA: Heinemann – Harvard University Press (Loeb), 1971).

Levi, Israel, ed., *The Hebrew Text of The Book of Ecclesiasticus* (Leiden: Brill, 1951).

Martinez, Florentino García, and Tigchelaar, Eibert J. C., *The Dead Sea Scrolls Study Edition*, vols 1–2 (Leiden and Grand Rapids, MI: Brill and Eerdmans Publishing Co., 1997–8).

Medieval Sources

Albert the Great, *Summa Theologia*, in *Opera Omnia*, ed. S. C. A. Borgnet, vols 31–3 (Paris: Vivès, 1895).

Alcuin (?), *De dignitate conditionis humanae* in *Patrologia Latina*, vol. 17, columns 1106–8 (taken to be of Ambrose). As a pseudo-Augustinian text *Patrologia Latina* 40, 1213–14 (*De creatione primi hominis*), as Albinus in *Patrologia Latina* 100, 565–68 (*Dicta Albini de imagine Dei*).

Alexander of Hales, *Glossa in libros Sententiarum* (Florence: Quaracchi, 1951–7).

——, *Summa Theologica*, ed. P. B. Klumper (Florence: Quaracchi, 1924).

Ambrose, *De Officiis*, ed. and trans. I. J. Davidson (Oxford: Oxford University Press, 2001).

Augustine, *The City of God against the Pagans*, trans. David E. Wiesen, vol. III, Loeb Classical Library (Cambridge, MA and London: Harvard University Press and William Heinemann, 1968).

——, Sermon 250, *Patrologia Latina*, 38, coll. 1163.

Basil de Césarée, *Sur l'origine de l'homme* (Hom. X et XI de l'Hexaémeron), ed. and trans. Alexis Smets S. J. and Michel Esbroeck, S. J., *Sources Chrétiennes* 160, 1970.

Bernard of Clairvaux, *Concerning Grace and Free Will*, trans. Watkin W. Williams (London and New York: Society for Promoting Christian Knowledge and The Macmillan Company, 1920).

——, *De cognitione humanae conditionis*, *Patrologia Latina*, Vol. 184, columns 485–508.

——, *De diligendo Deo*, Sancti Bernardii Opera III, Tractatus et Opuscula, eds J. Leclercq OSB and H.M Rochais OSB (Rome: Editiones Cisterciences, 1963).

——, *In Nativitate Domino*, serm. 2, 1, *Patrologia Latina*, Vol. 183, column 120 A.

——, *On Loving God* with an analytical commentary by Emero Stiegman, trans. Jean Leclercq OSB, Cistercian Fathers Series: 13 (Rome: Cistercian Publications Inc., 1973/1995).

Birgitta of Sweden, *Life and Selected Revelations*, Classics of Western Spirituality (New York: Paulist Press, 1990).

——, *Revelaciones*, V and VII, critically edited by Birger Bergh, *Samlinger utgivne av svenska fornskriftsällskapet, andra serien latiska skrifter* (Stockholm and Uppsala: Almquist och Wiksells, 1967–71).

Boethius, *The Consolation of Philosophy of Boethius*, trans. P. G. Walsh (Oxford: Clarendon Press, 1999).

——, *De Consolatione Philosophiae*, ed. A. Forti Scuto (London: Burns, Oates and Washbourne, 1925), re-edited with amendments by G. D. Smith (Hildesheim – New York: Georg Olms Verlag, 1976).

Bonaventura, *In Sententibus*, in *Opera Omnia*, ed. Collegii s. Bonaventura, vols 1–4 (Florence: Quarracchi, 1882).

Caterina di Siena, *The Dialogue*, translation and introduction by Suzanne Noffke, OP, Classics of Western Spirituality (New York and Mahwah, NJ: Paulist Press, 1980).

——, *Il Dialogo della Divina Provvidenza ovvero Libro della Divina Dottrina*, ed. Guiliana Cavallini (Rome: Edizioni Cateriniane, 1968).

Dante Alighieri, *The Divine Comedy* (Inferno, 1), trans. C. S. Singleton (Princeton, NJ: Princeton University Press, 1970, 2nd printing with corrections 1977).

Gertrud von Helfta Botschaft von Gottes Güte, Bd. 1–4, lateinisch-deutsch, ed. Maria Hildegard Brem (Heiligenkreuz, BeundBe Verlag, 2013).

——, *The Herald of Divine Love*, trans. and ed. Margeret Winkworth, introduced by Sr. M. Marnau, Classics of Western Spirituality (New York and Mahwah, NJ: Paulist Press, 1993).

Hildegard of Bingen, *Symphonia. A Critical Edition of the Symphonia armonie celestium revelationum* by Barbara Newman (Ithaca, NY and London: Cornell University Press, 1988).

John the Scot, Iohannis Scotti seu Eriugenae, *Periphyseon, Liber secundus*, curavit Edvardvs A Jeauneau (Tvrnholti: Typographi Brepols Editores Pontificii, 1997).

——, *Periphyseon. On the Division of Nature*, trans. Myra L. Uhlfelder, with summaries by Jean A. Potter, The Library of Liberal Arts (Indianapolis: The Bobbs-Merrill Company, inc., 1976).

Lebech, Mette, and James McEvoy†, 'A Latin liturgical source contributing to the conceptualization history of human dignity', *Maynooth Philosophical Papers* 2019, forthcoming.

Lebech, Mette, and James McEvoy with John Flood, '*De dignitate conditionis humanae*: Translation, Commentary, and Reception History of the Dicta Albini (Ps.-Alcuin) and the Dicta Candidi', *Viator*, Volume 40, 2 (2009), 1–34.

Leo the Great, *Sermons*, trans. Jane Patricia Freeland C. S. J. B. and Agnes Josephine Conway S. S. J. (Washington, DC: Catholic University of America Press, 1996).

——, *Sermon* 21 and 27, Corpus Christianorum, vol. 138, 88 and 137.

Missale Romanum ex decreto sacrosancta concilii Tridentini, Urban VIII, Dublin 1804.

Richard of St Victor, *De gratia contemplationis, Patrologia Latina*, vol. 196, column 123 A.

Robert Grosseteste, *De decem mandatis*, eds Richard C. Dales and Edward B. King, Auctores brittannici medii aevi X (Oxford: British Academy – Oxford University Press, 1987).

——, *Tabula*, ed. Philipp Rosemann, Opera Roberti Grosseteste Lincolniensis, V. I, Corpus Christianorum, vol. 130.

——, *Epistola Prima*, ed. Henry Richard Luard, Roberti Grosseteste Epistolae, Rerum brittannicarum medii aevi scriptores (London: Longman, Green, Longman and Roberts, 1861).

——, *Hexaëmeron*, eds Richard C. Dales and Servus Gieben O. F. M. Cap., Auctores britannici medii aevi VI (Oxford: British Academy – Oxford University Press, 1982.

——, *On the Six days of Creation*. A Translation of the *Hexaëmeron* by C. F. J. Martin, Auctores britannici medii aevi VI (2) (Oxford: British Academy – Oxford University Press, 1996).

——, 'Robert Grosseteste's Treatise on Confession, "Deus Est"', ed. Siegfried Wenzel, in *Franciscan Studies*, vol. 30 (1970), 218–93.

——, Rosenfeld, Randall, and Goering, Joseph, 'The Tongue is a Pen: Robert Grosseteste's Dictum 54 and Scribal Technology' in *The Journal of Medieval Latin*, Vol. 12 (2002), 114–40, no. 15.

Sancti Columbani Opera, Scriptores Latini Hiberniae, Vol. II, ed. G. S. M. Walker (Dublin: The Dublin Institute for Advanced Studies, 1957).

Thomas Aquinas, *Opera Omnia, iussu impensaque Leonis XIII P. M. edita*, ex typographia polyglotta S. C. de Propaganda Fide, 1882–1992.

——, *Summa Theologiae*, Latin text and English translation, introductions, notes, appendices and glossaries, Blackfriars in conjunction with Eyres and Spottiswoode/McGraw Hill Book Company, 1965–75.

——, *The Summa Theologica of St. Thomas Aquinas*, Literally translated by the fathers of the English Dominican Province (Shapcote) (London and New York: R. and T. Washbourne, LTD – Benziger Brothers, 1918). Available at: <http://www.ccel.org/a/aquinas/summa/home.htlm>.

Early Modern and Modern Sources

Arendt, Hannah, *The Burden of our Time* (alias first edition of *The Origins of Totalitarianism*) (London: Secker and Warburg, 1951).

——, *Denktagebuch: 1950–73*, eds Ursula Ludz and Ingeborg Nodmann, 2 vols (Munich: Piper, 2003).

——, *Hannah Arendt/Karl Jaspers Correspondence, 1926–69*, eds Lotte Köhler and Hans Saner, trans. Robert and Rita Kimber (New York: Harcourt Brace Jovanovich, 1992).

——, *Life of the Mind* (San Diego, CA: Harcourt and Brace, 1971).

——, *The Origins of Totalitarianism* (San Diego, CA: Harcourt Brace Jovanovich, 1968).

——, 'What is Existenz Philosophy?' in *Essays in Understanding, 1930–54: Formation, Exile and Totalitarianism*, ed. Jerome Kohn (New York: Harcourt, Brace and Co.1994).

Bloch, Ernst, *Natural Law and Human Dignity* (Cambridge, MA: MIT Press, 1986).

——, *Naturrecht und menschlicher Würde* (Frankfurt A. M.: Suhrkamp, 1985).

Burgh, James, *The Dignity of Human Nature. Or a brief account of the certain and established means for attaining the true end of our existence.* (London: W. B., 1754)

Burke, Edmund, *Reflections on the Revolution in France*, ed. J. C. D. Clark (Stanford, CA: Stanford University Press, 2001).

Brownlie, Ian, ed., *Basic Documents on Human Rights*, 2nd edn (Oxford: Clarendon Press, 1981).

A Compilation of International Instruments vol. 1 (1–2) Universal Instruments (New York and Geneva: United Nations, 1994).

Conway, Anne Finch, *Principles of the most ancient and modern philosophy*, in *An Unconventional History of Western Philosophy*, ed. Karen J. Warren (Lanham, MD: Roman and Littlefield, 2009), pp. 263–76.

Dupuis, Roger, and Paul Celier, *Courtoisie chrétienne et dignité humaine* (Paris: Mame, 1954).

Erasmus, Enchiridion militis christiani. An English Version, Early English Texts Society, no. 282, ed. Anne M. O'Donnell, S.N.D. (Oxford: Oxford University Press, 1981).

Erasmus von Rotterdam, *Enchiridion militis christiani*, in *Ausgewählte Schriften*, Acht Bände Lateinisch und Deutsch, vol. 1., trans. and ed. Werner Welzig (Darmstadt: Wissenschaftliche Buchgesellschaft Darmstadt, 1995).

Facio, Bartolomeo, *De dignitate et praestantia hominis*, written 1447/8, printed in 1611.

'A Gentleman', 'Man superior to Woman, or, the Natural Right of the Men to Sovereign Authority over the Women' (London: T. Cooper, 1739) (response to Sophia).

Greenville, J. A. S., *The Major International Treatises 1914–73. A History and Guide with Texts* (London: Methuen and co. Ltd, 1974).

Gouges, Olympe de, *Œuvres*. Présentés par Benoite Groult, Collection Mille et une Femmes (Paris: Mercure de France, 1986).

Grotius, Hugo, *Inleidinghe tot de Hollandsche Rechts-gheleertheyd* (Arnheim: P. Gouda Quint, 1895).

——*The Jurisprudence of Holland*, I, ed. R. W. Lee (Oxford: Clarendon Press, 1926).

Habermas, Jürgen, *The Future of Human Nature* (Cambridge: Polity, 2003).

Herder, Johann Gottfried, *Briefe zur Beförderung der Humanität*, ed. Michael Holzinger (Berlin: Holzinger, 2013).

——, *Ideen zur Philosophie der Geschichte der Menschheit*, Hofenberger Sonderausgabe (Berlin: Verlag der Contumax GmbH et Co., 2017).

Heydenreich, K. H., *Betrachtungen über die Würde des Menschen im Geiste der Kantischen Sitten – und Religionslehre mit Zollikofers Darstellungen über denselben Gegenstand*. Herausgegeben und nach Heydenreichs Grundlinien einer geistlichen Redekunst mit einigen Winken zu einer Parallele zwischen Heydenreichs und Zollikofers Ideen begleitet von J. G. Gruber (Leipzig: I. B. Schiegg, 1803).

Hobbes, Thomas, *Leviathan*, ed. Richard Tuck (Cambridge: Cambridge University Press, 1991).

Humboldt, Wilhelm von, *Über den Geist der Menschheit*, in *Werke in fünf Bänden*. eds Andreas Flitner and Klaus Giel, vol. 1 (Stuttgart: Cotta, 1960).

Hume, David, 'Of the Dignity or Meanness of Human Nature', Essay no. XI in *Essays Moral, Political and Literary*. ed. Eugene F. Miller (Indianapolis: Liberty Classics, 1987).

Kant, Immanuel, *Akademie Textausgabe*, Unveränderter photomechanischer Abdruck des Textes der von der Preußischen Akademie der Wissenschaften 1902 begonnenen Ausgabe von Kants gesammelte Schriften (Berlin: Walter de Guyter & Co., 1968).

——, 'Anthropology from a pragmatic point of view', trans. Robert B. Louden in *The Cambridge Edition of the Works of Immanuel Kant. Anthropology, History, and Education*, eds Günter Zöller and Robert B. Louden (Cambridge: Cambridge University Press, 2007).

——, *Critique of Pure Reason, Unified Edition*, trans. W. Pluhar (Indianapolis and Cambridge: Hackett, 1996).

——, *Critique of Teleological Judgement*, ed. J. C. Meredith (Oxford: Clarendon Press, 1928).

——, *Gesammelte Schriften* (Berlin: Königlich Preußischen Akademie der Wissenschaften, 1902–23).

——, *Grundlegung zur Metaphysik der Sitten* (Hamburg: Meiner, 2016).

——, *Metaphysische Anfangsgründe der Rechtslehre* (Hamburg: Meiner, 1986).

——, *Metaphysische Anfangsgrunde der Tugendlehre* (Hamburg: Meiner, 1990).

——, *Practical Philosophy*, ed. Mary Gregor (Cambridge: Cambridge University Press, 1996).

Karrer, Otto, *Schicksal und Würde des Menschen. Die Frohbotschaft Christi*, 2nd edn (Köln: Benziger et Co. AG, 1941), in particular II, 6: 'Die Würde der Menschlichen Person.'

Las Casas, Bortolomé de, *Obras Completas*, vol. 2 (Madrid: Alianza Editorial, 1990).

——, *Obras Completas*, vol. 13 (Madrid: Alianza Editorial, 1995).

——, *The Only Way (to Draw all People to a Living Faith)*, ed. Helen Rand Parish, trans. Francis Patrick Sullivan, S. J., Sources of American Spirituality (Mahwah: Paulist Press, 1992).

Lassalle, Ferdinand, 'Arbeiterprogramm' in *Reden und Schriften*. ed. Friedrich Jenaczek (München: Deutcher Taschenbuch Verlag, 1970).

——, *The Working Man's Programme*, trans. Edward Peeters (London: The Modern Press, 1884).

Leo XIII, pope, 'The Condition of the Workingman' in *Social Wellsprings. Fourteen Epochal Documents by Pope Leo XIII*, ed. Joseph Husslein, S. J. (Milwaukee: The Bruce Publishing Company, 1940).

The London Philanthropic Society (London, 18 July, 1789). Eighteen Century Collections Online (accessed November 2017).

Manetti, Gianozzo, *De dignitate et excellentia hominis*, ed. Elisabeth Riley Leonard (Padua: Editrice Atenore, 1975).

Marcel, Gabriel, *The Existential Background of Human Dignity* (Cambridge, MA: Harvard University Press, 1963).

——, *La dignité humaine et ses assises exstentielles* (Paris: Aubier, 1964).

Martin, Martin, *A voyage to St Kilda the remotest of all the Hebrides; or, Western Isles of Scotland. Giving an account of the very remarkable inhabitants of that place; their Beauty and singular Chastity: (Fornication and Adultery being unknown among them) their genius for Poetry, Musick, Dancing; their surprising Dexterity in climbing the Rocks and Walls of Houses; Diversions, Habits, Food, Language, Diseases and Methods of Cure; their extensive Charity; their Contempt of Gold and Silver as below the Dignity of Human Nature; their religious Ceremonies, Notions of Spirits and Visions etc etc.* (London: printed for R. Griffith, at the Dunciad in Ludgate Street, 1749) (3rd edn, 1st edn 1698), Eighteenth Century Collections Online (accessed 2 November 2017).

More, Hannah, *An Estimate of the Religion of the Fashionable World* (London: printed for T. Cadell, 1791), Eighteenth Century Collections Online (accessed November 2017).

——, *The Spirit of Prayer*, The Complete Works of Hannah More in seven volumes (New York: Harper and Brothers, Cliff Street, 1835), vol. 7 (digitised by Google, accessed 29 August 2018).

——, *Strictures on the Modern System of Female Education with a View of the Principles and Conduct Prevalent among Women of Rank and Fortune*, I–II, vol. 2, 3rd edn (London: printed for T. Cadell, Jun. and Davies, 1799), Eighteenth Century Collections Online (accessed 2 November 2017).

Nietzsche, Friedrich, *Early Greek Philosophy and Other Essays*, trans. Maximilian A. Mügge, in *The Complete Works of Friedrich Nietzsche*. ed. Oscar Levy, vol. 2 (New York: The Macmillan Company, 1911).

——, *Fünf Vorreden zu fünf ungeschriebene Büchern (3), Kritische Studienausgabe*, vol. 1, eds Giorgio Colli and Mazzino Montinari, vol. 3. (Berlin and New York: Deutscher Taschenbuch-Verlag and de Gruyter, 1988).

Paine, Thomas, *The Rights of Man*, Wordsworth Classics of World Literature (Ware: Wordsworth Editions Limited, 1996).

Pascal, *Œuvres Complètes* (Paris: Gallimard, 2000).

Peaslee, Amos J., *Constitutions of Nations*. 3rd revised edn prepared by Dorothy Peaslee Xydis in four volumes (The Hague: Martinus Nijhoff, 1964–8).

Perez de Oliva, F., *Diálogo del dignidad del hombre*, ed. Ma Luisa Cérron Puga (Madrid: Cátedra, 1995).

Pico della Mirandola, *Discorso sulla dignità dell'uomo*, ed. Francesco Bausi (Rome?: Fondazione Pietro Bembo, 2014).

——, *On the Dignity of Man, On Being and the One, Heptaplus*, trans. C. G. Wallis, P. J. W. Miller and D. Carmichael, The Library of Liberal Arts (Indianapolis, IN and New York: The Bobbs-Merrill Company, 1940 (repr. 1965)).

——, *Oratio de dignitate hominis*, <http://www.brown.edu/Departments/Italian_Studies/pico/>.

——, *Oratio de dignitate hominis*, ed. Eugenio Garin, Edizione Nationale dei Classici del Pensiero Italiano (Florence: Vallecchi, 1942).

——, *Oration on the dignity of man*, eds Francesco Borghesi, Michael Papio and Massimo Riva (Cambridge: Cambridge University Press: 2012).

——, 'Oration on the Dignity of Man', trans. Elisabeth Livermore Forbes, in *The Renaissance Philosophy of Man*, eds Cassirer, Kristeller and Randall (Chicago and London: University of Chicago Press, 1948).

——, הנאום על כבוד האדם, trans. Gayo Shiloni (Jerusalem: Carmel Publishing House, 1990).

Prince, Mary, *The History of Mary Prince*, ed. Sarah Salih (London: Penguin Classics, 2004 (first published 1831)).

Proudhon, P. J., *De la Justice dans la revolution et dans l'Eglise*, in *Œuvres Complètes de P. J. Proudhon*, vol. 4–8 (Paris: Garnier Frères, 1858).

Pufendorf, Samuel, *De Jure naturae et gentium Libro octo*, Publications of the Carnegie Endowment for International Peace, The Classics of International Law, vol. I, Photographic Reproduction of the Edition of 1688, with an Introduction by Simons Walter. Vol. II: Translation, by Oldfather C. H. and Oldfather W. A. (Oxford: Clarendon Press, 1934).

Reyntjens, F., ed., *Constitutiones Africae* (Bruxelles and Paris : Bruylant and Pedone, 1988).

Roman Missal, renewed by decree of the most holy second ecumenical council of the Vatican. Promulgated by authority of Pope Paul VI and revised at the direction of Pope John Paul II. English translation according to the third typical edition (Dublin: Veritas, 2011).

Schiller, Friedrich, *Über Anmut und Würde,* in *Samtliche Werke,* vol. V, ed. Perfahl (München: Winkler Verlag, 1968).

Sophia, *Woman not Inferior to Man, or, A Short and Modest Vindication of the Natural Right of the Fair Sex to a Perfect Equality of Power, Dignity and Esteem with the Men* (London: Fowler's Walk, 1739, reprinted by Brentham in 1975).

Stein, Edith, *Aus dem Leben einer jüdischen Familie,* Edith Stein Gesamtausgabe 1 (Freiburg: Herder, 2002).

——, *Life in a Jewish Family,* trans. Josephine Koeppel, OCD (Washington, DC: Institute of Carmelite Studies Publications, 1986).

——, *Potency and Act,* trans. Walter Redmond, The Collected Works of Edith Stein XI (Washington, DC: Institute of Carmelite Studies Publications, 2009).

——, *Potenz und Akt,* Edith Stein Gesamtausgabe 10 (Freiburg: Herder, 2005).

——, 'Probleme der neueren Mädchenbildung', in Edith Stein Gesamtausgabe 13 (Freiburg: Herder, 2000), 127–208.

——, *Was ist der Mensch?,* Edith Stein Gesamtausgabe 15 (Freiburg: Herder, 2005).

Stuart Mill, John, 'Utilitarianism' in *Collected Works of John Stuart Mill,* vol. X: Essays on Ethics, Religion and Society (Toronto and London: University of Toronto Press and Routledge and Kegan Paul, 1969).

Vatican II, *Dignitatis Humanae, Declaration on Religious Liberty,* in *Vatican Council II, The Conciliar and the Post Conciliar Documents,* ed. Austin Flannery O. P. (Northport, NY: Costello Publishing Company, 1975), pp. 799–812. Also <http://www.vatican.va>archive>documents>.

Wesley, John, *The Dignity of Human Nature* (Bristol, 1762) Eighteenth Century Collections Online (accessed 2 November 2017).

Wilson Justice James, *Chisholm v. Georgia* 2 U. S. (2 Dall.) 419, United States Supreme Court Reports, Lawyers' Edition 440; 1793 U. S. LEXIS 249.

Wollstonecraft, Mary, *A Critical Edition of Mary Wollstonecraft's A Vindication of the Rights of Women With Strictures on Political and Moral Subjects,* ed. Ulrich Hardt (New York: The Whitston Publishing Company, 1982).

——, *A Vindication of the Rights of Men A Vindication of the Rights of Woman An Historical and Moral View of the French Revolution,* ed. Janet Todd, Oxford World Classics (Oxford: Oxford University Press, 1993).

Zollikofer, Georg Joachim, *Predigten über die Würde des Menschen, und den Werth der vornehmsten Dinge, die zur Menschlichen Glückseligkeit gehören, oder dazu gerechnet werden*, vol. I–II (Leipzig: Weidmanns Erben und Reich, 1788 and 1784, 1st edn 1783. Nabu public Domain reprints).

——, *Sermons on the Dignity of Man and the value of the objects principally relating to human happiness*, trans. William Tooke (London: printed by A. Strahan for T. N. Longman and O. Rees, 1802). 1st edn 1783.

Studies

Allen, Prudence, *The Concept of Woman. The Aristotelian Revolution 750 BC – AD 1250* (Grand Rapids, MI: Eerdmans, 1985).

Amiot, François, *History of the Mass* (London: Burns and Oates, 1959).

Ammicht-Quin, Regina, Maureen Juncker-Kenny and Elsa Tamez, *The Discourse of Human Dignity* (London: SCM Press, 2003).

Andorno, Roberto, *La bioethique et la dignite de la personne* (Paris: PUF, 1997).

——, 'The paradoxical nature of human dignity', *Rivista internazionale di filosofia del diritto*, no. 2 (2001) 151–68.

Anscombe, G. Elisabeth M., 'The Dignity of the Human Being' in *Human Life, Action and Ethics. Essays by G. E. M. Anscombe*, eds Mary Geach and Luke Gormally (St Andrews: Imprint Academic, 2006) 67–73.

Arendt, Hannah, *The Human Condition*, Doubleday, New York, 1959.

——, *Lectures on Kant's Political Philosophy*, edited with an interpretative essay by R. Beiner (Chicago: University of Chicago Press, 1992).

Azikiwe, Nnamdi, *Respect for Human Dignity* (Onitsha: Union Publishing, 16 October 1960).

Azzola, Axel, et al., *Kommentar zum Grundgesetz für die Bundesrepublik Deutschland*, Bd. 1–2 (Munich: Luchterhand, 1984).

Baker, Hershel Clay, *The Dignity of Man: Studies in the Persistence of an Idea* (Cambridge, MA: Harvard University Press, 1947, repr. New York, 1961).

Barak, Aharon, *Human Dignity. The Constitutional Value and the Constitutional Right* (Cambridge: Cambridge University Press, 2015).

Baldus, Manfred, *Kämpfe um die Menschenwürde. Die Debatten seit 1949* (Berlin: Suhrkamp, 2016).

Bayertz, Kurt, ed., *Sanctity of Life and Human Dignity* (Dordrecht: Kluwer, 1996).

Bedjaoui, Mohammed, ed., *International Law: Achievements and Prospects*, UNESCO (Dordrecht, Boston, MA and London: Martinus Nijhoff, 1991).

Bednar, Miloslav, *Human Dignity: Values and Justice*, Czeck Philosophical Studies III, The Council for Research in Values and Philosophy, Series VIA, vol. 18, Washington, DC, 1999.

Benda, Ernst, 'Die Menschenwürde' in *Handbuch des Verfassungsrechts*, Gruyter, 1983, 107–28.

——, 'Die Würde des Menschen ist unantastbar' *in Beiträge zur Rechtsanthropologie*, ed. Ernst-Joachim Lampe (Stuttgart: Steiner Verlag, 1985).

Benestad, J. B., 'Dignity in the United Nations Declaration of Human Rights', *Natura e Dignita Della Persona Umana A Fondamento Del Diritto Alla Vita. Le Sfide Del Contesto Culturale Contemporaneo*, eds Vial Correa and Sgreccia (Rome: Libreria Editrice Vaticana, 2003), 133–42.

Benhabib, Seyla, *Dignity in Adversity: Human Rights in Troubled Times* (Malden: Polity, 2011).

Beyleweld, Deryck, and Roger Brownsword, *Human Dignity in Bioethics and Biolaw* (Oxford: Oxford University Press, 2001).

Bielefeldt, Heiner, *Menschenwürde. Der Grund der Menschenrechte* (Berlin: Deutsches Institut für Menschenrechte, 2008).

Böckenförde, Ernst-Wolfgang, and Robert Spaemann, eds, *Menschenrechte und Menschenwürde. Historische Voraussetzungen – säkulare Gestalt – christliches Verständniss* (Stuttgart: Klett-Cotta, 1987).

Böhr, Christoph, 'Die Würde des Menschen – ein säkularer begriff mit absoluter Geltung. Zur religiösen Fundierung des politischen Pluralismus im demokratischen Staat' in *Religion und politische Kultur: Ost trifft West/Religione e cultura politica: l'Est incontra l'Ovest* eds Markus Krienke and Wilhelm Staudacher (Rome: Soveria Manelli, 2010), 91–113.

——, 'Menschenwürde und Menschenrechte', 2013, <http://www.katholischeaerztearbeit.de/uploads/pdf/boehr>.

——, 'Wert und Würde. Vielfalt des Pluralismus und Beglaubigung des Absoluten: Ein Wiederspruch' in *Alte Werte – Neue Werte. Schlaglichter des Wertewandels*, eds Andreas Rödder and Wollfgang Elz (Göttingen: Vandenhoeck und Ruprecht, 2008), 181–8.

Brierly, J. L., *The Outlook for International Law* (Oxford: Clarendon Press, 1944).

Broad, Jacqueline, 'The early modern period: dignity and the foundation of women's rights' in *The Wollstonecraftian Mind*, eds Sandrine Bergès, Eileen Hunt Botting and Allan Coffee (London and New York: Routledge, forthcoming).

Brock, Stephen L., 'Is uniqueness at the root of personal dignity? John Crosby and Thomas Aquinas' in *The Thomist* 69 (2005) 173–201.

Brose, Thomas, and Matthias Lutz-Bachmann, *Umstrittene Menschenwürde. Beiträge zur ethischen Debatte der Gegenwart* (Hildesheim: Benno-Bernward-Morus mbH, 1994).

Cassiers, Leon, and Michel Dupuis (co-ordinators), 'Thème : Une dignité à inventer', in *Louvain* 129, June 2002.

Collste, Göran, *Is Human Life Special? Religious and Philosophical Perspectives on the Principle of Human Dignity* (Bern: Peter Lang, 2002).

Crespo, Mariano, *Menschenwürde: Metaphysik und Ethik* (Heidelberg: Universitäts-verlag C. Winther, 1998).

Debes, Remy, ed., *Dignity. A History* (Oxford: Oxford University Press, 2016).

Delacampagne, Christian, *Geschichte der Sklaverei*, trans. Ursula Vones-Liebenstein, Wissenschaftliche Buchgesellschaft (Düsseldorf – Zürich: Artemie et Winkler Verlag, 2004).

DeKoninck, Thomas, *De la dignité humaine* (Paris: Presses Universitaires de France, 1995).

——, and Gilbert Larochelle, co-ordinators, *La dignité humaine. Philosophie, droit, politique, économie, médicine* (Paris: Presses Universitaires de France, 2005).

Dennehy, Raymond, *Reason and Dignity* (Washington, DC: University of America Press, 1981).

Desmet, Marc, *Souffrance et dignité humaine* (Namur and Paris: Fidelité, 2002).

Dignité, perte de dignité. Acceuillir tout humain, in *Laennec. Medicine, santé, éthique*, no 3–4, March 93.

Dignité humaine des souffrants, Dossier: la notion de dignité, Le Supplement, no. 191, December 1994.

Dowrick, F. E., ed., *Human Rights. Problems, Perspectives and Texts* (University of Durham: Saxon House, 1979).

Droit et dignité de la personne humaine, special issue of *Gregorianum*, vol. 65 (1984), fasc. II/III.

Dworkin, Ronald, *Taking Rights Seriously* (Cambridge, MA: Harvard University Press, 1977).

Edelman, Bernard, 'La dignité de la personne humaine, un concept nouveau' in *Receuil Dalloz 1997*, 23e Cahier, chronique, 185–8.

Egonsson, Dan, *Dimensions of Dignity. The Moral Importance of Being Human* (Dordrecht: Kluwer, 1999).

Eibach, Ulrich, *Medizin und Menschenwürde. Ethische Probleme in der Medizin aus christlicher Sicht* (Wuppertal: R. Brockhaus Verlag, 1988).

European Commission for Democracy through Law, *The Principle of Respect for Human Dignity. Proceedings of the UniDem Seminar organised in Montpellier (France) from 2 to 6 July 1998 in co-operation with the 'Pôle universitaire européen*

de Montpellier et du Languedoc-Roussillon' and the Faculty of Law – CERCOP, *University of Montpellier I* (Strasbourg: Council of Europe Publishing, 1999).

Fagermoen, Solveig, 'Professional identity: values embedded in meaningful nursing practice', in *Journal of Advanced Nursing*, 1997, 25, 434–41.

Fawchett, J. E. S., *The Law of Nations* (Harmondsworth: Penguin, 1971).

Feldman, David, 'Human Dignity as a Legal Value – part I' and 'II', in *Public Law*, Winter 1999, p. 682–702 and Spring 2000, 61–76.

Finnis, John, *Aquinas. Natural Law and Natural Rights* (Oxford: Oxford University Press, 1980).

——, *Moral, Legal and Political Theory* (Oxford: Oxford University Press, 1998).

Fischer, Michael, ed., *Der Begriff der Menschenwürde* (Bern: Peter Lang, 2005).

Fischer, Tina-Louise, *Menschen- und Personenwürde. Über die Notwendigkeit eines neuen Würdebegriffs* (Berlin: Lit. Verlag Dr. W. Hopf, 2008).

Fletcher-Louis, Crispin H. T., *All the Glory of Adam. Liturgical Anthropology in the Dead Sea Scrolls* (Leiden: Brill, 2002).

Gerhard, Ute, 'Equality and/or difference criteria for a different law for women: freedom, equality and dignity' in Yotopoulos-Marengopoulos, A., ed., *Women's Rights Human Rights* (Athens: Hestia Publications, 1994).

Gimeno-Cabrera, Veronique, *Le Traitement Jurisprudentiel de Principe de dignité de la personne humaine* (Paris: L. G. D. J., 2004).

Glendon, Mary Ann, *Rights Talk. The Impoverishment of Political Discourse* (New York and Toronto: The Free Press, Collier MacMillan and Maxwell MacMillan, 1991).

——, *A World Made New. Eleanor Roosevelt and the Universal Declaration of Human Rights* (New York: Random House, 2001).

Goldgar, Bertrand A., 'Satires on Man and "The Dignity of Human Nature"', in *Papers of the Modern Language Association*, 80/5 (December 1965), 353–541.

Gotesky, Rubin, and Ervin Laszlo, *Human Dignity: This Century and the Next. An Interdisciplinary Inquiry into Human Rights, Technology, War and the Ideal Society* (London, New York and Paris: Gordon and Breach, 1970).

Green, Richard, *The works of John and Charles Wesley; a bibliography, containing an exact account of all the publications issued by the brothers Wesley, arranged in chronological order, with a list of the early editions, and descriptive and illustrative notes* (London: Methodist Pub. House, 1906).

Gregor, Mary, *Laws of Freedom. A Study of Kant's Method of Applying the Categorical Imperative in the* Metaphysik der Sitten (Oxford: Blackwell, 1963).

Guerrero van der Meijden, Jadwiga, *The Concept of the Human Person in Edith Stein's Philosophical Anthropology and the Christian Notion of Human Dignity*, PhD thesis, Institute of Philosophy, Jagiellonian University Krakow, 2018.

Gurmin, John Haydn, *A Study of the Development and Significance of the Idea of the 'Image of God' from its Origins in Genesis through its Historical-Philosophical Interpretations to Contemporary Concerns in Science and Phenomenology*. PhD thesis, National University of Ireland Maynooth, 2010.

Haakonsson, Knud, *Natural Law and Moral Philosophy. From Grotius to the Scottish Enlightenment* (Cambridge: Cambridge University Press, 1996).

Haesrahi, Pepita, 'The Avowed and the Unavowed Sources of Kant's Theory of Ethics', in *Ethics*, April 1952, Vol. LXII, No. 3, 157–68.

——, 'The Concept of Man as an End in Himself' in Robert Paul Wolff, ed., *Kant. A Collection of Critical Essays* (London and Melbourne: Macmillan, 1968), 291–314, reprinted from *Kant-Studien* 53 (1962), and *Kant: the Foundations of the Metaphysics of Morals Text and Critical Essays*, ed. Robert Paul Wolff (Indianapolis: Bobbs-Merrill Educational Publishing, 1969).

Haffner, Sebastian, *The Rise and Fall of Prussia*, trans. E. Osers (London: Weidenfeld and Nicolson, 1980).

Hanke, Lewis, *Aristotle and the American Indians* (Chicago: Henry Regnery Company, 1959).

Hansson, Mats, *Human Dignity and Animal Well-Being. A Kantian Contribution to Biomedical Ethics* (Uppsala: Almquist ock Wiksel, 1991).

Härle, Wilfried, and Bernhard Vogel, eds, *Begründung von Menschenwürde und Menschenrechten* (Freiburg: Herder, 2008).

Hartman, Robert S., 'Four Axiological Proofs of the Infinite Value of Man' in Katz, Marwin Charles, ed., *Sciences of Man and Social Ethics. Variations on the Theme of Human Dignity* (Boston, MA: Branden Press, 1969).

Hill, Thomas, *Dignity and Practical Reason in Kant's Moral Theory* (Ithaca, NY and London: Cornell University Press, 1992).

Hirsch, Emmanuel, 'Humanité et dignité' in *Prévenir*, no. 22, 1992.

Höffner, J., *Christentum und Menschenwürde. Das Anliegen der spanischen Kolonialethik im goldenen Zeitalter* (Trier: Paulinus Verlag, 1947).

Holderegger, A., Ruedi Imbach, and Raul Suarez de Miguel, eds, *De Dignitate Hominis. Mélanges offertes à Carlos-Josaphat Pinto de Oliveira* (Freiburg and Wien: Universitäts Verlag Freiburg Schweiz and Verlag Herder, 1987).

Iglesias, Teresa, The *Dignity of the Individual. Issues in Bioethics and Law* (Dublin: Pleroma Press, 2001).

International Auschwitz Committee, *In Hell They Preserved Human Dignity*. Anthology, Vol. 2, Part 3 (Warsaw: Auschwitz, 1971).

International Theological Commission, *Propositions on Dignity and Rights of the Human Person* (Maynooth: Furrow Trust, 1985).

Israel, State of, Basic Law: *Human Dignity and Liberty*, <https://www.knesset.gov. il/laws/special/eng/basic3_eng.htm> (accessed 1 September 2018).

Javelet, Robert, *Image et ressemblance au douzième siècle de saint Anselme à Alain de Lille*, vols I–II (Université de Strassbourg, Thèse de Doctorat, 1967).

Joas, Hans, 'Die Logik der Gabe und das Postulat der Menschenwürde' in *Von der Ursprünglichkeit der Gabe: Jean-Luc Marions Phänomenologie in der Diskussion* (*Scientia et Religio*), eds Michael Gabel and Hans Joas (Freiburg: Verlag Karl Alber, 2007).

Josaphat, Carlos, O. P., 'Las Casas. Prophet of Full Rights for All' in *Justice, Peace and Dominicans: 1216–2001*, ed. John Orme Mills (Dublin: Dominican Publications, 2001) 97–117.

Kaczor, Christopher, *The Edge of Life. Human Dignity in Contemporary Bioethics* (Dordrecht: Springer, 2005).

Kadish, Doris Y., and Françoise Massardier-Kenney, eds, *Translating Slavery, Gender and Race in French Women's Writing 1783–1823* (Kent, OH: The Kent State University Press, 1994).

Kamali, Mohammad Hashim, *The Dignity of Man. An Islamic Perspective* (Cambridge: The Islamic Texts Society, 2002).

Kantorowicz, Ernst H., 'Dignitas non moritur' in *The King's Two Bodies. A Study in Mediaeval Political Theology* (Princeton, NJ: Princeton University Press, 1957) 383–450.

Kass, Leon R., *Life, Liberty and the Defense of Dignity. The Challenge for Bioethics* (San Francisco, CA: Encounter Books, 2002).

Kaunda, Kenneth, *The Imperative of Human Dignity* (Lusaka: Neczam, 1968).

Kelly, Thomas A. F., 'The Ontology of Freedom as Foundation for a Theory of Human Dignity', in *Maynooth Philosophical Papers* 2 (2004) 39–50.

Kemp, Peter, Mette Lebech and Jacob Rendtorff, *Den bioetiske vending. En grundbog i bioetik* (København: Spektrum, 1998).

——, and Jacob Dahl Rendtorff, *Basic Ethical Principles in European Bioethics and Biolaw*, vol. I: *Autonomy, Dignity, Integrity and Vulnerability*, Report to the European Commission of the BIOMED II Project 'Basic Ethical Principles in Bioethics and Biolaw' 1995–8 (København: Centre for Ethics and Law, 1999).

——, Jacob Dahl Rendtorff and Niels M. Johansen, *Bioethics and Biolaw*, vol. I–II (København: Centre for Ethics and Law – Rhodos, 2000).

Kendall Soulen, R., and Linda Woodhead, eds, *God and Human Dignity* (Grand Rapids, MI: William B. Eerdmans Publishing Company, 2006).

Kielkopf, Charles F., 'The pure human dignity of the mentally retarded' in *World Futures. The Journal of New Paradigm Research*, vol. 9/1–2 (1971), 106–13.

King, Martin Luther, 'Letters from a Birmingham Jail' in *A Peace Reader. Essential Readings on War, Justice, Non-Violence and World Order*, eds J. J. Fahey and R. Armstrong (New York: Paulist Press, 1992).

Knoepffler, Nikolaus, *Menschenwürde in der Bioethik* (Berlin: Springer, 2004).

Kolnay, Aurel, 'Dignity', in *Philosophy*, 51 (1976) 251–71. Also in Robin Dillon (ed.), *Dignity, Character and Self-Respect* (New York: Routledge, 1995).

Korsgaard, C., 'Kant's Formula of Humanity' in: *Immanuel Kant. Critical Assessments*, ed. R. Chadwick, vol. III: Kant's Moral and Political Philosophy (London and New York: Routledge, 1992), 157–81. Also in *Kant-Studien* 77 (1986).

Kössler, H., ed., *Die Würde des Menschen* (Erlangen: Universitätsbund Erlangen-Nürnberg, 1998).

Kothen, Robert, 'Dignité de la Personne' in *L'Enseignement Social de l'Eglise* (Louvain: Em Warny, 1949), 143–58.

Kretzmer, David, and Eckart Klein, *The Concept of Human Dignity in Human Rights Discourse* (The Hague: Kluwer Law International, 2002).

Kristeller, Oskar, *Renaissance Concepts of Man and other Essays* (New York: Harper and Row, 1972).

Kugel, J. L., *Traditions of the Bible* (Cambridge, MA: Harvard University Press, 1998).

Langlois, Anne, 'Dignité humaine' in G. Hottois, and J. M. Missa, eds, *Nouvelle Encyclopedie de Bioethique* (Bruxelles: De Boeck, 2001) 281–84.

Lauterpacht, H., *International Law and Human Rights* (London: Stevens and Sons Ltd, 1950).

Lebech, Mette, 'Menschenwürde im Lichte der Philosophie Edith Steins' in *Edith Stein Jahrbuch* 2015, 179–93.

——, *On the Problem of Human Dignity. A Hermeneutical and Phenomenological Investigation* (Würzburg: Königshausen und Neumann, 2009).

——, and James McEvoy, 'Robert Grosseteste's Understanding of Human Dignity' in *Grosseteste and His Intellectual Milieu*, ed. James Ginther, John Flood and Joseph Goering (Toronto: PIMS – Brepols, 2013), 34–64.

Lloyd, Dennis, *The Idea of Law* (Harmondsworth: Penguin, 1st edn 1964, reprinted 1974 (with revisions)).

Lorberbaum, Jair, 'Human dignity in the Jewish tradition', *The Cambridge Handbook of Human Dignity*, eds Marcus Düwell, Jens Braarvig, Roger Browsword and Dietmar Mieth (Cambridge: Cambridge University Press, 2014), 135–44.

Luhmannn, Niklas, *A Sociological Theory of Law*, trans. E. King and M. Albrow (London and Boston, MA: Routledge and Kegan Paul, 1985).

McCrudden, Christopher, ed., *Understanding Human Dignity* (Oxford: Oxford University Press, 2013).

McDougal, Myres S., Harold D. Lasswell, and Lung-Chu Chen: *Human Rights and World Public Order: The Basic Policies of an International Law of Human Dignity* (New Haven, CT and London: Yale University Press, 1980).

McEvoy, James, '*Dignitas humana*: The Equal Dignity of Man and Woman through their Creation in the Image of God: Basil the Great's Outlook and Robert Grosseteste's reception of it', in *Maynooth Philosophical Papers* 2 (2004), 84–8.

——, *The Philosophy of Robert Grosseteste* (Oxford: Clarendon, 1982, reprinted 1986).

——, *Robert Grosseteste: Exegete and Philosopher*, Variorum, Aldershot, 1994.

MacIntyre, Alasdair, *After Virtue* (London: Duckworth, 1981).

——, *Three Rival Versions of Moral Enquiry* (London: Duckworth, 1990).

——, *Whose Justice? Which Rationality?* (London: Duckworth, 1988).

MacKendrick, Paul, *The Philosophical Books of Cicero* (London: Duckworth, 1989).

MacKenzie, Catriona, 'Reason and Sensibility: The Ideal of Women's Self-Governance in the Writings of Mary Wollstonecraft' in *Hypatia*, 8/4 (1993), 35–55.

McLaughlin, Mary Martin, 'Peter Abelard and the Dignity of the Women: Twelfth Century "Feminism" in Theory and Practice' in Pierre Abelard, *Pierre le Venerable: Les courants philosophiques, litteraires et artistiques en Occident au milieu du XIIe siècle* (Paris: CNRS, 1975), 287–334.

McNamara, Jo Ann, *Sisters in Arms. Catholic Nuns through Two Millennia* (Cambridge, MA: Harvard University Press, 1996).

Maihofer, Werner, 'Die Würde des Menschen als Zweck des Staates', in *An Cated Suarez*, 12 (1972) 37–62.

Malpas, Jeff, and Norelle Lickiss, eds, *Perspectives on Human Dignity: A Conversation* (Dordrecht: Springer, 2007).

Marenbon, John, *From the Circle of Alcuin to the School of Auxerre. Logic, Theology and Philosophy in the Early Middle Ages* (Cambridge: Cambridge University Press, 1981), 30–43 and 144–63.

Marin, Isabelle, 'La dignité humaine, un consensus?' in *Esprit*, February 1991, 97–101.

Maritain, Jacques, *The Rights of Man and Natural Law* (London: The Centenary Press, 1944).

Mathieu, Bertrand, 'La dignité de la personne humaine: quel droit? quel titulaire?' in *Receuil Dalloz Sirey*, 1996, 33e Cahier, 282–6.

Maurer, Béatrice, *Le principe de respect de la dignité humaine et la Convention européenne des droits de l'homme* (Paris: La Documentation Française, 1999).

Menschenwürde, Zeitschrift für Menschenrechte, 4/2010, 1.

Meyer, Michael J., 'Dignity, Death and Modern Virtue', *American Philosophical Quarterly*, 32/1 (1995) 45–55.

——, 'Kant's Concept of Dignity and Modern Political Thought', *History of European Ideas*, 8, 1987, 319–32.

——, and W. A. Parent, *The Constitution of Rights. Human Dignity and American Values* (Ithaca, NY and London: Cornell University Press, 1992).

Migiel, Marilyn, 'The Dignity of Man: A Feminist Perspective' in *Refiguring Woman. Perspectives on Gender and the Italian Renaissance*, eds Marily Migiel and Juliana Schiesari (New York: Cornell University Press, 1991).

Morewedge, Parviz, *The Metaphysica of Avicenna (Ibn Sina): A Critical Translation-Commentary and Analysis of the Fundamental Arguments in Avicenna's Metaphysica in the Danish Nama (The Book of Scientific Knowledge)* (London: Routledge and Kegan Paul, 1973).

Morgan, Rabbi Fred, 'The Notion of Human Dignity in Jewish Tradition', Faculty of Theology and Philosophy, Australian Catholic University, <https://leocontent.acu.edu.au/file/44acd9ef-4eb7-44cb-b081-98da4d4dc095/6/docs/m2-Fred-Morgan.pdf> (accessed 1 September 2018).

Morsink, Johannes, *The Universal Declaration of Human Rights. Origins, Drafting and Intent* (Philadelphia: University of Pennsylvania Press, 1999).

Netzelgang, Véra, and Clara Frost, *Soigner à tout casser. La dignité de la personne à l'épreuve de la psychiatrie lourde* (no place: Bernard Gilson Éditeur, 2006).

Neuner, J., and J. Dupuis, eds, *The Christian Faith in the Doctrinal Documents of the Catholic Church* (Sydney: Collins, 2001).

Nseka, Donatien Banona, *Technique et dignité humaine. Perspectives contemporains à partir de Gabriel Marcel* (Louvain-la-Neuve: Bruylant-Academia s.a., 1997).

Nussbaum, Martha, 'Political animals: Luck, love and dignity', in *Metaphilosophy*, 29/4 (1998), 273–87.

O'Donovan, Joan Lockwood, 'Historical Prolegomena to a Theological Review of Human Rights' in *Studies in Christian Ethics*, 9/2, 52–65.

O'Flaherty, Michael, *Human Rights and the UN Practice before the Treaty Bodies* (London: Sweet and Maxwell, 1996).

Paine, Thomas, *Rights of Man*, with an Introduction by Derek Matravers (Ware: Wordsworth Editions, 1996).

Pédrot, Philippe, ed., *Ethique, Droit et Dignité de la Personne. Mélanges Christian Bolze* (Paris: Economica, 1999).

Pohier, Jacques, and Dietmar Mieth, eds, *The Dignity of the Despised of the Earth*, *Concilium* 130 (New York: Seabury Press, 1979).

Pokorny, J., *Indogermanisches Etymologisches Wörterbuch* (Bern-München: Franke Verlag, 1959).

Portelli, Hugues, *Droit constitutionnel* (Paris, Dalloz: 1996).

Rawls, John, *A Theory of Justice* (Oxford: Oxford University Press, 1972).

Rotenstreich, Nathan, *Man and His Dignity* (Jerusalem: The Magnes Press – the Hebrew University, 1983).

Rousseau, Dominique, *Les Libertés individuelles et la dignité de la personne humaine*. Préparation au C. R. F. P. A. Libertés et droits fondamentaux (Paris: Editions Montcrestien, 1998).

Sahlin, Claire L., "'A Marvellous and Great Exultation of the Heart'': Mystical Pregnancy and Marian Devotion in Bridget of Sweden's *Revelations*' in *Studies in St Birgitta and the Brigittine Order*, Vol. 1 (New York: Edwin Mellen Press, 1993).

Said, Abdul Aziz, 'Pursuing Human Dignity' in *Human Rights and World Order*, ed. Abdul A. Said (New York: Praeger Publishers, 1978).

Schaber, Peter, *Menschenwürde* (Stuttgart: Reclam, 2012).

Schattner, Mikaël, *Souffrance et dignité humaine* (Condé-sur-Noireau: Mame, 1995).

Schmidt-Bleibtreu, B., and E. Klein, *Kommentar zum Grundgesetz für die Bundesrepublik Deutschland*, 6. Auflage (Neuwied: Luchterhand, 1983).

Schroeder, Doris, 'A Child's life or a "little bit of torture"? State-sanctioned Violence and Dignity', in *Cambridge Quarterly of Healthcare Ethics* (2006), 15, 188–201.

Schweidler, Walther, *Über Menschenwürde. Der Ursprung der Person und die Kultur des Lebens* (Wiesbaden: VS Verlag, 2012).

Sebag-Lanoë, Renée, 'Le prix de la dignité' in *Etudes*, 3793/September (1993), 173–80.

Seelmann, Kurt, ed., *Menschenwürde als Rechtsbegriff. Tagung der Internationalen Vereinigung für Rechts- und Sozialphilosophie (IVR), Schweizer Sektion Basel, 25. Bis 28. Juni 2003* (Wiesbaden: Franz Steiner Verlag, 2004).

Seifert, Josef, 'Die vierfache Quelle der Menschenwürde als Fundament der Menschenrechte', in *Staatsphilosophie und Rechtspolitik*, ed. Burkhardt Ziemske (München: Verlag C. H. Beck, 1997), 165–85.

——, 'The Right to Life and the Fourfold Root of Human Dignity', in *The Nature and Dignity of the Human Person*, eds Vial Correa and Sgreccia (Rome: Libreria Editrice Vaticana, 2003), 183–215.

Sensen, Oliver, *Kant on Human Dignity* (Berlin: De Gruyter, 2011).

Siegetsleitner, Anne, and Nikolaus Knoepffler, eds, *Menschenwürde im interkulturellen Dialog* (Freiburg and München: Alber Verlag, 2005).

Skinner, B. F., *Beyond Freedom and Dignity* (London: Cape, 1972).

Skinner, Quentin, *The Foundations of Modern Political Thought* (New York: Cambridge University Press, 1978).

Soulen, R. Kendall, and Linda Woodhead, *God and Human Dignity* (Grand Rapids, MI: Eerdmans Publishing Company, 2006).

Sozzi, Lionello, *La 'dignité de l'homme' à la renaissance* (Torino: G. Giappichelli, 1982), also in *Humanism in France at the end of the Middle Ages and in the Early Renaissance*, ed. A. H. T. Levi (New York and Manchester: Manchester University Press and Barnes and Noble, 1970), 176–198.

Spiegelberg, Herbert, 'Human Dignity: A Challenge to Contemporary Philosophy', in Gotesky, R., and A. Lazlo, eds, *Human Dignity* (New York: Gordon and Breach, 1971); reprinted in Herbert Spiegelberg, *Steppingstones towards an Ethics for Fellow Existers: Essays 1944–83* (The Hague: Nijhof, 1981), 175–198, and again (Dordrecht: Martinus Nijhoff – Kluwer, 1986).

Staab, Giles, *The Dignity of Man in Modern Papal Doctrine: Leo XIII to Pius XII, 1875–1955* (Washington, DC: Catholic University of America Press, 1957).

Stark, Caroline, 'Renaissance Anthropologies and the Conception of Man' in *New Worlds and the Italian Renaissance: Contributions to the History of European Intellectual Culture*, eds Andrea Moudarres and Christiana Purdy Moudarres (Leiden: Brill, 2014), 173–94.

Stark, Rodney, 'God's Justice: The Sin of Slavery' in *For the Glory of God* (Princeton, NJ: Princeton University Press, 2003), 291–366.

Stein, Edith, *An Investigation concerning the State*, trans. Marianne Sawicki (Washington, DC: Institute of Carmelite Studies Publications, 2006).

Steinvorth, Ulrich, 'Problems of understanding human dignity' in *Philosophy and Culture, Proceedings of the 17th World Congress of Philosophy*, 33 (1983), 393–8.

Stern, Axel, 'On Value and Human Dignity' in *Listening*, spring (1975), 74–90.

Stoecker, Ralf, ed., *Menschenwürde. Annäherung an einen Begriff* (Vienna: öbv et hpt Verlagsgesellschaft, without date, approx. 2004).

Tamm, Ditlev, *Roman Law and European Legal History* (University of Copenhagen: Faculty of Law, 1996).

Taureck, Bernhard H. F., *Die Menschenwürde im Zeitalter ihrer Abschaffung. Eine Streitschrift* (Hanburg: Merus Verlag, 2006).

Tellegen-Couperous, Olga E., *A Short History of Roman Law* (London and New York, Routledge, 1993).

Thies, Christian, ed., *Der Wert der Menschenwürde* (Paderborn: Ferdinand Schöningh, 2009).

Tiedemann, Paul, 'Der Begriff der Menschenwürde. Eine Anfrage an die Sozialphilosophie' *e-Journal Philosophie der Psychologie*, Oct. (2006), 1–18.

——, *Was ist Menschenwürde?* (Darmstadt: Wissenschaftliche Buchgesellschaft, 2006).

Timmons, Mark, *Kant's Metaphysics of Morals. Interpretative Essays* (Oxford: Oxford University Press, 2002).

Todd, Stephen, *The Shape of Athenian Law* (Oxford: Clarendon Press, 1993).

Tonti-Filipini, Nicholas, 'The Concept of Human Dignity in the International Human Rights Instruments' in *Identity and Statute of Human Embryo*. Proceedings of Third Assembly of the Pontifical Academy for Life 1997, eds Vial Correa and Sgreccia (Rome: Libreria Editrice Vaticana, 1998).

Trinkaus, C., *In Our Image and Likeness Humanity and Divinity in Italian Humanist Thought*, Vols I–II (Chicago: University of Chicago Press, 1970).

Tuck, Richard, *Natural Right Theories. Their Origin and Development* (Oxford: Oxford University Press, 1979).

UNESCO, ed., *Human Rights. Comments and Interpretations*, with an Introduction by Jacques Maritain (London and New York: Allen Wingate, 1949).

Unterburger, Klaus, 'Gnade und entscheidendes Christentum. Innerkatholische Konflikte des 18. Jahrhunderts als lange verkannte Wurzel des Menschenrechtediskurses', in Bernard Laux, ed., *Heiligkeit und Menschenwürde. Hans Joas' neue Genealogie der Menschenrechte im theologischen Gespräch* (Freiburg etc.: Herder, 2013).

Vallat, Francis, ed., *An Introduction to the Study of Human Rights. Based on a Series of lectures Delivered at King's College, London in the Autumn of 1970* (London: Europa Publications, 1970).

Verbeke, Gerard, 'Man as a "frontier" according to Aquinas' in *St Thomas and his Times*, eds G. Verbeke and D. Verhelst (Leuven: Leuven University Press, 1976), 195–223.

Verdoodt, Albert, *Naissance et signification de la déclaration universelle des droits de l'homme* (Louvain and Paris: Editions Nauwelaerts, 1964).

Verspieren, Patrick, SJ, '*Dignity* in Political and Bioethical Debates' in *Concilium* 2 (2003), 13–22.

Vial Correa, Juan de Dios, and Elio Sgreccia, eds, *The Nature and Dignity of the Human Person and the Foundation of the Right to Life. The Challenges of the Contemporary Cultural Context* (Citta del Vaticano: Libreria Editrice Vaticana, 2003).

Volp, Ulrich, *Die Würde des Menschen. Ein Beitrag zur Anthropologie in der Alten Kirche* (Leiden and Boston, MA: Brill, 2006).

Waithe, Mary Ellen, ed., *A History of Women Philosophers* Vols I–IV (Dordrecht: Kluwer, 1987).

Walde, Alois, and J. B. Hofmann, *Lateinisches Etymologisches Wörterbuch* (Heidelberg: Carl Winther Universitätsverlag, 1982).

Warren, Mary Anne, *Moral Status. Obligations to Persons and Other Living Things* (Oxford: Oxford University Press, 1997).

Weber-Guskar, Eva, *Würde als Haltung. Eine philosophische Untersuchung zum Begriff der Menschenwürde* (Münster: Mentis, 2016).

——, and Brandhorst, Mario, eds, *Menschenwürde. Eine Philosophische Debatte über Dimensionen ihrer Kontingenz* (Berlin: Suhrkamp, 2017).

Weinland, James D. Davis, *Counsciousness, Freedom, and Dignity* (Philadelphia, PA: Dorrace, 1974).

Weinreb, Lloyd L., *Natural Law and Justice* (London: Harvard University Press, 1987).

Wetz, Franz Josef, *Illusion Menschenwürde. Aufstieg und Fall eines Grundwerts* (Stuttgart: Klett-Cotta, 2005).

Wils, Jean-Pierre, 'The End of "Human Dignity" in Ethics?' in *Ethics in the Natural Sciences*, eds D. Mieth and J. Pohier, *Concilium*, June (1989), 39–54.

——, 'Zur Typologie und Verwendung der Katergorie "Menschenwürde"' in J. P. Wils and D. Mieth (eds), *Ethik ohne Chance? Erkundungen im technologischen Zeitalter* (Tübingen: Attempto Verlag, 1991), 130–57.

Zaruk, David, *The Dignity of Humanity in one's Person. An Analysis of Kant's Concept of Dignity*, PhD thesis, KUL, HIW, Leuven, 2001.

Zimmern, Alfred, *The League of Nations and the Rule of Law 1918–35* (London: Macmillan and Co., 1936).

Index

a priori 200, 201, 202–9, 209, 215, 268, 278

Abélard, Pierre 83–4

abolition (of slavery), abolitionism 6, 171, 193, 234, 237, 260, 266

abortion 4

absolute 165–6

activity 177–8, 185

addiction 278

adultery 89

advantage, advantageous 29–36, 169

Alcuin (=Albinus) 74–80

Ambrose, St 74, 75

American Indians 129, 131, 150–2, 171

anarchism, -ist 6, 270

angel(s) 66, 134, 184, 279

    angelic state 132, 144

    angelomorphism 58

animals 122, 170, 188, 256

anthropology 1

    Christian 284

    pragmatic 200, 232

Anthropology from a Pragmatic Point of View (Kant) 232

Antigone 234

anxiety 44

Arendt, Hannah 272, 303–6

aristocracy 6, 11, 23, 27, 38, 40, 42, 65, 199, 165, 271, 276–7

    aristocrat(s) 23, 235, 283

Aristotle 11–26, 27, 63, 94, 110, 111, 153, 201

    Aristotelian 83

arrogance 227, 229

Athens 11, 39

Athenians 40

atrocities 291

Augustine of Hippo 65, 66–68, 74, 75, 88, 110

Auschwitz 3

authority 12, 29, 93, 112–8, 119, 167

autonomy 3, 132, 201, 207

axiology 21

axioma, axiom 9, 11–17, 19, 39, 102–3

baptism 6, 65

Basil, St 93

beasts 172, 174–5

    see also brutish state

beginning(s) 11, 16, 102

Bernard of Clairvaux 83, 85–8, 89

Bildung 195

Birgitta of Sweden 120, 125–6

Bloch, Ernst 297–300

Blue Stocking Society 260

body 90

Boethius 29, 65, 70–2, 73, 94, 98, 101, 232

brotherhood of men 284–90, 300

    see also fraternity

brutish state 48, 80, 110, 132, 134, 162, 164

burden 2, 80

Burke, Edmund 235, 236, 237

calumniating 89, 229

Candidus 74

categorical imperative 199, 201, 202–9, 211, 216

Catherine of Siena 120, 126–8

character 235–45

children 260, 295, 301

Christ 163–4
  see also Jesus Christ
Christian(s) 65, 68, 93, 284–90
  anthropology 284
  bad 270
  dignity 65, 68
  modish 262
  nominal 263
  sociology 284
Christianity 63, 189–92, 260–3
choice of one's own nature or status 3,
  132–47
Church 6, 65
  Catholic 3
Cicero 27–55, 63, 65, 70, 93, 108, 111, 153,
  163, 232
  Ciceronian 83, 199
citizen, citizenship 1, 5, 6, 7, 8, 195, 200,
  216, 217–21, 310
civilisation 9
claim 17, 19, 20, 23, 25–6, 106, 117, 119
  claimants 21
  see also desert; merit
coercion 307–8
colonies 6
Columban, St 73
common good 290–1
community 287, 303, 304
The Community Rule (Qumran) 57–60
complaints 22
Concerning grace and free will
  (St Bernard) 87–8
condemnation 303
conflict 2
conscience 285, 287, 292
consequences 25
The Consolation of Philosophy
  (Boethius) 70–2
constitutional change 193
constitutional limits 307
consultation 75, 92

contemplation 212
contempt 228, 241
contradiction 13–4
conversion 286
Conway, Anne Finch 162–4
corruption 70, 164
cosmopolitan, -ism 27, 258
courage 32
covenant 60
crime 219–21, 283, 287, 290
Critique of Judgement (Kant) 202,
  211–16
Critique of Practical Reason (Kant) 209
Critique of Pure Reason (Kant) 201
cruelty 292
culture 254, 274–5
cursus honorum 39–40, 42, 55, 65
customs 7, 31, 236

The Damascus Document
  (Qumran) 57–60
Darwin, Charles 163
De civitate Dei (Augustine) 67
De decem mandatis (Grosseteste) 89
De dignitate conditionis humanae
  (Alcuin?) 74–80
De dignitate et excellentia hominis
  (Manetti) 132
De dignitate et praestantia hominis
  (Facio) 132
De Gouges, Olympe 195, 232–4
De inventione (Cicero) 28–36
De jure naturae et gentium
  (Pufendorf) 161–2
De legibus (Cicero) 41–44
De miseria humanae conditionis (Inno-
  cent III) 74, 132
De officiis (Cicero) 47–55
De oratore (Cicero) 36–8
De re publica (Cicero) 38–41
De unico vocationis modo (Las Casas) 151

death 3, 44, 278
  deserving 110
debt 116
Declaration of man and of the citizen
  (1789) 233–4
Declaration of the rights of woman and of
  the (woman) citizen (Olympe de
  Gouges) 232–4
decorum, decorous 44–7, 48–55
Decree abolishing slavery throughout the
  French Empire (1848) 266
defamation 200
definitio magistralis 83, 94, 98, 99, 101–2,
  278
definitions 14, 93–4
degradation 44, 164, 187, 224, 292, 297
deism 195
democracy 6, 11, 22, 38, 39, 194, 165, 275,
  283
  democrats 23
  democratisation 193
demons 67
demonstration 12–7
Denktagebuch (Arendt) 305
Descartes, René 159
desert 17, 18, 19, 20, 26
  see also claim; merit
Deus est (Grosseteste) 90
Deus qui humanae substantia dignitatem
  (Leo the Great?) 3, 4, 63, 69–70
  see also prayer
dialectics, dialectical 120, 143
Diálogo del dignidad del hombre (Perez
  de Oliva)
Dicta Albini 65, 75
Dicta Candidi 75
Dictum 54 (Grosseteste) 91
dignatione 120–25
dignitary 106–9
dignitas 11–17
  as bodily beauty 36, 52, 55

etymological connection with
  decus 44
as office 27, 29, 47–55
as a prerogative of man 54–5
as qualification 104–9
as rank 34
as stateliness 54
Dignitatis Humanae (Vatican II) 307–8
dignity 15
  as advantageous 29
  of character 238–40
  concept of 27
  conscious 240–5
  distinctions in 38, 39, 40
  as economy or super-utility 36–8
  as 'fundamentality' 25
  of God 109
  of human nature 70, 81, 166, 169, 263
  of the human person 284–90
  of humanity 225, 227–8
  of man (as distinct from woman) 55
  native 237–45
  as what ought to command
    respect 39
  of work 271
'*The Dignity of Human Nature*'
  (Wesley?) 170–1
The Dignity of the Human Person
  (Karrer) 284–90
discrimination 104–9, 292–3
disgrace 45, 71, 80, 251
distinctions in status or worth 43, 72,
  292
  see also cursus honorum; rank
divine nature 68
divine state 147
  see also Deus qui humanae dignitate,
    prayer
Doctrine of Rights (Kant) 216–21
Doctrine of Virtue (Kant) 221–31
double standards 7

drunkards 281
dust 191
duties 29–36, 47–55, 205, 208, 296

Ecclesiasticus 61
economy 6, 299–300
   economic liberation 298
education 240, 295
egalitarian, -ism 25, 27, 39
end 280
   of Creation 212, 213
   final 213–6
   in itself 204–9
   ultimate 214
Enlightenment 259
entitlement 26
Epicure, Epicurean, Epicureanism 44–5
equality 21–2, 39–41, 55, 235–45, 274,
   280, 302
   abstract 300
   before the law 293
   inequality 218, 280
   socially engineered 193
Erasmus of Rotterdam 131, 148–9
Eriugena, Joannes Scottus 65, 81, 83, 89, 163
Essenes 57–61
esteem 25
An Estimate of the Religion of the Fashion-
   able World (More) 260–2
etymology, etymological 8, 44
evil 45, 110, 305–6
excellence 20, 24, 39
The Existential Background of Human
   Dignity (Marcel) 300–3

Facio, Bartolomeo 132
fall 2, 58
fairness 41
   unfair discrimination 104–9
   see also discrimination; person(s),
      respect for

fatherhood of God 284–90
Fathers of the Church 43
feudalism 65
foreigner(s) 5, 11
formalism 301
fortune 47
fraternity 303
   see also brotherhood of men
freedom 3, 42, 174, 287, 291, 307
   moral 175–7, 185
French revolution 6, 129, 193
friendship 23–5, 29, 30, 34–5

genius 165, 271, 275, 277
Gertrude the Great (of Helfta) 119–25,
   275
glory 29, 34, 63, 57–61
goal, last or final 245, 249, 253
   see also end
God 41, 43, 58–61, 75, 85–7, 97–99,
   163–4, 190, 211, 214–15, 240, 242,
   310
   children of 280, 287
   relationship to 174, 187, 190–2, 286
gods 41
   descent from the 42
Goethe 163
Goethe and Tolstoi (Mann) 276
good, the 21, 23
   human being 254
   see also common good
good(s) 46–7
   exterior, external 17, 19, 25–6
grace 2, 73, 85
gratitude 31–2
great-souled, the 17–8
   see also magnanimity
Greek(s) 11, 12, 93, 272–5
   imperial power 10
The Greek State (Nietzsche) 272–5
Grosseteste, Robert 83, 88–93

Grotius, Hugo 153–4, 161, 199
Groundwork of the Metaphysics of Morals
    (Kant) 200, 201–9
guilt 287

Handbook of a Christian Soldier
    (Erasmus) 148–9
happiness 46, 197, 201, 212–6, 241, 242,
    253, 254, 257, 298–300
Hegel, Georg Wilhelm Friedrich 165–6
Héloïse 84
Henriette (Hortense Wild) 269–70
Herder, Johann Gottfried 195–9
hereditary honours and property 236
Hexaëmeron (Grosseteste) 91–3
Heydenreich, Karl Heinrich 171, 195,
    246–60, 267
highmindedness (*magnificientia*) 32
Hildegard von Bingen 83, 84
Hobbes, Thomas 129, 155–8, 161, 165, 167,
    169, 171
holocaust 283
honour(s) 17, 19, 27, 63, 106, 109, 114–18,
    157–8
    honourable 29–36, 46, 157–8, 174
human being(s) 2, 3, 5, 195, 222, 310
    as such of noble rank 41
human dignity
    Aristotle's understanding of 25
    as a basic principle 193
    conceptions of 6, 27
    conceptualisation as a constitutional
        principle 283
    conceptualisation history of 1, 3, 4,
        309
    as a constitutional principle 83, 129,
        199, 165, 297
    deformation of 2
    as *Ersatz*-Christianity 195
    feeling of 247–60, 267–9
    foundational for law 1, 27

as the glory of Adam 57–61
    idea of 25–6, 272
    intuition of 309
    as a legal principle 130
    linguistic expression of 8
    phrase of 27
    recognition of 8
    sacral quality of 301
    status of 25
    understandings of 7, 25, 55
    as a useless or meaningless
        concept 309–10
human nature 9, 27, 41, 201, 280
    corruption of 9
humanism, -ist(s) 277
humanity 25, 57, 196–9, 201, 208, 222,
    223, 236, 256–60, 269, 285–90,
    299
Humboldt, Wilhelm von 195
Hume, David 165, 169–70, 171
humility 120, 225
    false 224

iconicity (the human being as the image
    of God) 4, 9, 43, 69, 73, 74–80,
    87, 90, 119, 179, 287
    aiming at 263
*Ideas on the Philosophy of the History of
    Humanity* (Herder)
Il dialogo (Catherine of Siena) 127–8
illness 64, 119–25,
    as spirit 276–8
immortality 58, 178, 186–7, 254–60,
    286–90
importance 11, 12, 66
inalienability 283, 290
    of dignity 225
    of human rights 110, 291
    of the value of the human being 300
inclusion 6, 7
indigenous peoples 129

see also American Indians
individuality 95–102, 163–4, 279
induction 11, 310
infinity 254–5
inherency (of human dignity) 283,
        290–1
inner man 75
intellect (intelligence, thought, under-
        standing) 9, 41, 74, 76, 159–60,
        161, 174–5, 184–5
intolerance 258
intuition 16, 25, 309
        of categorical imperative
        of dignity 12
        of first principles 11
isonomia 11
ius 21, 153–4

Jesus Christ 61, 65, 66, 70, 84, 174, 180,
        190, 290, 309
Jew(s), Jewish 9, 10, 57–61, 63, 129, 283
see also tradition
The Jurisprudence of Holland
        (Grotius) 154
justice 112, 268–9
        as defined by dignity 24, 93
        as the feeling of human dignity 268
        *to give everyone according to their dig-
        nity* 21, 94–5, 104–9
        *a habit of mind which gives every man
        his desert while preserving the
        common advantage* 31, 43,
        51, 112
        injustice of equality 39
        just, the 22–3
        justifiable to kill a sinner 110
        legal 112
        sense of 41, 298
        unjust, the 21
Justice in the Revolution and in the Church
        (Proudhon) 267–9

Kant, Immanuel 24, 161, 195, 199–232,
        232, 234, 245, 246, 297, 305–6
Kantian(ism) 65, 300
Karrer, Otto 284–90
knowledge 85
Kvod ha-adam 10, 57–61

labour 272–5
Las Casas, Bartholomé de 129, 131, 150–2
Lassalle, Ferdinand 270–1
law(s) 9, 41–44, 64, 216, 233, 280, 291
        constitutional 5, 6, 129, 131, 193, 308
        history of 1
        see also constitutional change
        customary 32
        in common with the gods 42
        international 129
        maternal 298–300
        moral 209, 213, 215, 225
        natural 9, 31, 155, 297, 298–300
        of nature 31, 41, 72
        positive 5, 9, 25, 161
        practical 209
        subjection to 208
        universal law of nature 208
        see also legal protection
        universal practical 205, 207
leadership 7
Lebech, Mette 74, 75, 93
Lectures on the Philosophy of Religion
        (Hegel) 165–6
legacy (the glory of Adam=human dig-
        nity as a legacy) 60
legal protection 293
Legatus (Gertrude of Helfta) 120–5
Leo the Great, St 65, 68–70, 85, 307
Letter to Karl Jaspers (Arendt) 305
Letter to the Emperor (Las Casas) 151–2
Letters on the Advancement of Humanity
        (Herder) 198–9
Leviathan (Hobbes) 156–8

Liber de diligendo deo
  (St Bernard) 85–7
liberal(ism), 6
liberty 166
Life of the Mind (Arendt) 306
Life in a Jewish Family (Stein) 280–1
likeness (to God), 73, 75, 79
linguistic ancestry 4
  see also etymology
liturgical anthropology 58
liturgical order 65
liturgical reforms of Charlemagne 3
love 24–5, 78–80

The Magic Mountain (Mann) 277–8
magnanimity 18–20
Manetti, Gianozzo 132
manipulation 288
Mann, Thomas 275–8
Marcel, Gabriel 300–3
Maritain, Jacques 2
Martin, Martin 166
Marx, Karl 297, 300
Mary, Mother of God 120, 125–6, 306
men, man 5, 167–8
Mendel, Gregor 163
merit 11, 17, 19, 22, 25, 30, 95, 108, 160
  translating *dignitas* 29
  see also claim; desert
meritocracy 39, 42, 111
metaphysics, metaphysical 199, 200, 235,
  237, 303
microcosmism 4, 81, 89, 90, 92, 163, 200
missionaries 131
mockery 230
monarchy 38, 39, 155
money 30, 35
moral
  being 214, 222
  capacity 217
  goodness 17

maturation 286
nature of human beings 248
perfection 286
morality 206, 256
morals 47, 201, 236
More, Hannah 195, 260–3
mother(s) 7
motherhood 120, 295

nationalism 6
Natural Law and Human Dignity
  (Bloch) 297–300
nature 9, 10, 51–3
  natural greatness 17
  natural order 9
  natural justice 11
  natural law 31
  nature's law 52
Nicomachean Ethics (Aristotle) 17–27
Nietzsche, Friedrich 119, 165, 271–5, 275,
  277, 302, 303
nobility 47, 199
normality 3
nudity 301

obedience 280
*Of the Dignity and Meanness of Human
  Nature* (Hume) 169–70
office(s) 29, 63, 65, 70, 71, 84, 106, 119,
  168, 219, 233–4
officium 47–55
oligarchy 11, 22
On the Problem of Human Dignity
  (Lebech) 1, 2
On the Spirit of Humanity
  (Humboldt) 245
ontology 5
  ontological anchorage 159
  ontological mobility 132
oppression 291, 303

Oration on the Dignity of Man
   (Pico) 132–47
The Origins of Totalitarianism
   (Arendt) 304–5
   others 306, 310

pain 44–7
Paine, Thomas 235
parental project 2
Pascal, Blaise 159–60, 161
passions 27, 44, 48–9
patriotism 111
Paul, St 65
peace 2, 291
Peaceful Democracy (Henriette) 269–70
peasant(s) 5, 6
Pensées (Pascal) 159–60
Perez de Oliva 132
perfection 192
   striving for 178, 186
Periphyseon (Eriugena) 81
perpetrator(s) 283
persecution 293
person(s) 63, 74, 83, 94, 204, 222, 232,
   267, 278
   respect for 104–9
   see also fairness, unfair discrimination
personhood, definition of 95–102
philosophy 132, 144–8
   first 200
Pico della Mirandola 57, 66, 131, 132–47,
   162, 200
piety 111–18
pleasure 149
   sensual 53
political institutions 5
political realism 153, 155
politics 9
pomp 301
poor, the 64, 239, 271, 300, 301
position(s) 19, 72, 81, 111, 114

Posterior Analytics (Aristotle) 12–17
Potency and Act (Stein) 278–9
power 35, 106, 115, 156–8, 274, 280, 301
   of domination, dignity as 86
   of government 307
   prayer 263
   *see also Deus qui humanae substantiae
      dignitatem*
pregnancy 64
priesthood 65, 120, 126–8, 180, 189
primitive(s) 13, 14, 16
prince 12
principle 9, 12
   abstract 3
   basic 2, 3, 11, 13, 15, 193
   constitutional 1, 4, 5, 25, 83, 171, 193,
      283, 309
      see also constitutional change; law
   non-demonstrable 11, 103
   of principles 16
   as relational 17
   unfounded 13
*Principles of the Most Ancient and Modern
   Philosophy* (Conway) 162
privilege(s) 174, 175, 182, 189, 234
   of dignity 75
   of the landed classes 6
The Problems of Educating Girls Today
   (Stein) 279–80
professions, professionalisation 6, 260,
   262
progress 248, 257, 306
   social 291
property 154, 299
proposition(s) 13–4
propriety 49–52
   see also decorum, decorous
Proudhon, Pierre-Joseph 193, 267–9
Pseudo-Dionysius 94–5
Pufendorf, Samuel 161–2, 199

racial mythology 285
rank 63, 94, 98, 108, 111, 170, 234, 239–40
rational
   animal(s) 12, 16, 25–6, 102, 110
   being(s) 205–9, 211, 215, 301
   nature 207
   soul 66, 67
rationalism 300–3
rationality 3, 11, 12, 16, 17, 25, 68
   irrational acts undoing human
      dignity 110
reason 9, 10, 25, 42, 52, 68, 197, 205–9,
   209, 235–45, 269, 292
   human dignity known through 307
   may become sham and parody 302
   recognition 48, 64, 292
   secularisation of 302
redemption 65, 132
   redeemed 58, 66
Reflections on Human Dignity
   (Heydenreich) 246–60
Reflections on the Revolution in France
   (Burke) 235
relation, category of 17
religion 1, 6, 9, 31
   religious freedom 294, 307
The Republic (Plato) 21
reputation 29, 30
Rerum Novarum (Pope Leo XIII) 272
respect 11, 24, 27, 95, 111–8, 288–90, 309
   for persons 104–9
   see also fairness, unfair discrimination
responsibility 287
restoration (of image, of dignity) 3, 4, 63,
   69–70, 73, 110, 291, 307, 309
resurrection 287
Revelaciones (Birgitta of Sweden) 126
revenge 31
reverence 32, 51
Richard of St Victor 85
ridicule 200

right(s) 29, 64, 235–45, 165, 278, 280,
   287, 291–7
   civil 308
   definition of 267
   -language 165, 167, 193
   human 1, 2, 290–300, 304
   to life, misuse of 288
   of men 236, 274
   political 23
   subjective 299
   translation of *'ius'*
righteousness 58, 65
Rights of Man (Paine) 235
rival interpretations 2
Roman(s), 12
   cult of honour, rank and dignity 64, 65
   empire, Western 63, 65
   imperial power, imperialism 10, 27
   law 27, 63, 94

sacrament(s) 6
sacrifice 286
salvation 2
science 9, 15–16, 78, 157
   fiction 3
Second Vatican Council 3, 306–8
secularism 307
security 29, 35
   of property 237
self-contempt 226
self-control 10, 48, 50, 52, 63
Sermon XI (Columban) 73
Sermon XIII (Abélard) 84
Sermon 21 (Leo the Great) 68
Sermon 27 (Leo the Great) 69
Sermon 250 (Augustine) 66
Sermons on the Dignity of Man
   (Zollikofer) 172–92
servility 200, 225–6, 288
silence 3
sin 58, 104–9, 110, 131, 148–9, 260–3

original 170–1, 262
slave(s) 5, 6, 129, 243, 165, 271–5
slave trade 237, 250, 292
slavery 25, 150, 216, 220, 234, 246, 258,
  266, 292
social construction 5
  of dignity 104
  of standards of value 11
  of state 7
social doctrine of the Catholic
  Church 272
social dynamics 48
social organisation 9
social problems 129
socialist, -ism 6, 270, 270–1, 274
  see also tradition, left wing
Sophia (Mary Montagu or Sophia
  Fermor) 167
soul 43, 76–80, 89, 161–2
  preservation of one's and human
    dignity 288
sovereignty 216–7, 268
species 163–4
spirit 276–8
  divine 286
  human 307
The Spirit of Prayer (More) 263
spouse 145
  dignity of 120
state(s), 7, 8, 27, 39, 64, 199, 292
  conception of 5
  constitution of 1
  emergence of modern 6, 63
  interests of 7
  nation 283
  universal 260
station, standing 104
status 23, 25, 28, 67
  citizenship 5, 200
  as human beings 309
  ontological 5, 130, 169

political 1, 54, 130, 169
Stein, Edith 5, 278–81, 310
Stern, Axel 1, 2
Stoics 46
*Strictures on the Modern System of Female
  Education* (More) 262–3
subjectivity 99
substance 17
suffering 44, 119–20, 281, 286, 287
suicide 44
Summa theologiae (Thomas
  Aquinas) 94–118
superior(s), superiority 53, 119, 167, 172
  logical 201
superstition 258

teleology 14, 54, 303
  moral 211, 215
  physical 214, 215
telos 43, 195, 196
  man as, of the universe 181–2
temperance 33, 50
Temple worship 58
tension(s) 3, 6, 7
The Thanksgiving Hymns/Hodayot
  (Qumran) 57–61
theft 89
theosis 58–61
  see also *Deus qui humana substantiae
    dignitatem*
Thomas Aquinas 93–118, 278, 279
topos 2
totalitarianism 194, 304
tradition(s) 2, 3, 199, 278, 309
  Christian 2, 3, 129, 131–2, 278, 309
  classical 132–3, 278
  conservative 3, 42, 155, (165), (271–5),
  esoteric 3, 129
  of human dignity 277
  human rights 3, 307
  Islamic 3

Jewish 3, 57–61, 129, 132, 162
left-wing 3, (267–70), (270–1), (271)
liberal 3, (274)
masonic 3, 195, 267
modern 278
right-wing 3
secular 2, 3, (302)
transmutation of species 163–4
trauma 283
tribal loyalties 5
Trinity 74–80
truth 30, 32, 308
Tusculan Disputations (Cicero) 44–7
tyranny 11, 25, 241, 243, 291

United Nations 3, 193, 290–6, 307, 310
universal, the 11, 16
*The Universal Declaration of Human
    Rights* (1948) 291–6
untouchability 283
useful 29, 66, 167
utopian, -ism 25, 39, 42, 55, 271, 297,
    298–300

valuer 2, 23
values 9, 17, 21, 66, 68, 157, 174, 198, 202,
    273, 287, 307
    basic 11
    fundamental 1, 2, 4, 7
    of human beings 23, 309
    of human dignity 119
    as intelligible by their motivating
        power 310
    intrinsic 2, 240
    intuition of 1
    standards of 67
vanity 18
victim 283
vindication 64, 85, 165, 167–8, 193, 216,
    235–45, 165, 300
A Vindication of the Rights of Men
    (Wollstonecraft) 235–40

A Vindication of the Rights of Woman
    (Wollstonecraft) 240–5
virtue 21, 30, 40, 46–7, 48, 50, 65, 80, 85,
    106, 109, 111–8, 169, 221–31
    bodily -, dignity as 35
    moral 29
Von Humboldt, Wilhelm 245–6
vote, the 219
A Voyage to St Kilda (Martin) 166
vulnerability 64

war(s) 283
    Second World 2, 6, 290
weakness 89, 93, 119, 170, 241, 243,
    301–3
    the weak, dignity of 131, 300
Wesley, John 165, 170–1
What is Existenz Philosophy?
    (Arendt) 304
What is the Human Being? (Stein) 280
will 41
    united, of all 216–17
wisdom 2, 33, 42, 44, 77, 88, 90, 170
Wollstonecraft, Mary 195, 216, 235–45
Woman not Inferior to Man (Sophia) 167
women 5, 6, 7, 25, 54, 64, 83–4, 89, 93,
    94, 119–20, 129, 130, 131, 165,
    193–4, 195, 199, 216, 218, 232–4,
    260, 265, 269–70, 278
    womanly 280
word 89, 91, 268
workers 129, 193–4, 199, 218, 265, 270–1
The Working Man's Programme
    (Lassalle) 270–1
worth 21, 24–5, 30, 34, 47, 71
    social 105–9
worthy 18, 20, 24, 43
    unworthy 45–7, 71

Zeno 46
Zollikofer, Georg Joachim 165, 171–92,
    195, 202, 245, 246

Printed in Great Britain
by Amazon